D0225962

DATE DUE

FOR CANADA'S SAKE

MCGILL-QUEEN'S STUDIES IN THE HISTORY OF RELIGION

Volumes in this series have been supported by the Jackman Foundation of Toronto.

SERIES TWO   In memory of George Rawlyk
Donald Harman Akenson, Editor

For Canada's Sake

Public Religion,
Centennial Celebrations,
and the Re-making of
Canada in the 1960s

GARY R. MIEDEMA

McGill-Queen's University Press
Montreal & Kingston · London · Ithaca

© McGill-Queen's University Press 2005
ISBN 0-7735-2877-6

Legal deposit fourth quarter 2005
Bibliothèque nationale du Québec

Printed in Canada on acid-free paper that is 100% ancient forest free
(100% post-consumer recycled), processed chlorine free.

This book has been published with the help of a grant from the Canadian
Federation for the Humanities and Social Sciences, through the Aid to
Scholarly Publications Programme, using funds provided by the Social
Sciences and Humanities Research Council of Canada.

McGill-Queen's University Press acknowledges the support of the Canada
Council for the Arts for our publishing program. We also acknowledge the
financial support of the Government of Canada through the Book Publishing
Industry Development Program (BPIDP) for our publishing activities.

Library and Archives Canada Cataloguing in Publication

Miedema, Gary R. (Gary Richard), 1970–
For Canada's sake: Public Religion, centennial celebrations,
and the re-making of Canada in the 1960s/Gary R. Miedema.

(McGill-Queen's studies in the history of religion; 34)
Includes bibliographical references and index.
ISBN 0-7735-2877-6

1. Religious pluralism – Canada. 2. Christianity – Canada – 20th century.
3. Expo 67 (Montréal, Québec) I. Title II. Series.

FC623.C4M53 2005   200'.971   c2005–901666-3

This book was typeset by Interscript in 10/12 Palatino.

Contents

Acknowledgments

This is my chance to express my appreciation for the many people and institutions who have contributed to this project. Before publishing was dreamed of, many archivists and archival institutions gave me access to their collections of primary sources upon which the arguments of this book are based. I wish to thank the staff at the National Archives in Ottawa and those at the many religious institutions who also opened their doors and answered my questions – the national archives of the Anglican, Presbyterian, and United Churches of Canada and of the Pentecostal Assemblies of Canada in Toronto, the archives of the Baptist Federation of Canada, located in Hamilton, the archives of the Canadian Conference of Catholic Bishops and of the Canadian Council of Churches in Ottawa, and the archives of the Montreal/Ottawa Conference of the United Church of Canada in Montreal. Thanks, in particular, to Janis Rosen at the archives of the Canadian Jewish Congress, Glen Smith of Christian Direction, and Bernice Baranowski at the Canadian Centre for Ecumenism, all in Montreal.

The final written form of this study is embarrassingly stronger than it once was, thanks to the constructive criticisms of many. First and foremost, thank you to Marguerite Van Die and Ian McKay, two people whose scholarship I admire and whose supervision was exemplary. Brian Clarke, Jane Errington, Elsbeth Heaman, and William C. James also gave exceptional feedback, as did the anonymous readers for the Aid for Scholarly Publications Program of the Humanities and Social Sciences Federation of Canada.

Many others have contributed, wittingly or unwittingly, to making this book possible. Thank you to my family for their support and to friends and colleagues Kevin Kee, Catherine Gidney, Mike Dawson, Elizabeth Davey, George Sweetman, Gordon Heath, Richard Davis, Wil Katerberg, Bill VanGroningen, and the First Toronto group. Most of all, thank you to my partner Jen, the one who freely gave and endured the most to allow me to get this book done.

Finally, I wish to dedicate this book to the reader I most had in mind while writing it: my father, Samuel Miedema. Diagnosed with ALS two years before this study began, he lived to see it completed in dissertation form. Never much for academic historical studies, he was nonetheless determined to read this one. Sitting in front of the living room window in his wheelchair, he worked his way through half of it before the disease no longer made reading possible.

He even said he enjoyed it.

He is sorely missed.

Toronto, April 2004

Introduction

On Saturday, 1 July 1967, Canadians gathered on Parliament Hill to celebrate their country's one hundredth birthday.[1] The first eager citizens, encouraged by blue skies, a slight breeze, and temperatures forecast to be in the eighties, began to appear around 9:30 A.M. The best spots close to the freshly built platform were quickly taken. In the next hour, the rear edge of the crowd moved slowly back until the lawns were covered with an estimated twenty to twenty-five thousand people.

The growing crowd was entertained by the Canadian Guards band and the Peace Tower carillon, as well as by last-minute sound checks. The real centre of attention, however, was the dais. Standing below and in front of the Peace Tower on the edge of the lawns, the platform caught the eye with its crimson canopy and imitation-stone facia. Fences patrolled by red-coated Mounties stretched out from the sides of the stage, keeping the crowds at a safe distance from the platform. Prominently displayed on the canopy was the royal standard and on the platform the royal thrones brought from Canada's Senate chamber. Nine other chairs and a podium filled out the decor. It was a stage fit for the queen.

At 10:00 A.M., with anticipation building, the crowd focused its attention on the arrival of members of parliament, senators, and their guests as they took their seats on reserved platforms to the front and sides of the dais. The band and the Centennial Choir were already positioned behind the dignitaries, facing the stage. A few minutes later, people strained to see the arrival of the prime minister, the leader of the opposition, and members of Cabinet. Then came the speaker and officials of the House of Commons, then their counterparts from the Senate, then the governor general. Then, finally, the excitement of the crowd peaked as a black open limousine followed by the throngs that had lined the streets to see it brought the queen and the prince to Parliament Hill.

When the two royals emerged from their car, they were met by eight clergymen and walked to a platform at the side of the dais where they were seated. The clergymen then ascended the dais and, joined by Prime Minister Lester B. Pearson, filled the nine chairs. In the half-hour, nationally televised ceremony that followed, Canadians across the country began their Canada Day celebrations of the country's one hundredth birthday with prayer, Bible reading, and song. "A hundred years ago today," read the distributed programs, "our ancestors witnessed the birth of a new nation. Now a century later, some twenty million Canadians share the heritage of freedom and material prosperity for which, on this historic occasion, all will wish to join in thanksgiving to God."

The eight clergymen on the dais represented a number of distinctive religious traditions. The Right Reverend Wilfred C. Lockhart, Moderator of the United Church of Canada, the Right Reverend John Logan-Vencta, Moderator of the Presbyterian Church of Canada, His Eminence Cardinal Maurice Roy, Archbishop of Quebec and Roman Catholic Primate of Canada, and the Most Reverend H.H. Clark, Anglican Archbishop of Rupert's Land and Primate of All Canada symbolized the presence of the largest and most historically significant Christian churches in the country.

Joining Roy, Clark, Lockhart, and Logan-Vencta were others less familiar to the Canadian public. Dressed in the distinctive robes of his office, the Right Reverend Timotheos, Bishop of Rodolstolon, represented the Ukrainian Orthodox Church. The Reverend D.P. Neufeld represented the Mennonite Central Committee, a relief organization of Canadian Mennonites that had only recently gained respect and attention outside Mennonite circles. Rabbi S.M. Zambrowsky represented the Canadian Jewish Congress, a parliament of Canadian Jews that involved those of orthodox, reform, and conservative persuasions in common projects and programs. The last religious representative on the podium was not, in fact, there as a clergyman at all. Mr Lavy N. Becker, a prominent member of the Jewish community in Montreal and the proprietor of a small business, represented the Canadian Interfaith Conference, of which he was the chairman.

It was Becker who approached the podium first and began the service with the Call to Worship from Psalms 33 and 95.[2] "Blessed is the nation whose God is the Lord, and the people whom He hath chosen for his own inheritance. O come, let us worship and bow down and kneel before the Lord, our Maker." Following Becker, the Centennial Choir led the audience in the singing of the hymn "O Lord My God." Replacing Becker at the podium, the Right Reverend Timotheos implored God in prayer to "Cleanse us from our sins and from every thought displeasing to Thy goodness." The crowd then joined Lockhart in reciting the Lord's Prayer and Neufeld and Logan-Vencta in a responsive reading. "I will lift up mine eyes unto the hills, from whence cometh my help," read the clergy. From all over the hill came the response, "My help cometh from the Lord, which made heaven and earth."

The responsive reading was followed by another hymn, "Know that the Lord is God indeed," and then the prime minister took his turn at the podium. Reading from 1 Peter 3:8–14, Pearson's familiar voice echoed off the stone walls of the Parliament buildings: "Be ye all of one mind, having compassion one of another … For the eyes of the Lord are over the righteous, and his ears are open to their prayers; but the face of the Lord is against them that do evil." "Be forbearing and charitable with one another," read Cardinal Roy next. "So shall we all at last attain to the unity inherent in our faith and our knowledge of the Son of God – to mature manhood, measured by nothing less than the full stature of Christ. Let us speak the truth in love; so that we shall fully grow up into Christ. He is the head and on him the whole body depends." Following the singing of the Centennial Hymn, the Most Reverend Clark prayed, "With Thy blessings, bless Thy servant Elizabeth, our Queen, with all members of the Royal House." Then the tens of thousands of voices again joined in a litany. "We re-dedicate ourselves, O Lord," chanted Canadians in repeated response to statements of the clergy. After another hymn, Clark read the benediction.

The formal service was over, but the ceremonies were not. After the clergymen had exited the stage, another colourful procession moved to take their place. Amidst a fanfare of trumpets, her majesty and the duke of Edinburgh moved onto the dais. The familiar and stirring notes of "God Save the Queen" took to the air, and only after the anthem had been sung did the queen and the crowd take their seats. Led by their officials and respective maces, the speaker of the Senate, Sydney Smith, and the Commons speaker, Lucien Lamoureaux, then followed the queen to the dais. Addressing the queen as, among other things, "Defender of the Faith," they delivered formal greetings on behalf of the Canadian people.

Following their words, Queen Elizabeth herself moved to the podium. Her speech was evidently the highlight of the morning's ceremonies and was closely reported by the press. Standing before the massive crowd, underneath the crimson canopy, and in a blue and white gown and diamond tiara, she spoke in English and French. Canada was richly blessed, she said, but its power and authority depended on internal unity, particularly between French and English Canadians. If Canadians could unite, she urged, they might attain even higher levels of greatness. Under the blue sky, before the colour and pageantry of the royal persons, the dais, and the Parliament buildings topped by dancing Canadian flags, the assembled crowd responded to her address with an emotional and fervent singing of "O Canada." The queen and the duke then proceeded down the broad walk to the Centennial Flame, where they were again greeted by a fanfare of trumpets, then whisked away in the open limousine, leaving the guests and crowd to celebrate their country and themselves.

What should we make of such an event? In the study that follows, I argue that we should make a good deal of it indeed. Under the bright sun and clear blue skies that Saturday morning, in the ritual and hymns and prayers and readings, in who said what and who stood where, something important was being said about Canada and Canadians. As we look back from a now-distant time and place, the prayer service on Parliament Hill can tell us a good deal about the people that planned it, about those that gathered on the Hill on 1 July 1967 and about the country they gathered to celebrate. On the surface, the service suggests something very simple. Since it was carefully organized by federal centennial planners and orchestrated for the benefit not just of those in attendance but, by television, for the benefit of all Canadians, it is significant that the service was religious. When Canadians celebrated their Centennial in 1967, expressions of religious faith played an important role in those celebrations.

Beyond that, the service conveyed some very strong messages about what this celebrated country of Canada was. It not only declared that it was a religious country; it characterized it as broadly Christian. That message was obvious in the readings, all of which were from the Bible (the King James Version, even in the midst of the "hip" sixties). Cardinal Roy, in fact, read from a New Testament passage that repeatedly referred to Christ, while the Lord's Prayer and the responsive readings put the language of the Christian faith into the mouths of the crowd. Except for the Centennial Hymn and including "O Canada," all songs were from the Christian tradition.[3] After the service was over, the queen was greeted as the "Defender of the Faith."

That verbal message was backed up visually. In the prime minister and the queen, two of the strongest symbols of Canadian nationhood found themselves shoulder to shoulder not with businessmen or professors or soldiers but with religious men – leaders in faith. The first people to greet the queen on that Centennial morning were clergymen. As the prime minister read the New Testament lesson, the boundaries between politician and clergyman became blurred, then briefly blended into one. It was on a stage sacralized by religious observance, prayer, and "God Save the Queen," an anthem that was itself a prayer, that the queen addressed the nation. In the presence of tens of thousands of Canadians nation-wide, the country and its leaders were symbolically declared religious, and, within that, Christian.

That said, more was going on in the prayer service than the simple affirmation of a relationship between Christianity and the people of Canada. On closer examination, the exclusively Christian nature of the service was qualified by the planners themselves. Beside the representations of Christian dominance in national public life were those of a more pluralistic nation. There on the podium, after all, sat Rabbi S.M. Zambrowsky and Lavy Becker. Rabbi Zambrowsky's Jewish identity was obvious. Becker, though Jewish himself, represented the Canadian Interfaith Conference, an organization involving over thirty Christian and non-Christian Canadian faith groups that together had planned interfaith celebrations of the Centennial. The display of religious pluralism that these men presented was obviously limited, however. The presence of Jewish representatives in national expressions of public religion had not been uncommon in previous years,[4] and what Zambrowsky and Becker said easily fit within a larger Christian framework. Nonetheless, the service did also give a very significant nod to religious pluralism in Canada. For eyes and ears outside the historic Christian denominations, Lavy Becker, on behalf of the Canadian Interfaith Conference, gave public representation to an unprecedented breadth of religious groups. Canada was predominantly Christian, to be sure, but it was also making new room in national public life for other religious persuasions.

In this regard, the prayer service on Parliament Hill captured something very important indeed on that Saturday morning in 1967. It hinted visually at an important change in the way religion would publicly inform Canadian national identities in the future. Into the 1960s, everything from CBC programming to prime ministerial speeches was explicitly marked by the privileging of the faith of Canada's largest Christian churches. While other expressions of faith from outside those churches were occasionally given public recognition before the 1960s, their secondary status remained clear. In the 1960s, however, many of the demarcations of Christian privilege in Canadian public life either dramatically disappeared or were transformed into declarations of a new Canadian "religious neutrality" that attempted, at least visually, to give equal status to all faith groups in Canada. Though still very much in progress, that shift was arguably one of the most significant adjustments in understandings of Canada in the history of the nation.

These generalisations might seem like a lot to pull from a thirty-minute prayer service, especially considering that it was followed on Parliament Hill by 1 July celebrations that involved much less religious expression and much larger crowds. While an estimated twenty to twenty-five thousand came out for the prayer service (and some of them simply to see the Queen), between thirty-five and fifty thousand showed up later in the day for the royal cutting of the enormous Centennial Birthday Cake. That evening, some seventy-five thousand people massed onto the Hill for music and fireworks. The Canadians gathered on that 1 July Saturday went on to party in a manner that quickly eclipsed the prayer service and had the newspapers gushing.[5]

Putting the prayer service in that context cautions us from implying too much about the importance of public religion to Canadian citizens on 1 July 1967. It should not, however, lead us to dismiss that display of public religion altogether, for the service did not stand alone. On the 1 July weekend itself, the Queen's presence in church on Sunday morning was noted by the press, as was a much more relaxed national youth service, complete with guitars, on the Hill Sunday evening. More significantly, the 1 and 2 July services took place in the middle of a year dedicated to the celebration of one hundred years of Canadian Confederation. Not just on Parliament Hill but across the country, the Centennial year, as it was called, inspired a whole variety of events marked by public expressions of religion. From canoe races and privy parades begun by prayer, to open houses in religious sanctuaries, to religious pavilions specially built at a world's fair in Montreal, Canadians included religion in their public celebrations and exhibitions. On Parliament Hill on 1 July, the holiest of days during the Centennial year, the prayer service was no doubt the national pinnacle of religious events. It was not, however, alone.

The larger 1967 Centennial celebrations and Expo 67, the Universal and World Exhibition held in Montreal in the Centennial year, will provide the subject matter for much of this study. Those two events both reflected their sociopolitical context and became in turn important tools in efforts to shape it. More particularly, they were nation-building moments, events devised not only to entertain Canadians and the world but also to instil in Canadian minds an understanding of their country and of themselves. In those two large-scale public events, Canadians certainly had a good time. More importantly for this study, they also revealed in their public symbols, rituals, celebrations, and exhibitions just what they thought of themselves, their country, and their future. In doing so, they provided subsequent generations with an intriguing entranceway into their complex 1960s world.[6]

More specifically, the Centennial celebrations and Expo 67 will focus our attention on one often overlooked and yet vital aspect of that world: religion. For that reason, the celebrations and Expo 67 will only briefly appear in their entirety in this study. More sustained attention will be given to those parts, like the prayer service, that explicitly involved religion. They will be examined in order to understand the way religion publicly informed Canadian identities and the way those identities shaped public religion.

That Canadians used the Centennial celebrations and Expo 67 to express visions of themselves and their country should come as no surprise. First, exhibitions and public celebrations have always served as powerful means of cultural expression and have often crystallized public debates.[7] Second, in the 1950s and 1960s Canadians found themselves immersed in a very lively and difficult debate about issues of national identity, a debate that almost inevitably revealed itself in their public celebrations. In those decades and into the 1970s, Canadians and their social, cultural, and political institutions struggled through a period of dramatic and intense change. At the very moment that Canadians entered into year-long celebrations and representations of their country, how one defined "Canada" or "Canadian" was in dispute.[8]

So too was the role of religious identity in that definition. Both the turmoil of the 1960s and the debate about national identity explicitly involved religion and indicated a profound transformation in how Canadians were understanding – and being asked to understand – their country, their institutions, and themselves. Amidst the confusion of the 1960s and as part of a long process reaching back into the beginning of the century, Canada was very visibly slipping away from its historic and public Christian moorings.[9] In the postwar period, historians have contended, the increasingly more egalitarian and less conservative attitudes and values of Canadians combined with an ever more pluralist society to push many citizens, both in the churches and the state, to move their conception of Canada towards a "religiously neutral" position. That shift represented nothing less, in the words of one historian, than the end of Christendom in Canada.[10]

This study will explore in some detail what that adjustment looked like and how and why it took place. In the 1960s, I will argue, long existent but subtle trends and patterns of change led federal politicians and state officials, in particular, to attempt to very visibly rewrite the public image of Canada. To accommodate the growing demand for an end to racial and religious discrimination in public life, they began to reshape Canada into a country welcoming of all, yet "united in its diversity." Instead of presenting Canada as a nation closely associated with particular ethnic groups (French and British) and a particular religion (Christianity), as the federal state had historically done, politicians and bureaucrats made explicit and dramatic moves to reimagine their country as a more inclusive and tolerant "nation" built upon the secure foundation of religious and ethnic pluralism.

That attempt to forge a new understanding of a diverse and pluralist Canada was not without paradox and irony. Not all diverse groups and voices were willing to put their own particular agendas behind the national unity agenda of the federal state. Not surprisingly, then, state officials working to end religious and ethnic discrimination in national public life found themselves discriminating against those who wanted to use their newfound public voice for their own expansive purposes, not for those of the state. Trying to forge a new national *unity* by emphasizing *pluralism* and *diversity* was, to say the least, potentially contradictory.[11]

That said, the large-scale Centennial celebrations and the world exposition, planned explicitly by a government commission and corporation to include religion, caught the transition from a Christian to a religiously plural Canada in mid-step and, with all its ambiguities and ironies, threw it into bold relief. The Centennial and Expo 67 demonstrate that in the 1960s the religious identity of the country was subjected with virtually everything else to the tumult and challenges of what one historian has called the "years of uncertainty and innovation."[12] In the midst of that tumult, a religiously and ethnically neutral vision of Canada moved from the periphery to the centre of the political and cultural fray and competed vigorously with older visions for the hearts and minds of Canadians. If officials of the federal state worked hard to reshape the way Canada was defined religiously, others made their own connections between religion and their country and made sure to have those reflected, too, in public life. In the 1960s, in a process that had begun long before and continued long after, the religious component of the terms "Canada" and "Canadian" was being officially redefined. The complicated and conflicted nature of that process makes for a compelling and important story.

The argument of this study will proceed as follows. For those interested in its theoretical foundations, chapter 1 explores the meaning behind such terms as "public religion" and explains how public celebrations and exhibitions, including the symbols and rituals that make them up, can be fruitfully interpreted, and, it is to be hoped, not misinterpreted, by the historian.

To provide a better understanding of the public and explicit connections made between Christianity and national public life across the country in 1967, chapter 2 puts those connections into their historical context. Based largely on secondary sources, with some primary materials from the archives of the Presbyterian, Anglican, and United Churches and the Pentecostal Assemblies of Canada, chapter 2 examines the official, or dominant, model for understanding Canada in national public life until the Second World War: that of a Christian and British country with a French minority. Already in the interwar period, the ability of that model to reflect reality and to unify and stabilize Canada was showing signs of strain. Chapter 2 also considers, then, how during the rapid socioeconomic development of the postwar period, the privileged position of Christianity in Canadian public life began to blur and then fade.

How the federal arm of the Canadian state and the mainline[13] Christian churches shaped and responded to the growing challenges to the historic privileging of Christianity in Canadian public life is the subject of chapter 3. Building on the analysis of chapter 2, it will argue that as Canadian society became increasingly diverse and as public opinion liberalized in the postwar period, a religiously and racially exclusive image of Canada irritated and alienated a growing proportion of the population. Within the federal state and also within the mainline churches, a dominant reformist mentality, bolstered by the affluence and progressivism of the 1950s and 1960s, resulted not in the defense of the status quo, but in the gradual weakening of the privileged position of Christianity in the dominant culture of the country and the dismantling of the symbols and structures that represented that position and the racially and ethnically discriminatory legislation that had supported it. Reformers worked to accommodate their institutions to the changing times and in doing so, found themselves caught in a cross-fire between those who supported their efforts at reform and those who adamantly rejected them.

Chapter 4 picks up the reaction of Prime Minister Pearson (1963–67) and his governing federal Liberal Party, in particular, to the changes of the postwar period and places their initiatives in the context of nation-building. It contends that in a country shaken by a dissatisfied Quebec and faced with the discontent of other ethnic and religious minorities, the celebrations of 1967 became part of a larger effort to reimagine Canada as a pluralistic country, yet one united in its diversity. With other government initiatives, the celebrations worked hard to get people involved in and enthusiastic about the public life of a more inclusive Canada. Not surprisingly, that focus shaped the way religion was welcomed within them. Instead of presenting a uniquely Christian Canada to Canadians, federal state planners formed and funded the Canadian Interfaith Conference (CIC), an organization which attempted to represent and involve in the Centennial celebrations every organized faith group in the country. The records of the CIC and its interactions with the Centennial Commission, gleaned from both the National Archives of Canada and the Centennial files of the various member faiths, form the basis for this chapter.

The attempt to use the Centennial celebrations and the CIC to translate Canada from a Christian and British-French to an inclusive and pluralistic country was a massive project of public persuasion. It meant changing people's minds. Chapter 5 of this study focuses on the Canadian Interfaith Conference again, but this time from the perspective of the various faith groups involved. Why did some thirty-three religious groups say yes to the CIC? How did people worshipping on prayer mats or in pews across the country respond to its message of a religiously inclusive Canada? To answer those questions, chapter 5 returns to the rich records of the CIC and to the Centennial files kept by the Canadian Council of Catholic Bishops, the Canadian Jewish Congress, the Baptist Federation of Canada, and the Anglican, Presbyterian, United, and Pentecostal Churches.

Chapters 6, 7, and 8 carry the same themes into an examination of Expo 67 in Montreal. They rely heavily on the voluminous and thorough records of the Canadian Corporation for the 1967 World Exposition found in the National Archives of Canada. They also use records for the Sermons from Science Pavilion, the Christian Pavilion, and the Pavilion of Judaism found, respectively, in the archives of an organization called Christian Direction, the Canadian Centre for Ecumenism, and the Canadian Jewish Congress, all located in Montreal. Several personal interviews with pavilion organizers helped fill in some gaps.

At Expo, as in the Centennial celebrations, a federal corporation sought to present an image of Canada that erased a British-French and Christian past and that highlighted an inclusive and pluralistic present and future. There, too, as I will argue in chapter 7, a state corporation found itself trying to shape public expressions of religion in ways that celebrated pluralism and "unity in diversity." There, too, the official approach to public religion found only partial support among Canada's religious groups and was flatly rejected by others determined to present to the world a Canada that was still particularly Christian. In chapter 8, an examination of two Christian pavilions and the Pavilion of Judaism at Expo, constructed by religious groups themselves, will demonstrate again that those groups were divided on how best to adjust to a pluralistic Canada. They were determined, nonetheless, to publicly present their own religious messages, and not simply those wished for by the state, to the world at Expo 67. A conclusion will draw out the key themes of this study and then offer some reflections on how those themes can inform our understanding of public expressions of religion in Canada in the 1960s.

Mr. John Fisher proudly displays his giant-size mallet, which bears the inscription "Mr. John Fisher – presented by the Hon. Luther H. Hodges, Governor of the Toastmasters, District 37, and Ted Davis, Gov. T.N. Raleigh, N.C." Centennial Commission staff, *from left to right*: Robbins Elliott, Peter H. Aykroyd, Claude Gauthier, John Fisher, Robert Choquette, Jean-Pierre Houle.

Expo 67's Man the Producer Pavilion. National Archives of Canada, PA-145603

Crowd in front of the Canada Pavilion at Expo 67. National Archives of Canada, e001096693

Crowd in Katimatik at Expo 67. National Archives of Canada, e001096696

The final model of the Christian Pavilion, Expo 67. Canadian Centre for Ecumenism, Montreal

The Christian Pavilion Board of Directors in front of the pavilion's Tau cross. *From left to right*: Rev. E.M. Jenkins, Rev. G.M. Morrison, Rev. T.P. Theophilos, Very Rev. William Bothwell, Rev. Earl J. Treusch, Rév. Père Irénée Beaubien, Rev. H.E. Bartsch, Mme Thérèrse Demers, Rev. Douglas Smith, Rev. Dr. C. Ritchie Bell, Mr L. Buzzell, M. Horace Boivin. Canadian Centre for Ecumenism, Montreal

Inside the Christian Pavilion courtyard: the garden. Canadian Centre for Ecumenism, Montreal

Inside the Christian Pavilion, Zone 1: photographs everywhere. Canadian Centre for Ecumenism, Montreal

Inside the Christian Pavilion: descending to Zone 2. Canadian Centre for Ecumenism, Montreal

Inside the Christian Pavilion, Zone 3: a place to recover and reflect. Canadian Centre for Ecumenism, Montreal

Inside the Christian Pavilion, Zone 3: under this photograph were the words "Why do you look for me among the dead? I am with you always." Canadian Centre for Ecumenism, Montreal

The Sermons from Science Pavilion, complete with line-ups and the clock on the right giving the time of the next performance. Christian Direction, Inc., Montreal

The Sermons from Science Pavilion's founding group of directors. *From left to right*: Joe Kass, Bill Weaver, Malcolm Spankie, Don Robertson, Alastair Hamilton, Keith Price. Christian Direction, Inc., Montreal

Sermons from Science Pavilion, the first auditorium filled to capacity. Note the state-of-the-art translation headphones. Christian Direction, Inc., Montreal

Sermons from Science Pavilion, some counselling with scattered groups after the second Leighton Ford film presentation. Christian Direction, Inc., Montreal

The Pavilion of Judaism. Canadian Jewish Congress Archives, Montreal

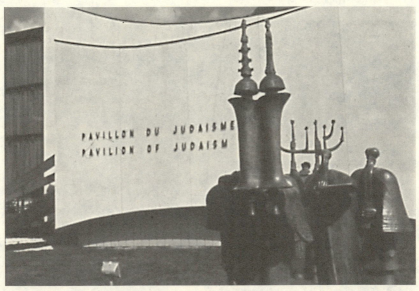

The Procession, on the lawns in front of the Pavilion of Judaism. Canadian Jewish
Congress Archives, Montreal

Deputy Commissioner General Robert Shaw visits the Pavilion of Judaism.
From left to right: architect Harry Stillman; Dr S. Levine; pavilion director Mordecai Kessler; Rabbi Simor Zambrowsky; artist of the temple reconstruction, Lazare Halberthal; Expo representative Stan Turner; director of Canadian Exhibits, Drummond Giles; deputy commissioner general at Expo, Robert Shaw; the most significant financial organizer of the pavilion, Mr Sam Steinberg; director of exhibits at the Pavilion of Judaism, Igor Kuchinsky; architect Max Roth, who designed the exhibits at the pavilion; and Rabbi Wilfred Shuchat.
Canadian Jewish Congress Archives, Montreal

Cardinal Léger (far left in group of four on the right) is shown the Pavilion of Judaism's scale-model reconstruction of Solomon's temple by its creator, Judge Lazarre Haberthal. Canadian Jewish Congress Archives, Montreal

FOR CANADA'S SAKE

1

Public Religion, Public Celebrations, and the Construction of Nations:

Theoretical Considerations

This study uses public exhibitions and celebrations to highlight the ways in which understandings of Canada in the 1960s included religious understandings, as well as the ways in which both changed. Without doubt, that is an ambitious and slippery task that raises several important questions. How do we understand public religion? What is it, and what does it do? What do we mean when we talk about changing understandings of Canada? Is it even possible to define national identities – identities that might arguably have a thousand definitions instead of one? For that matter, how can we make sense of such elusive things as public ritual and symbolism, or centennial celebrations and world fairs?

It is much easier, of course, to raise such questions than to answer them. For the purpose of analytical clarity, however, answers are important. This chapter turns first to an analysis of public religion, then to a discussion of its inclusion in "constructed" national identities, and finally to a discussion of how public religion and national identities are expressed through public ritual, symbols, celebrations, and exhibitions.

In recent years, Canadian historical scholarship focused on religion has been dominated by "the secularization debate."[1] Prominent scholars have argued eloquently about when organized institutional religion, represented by Canada's largest Christian churches, lost its influence over Canadians. Was it in the first decades of the last century that personal faith and belief became privatized and therefore less publicly significant?[2] Or, misinterpreting change for decline, have historians missed the signs that those churches actually gained in strength and influence into the Great Depression?

While that debate has been extraordinarily fruitful and engaging, I take a different approach here. First, while studies of secularization have tended to try to assess the health of key church institutions by analysing

changes in individual Christian belief and theology, I attempt to examine
the very different question of how Canadians attached religion to their
national identities. For this book to be properly understood, the latter
point is particularly significant. Changes in the theology of Christian
church institutions will be addressed, but in the context of how they affected the religious identities of communities and the country of Canada.
An examination of Christian belief and practice will help lay the foundation for the much broader central focus of this study: an assessment of
how religious identities, both Christian and otherwise, helped shape and
were shaped in turn by changing understandings of Canada in the 1950s
and 1960s.[3]

While shifting the focus to the relationship between religious and national identities, I also shift the time frame from the first half of the twentieth century to the relatively untouched 1945–70 period. While many
studies have fruitfully debated the long process of secularization in Canada from the Victorian period on, I argue here that after years of ebbs
and flows, it was mainly in the postwar period, and more particularly in
the 1960s, that the historic privileging of Christianity in Canadian national public life began very visibly to crumble. Even then, however, in
the celebrations and expositions of 1967, Canadian public religion was
becoming more diverse, not disappearing.[4]

The evidence for that argument is growing, and it is impressive. For
many years, historians have noted that the Roman Catholic Church, in
particular, continued to have a remarkable degree of influence in Quebec and in French Canadian culture into the 1960s. It was in that decade of the Quiet Revolution that the Church was most visibly forced
to relinquish much of its control over social programs in Quebec and
that French Canadians in significant numbers let go of the Roman
Catholic Church as a central pillar of their cultural identities.[5] Outside
Quebec and Roman Catholicism, too, a good number of historians of
religion have pointed to the 1960s as a fundamental turning point in
the relationship between religion and culture. Already in 1972, John
Webster Grant noted that as a result of the events of earlier decades, it
was the 1960s that saw the most dramatic "disestablishment" of the
mainline Christian churches in Canada. Whereas they had once been
some of the most important and influential institutions in shaping the
public life of the nation, Grant argued that by the end of the 1960s they
were "no longer the keeper of the nation's conscience, and few Canadians seemed to regret [their] dethronement."[6] The one "fundamental"
and "irrevocable" change since the 1960s, the most recent survey of Canadian Christianity has argued, is that "the concept of 'Christendom' –
that is, of a society where Christianity and culture are essentially integrated – is gone forever in Canada."[7]

In pointing to the 1960s as a dramatic turning point away from the historic privileging of Christianity in Canadian public life, then, I take a particular angle on the relationship between religion and culture in Canada that remains relatively unexplored. Though studies of theology, doctrine, and individuals have been central to much of the historiography surrounding Canadian religion, such things are of secondary interest here. Of fundamental importance to this study is the very different question of how public expressions of religion (including Christian and non-Christian faiths) shed light on the subtle relationship between religious and national identities in Canada in the 1960s.[8]

In choosing to examine what might be called public religion, I am entering a field of relative scarcity in Canada, but one of overabundance in the United States. While Canadians and Canadian scholars have generally expressed little interest in public religion, American scholars have been studying the field very carefully, and very thoroughly, for well over thirty years. At the very least, one learns from reading their work that care and clarity in terminology and language is crucial in any examination of public expressions of religion.[9]

So what do I mean by "public religion"? We might begin with some obvious examples. The 1 July prayer service can serve us yet again. Staged on Parliament Hill (one of Canada's most recognizable public sites), involving Canada's highest public officials, and aimed at every Canadian, public it surely was. It was also indisputably religious, involving prayer, the reading of sacred texts, and appeals to divinity. Religious pavilions on the Expo 67 site, also to be considered in this study, were equally obvious and explicit representations in public of what we would commonly understand to be religion. Expressions of religion in public life need not always be embodied in such explicit and obvious forms, of course. Such things as the hope for progress and faith in technology can equally serve the role of religious belief in public life.[10] Nonetheless, it is precisely such traditional public expressions of religion – prayers on behalf of "the nation," the embedded nature of Christianity in laws and school textbooks, and religious representations at public exhibitions – that are the central focus of this study.

Religion in the prayer service and at Expo 67 was public, of course, simply because it was often in an open and accessible space and involved an unrestricted number of people. It was, in Robert Wuthnow's words, "out in the open, rather than being buried in the subjective consciousness of the individual."[11] We need to be careful here, however, to note that religion can be public – "out in the open" – in very different ways. While the Prayer Service and the religious pavilions at Expo 67 were both public expressions of religion, and while they both attempted to engage "the public",[12] they were also quite distinct in terms of their content and purpose.

Again, the ongoing debate about public religion in the United States has helped to make this point clear.[13] Public expressions of religion, it should be remembered, can be as varied in their style, content, and purpose as private expressions of religious belief. They might have as their object of veneration everything from society itself, to certain values and assumptions embedded in a culture, to a political party, to a transcendent divine being.[14] Choosing to declare very different things sacred, public expressions of religion might also do so for very different reasons. A national celebration, for example, might attempt to make a nation appear "holy" in order to disarm and dissolve attempts to break that nation apart. During the same celebration, however, a preacher might stand on a soap box in the middle of the crowd and declare his religious belief system (which might have no explicit connection to the nation) as the true religion – all in the attempt to use the large gathering as a forum to convince others to adopt that belief system as their own. Those are very different forms of public religion, indeed.

Such distinctions are not merely academic abstractions. They help direct us to the importance of context, including authorial intent, in the interpretation of public expressions of religion and in doing so, help us to better understand those expressions themselves. They allow us to note, for example, that while both the prayer service on Parliament Hill and the religious pavilions at Expo 67 said something important about changing patterns of Canadian public religion in the 1960s, they did so in significantly different ways. The prayer service connected religion directly to the political leadership of the country by the presence of politicians and the queen and employed religion for the purposes of the state. The three religious pavilions on the Expo site, on the other hand, attempted to shape the Canadian public without direct connections to the state or to the political stability of the country. The Prayer Service was designed to unite all Canadians together in an expression of thanks for, and a rededication to, the welfare of their country.[15] At Expo, religious organizations attempted to inspire everything from a broad concern for social justice, to a respect for particular faith traditions, to a dramatic and life-changing conversion to particular doctrines and beliefs.[16] Without understanding those distinctions, interpreting the prayer service and the Expo pavilions would be a difficult task indeed.

The term "public religion," then, may refer to a wide range of public expressions of religion, some directly sponsored and sanctioned by the state and others representing more particular and certainly un-official forms of religion in public life. If we are to try to understand how religious identities informed Canadian national identities, we will need to recognize public religion in all its forms. Examining only state-sponsored public expressions of religion, after all, would leave us listening to only a few dominant voices and blocking many quieter ones out. Casting our net more widely, we will discover that official expressions of religion in public life sometimes varied significantly from others that also had something to say about the religious iden-tity of the country. How they varied, in fact, can sometimes tell us far more than the individual expressions of public religion themselves.

Having, I hope, clarified the meaning and scope of the term "public religion," I face another question: Why bother writing a book about it? My answer is two-fold. First, public expressions of religion can provide us with colourful and captivating visual descriptions of the individuals and communities that formed them. The public privileg-ing of Christianity in Canada in the 1960s, for example, can be read partly as a reflection of the fact that the vast majority of Canadians described themselves as Christian in that period. But public expres-sions of religion can do more than tell us about the way things were. They can also tell us about how the people of the past wished them to be. Public expressions of religion, in other words, will be far more than a description of their context. They will also be a prescription – an attempt to shape a community or society into an ideal, to impose on that society values considered sacred or transcendent by some, but not necessarily by all. The historic public privileging of Christianity in Canada, for example, accurately reflected the fact that the vast ma-jority of Canadians were affiliated with a Christian church. At the same time, it prescribed a religious vision of the country that sought to make Canadians into something they often were not: a united, loyal, honest, and obedient community of publicly minded citizens.

To understand the prescriptive nature of public religion, we need to understand that it is a constructed entity. It is constructed, we might say, because it is the product of human creativity and organiza-tion – the result of a choice to place religion in public life in the first place and of a further selection of the form it should take. In some contexts, such choices might seem implicit or commonsensical, mak-ing public expressions of religion seem natural or normal. Forms of public religion, like all aspects of culture, however, are indeed created in particular times for particular reasons.

To make that point clear, we might consider the constructed nature of public identities, of which public religion has historically been a part, as well as the dominant cultures that have helped to create and maintain those identities. Though designed to seem incontrovertible and common-sense, nations and nationalisms have in fact been products of human invention. "All communities larger than primordial villages of face-to-face contact (and perhaps even these) are imagined," Benedict Anderson argues in his seminal book, *Imagined Communities*.[17] "The members of even the smallest nation will never know most of their fellow-members, meet them, or even hear of them," he writes, "yet in the minds of each lives the image of their communion."[18]

As constructed or imagined entities, nations and national identities have naturally reflected the visions and goals of those who have created them. Not surprisingly, perhaps, nationalisms and national identities constructed by cultural, political, and economic elites have often gained a kind of dominant or official status.[19] Since those elites had the power to shape and maintain the dominant culture of their societies, they could use that culture to reflect their own identities and values and to convince others to adopt them. In sum, nationalisms and national identities have historically been shaped by the particular needs of their creators and have served their particular ends.[20]

One must be careful, of course, when speaking about dominant or official national identities and cultures. The regionally and ethnically fractured nature of Canadian national life has quite appropriately made scholars writing about Canada, in particular, wary of those claiming anything to be national, let alone dominant. That said, references to a dominant culture in Canada and to the official national identity that it shapes will appear in this study as useful ways to represent one among many Canadian cultures, and a particularly influential one at that.[21] Cultural theorist Raymond Williams argues that in "any society, in any period, there is a central system of practices, meanings and values, which we can properly call dominant and effective."[22] Such dominant cultures are not static and all-pervasive but hegemonically fluid and changing as they attempt to adapt to, absorb, or overcome opposition within their societies. Translating this idea into our Canadian context, then, the term "dominant culture" will be used in this study to describe the culture that is shaped and formed by national elites most often centred in central Canada, a culture that is more or less diffused through those elites and their institutions across the country. Though that culture is associated with political, economic, and cultural power, the term "dominant" does not imply a lack of adaptability, nor does it imply that it is not challenged by other cultures within the borders of Canada.[23] Instead, it refers to its ability to infuse its particular understanding of the world into national institutions and to accommodate challenges as they come.

Historically, official national identities and the dominant cultures of which they are a part have carried a significant religious component. In an important study, Linda Colley describes the importance of Protestantism as a defining component in the shaping of a British identity.[24] Others have argued convincingly that religion can play both a "priestly (legitimating)" and a "prophetic (critical)" role in the formation of communal identities. It can both make some ideas and structures more secure by declaring them holy and undercut others by declaring them morally and religiously wrong.[25] In its ability to do so, religion "has been the historically most widespread and effective instrumentality of legitimation," sociologist Peter Berger argues, a force that, by locating social institutions "within a sacred and cosmic frame of reference," could play a powerful role in building allegiance to "the established order of society and the state."[26] If the state could be positively associated with the will of God, Berger notes, then few God-fearing people would cause it ill. By connecting institutions and identities with something transcendent, public expressions of religion have helped make them worthy of devotion, loyalty, and support.

Like the nations and national identities of which it is often a part, then, public religion is a constructed, malleable entity that serves the needs of its creators. If we are to understand the significant presence of religion in Canadian public life in the 1960s, we will need to understand it precisely in this historical and theoretical context. How public religion has been formed and structured can say a great deal about the citizens and elites who have both shaped it and been shaped by it. As a cultural artifact, both descriptive and prescriptive in form and content, public religion as a component of national identities can be an important window through which we can view and understand the past.

In analyzing the Centennial celebrations and Expo 67, I will draw heavily on the work of scholars who have pioneered a thoughtful and careful approach to the study of public ritual and symbol, the building blocks of exhibitions and anniversary celebrations. Sociologists, anthropologists, cultural theorists, and, more recently, historians have argued in a multitude of studies that the ritual and symbolism of such occasions, religious and otherwise, should not be dismissed as the fluff of history but should instead be carefully examined as important tools of cultural formation and maintenance.[27] "Public rituals are simply more formalized and elaborated versions of behaviours in ordinary life, such as tidying one's room or tipping one's hat, that also help align our relations with other people and ourselves," Robert Wuthnow argues.[28] In the words of another observer, public ritual and

symbols play "a cognitive role, rendering intelligible society and social relationships, serving to organize people's knowledge of the past
and present and their capacity to imagine the future."[29] Carefully
planned, self-consciously orchestrated, and often involving the participation of tens if not hundreds of thousands of persons, public ritual
and symbol can help shape personal and collective identities. They
can help convince and reassure us of an understanding of ourselves,
our neighbours, and our communities.

In its study of public religion in public symbol and ritual, this
book has been inspired, in particular, by the insights and analysis of
Raymond Breton, an anthropologist who argues in a series of articles
that changes to what he calls Canada's "symbolic order" since the
1960s were in fact some of the most controversial political developments of the late twentieth century.[30] Why? Drawing on the work of
others, Breton argues that the symbolic order of a nation includes its
"collective identity ... represented in the multiplicity of symbols surrounding the rituals of public life, the functioning of institutions,
and the public celebration of events, groups and individuals." It includes the values and norms and customs and ways of doing things
of a nation that are most importantly "embedded in the forms and
style of public institutions" such as government, school curricula,
and the administration of justice.[31] "The symbolic construction in-
volves defining the socio-cultural character of the collectivity: the set
of ideas and symbols that articulate its basic understandings about
itself, its place in the surrounding world, and its constituent groups
and social categories and the relations among them. This is especially the case for large collectivities whose members do not and will
never know most of their fellow members. The identity and boundaries of the collectivity are symbolically defined: [through them]
members acquire a conception of the group's identity".[32] Drawing
on the work of Anthony Cohen, Breton goes on to argue that a country's public symbols and rituals act as boundaries for its identity – as
gatekeepers defining who is allowed in and who must be kept out,
whose voice will be heard and whose will be ignored.[33] And following Jeffrey Alexander, he contends that public symbols ascribe recognition, status, and value to those groups who find their beliefs and
cultural traditions within those symbols and deny status and value
to those whose beliefs and cultural traditions are left out.[34]

By extension, we can argue that the religious elements of public rituals and symbols can represent visually the way religious identities
inform Canadian national identities. They offer clues, sometimes subtle and sometimes explicit, about which people and which beliefs can
be considered legitimate in the country and which cannot. In doing

so, they hold a degree of cultural power, reflecting and shaping the identity not just of the country but of its individual citizens as well.

Given the significance of public rituals and symbols, then, they are an excellent place to begin a study of the way public religion has informed communal and, in our case, national identities. Anniversary celebrations and world fairs are, in turn, a fine place to go in search of public rituals and symbols. In her recent book, *Nation and Commemoration: Creating National Identities in the United States and Australia*, Lyn Spillman has carefully and convincingly analyzed centennial and bicentennial celebrations in both Australia and the United States to observe how the national identities of those two nations have changed over time. "Centennial celebrations," she notes, "seem to be important – and largely neglected – moments in the process by which American and Australian identities were formed."[35] In the past few years, in fact, that neglect has been waning, and excellent studies not only of Canadian anniversary celebrations but also of public exhibitions have emerged. Four book-length studies, by Elsbeth Heaman, Keith Walden, H.V. Nelles, and Ronald Rudin, have investigated, respectively, Canadian exhibitions in the nineteenth century, the Toronto Industrial Exhibition (precursor to the Canadian National Exhibition, or CNE), the 1908 tercentenary celebrations of the founding of Quebec, and commemorations of the lives of Samuel de Champlain and Mgr Francois de Laval in Quebec City from 1878 to 1908.[36]

These studies and others confirm and expand upon our earlier insights in two particularly significant ways. They demonstrate again how public anniversaries and exhibitions have been used by elites to present an official version of national or local identity to celebrants and fairgoers. For that reason Heaman, Walden, Nelles, Rudin, and others have all refused to view those events simply as a snapshot of the culture that created them, or, in Heaman's words, as "a cross-section of past culture frozen in time."[37] Instead, each has argued that they were, among other things, tools used by their developers to shape and influence their societies.

If these events have attempted to shape their visitors as well as their social, political, and economic context, they must not be seen simply as sites of one-way communication and indoctrination. They are all the more interesting because they are "contested grounds" where participants and visitors develop and offer their own meaning of the events, sometimes in direct challenge to the official message.[38] Public rituals planned by the state "have an 'official' form and rationale," one scholar has concisely argued, "but their participants may well find in them quite different meaning and experience."[39] Carefully planned and densely packed with symbol and ritual, they have been crucial sites for the study of cultures – important places to turn to in order to discover how planners *and* citizens understood themselves and their societal context, religion and all.

One more nagging – and closely related – question remains. Symbols and rituals, by their very nature, tend to be vague and ill-defined. In the attempt to embody visually the common identity of millions of people, specificity is not a virtue. Indeterminacy is. Add to that the ability of different persons to make different meanings of the same event, and the complexity builds. How then, can we know that any interpretation of symbols and rituals is correct? How can we know the significance of a prayer service? What can we "read into" symbols and rituals, and what can we not?

There is no easy answer to these questions, but there is one important principle of historical interpretation that applies here as elsewhere: the need to study pieces of the past in their historical context. As cultural theorist Stuart Hall has argued, visual signs can, theoretically, have any number of meanings.[40] Placed in their own cultural context, however, their meanings are limited. Communication is invariably coded, laden with biases, assumptions, and goals, without which the message cannot be properly understood. Those codes, in the form of alphabets and grammatical rules, are easily identified in written or spoken language. They are equally important to visual communication. Just as the written word, placed in the context of its culture, is limited in its meaning by the sentence and language of which it is a part, so too are visual images, rituals, and symbols.

As Hall argues well, communication through visual signs is not a precise science. While it is generally not difficult to discover, through paper trails, what such signs were intended to mean by their creators, it is much more difficult to say what the often anonymous people who viewed them actually took from them. Human variability makes sure of that. But neither is discerning the meaning of visual signs and events purely a game of chance, without rules by which it might be understood and played with success. The ambiguity and imprecision of public symbols and rituals must be respected, but the restraining value of historical context should prevent us from despair.

Those insights will form the foundation of this study. Grounding the analysis that follows, they contend that the Canada that was celebrated and sacralized in the prayer service on 1 July 1967 was a constructed entity. It had been constructed in a geographical and institutional sense, of course, a century earlier by a small group of men in the years preceding 1867 and had been brought to its present form through many more negotiations in the years since. But Canada was also constructed in the sense that it was an "imagined community" as much as a physical one. What it meant to be Canadian was what Canadians *thought* it meant. Geographical location was included, but definitions of Canada rarely left it at that. Canadian nationality, various citizens have argued over time, has also been about such concepts as British-ness, Christianity, and masculinity or, in more recent times, about humility, generosity, and plurality.[41] Like all thoughts, definitions of Canada and Canadian, including the important component of public religion, have been susceptible to change.

With others, this study contends that it was in the 1960s that the important privileging of Christianity in national public life began to very visibly fall apart. As we will now see, what first emerged from the "official de-Christianization" of Canada was not a secular but rather an officially multifaith Canada.

2

"The Things That We Believe in in This Country Stand for Christianity":

Christian Canada to the 1960s

As the 1 July prayer service on Parliament Hill explicitly revealed, religion played an impressive role in the state-sponsored, public celebrations of the Centennial of Canadian Confederation in 1967. More specifically, while the service continued to be recognizably Christian, it also hinted that the privileging of Christianity in Canadian national public life was not without challenge.

To understand that challenge, we need to first understand why and how Christianity came to be publicly privileged in Canada in the first place. At its heart, the public identity of Canada as a Christian country was, like other such identities, shaped by human relationships, embedded in culture, rooted in history, and susceptible to change.[1] More specifically, at the heart of the explicit and exclusive public relationship between Christianity and Canada was a shared understanding among Canada's political and cultural elites, including the leadership of Canada's largest churches. Those elites were largely responsible for the dominant forms of public religion in the country, and it was their generally positive view of the influence of Christianity on Canadian society that not only connected the two but also helped to build the close historical relationship between the Canadian state and Canada's mainline Christian churches.

In fact, at the foundation of a Christian Canada was not just a close relationship between the Canadian state and Christianity but a more specific privileging of Canada's largest and most "respectable" Christian denominations, the mainline Protestant churches and the Roman Catholic Church. In the sensitive and difficult project of Canadian nation-building, those wishing to build a united nation emphasized broad public expressions of religion, that is, expressions that were able to reach as many Canadians as possible, regardless of their particular denominational affiliation. Ironically, that approach left out of the dominant culture not only individuals of non-Christian faiths but also a significant number of Christian faith groups as well.

Into the 1960s, the public privileging of a broad Christianity and Canada's mainline Christian churches was revealed in everything from royal commissions to public radio to immigration regulations. By that decade, however, Canada's close public identification with Christianity faced formidable challenges. In the 1950s and 1960s, Canada was in transition, and the national, public manifestations of a Christian Canadian national identity – always contingent – were eroded visibly and quickly. The representations of a Christian Canada in Canadian public life became contested as never before.

In 1956, the province of Quebec's Royal Commission on Constitutional Problems submitted its five-volume report to Premier Maurice Duplessis.[2] Appointed three years earlier to study federal-provincial relations with specific regard to taxation, the Tremblay Commission, as it was popularly called, had received about 250 briefs and had travelled across the province to gather testimony from hundreds of Quebeckers. The result of its work has been described as "one of the landmark events of the period,"[3] "a massive document detailing the philosophical, sociological, even theological reasons for Quebec's distinctiveness."[4]

Those theological reasons, in fact, played an important role in the report. The commissioners characterized French and English Canada by language, ethnic origin and religion. Primary responsibility for the differences in French and English culture, however, was attributed to religion. Roman Catholicism had fostered a social order in Quebec that was based on the dignity of the common person, the report argued. Protestantism, on the other hand, had infused English Canadian culture with pragmatism, an acquisitive instinct, and a lack of concern about principles. In French Canada, as a result, liberty was defined by the common good; in English Canada, by materialism.[5]

Until very recent times, ethnicity and religion have been tightly linked in the minds of Canadians. French Canadians, as the Tremblay Report argued, were Roman Catholics. English Canadians were Protestants. Those were gross generalizations, of course, and the Tremblay Report was by no means unbiased.[6] Nonetheless, that there was a link between ethnicity and religion remained a popular assumption. English and Irish Protestants were largely Anglican or United, Scots were Presbyterians, Ukrainians either Ukrainian Orthodox or Ukrainian Roman Catholics, and Italians, Roman Catholic. What was no doubt intended to be a harmless joke in the *United Church Observer* in 1958 made the point perfectly clear. Introducing a new journalist by the name of Michael Pengelley to its readers, the editor included the comment, "Despite that name, Mike is a Protestant."[7]

If religion and ethnicity were intertwined, so were Christianity and the concept of Canada. Into the postwar period, everyone from prime ministers to editors of church periodicals considered Canada a Christian country, and they had good reason to do so. Demographically, 94 percent of Canadians were affiliated with a Christian church in 1961, with the largest non-Christian religion, Judaism, claiming only 1.3 percent of the population.[8] Culturally, too, Christianity was everywhere. Until the early 1960s, a daily feature of CBC radio in Toronto was *Plain Talk*, a ten-minute morning devotion read by a Christian minister, just before the 8:00 A.M. news.[9]

Canada's provincial education systems, arguably the central institutions of social reproduction, also backed up the point. Into the 1960s in Quebec, education was virtually controlled by two religious boards, one Roman Catholic and one Protestant. In Newfoundland, the newest Canadian province, the education system had been set up in 1949 on a denominational basis, with schools run by the Anglican Church and the Salvation Army, for example, but without any secular or religiously neutral schools. In the midst of World War II, Ontario moved to make its education system even more Christian. In 1944, Premier George Drew saw to it that two thirty minute classes of education in the Christian religion were added to the curriculum in public schools. Taught by regular teachers or clergymen, they remained there into the 1970s.[10]

Even Canada's legal system reflected the formative influence of the Christian churches in the construction of the nation. In 1964, adoption laws in some provinces made it illegal for Protestants to adopt Roman Catholic children, and vice versa.[11] Canada's citizenship laws bore a Christian imprint too, a fact that was well publicized when a Dutch couple, both atheists, were denied citizenship in 1964.[12] Though having lived in Ontario for the previous nine years as landed immigrants, the couple was criticized by an Ontario judge for their lack of church affiliation and lack of faith. The citizenship oath, ending "so help me God," could mean nothing to them, he argued. "The things that we believe in in this country stand for Christianity – being honest and being kind – believing in Christ's teachings ... Not everybody follows this but that is what we try to attain in this country, the Christian way of life."

The law enshrined still other privileges for the Christian faith, though in a more subtle way. Federal regulation of immigration to Canada well into the postwar period reflected the concern to keep Canada both white and Christian. In 1947, in the midst of a debate on his own government's immigration policy, Prime Minister Mackenzie King argued to the House of Commons that "the people of Canada do not wish, as a result of mass immigration, to make a fundamental alteration in the character of our population ... Any considerable Oriental immigration would ... be certain to give rise to social and economic problems."[13] Coming from a Liberal politician, that was a strikingly illiberal statement, but it was hardly outrageous for its time. It was reflected in Canadian policies that favoured immigrants of Anglo-Saxon and Christian background and that discriminated heavily against immigrants of Asian and largely non-Christian origins. A new Immigration Act in 1952 continued to be discriminatory with regard to race and nationality in its categorization of prospective immigrants by nation. British subjects were preferred most of all along with citizens of Ireland, the United States, and France. Last on the list were South Asian (and overwhelmingly non-Christian) nationalities. Among others, one order-in-council limited immigrants from India, Pakistan, and Ceylon to 150, 100, and 50 people per year, respectively.[14] As Lester B. Pearson described them, Canada's immigration policies in the 1950s were designed to prevent "major change in the racial, religious, or social constitution of the country."[15]

The understanding of Canada as a country that "stands for Christianity," then, was displayed in the privileging of Christianity in demographics, educational structures, and law. It was also clear to commentators of the time. In his study of church-state relations in Canada, published in 1967, J.S. Moir noted the important place that churches continued to hold in public life in his own day. Canadians assumed "the presence of an unwritten separation of church and state, without denying an essential connection between religious principles and national life or the right of the churches to speak out on matters of public importance."[16] Another scholar, E.R. Norman, was more direct and argued in 1968 that an "establishment of non-sectarian Christianity" in Canadian public life was still alive.[17] Into the 1960s, dominant understandings of the Canadian nation included a strong religious, and more particularly Christian, component.

How had that equation of Christianity and Canada in the dominant culture come to be? First and foremost, behind the very visible manifestations of Christianity in public life stood the nearly total monopoly of that faith among Canadians. More specifically, it was the importance of Christianity to the upper and growing middle classes of Canadian society after the 1850s – to those who created and controlled the dominant culture in their communities – that helped to firmly place Christianity within it.[18] As Canada developed its own dreams of nationhood after 1867, the Canadians who dreamed those dreams conceived of both their church and their state as nation-building institutions. For their part, leaders of the mainline churches and state institutions imagined themselves as often working towards the same nation-building goals.[19]

They often were, and for good reason. In the nineteenth century
and well into the twentieth, they drew on the same educated citizens
from the same Anglo-Protestant and French Roman Catholic communities. Canada's cultural and political elite was demographically
small and interconnected, often educated in the same limited number
of universities, which remained imbued with a broadly Christian atmosphere and which graduated clergy as well as political, economic,
and cultural leaders.[20] Into the mid-1950s, Canada's elites remained
strikingly homogenous. Not only were Canadians of British descent
vastly overrepresented in their ranks, but so were Canadians belonging to the United, Anglican, Presbyterian, and Baptist Churches.[21]
Leaders of church and state institutions communicated easily and
shared similar perspectives, in part because they were members of
the same cultural elite, educated in the same institutions, and shaped
by a similar cultural vision for the future of their country.

Through everything from evangelistic campaigns to social reform
agencies, middle and upper class Canadians, in particular, sought
ways of making Christianity an important element of their communities and their country from the middle of the nineteenth century and
into the middle of the twentieth. Many of the politicians who argued
in the country's legislatures also sat in one of the largest Christian
churches on Sundays. Their country, many Canadians believed, had a
great deal to gain from being Christian, and a great deal to lose if that
faith was lost.

In his study of religion and culture in nineteenth-century Ontario, for
example, William Westfall has noted the importance of the commonly
held assumption that "a religious population would be a loyal population."[22] The welfare of the state and of society, it was believed, could be
enhanced by the Christian emphasis on submission to authority, a commitment to the common good, and other such state-friendly ideas. Into
the second half of the twentieth century, the perception that Christianity
was a necessary component of a stable and healthy democratic society
remained firm in Canada and was in fact, enhanced by the Cold War.
After 1945, Canada's cultural and political elites often shared a common
concern with church officials that a "spiritual component" was necessary to raise Canadian culture above crass materialism to greatness.[23]
Christianity was widely deemed to be the bedrock of Western democracies, the necessary guarantor of the moral responsibility of each individual and of the freedom to use it that democratic societies required. In the
first half of the twentieth century, Canada's religious and political leaders commonly referred to Christianity as the repository of the highest
values of Western civilization.[24] In French Canadian Roman Catholic
circles, where until the 1960s the principles of a liberal democracy were

not as important as they were among Anglo-Protestants, Roman Catholicism was nonetheless considered one of the key pillars of the French Canadian identity – dominant cultural elites considered it to be essential to the survival of the "French fact" in Canada.[25]

As the institutions primarily responsible for representing the Christian religion in Canada, the mainline Protestant and Roman Catholic churches, in particular, played a key role in ensuring the powerful presence of Christianity in the dominant culture and benefited a great deal from it. The common belief that Christianity would be a positive and necessary element of nation-building in Canada was, in fact, admirably represented in the claim those churches made on both the nation and the state. They clearly shared what might be called an establishment mentality, possessing an acute sense that Canada and its citizens somehow belonged to them – that the churches bore responsibility for the welfare of the nation. That mentality was never far from view. In 1953, it gave Paul-Émile Léger, named Cardinal of the Roman Catholic Church in Canada in that year, the confidence to call himself the ecclesiastical prince, not just of the Catholics in his city of Montreal, but of the city itself.[26] That same deep sense of connection to all citizens of a city or region or of Canada itself was exemplified in the United Church of Canada's report to the Massey Commission (1949–51), prepared by the church's Commission on Culture. "Whatever will advance our national welfare and cultural development will also advance the interests of the United Church,"[27] the report bluntly stated.[28] In 1960, a booklet published by the United Church noted that the "church should avoid identification with any political party" but that it "may exert an important influence [in politics] by showing the bearing of Christian principles upon the issues of the day." In a memorable phrase, it claimed the church to be "the conscience of the state."[29]

The latter phrase summed up better than most, perhaps, how religious elites viewed the relationship between their churches and their country of Canada. It demonstrated their firm conviction that religion had implications not just for the private life of the individual but for the public life of the community as well. As the conscience of the state, the mainline Protestant and Roman Catholic churches assumed themselves to be the nation's privileged possessors of moral authority, ready and willing to guide its development towards a truly Christian existence. To be sure, there were important differences of opinion about church-state relations among Canada's largest Christian denominations.[30] Nonetheless, their leaders expected a privileged place for themselves and for Christianity in the dominant Canadian culture that they had helped shape.

If shared goals and visions ensured that Christianity had a privileged position in Canadian public life. Theological, racial, and class differences

within Canadian society and within and among Canadian denominations did however, shape federal state-sponsored public religion into
particular forms. Church-state relations and efforts to Christianize Canada were tempered by disagreement about what a "Christian Canada"
would look like. At the heart of the matter were varying definitions of
the adjective "Christian." Protestant efforts to Christianize Canada in the
late nineteenth and early twentieth centuries, for example, differed significantly from the efforts of French Roman Catholics,[31] and the more
particular the "Christianizing" programs were – for example, with respect to the prohibition of alcohol – the more room there was for disagreement even within Canada's mainline Protestant churches.[32] Many
francophone Roman Catholics hoped for a bilingual and bicultural country where French and English, Roman Catholic and Protestant would receive equal rights and equal treatment.[33] English-speaking Protestants,
on the other hand, commonly understood their country as a predominantly Protestant, British nation, though with a Roman Catholic minority.[34] Those different visions had very practical consequences. They led,
for example, to conflicts over the rights of French Roman Catholics to
their own publicly funded schools in New Brunswick (1870s), Manitoba
(1890s), and Ontario (the second decade of the twentieth century).

Disagreements within and between the various denominations
made public religion in Canada a potentially disruptive affair, especially at the federal level of politics. While the provincial consensus on
public religion was simpler within British Protestant-dominated Ontario or within French Roman Catholic-dominated Quebec, when such
differing visions of a Christian Canada met at the national level, the
tensions between them made one common vision difficult to achieve.[35]
The competing religious interests of Protestants and Roman Catholics
had to be handled most sensitively if the unity of the country was to be
maintained.[36] That said, Roman Catholics and Protestants, Anglicans
and Methodists did, after all, share elements of the Christian faith and
the widely held belief in the importance of religion to the nation, combined with a federal concern for national unity, made the inclusion of a
broad, mediating form of public Christianity a practical reality. Federal
legislation regulating adoption, divorce, contraception, and homosexuality, for example, reflected the influence of a Christian morality held in
common across the denominational spectrum.

A Christianity that avoided denominational differences also found itself displayed in public rituals, symbols, and speeches. The 1967 prayer
service on Parliament Hill is only one noteworthy mid-twentieth-
century example. Taking place two years earlier, the religious service
designed to dedicate the new Canadian flag in 1965 (a service requested
by the prime minister himself) is another.[37] Through the 1960s, the

opening ceremonies of the Canadian federal Parliament included the reciting of nonsectarian Christian prayers by the speaker of the House, a sacralizing and legitimating procedure done before the entrance of the mace, the symbol of political power in the nation. Less colourful or spectacular but equally significant were the more common events and statements connecting a nonsectarian Christianity and the Canadian nation. Broad appeals to religion continued to serve a legitimating role in Canadian public life into the middle decades of the twentieth century. "God and nature have made the two Canadas one," the leader of the opposition, the Honourable R.B. Hanson, said to the House on the occasion of the seventy-fifth anniversary of Confederation in 1942. "Let no factious men be allowed to put them asunder."[38]

Into the late 1950s, in fact, prime ministers declared Canada Christian in a manner that seemed to have little to do with sectarian Christian doctrines and much to do with such broad principles of political liberalism as the value of the individual person, honesty, and a commitment to the common good. In the federal parliamentary debate on the declaration of war in 1939, for example, Prime Minister Mackenzie King defined the importance of Christianity to Canada when he declared the war a struggle "between the pagan conception of a social order which ignores the individual and is based upon the doctrine of might, and a civilization based upon the Christian conception of the brotherhood of man with its regard for the sanctity of contractual relations, in the sacredness of human personality."[39] That war, and the Cold War that followed, further encouraged the equation of Christianity with the liberal democratic principles routinely hailed as the bedrock of Western civilization.[40] Confronted by the horrors of totalitarianism in the Nazi and atheistic communist regimes, Canadians as well as Americans defined themselves as Christians in a way that clearly set them apart from "the other."[41] The Cold War was perceived as a moral crusade, Doug Owram has argued, "evil against virtue, Christ against anti-Christ".[42] Supporting the teaching of Christianity in Ontario's public schools, the report of the Hope Commission in 1950 argued that "there are two virtues about which there can be no question – honesty, and Christian love." It went on to argue that "patterns of behaviour which are based on Christian ideals, and are acceptable to society, can be realized only through the co-operative efforts of the home, the school, and the church."[43] The duty of the Christian church in Canada, historian Arthur Lower argued in 1950, "has been to conserve and strengthen the ethical principle" defined broadly by the Hebrew prophet Micah as "to do justly and to love mercy and to walk humbly with thy God."[44]

To be sure, that broad interpretation of Christianity in public life may have masked Canada's religious divisions as much as it overcame them.[45] Nonetheless, through relations among elites, shared understandings grounded in the past, and the desire to use the benefits of religion to unite the nation, a nonsectarian Christianity was embedded in Canadian public identities into the postwar period. Religious conflict may have rendered national consensus on religious matters difficult and disruptive disagreement all too common, but the vast majority of Canadians were Christians, and where their interpretations of the Christian faith overlapped, that faith was easily entrenched in the laws, symbols, and language that helped define Canadian public life.

One more important point of clarification needs to be made with regard to the privileging of Christianity in Canadian public life. Even a broadly represented public Christianity was, of course, not able to include all Canadians. Ironically, in fact, despite all the efforts to find inclusive public expressions of Christianity, they continued to exclude many. Among those on the outside of a Christian Canada, quite obviously, were non-Christians, but less obviously, a significant number of Christian Canadians were excluded too. Together, Canada's political and cultural elites self-consciously defined the kind of religion that was welcome in public life to the exclusion of smaller, less "respectable" Christian denominations. In twentieth-century Canada, Christian denominations outside the mainline Protestant and Roman Catholic churches were often dismissed in the dominant culture as insignificant minorities or, worse, as groups of self-serving, deluded, and immature individuals. The title of an article published in 1960 in the United Church *Observer*, "The 'Have-Nots' of Religion," demonstrates well the not so subtle bias against such groups. Its author, Gordon Donaldson, went on to lump into that category Pentecostals, the Christian and Missionary Alliance, and the Amish, Mennonites, Doukhobors, Mormons, and Seventh-Day Adventists. Labelling them "sects," a favourite and clearly derogatory term of the day for smaller and more conservative faith groups, Donaldson then proceeded to write them off. "Many claim a monopoly on religious truth, often because of some quirk of Biblical interpretation," he wrote. Evidently unable to discern the impact of social position on his own faith, Donaldson went on to condescendingly argue that the "sects are fundamentalist, believing in literal interpretations of the Bible and usually stressing passages appropriate to the social needs and aspirations of the group concerned."[46]

Indeed, that paternalistic approach to smaller Christian denominations on the fringes of the dominant culture (as well as to those, like the Mormons, who were outside traditional Christian orthodoxy) was readily apparent outside the mainline churches as well. According to the authors of a historical survey of post-1945 Canada, "the press virtually ignored" conservative Christian groups in the 1950s and 1960s, choosing instead "to emphasize the progressive trends in modern religion."[47]

Scholarly publications were equally disparaging. Published in 1948, S.D. Clark's *Church and Sect in Canada* quickly became a foundational book in the study of religion in Canada.[48] Using the two terms of his title to analyze the development of religious groups in this country, he favoured those falling under the first category. Churches, he argued, were mature institutions dedicated to the betterment of society and involving people with high social status, good social connections, and stability. The mainline denominations belonged here. Sects, on the other hand, were equated with narrow conservatism, backwardness, low social position, and relative isolation. Caught up in other-worldly interests, they contributed little to the society around them. On Clark's evolutionary scale, the churches represented the pinnacle of religious development, while the sects were a few stages behind.[49]

Those cultural stereotypes had very real repercussions. In the early days of radio, for example, CBC officials declared that public expressions of religion on its stations were to emphasize what Canadians held in common, not what held them apart.[50] By that standard, religious groups that chose to attack others or emphasize difference in order to claim converts were given little free air-time on the CBC. In 1938 the CBC followed the model of the British Broadcasting Corporation in England, erecting the Religious Advisory Council, a body designed to screen out the kind of religion that would be unwelcome on public radio and to keep that screening at a safe distance from the CBC itself. Not surprisingly, it was the "respectable" mainline Protestant and Roman Catholic churches that were asked to run the council and that were given free airtime to distribute as they saw fit among the faith groups of Canada. They promptly proceeded to offer several Sunday service time slots a year to Jews, Lutherans, the Salvation Army, and Christian Scientists but clearly dismissed the requests for radio time from smaller, more conservative and fundamentalist Christian denominations.[51] As Russell Johnston has argued, "the council made it possible for the state to censor from its own transmitters any dissenting religious opinions, under the guise of a more 'open-minded' and innocuous inclusiveness."[52] The mainline churches and a broad, nonsectarian Christianity were welcome in Canadian public life simply because, for the most part, they were willing to appeal to "the eternal truths that unite us."[53] Smaller Christian denominations were most often relegated to paying for time on private commercial radio stations, where, presumably, their impact would be limited.[54]

Several complicated factors lay behind negative characterizations of religious groups that were not mainline and their exclusion from public life. Ethnicity, no doubt, played a role, keeping Christians of non-British or non-French descent, such as Russian Mennonites or Italian Roman Catholics, on Canada's cultural fringe. Class did too, relegating those

lower on the economic scale, including recent immigrants simply struggling to survive, to the same shadows. For some, exclusion from the public life of their country was self-imposed. Clark, after all, was close to the
mark on this point. Christians outside Canada's mainline churches often
did not share the same public interest and tradition of public service held
by the larger, more historic churches.[55]

But there was more to their public absence than that. The vigorous
and emotional style of conservative evangelical revivalistic preaching,
in particular, grated against the quieter, more "rational" modes of communication in the dominant culture.[56] Some denominations also raised
opposition within the mainline churches by considering them too liberal or, even worse, not Christian at all.[57] Furthermore, the exclusion of
conservative evangelicals from public life was no doubt related to their
outright rejection of some of the leading intellectual trends of the day.
In 1934, for example, the United Church's Board of Evangelism and Social Service boldly dismissed those who based their faith on the "rejection of a scientific view of the world" and who insisted on "unhistorical
methods of treating Holy Scripture."[58] The refusal of some Christian
groups to accept some of the more significant intellectual developments of even the late-Victorian period earned them the reputation of
being ignorant dwellers of Canada's cultural backwoods.

When conservative, minority Christian groups proclaimed their
Christian message in public life, then, they often did so in ways that were
simply out of step with Canada's political and cultural elites. As a result,
though cloaked under the veil of inclusivity and tolerance, a broad interpretation of Christianity in public life clearly declared that a certain kind
of Christianity, beneficial to the project of building national unity, was
welcome on the public stage and that anything other was not. In essence,
then, the assumption that a broad and inclusive Christianity would be a
positive force in national life led to the cooperation of Canada's largest
churches and the Canadian state both in defining "Christian" broadly
enough to include Protestants and Roman Catholics and in defining it
narrowly enough to ensure that only the voices of the most respectable
Christians would find themselves sanctioned in Canadian public life.

Built by common assumptions held by Canadian elites, grounded in history, and embedded in the dominant Canadian culture, the public privileging of Christianity in Canada was fundamentally challenged by the
rapid and remarkable development of Canadian culture and society, particularly after the Second World War. While the outward manifestations
of the close link between the mainline Christian churches and Canadian
public life continued to exist as they had before, the underpinnings of
those public symbols changed. In the years leading up to and following

the 1940s, the growth of the federal welfare state – and of the government bureaucracies that managed it – altered the relationship between it and the mainline churches. Behind the welfare state was a commitment to social scientific expertise, a commitment that, when combined with the impact of consumerism in a new postwar world of abundance, challenged the functional importance of religion not only in the corridors of the state but also in the individual lives of Canadians. Added to all this, the ability of a broad Christianity to serve as a lowest common religious denominator was undermined by growing cultural diversity and by the development of more cosmopolitan attitudes among the Canadian populace. The privileged public position of the mainline churches was, in turn, gradually dismantled by growing demands for equality, tolerance, and participatory democracy. From the 1940s and into the 1960s, the same trends and forces that transformed Canadian society in general also transformed how religion would be welcome in Canadian public life and the way it would inform understandings of Canada.

One key factor involved in the transformation after 1945 was the growth and development of the Canadian state. The various levels of the Canadian state entered the twentieth century as small laissez-faire administrative structures dedicated largely to ensuring the growth of commerce in Canada.[59] As such, they functioned largely by either contracting out the provision of services to private agencies or by simply expecting the private sector to take care of those services themselves.[60] In attempting to be as hands-off as possible, the state relied on those who were willing to be hands-on. For their part, the Canadian churches fulfilled their historical role as providers of needed social services, applying their finances, personnel, and organizational expertise to fill areas left empty by the state. Sometimes given state funding, sometimes not, they were left to themselves to run everything from schools to hospitals to welfare agencies.

Beginning in the 1920s and 1930s, that began to change. The federal level of the Canadian state began to leave its laissez-faire approach behind and to move in the direction of much greater involvement in the creation and administration of social programs in Canada and in Canadian culture. That move was exemplified by such things as the nationalization of public radio in 1932, the enactment of a federal program of unemployment insurance in 1940, and a program of universal old-age security in 1952. These programs, and many others not mentioned here, required an expanded budget and an expanded bureaucracy. Beginning in 1918, the federal government added to its customs and excise revenues moneys drawn from new personal income and corporate taxes. Between 1945 and 1975, the total number of federal government employees nearly tripled, rising from 115,908 to 319, 605.[61]

The explosive growth of the welfare state in the twentieth century had some important consequences for the old structures and relationships of Canada's dominant culture. The expansion of the state bureaucracy itself may have muted the effectiveness of older personal networks among Canada's cultural and political elites.[62] Equally important, the expansion of the state into all the traditional domains of the Christian churches of Canada – such as education, health care and welfare – removed those important areas of social influence from direct church control.[63] That was particularly the case in Quebec.[64] More wary of the state than the Protestant churches, the Roman Catholic Church had maintained a much heavier influence over education, health care and welfare in that province for much longer than had the Protestant churches elsewhere. In the 1960s, and in the midst of Quebec's Quiet Revolution, that influence was reduced quickly and dramatically when the provincial government moved into each of those fields.

In the rest of Canada, as in Quebec, when the influence of the Canadian state grew, that of the churches shrank. Something more significant was going on here than the mere shifting of administrative control from one set of institutions to another. Beneath that change was arguably a much bigger challenge for the public role of the mainline churches and for the privileging of Christianity. Undermining the public presence of religion in Canada were changes in the way Canadians approached religion itself. Trust and hope in the new social sciences and in technology and material abundance were weakening the importance of religion and morality as guides for the development of the country.[65] In the explosive economic and technological growth of the postwar period, scientific management, the quest for efficiency, and material abundance blossomed as they had not done before, and the churches found themselves preaching to Canadians who, in the words of one historian, had put "their faith for a better world" in material security, technology, and the welfare state.[66] "The Great God Gadget," one commentator noted in 1967, was a rival to the traditional Christian deity.[67] In a rapidly modernizing and differentiating society, the churches found their voices increasingly unheard in discussions of economic or political issues and increasingly restricted to the more subjective, private religious affairs of individuals.[68]

The growth of the welfare state, then, brought with it a number of significant challenges to the historic prominence of the mainline churches in public life and to the privileged position of Christianity in the dominant culture which they had helped to create. Further undermining those things was one of the most obvious trends of post-1945 Canada: the diversification of the Canadian population. A Christian Canada made some sense in a society and culture dominated by those of British and French descent and by those affiliated with one of Canada's largest mainline churches. When that dominance began to break down, however, so too did the idea that a broad Christianity was an important element of Canadian nation-building. By 1961, Canadians of British descent had not formed a majority of the population for over twenty years, and the French had slipped to form one-quarter of the population. As for religious affiliation, British and Irish Protestants made up 35 percent of the population, Roman Catholics of French descent made up 30 percent, and the remaining 35 percent belonged to other Christian and non-Christian faith groups (see table).[69]

Changing attitudes were another, perhaps more important, element. Before the Second World War Canada's growing ethnic diversity had little impact on the country's dominant culture. Although some Canadians had begun to speak of Canada as a collection of diverse peoples – a "mosaic" – as early as the 1920s and although their ideas gained popularity in the 1930s and 1940s,[70] up to and even after the 1960s, non-French and non-British Canadians wishing to maintain their own cultural identities were largely expected to do so in private. Public institutions and public life were based on what one scholar has aptly called "dominant conformity" – on the assumption that Canada was a British nation with a French minority, a Christian nation to which newcomers would have to adjust.[71] For their part, the Anglican, Presbyterian, Baptist, United, and Roman Catholic Churches continued to dominate Canadian religious life with little discussion into the postwar period. Those who did not fit their mould, such as Buddhists, fundamentalist Christian denominations, Jews, Hutterites, and Doukhobors, remained minorities in the shadows of public life. Some, like Buddhists and Jews, were even limited in their access as immigrants to Canada.[72] If Canada was a mosaic into the 1950s, the exclusive attitudes of those who defined Canadian public life made sure it was a mosaic within the boundaries of a Christian and largely British culture.

Much of that changed in postwar Canada, in no small part due to the war itself and the Cold War that followed it. A recent analysis of immigration policy in Canada has noted that, beyond wreaking havoc on global humanity and absorbing the human and material resources of many nations, World War II led to a "broad, albeit belated, public awareness of the horrors of Nazism and its racist implications [which, in turn,] led to increasing receptiveness to ... humanitarian views" in Canada and around the world. The desperate plight of displaced persons in war-torn Europe demanded a more open immigration policy and "Church, community, ethnic, and other public interest groups" arguing on behalf of the dispossessed helped to shift popular and political opinions in that

Population by Religious Denomination, Canada, 1901–71

Religious Denomination	1901	1911	1921	1931	1941	1951	1961	1971
Canada[1]	5,371,315	7,206,643	8,787,949	10,376,786	11,506,655	14,009,429	18,238,247	21,568,310
Adventist	8,092	10,462	14,200	16,058	18,485	21,398	25,999	28,590
Anglican Church of Canada	689,540	1,048,002	1,410,632	1,639,075	1,754,368	2,060,720	2,409,068	2,453,180
Baptist	319,234	384,152	422,312	443,944	484,465	519,585	593,553	667,245
Buddhist	10,531	10,072	11,316	15,921	15,676	8,184	11,611	16,175
Christian and Missionary Alliance	–	128	283	3,560	4,214	6,396	18,006	23,630
Christian Reformed[2]	–	–	–	–	–	–	–	83,390
Christian Science	2,644	5,099	13,856	18,499	20,261	20,795	19,466	–
Churches of Christ, Disciples	17,250	14,610	13,125	15,831	21,260	14,920	19,512	16,405
Confucian	5,171	14,652	27,185	24,253	22,282	5,791	5,089	2,165
Congregationalist[3]	28,504	34,215	30,788					
Doukhobor	8,858	10,616	12,674	14,978	16,878	13,175	13,234	9,170
Free Methodist Church of Canada	–	–	–	7,740	8,805	8,921	14,245	19,125
Greek Orthodox[4]	15,909	89,323	170,069	102,529	139,845	172,271	239,766	316,605
Hutterite[5]	7	7	7	7	7	7	7	13,650
Jehovah's Witnesses	101	938	6,689	13,582	7,007	34,596	68,018	174,810

Jewish	16,493	74,760	125,445	155,766	168,585	204,836	254,368	276,025
Lutheran	94,110	231,883	286,891	394,920	401,836	444,923	662,744	715,740
Mennonite	31,949	44,972	58,874	88,837	111,554	125,938	152,452	168,150
Methodist[6]	924,750	1,084	1,161,165					
Mormon	7,061	16,115	19,657	22,041	25,328	32,888	50,016	66,635
Pentecostal	—	515	7,012	26,349	57,742	95,131	143,877	220,390
Presbyterian	847,635	1,121,394	1,411,794	872,428	830,597	781,747	818,558	872,335
Roman Catholic	2,238,955	2,841,881	3,399,011	4,102,960	4,806,431	6,069,496	8,342,826	9,974,895
Salvation Army	10,360	18,909	24,771	30,773	33,609	70,275	92,054	119,665
Ukrainian (Greek) Catholic[7]	—	—	—	186,879	185,948	191,051	189,653	227,730
Unitarian	2,032	3,275	4,943	4,453	5,584	3,517	15,062	20,995
United Church of Canada	—	—	8,739	2,021,065	2,208,658	2,867,271	3,664,008	3,768,800
Other	92,136	145,975	146,518	154,345	157,237	235,604	415,062	293,240
No religion	—	—	21,819	21,155	19,161	59,679	94,763	929,575

Source: Census of Canada, 1961, 1971.

[1] Exclusive of Newfoundland in censuses prior to 1951.
[2] Figures not available for 1901 to 1961.
[3] Included with United Church of Canada, 1931–61; included with "other," 1971.
[4] Greek Catholic and Greek Orthodox combined under Greek Church, 1901–21.
[5] Included with "Mennonite," 1901 to 1961.
[6] Included with United Church of Canada, 1931–61; assigned alternatively to Free and Wesleyan Methodist, 1971.
[7] Includes other Greek Catholic.

direction.[73] Though racial and religious discrimination obviously continued, the war and its aftermath began to put that discrimination in a negative light and at least weakened its expression in public life.[74]

The postwar trend towards internationalism and globalization may
also have fostered more open and tolerant attitudes to diversity. The
war and the years leading up to it had been formative, pulling countries around the globe out of isolation and placing them on the world
stage. The Cold War, with its deep concern about the spread of communism, kept the spotlight on the international community, while
other factors also encouraged the recognition of humanity as a global
community. Allan Smith has noted, for example, that a more inclusive
perspective in postwar Canada was the result of "the simple need to
find a *modus vivendi* for living together as transportation, technology
and integrated economies drove the world's peoples closer to each
other."[75]

Just as importantly, the Second World War and the Cold War made
the defense of democracy a key theme in the 1940s and into the 1950s.[76]
As we have already seen, that theme originally gave added support to
the public privileging of a broadly defined Christianity. As opposed to
atheistic communist countries, Canada was declared Christian, and
Christianity was considered the bedrock of Western democratic values.
On the other hand, however, a deep interest in things democratic
helped lay the groundwork for an emphasis on equality, tolerance, and
anti-authoritarianism that, in the 1960s, would challenge the historically hierarchical and authoritative institutions of church and state. In
the 1940s and 1950s in Canada, Doug Owram has argued, democracy
meant cooperative relationships, and that principle found itself translated by experts into everything from family structure to education.
Child-rearing manuals emphasized the importance of democratic decision making in families, while the leading educational philosopher of
the day, John Dewey, spoke out against authoritarianism and sought to
find ways in which each individual child could have his or her needs
met in the classroom.[77] The theme of individual responsibility implicit
in the postwar emphasis on democracy and in the fear of totalitarianism was also embodied in growing interest in the 1950s in the plight
of the individual in "the mass age."[78] Encouraged by the dramatic
growth of corporations and bureaucracies in postwar North America,
by the growth of a mass consumer culture, by fear of communist totalitarianism, and by the expansion of automation in industry, an existentialist concern for individual responsibility became an important theme
of the 1950s and 1960s.[79] If democracy urged tolerance, it also urged
Canadians to be active, critically thinking individuals not particularly
attached to the status quo.

Underlying and supporting changing attitudes in the postwar period, as well, was unprecedented and sustained economic growth. It enabled the expansion of the Canadian state in the postwar period and encouraged the development of a consumerist ethic, but it also made possible a dramatic sense of optimism and interest in social and political reform. Although Canadians experienced a recession from the late 1950s to 1962, affluence was a dominant theme of cultural discussion in the 1950s and 1960s.[80] With economic abundance fueling unprecedented technological development, state growth, and individual wealth, an influential number of cultural and political elites aggressively embraced the future as open to change.[81] The 1960s, as a result, would be years of dramatic transformation in which the old ideas and structures of Canada's dominant culture would come under intense scrutiny and criticism.

Such broad changes also influenced attitudes of those who were left standing on the outside of public life, looking in. At the same time as more inclusive and tolerant attitudes were shaping Canadian society, ethnic and religious minorities began to demand that they be recognized, in all of their distinctiveness, in the public life of their country. The most powerful challenge to the Canadian status quo, of course, came from the province of Quebec. Under Maurice Duplessis' Union Nationale (1944–60), that province had demanded little more of the federal government than to be left alone to preserve a uniquely French Canadian and Roman Catholic culture within its borders. With the election of Jean Lesage's Liberals in 1960, however, things changed dramatically. The new provincial government was shaped by reformers who were frustrated by the subservience of French Canadians to English Canadians within and outside Quebec, as well as by the continuing power and influence of the Roman Catholic Church over the province's systems of education, health care, and social welfare.[82] With those reformers now in power, the relationship between the Roman Catholic Church and Quebec society, as well as the relationship between the province of Quebec and the rest of Canada, began to quickly change. Some separatists saw the Quiet Revolution in Quebec, in fact, as the Canadian manifestation of the world-wide trend toward decolonization.[83]

The French Canadian push to be regarded as equals in Canadian public life, and not simply as a peculiar minority, shook Quebec and the Canadian status quo. Dissent in Quebec, however, also found counterparts in some of Canada's non-French minority groups. In the late 1950s and 1960s, a new awareness of (and pride in) distinct ethnic identities marked Canada, as well as many other Western countries. Named a "revival of ethnicity" by one sociologist, it represented a politicization of ethnic groups in Canada – a refusal to give up distinctive traditions in order to be considered Canadian and a frustration with the way they had been previously ignored in public life. That revival of ethnicity has been traced not only to decolonization and wars of independence but also to tribal and ethnic conflict in newly independent countries, to the horrors of the apparent American imperialism in the Vietnam War, and to émigrés from Eastern Europe who feared that communist revolutions were obliterating national cultures and who sought to preserve those cultures on Canadian soil.[84]

Of the latter, Ukrainians are a case in point. Living through two world wars in which foreign-born Canadians were deemed highly suspect and sometimes physically penalized by the Canadian state, Ukrainian Canadians had learned to try to stay out of the state's disfavour by clearly expressing their loyalty to Canada and their primary interest in Canadian, not Ukrainian, affairs. Bolstered by their active service in the Canadian effort in the Second World War, however, some Ukrainian Canadians became less apologetic in the 1950s and 1960s about their rights as Canadians and less willing to try to blend into Canada's dominant British and largely Protestant culture. Members of the Canadian Ukrainian community were drawn further into a more active and demanding position with regard to their rights as Canadian citizens by an influx of displaced persons from Ukraine. Having witnessed the severe repression of the Ukrainian national identity in the USSR and having been formed into active Ukrainian nationalists in displaced persons camps in Europe, many came to Canada determined to defend their national identity here. When they did so, their bold actions and mannerisms initially threatened their Canadian-born Ukrainian hosts.[85] Eventually, however, they helped push the Canadian Ukrainian community in a more vocally nationalist direction.[86] By 1965, Paul Yuzyk, a Ukrainian in the Canadian senate, was boldly arguing that "as co-founders" of Canada, non-French and non-British ethnic groups "should be co-partners who would be guaranteed the right to perpetuate their mother tongues and cultures."[87]

In their dissent, Ukrainians were joined by the Jewish community, which also became increasingly active in the 1960s, partly in response to the prodding of newcomers to Canada among them.[88] In the same period, Canada's aboriginal peoples began to lobby effectively for an end to the discrimination they had long faced, and second-wave feminism made itself heard in protest against the inequities and discrimination faced by women in Canadian society.

It was also in the postwar years that religious groups that had been kept outside elite circles became increasingly unlikely to leave public life to others. For some, the ethnic revival and their demands for greater religious recognition went hand in hand. When Ukrainians in Canada, for example, argued for greater public recognition and influence, they did so also as Catholic and Orthodox Christians.[89] One scholar argued in 1966, for example, that Ukrainians were proud of their two members in the Canadian Senate (including Paul Yuzyk) not just because of their Ukrainian background but because of their religious affiliation. "As one is of the Ukrainian Roman Catholic and the other of the Ukrainian Orthodox faith," Elizabeth Wangenheim pointed out, "both of the large Ukrainian national churches are represented in the Canadian Senate."[90]

The Pentecostal Assemblies of Canada were another case in point. A revivalistic faith group placing heavy emphasis on the miraculous and on the need for a dramatic individual conversion experience, they had been fairly content to be kept on the edges of Canadian public life into the 1950s.[91] In the late 1950s and 1960s, however, they too became more visible and involved in Canadian public life. Their efforts were aided by surveys and polls that revealed that the Pentecostal Assemblies of God was one of the fastest-growing denominations in both Canada and the United States.[92] In 1958, hosting the World Conference of Pentecostalism in Toronto also raised their profile, while Pentecostals pointed with pride to two of their own, Phil Gagliardi and Everett Wood, who were elected to provincial legislatures in the late 1950s.[93] "Pentecostalism entered the 1960s with a new-found public acceptance and ecclesiastical respectability,"[94] Pentecostal historian Thomas Miller has argued.

All that attention apparently whetted the appetite of Pentecostals for public influence. Although editorials warned them of the temptations of worldliness, Pentecostals nonetheless began more confidently to add their voices and opinions to Canadian public life and to define themselves as important Canadians.[95] *The Pentecostal Testimony* seemed to take a greater interest in Dominion Day in the early 1960s,[96] and the publication also began to encourage a stronger social conscience among Pentecostals.[97] In 1964 the General Conference of the Pentecostal Assemblies of Canada (PAOC) passed the resolution "Discrimination re CBC-TV," which noted that the CBC's arm's-length National Religious Advisory Council had privileged the mainline Christian denominations that made up its membership.[98] In the same year, it also continued to lobby French-language Radio-Canada for airtime for francophone Protestants – airtime that had been prohibited due to the dominance of the Roman Catholic Church among French Canadians.[99]

Non-Christian groups also worked to make sometimes very old complaints finally heard in public life. An increasing resistance to the

Christian exclusivity of Canada's dominant culture among those outside the Christian churches was perhaps best exemplified in the controversy involving the teaching of the Christian religion as part of the
official curriculum of Ontario public schools.[100] In 1969, the Minister's Committee on Religion in Education concluded that the Christian faith should be removed from its place of privilege in the public
school curriculum.[101] Among the reasons for the change, the committee's report significantly referred to heavy postwar immigration that
"had brought in, year by year, representatives of faiths different from
the traditional denominations of Ontario."[102] Jews, in particular, were
mentioned.[103] Religious pluralism, like ethnic pluralism, was no
longer being ignored.

   All of this meant that the dominant cultural consensus, which un-
derpinned the public privileging of Christianity, was slowly melting
away. Not only were the mainline Protestant and Catholic churches
being pushed into narrower and less public roles in Canadian society
by the growth of the modern welfare state, but their cultural dominance was also being challenged by those they had kept out. In the
wake of the Second World War, exclusive racial and religious perspectives slipped under dark shadows as minority groups themselves began to demand their demise.

Though all these challenges to an ethnically and religiously exclusive
dominant culture had implications for Canadian institutions as a whole,
they had a particularly powerful effect on the mainline Protestant denominations and the Roman Catholic Church, which had directly benefited in prestige and influence from the old order. Notably, through the
1950s, Canadians in those churches, like most of their fellow citizens,
failed to see the dramatic changes of the 1960s on the horizon. With the
end of World War II and the beginning of the Cold War, in fact, the
country had seemed to experience a religious boom. The United and
Anglican Churches, in particular, were favoured with impressive
growth. Membership rolls rose to all-time highs. New churches were
springing up at astonishing rates and were being paid for, voluntarily,
with equal speed. Sales of religious publications soared, and news media took increasing interest in the "revival phenomenon."[104]

   Underneath the veneer of stability and growth, however, things
were clearly changing. In Quebec, the influence of the Roman Catholic
Church had been slipping, particularly since the Second World War
and especially in the major urban centres.[105] The postwar revival in the
Protestant churches, for its part, has since been described not as a genuine renewal of faith so much as a culturally determined "return to nor-
malcy" after five years of war and ten years of economic depression.[106]

Sensitized to the Christian foundations of Western civilization by the
threat of atheistic communism, large numbers of Canadians were returning to the comfort of the old institutions of church and home, not
necessarily to a more active or vital faith. Leaders of Canada's largest
denominations began to wonder out loud just how deep the revival really was.

They found out in the 1960s, when things seemed to change dramatically. Protestants in Canada had been slowing in their rate of weekly
attendance through the 1950s and into the 1960s,[107] but other key indi-
cators of church vitality also began to fall. In the Anglican Church, for
example, membership in men's and women's organizations peaked in
1963, as did, in 1964, the overall church population, the number of lay
readers, and the number of clergy. By 1968, membership in men's
groups had fallen by 40 percent from the previous high, while the
number of lay readers in Anglican churches had fallen by 38 percent.[108]
Among Roman Catholics, as late as 1965 polls found 83 percent in
church on a weekly basis. By 1975, that number had dropped to 61 percent. In Quebec the 1960s were a time of astoundingly rapid secularization and liberalization with regard to the role of the Roman Catholic
Church in provincial public life. Discontent with the church's virtual
monopoly over health care, welfare, and educational institutions in the
province had been voiced in previous decades, but it was only in the
early 1960s that the church's control of those public fields was restricted or removed and placed in the hands of the provincial government. Quebec's cultural and political elites, at least, argued that those
services were better run by the state, an institution that could legitimately represent all Quebeckers, not just Roman Catholics, and that
was better able to adapt to a rapidly changing society. As an exclusive
and conservative institution, the Roman Catholic Church was no
longer deemed able to lead and control what were considered public
aspects of an increasingly diverse and liberal society.[109]

In both the Protestant and Roman Catholic Churches there was an
unprecedented level of vocal criticism of the church as an institution. That criticism began earlier in the Roman Catholic Church in
Quebec, but by 1965 the Protestant churches, too, were in turmoil. In
the midst of the controversy, many of the key trends of the postwar
period emerged in full opposition to the privileged position of those
churches.

That controversy and that opposition were best demonstrated by
Pierre Berton's *The Comfortable Pew*. Published in 1965, that book was
nothing short of a systematic and comprehensive attack on the Anglican Church, in particular, and on the mainline churches of Canada
in general, institutions that Berton felt were stuck in the past and

increasingly irrelevant in the present.[110] Charging the Anglican Church with apathy and an unthinking defense of the status quo, he went after its complacent position on everything from nuclear arms to shady business deals, as well as its rejection of the sexual revolution. Underlying the complacency and conservatism, he argued, was "the worship of conformity and respectability" in the mainline churches, a greater concern for success and comfort than for the hard application of the "revolutionary" and "radical" teachings of Christ.[111] But Berton also railed against what he disdainfully called the churches' "pretensions to absolute rightness." Dogma, he argued, no longer made sense in "the space age ... Modern man has been taught to question, to probe, to weigh pieces of evidence rationally; a church that insists he accept certain tales and certain ideas [the Virgin Birth, the Creator God, and the divinity of Jesus Christ all fell into this category] without question or argument cannot hold his respect."[112] In the end, Berton argued, "the Christian philosophy and ethic has been shackled by its institutional chains ... [I]n its desperate effort to preserve its established entity, the Church has become fossilized and ... this fossilization has prevented it from moving with the world." Following a long-established pattern, Berton criticized the church by holding it up to its own standards and claiming that it was not Christian enough.[113] The only way forward, in his opinion, was for the church to relinquish an establishment mentality and to become flexible and in touch with the leading trends of its more liberal and inclusive culture.

As Berton's preface to the United States edition carefully detailed, the book was an immediate success in terms of sales when it hit the shelves in January 1965. By June of that year, 150,000 copies had been printed, setting a record that "no other book in the history of Canadian publishing had approached."[114] Perhaps feeling left out, the United Church quickly put together its own publication critiquing the mainline churches.[115] The strong response to *The Comfortable Pew* suggested, among other things, that Berton had tapped into a widespread sense of dissatisfaction with the role of the mainline Christian churches in Canadian society, dissatisfaction that until the publication of his book, had not been so concisely, forcefully, or publicly stated in English Canada.

In French Canada *The Comfortable Pew* had its Roman Catholic counterparts, which had argued for an end to the traditional public dominance of the Roman Catholic Church, particularly in Quebec.[116] In that province, too, they had argued that tolerance, inclusivity, and reasoned judgment were the keys to the future of public life in Quebec. With them, the argument of Berton's book – and the debate that engulfed

Canada's mainline churches in the mid-1960s – demonstrated well how precarious the public position of those churches had become. Once considered institutions essential to a future of national greatness, those churches were now increasingly perceived as conservative institutions imposing limits on personal and national development.

The significance of *The Comfortable Pew* to a discussion of the decline of Christian Canada, however, is larger yet. What Berton and many of his Roman Catholic counterparts had done was to argue that the Christian faith itself, and not just the institutional church, needed to be reworked. The deep significance of that point was brought out in the debate that the book inspired, as much as in the book itself. Alongside the many editorials, book reviews, and letters to the editor, several books were published in response to Berton's book. One of those, William Kilbourn's edited collection of essays appropriately titled *The Restless Church*, was particularly insightful.[117] The book contained arguments both for and against Berton's analysis from prominent international figures involved somehow in the contemporary study of religion, including Bishop John A.T. Robinson, Eugene Fairweather, Peter Berger, and the Jewish scholar Emil L. Fachenhiem. Robinson, already famous for his radical religious views, backed Berton completely. Fairweather, Berger, and Fachenhiem were not so positive. Significantly, however, they all agreed on what Berton was trying to do. In Robinson's words, he was "sharpening" or "stripping down" the Christian faith by "paring way" what was unessential: doctrine. Berton was after "religion without dogma." In that sense, he was a part of a much larger debate within the Christian faith about the nature of that faith itself. He was proposing that the faith had to be fundamentally reinterpreted – translated out of its ancient mythical and supernatural roots and into a modern, rational, ethical structure appropriate for a modern, rational "new age".

It was that argument that Fairweather, Berger, and Fachenhiem attempted to dissect. Each of them tried to say much the same thing, though in different ways. Christianity without doctrine, they argued, was not Christianity. Fairweather argued that Berton had really misunderstood the Christian faith and therefore had written off its doctrine on insufficient grounds. With a particularly biting tone, Berger placed both Berton and Robinson in a contemporary movement to applaud secularization, to empty the church of its distinctiveness, to subjectivize religion, and to turn it into psychology. Fachenhiem warned that Berton's "new church" was simply the handmaiden of secularist liberalism.

The insights of Berger and Fachenhiem, in particular, cut to the core of the threat that faced the privileging of Christianity in Canada's

dominant culture in the 1960s. Berton, Berger argued, was clearly uncomfortable with the exclusive claims to divine truth within Christianity, claims that no longer made sense to many immersed in historical
relativism, something Berger found understandable. What irritated
him was that instead of saying yes or no to Christianity on the basis of
those claims, Berton had emptied the faith of its historic meaning and
replaced it with his own version, neatly tailored to meet the broad re-
quirements of a tolerant and inclusive time. That approach, Berger
fumed, was dishonest. Motivated by that kind of Christianity, he argued, the churches would become useless institutions. Any other
worldview might also be used to inspire such a broad understanding
of justice and moral responsibility.

Significantly, Fachenhiem argued the same essential point from a
completely different perspective. In warning that Berton's "new
church" was simply the handmaiden of secularist liberalism, he too
argued that Berton had effectively emptied it of anything distinctly
Christian. The value of philosophical liberalism and the broad principles of freedom and equality that it endorsed, Fachenheim argued,
were not in question. Whether those principles defined Christianity
or were themselves defined by a much broader and deeper historic
Christian faith was in question. Philosophical liberalism, he argued,
had to be rooted in historic Christianity. Otherwise, he feared, secular
"Man" would become the judge of the churches, as Berton was, and
principles of freedom and equality would be set adrift, open to any
interpretation.

The debate between Berton, Robinson, and their critics was of real
consequence for the future of public religion in Canada. Berton's attempt to turn Christianity into a broad system of ethics was, in one
sense, nothing new. As we have seen, long before *The Comfortable Pew*
public officials in Canada had equated Christianity with the principles of a liberal democratic society and had done so in the belief that
the values essential to Western civilization and liberal democracies –
the moral responsibility of the individual and the freedom to excerise
that responsibility for the welfare of the community – could be found
only in the Christian faith. To call those values Christian, as Berton
did much later, was then considered natural and unquestioned.

By Berton's day, however, it was not. In the postwar period, the debate around his book indicated that an essential change had taken
place in the relationship between Christianity and ethics in Canadian
society. In and of themselves, both Berger and Fachenheim argued,
there was nothing uniquely Christian about the idea of justice, fair-
ness, or the love of neighbour. Many other worldviews could endorse
those ideas as well, Berger argued, while Fachenhiem associated

them with what he called secular liberalism as much as with Christianity. The values undergirding liberal democracies, they suggested, had become disengaged from the Christianity of their roots.

Theologian Pamela Dickey Young has made the same argument from the vantage point of the 1990s. The principles of justice, equity, and love, she has correctly argued, had been called Christian in the early twentieth century only "because it was simply assumed that they arose within Christianity rather than elsewhere."[118] In an ever more religiously and culturally diverse and internationally engaged Canada, and particularly after 1945, that assumption broke down. In an increasingly interconnected world, it seems, a growing number of Canadians found it awkward to insist that the success of their country rested on the Christian faith alone or that Christianity alone was the repository of goodness, not to mention good citizenship. In fact, in the report of its Commission on World Mission (1966), the United Church itself gave up on this point, acknowledging that other religions, too, could rightfully claim access to divine truth.[119] The exclusive claim of Christianity to the highest values of Western civilization was questioned by some leaders within the churches themselves as a misunderstanding fostered by imperialism, triumphalism, and cultural isolation. Many of those responsible for the maintenance of Canada's dominant culture came to realize that they could no longer assume "that all laudable values should be exclusively Christian."[120]

In the post-1945 period, Canadians seemed less and less willing to accept the exclusive privileging of the mainline Christian churches and to endorse Christianity as the dominant public religion. Increasingly suspicious of hierarchy, authority, and racial or religious exclusivity, younger Canadians and cultural elites turned against a wide range of Canadian institutions and social norms that seemed out of touch with modern realities. The mainline Christian churches were among those caught by the brunt of the attack, and because of the growing diversity of the country, they were having an increasingly difficult time providing a common enough religious denominator in public life. As a result, Christianity's role as the exclusive guarantor of a free and prosperous Canada was increasingly in doubt.

Though many of the challenges facing the mainline churches' control of public religion in Canada's dominant culture had been evident even before the Second World War, it was in the mid-to-late 1960s, – a dramatic period of social and political turmoil and reevaluation, of "uncertainty and innovation" – that they reached a crescendo. Broadly speaking, at the root of the turmoil and change of the period was what one study has called "the increasing social and political commitment during the 1960s to concepts of equality and non-discrimination."[121] In the words of another, the period saw "a broad societal shift towards liberalization."[122] For another, the "turmoil of the 1960s and early 1970s had at its roots a crisis of authority in Western social and political institutions."[123] According to Mark Noll, in both Canada and the United States the 1960s, which were marked by "moral revolution," were "simply a shock."[124] At bottom, he contends, "the changes that have most significantly shaped North American culture" since World War II and that contributed to the tumultuous sixties "have stressed technology instead of morality, personal enrichment instead of altruistic service, and the potential for individual development instead of the force of historical traditions."[125] Looking back on the 1960s some thirty years later, Pierre Berton perhaps summarized the period best. In that decade, he recalled, "Canadian manners and morals were on the cusp of change." "The world of 1967 was a world in which everything from sex to religion was being questioned, and the old answers were not working."[126]

In the midst of all of these challenges to the privileging of Christianity in Canadian national identities, what were the churches and the state doing? What role did those institutions play in the dramatic changes of the postwar period, and how did those changes affect the complex relations between church and state institutions that had encouraged the identification of Canada with a broadly defined Christianity? It is to those questions that I now turn.

3

An Inclusive State, a Servant Church, and the Waning of a Christian Canada

The public expressions of Christianity in the Centennial celebrations of 1967 had a long and cherished history in Canada's dominant culture. Until well after the Second World War, Christian identities were embedded in Canadian public life. Nonetheless, in the 1950s and 1960s Canada was a country in transition. The development of both church and state institutions altered the relations between them, changing demographics met with more inclusive attitudes to push Canada away from its racially and religiously exclusive representations, and minority groups seemed determined to end their exclusion from public life. The result was a list of serious challenges to the old privileging of a nonsectarian Christianity in Canada's dominant culture.

We need to recognize those challenges if we are to understand the public expressions of religion in 1967 that are at the core of this study. Equally important, however, is an understanding of how both the federal state and church institutions responded to those challenges. In the 1950s and 1960s both sets of institutions moved to rethink Canada's close symbolic association with Britain and the Christian faith. What, they asked, was Canada? Was it a Christian country dominated by a British and Protestant population with non-British, non-Protestant and non-Christian minorities? Or was it a more inclusive country in which every Canadian, regardless of his or her ethnicity and religion, could be welcomed into public life and reflected in public symbols and rituals?

The responses of those in church and federal state institutions varied, of course. Nonetheless, in the 1960s the federal government and the mainline Protestant and Roman Catholic churches came under the influence of a dominant mood of reform. Empowered by the affluence and optimism of their day and propelled by a concern to keep their institutions relevant to their rapidly changing Canadian context, leaders in both the churches and the federal government responded in innovative and progressive ways to the challenges they faced. Respect for difference and democratic participation became two of their defining principles and underlined their efforts to make their institutions and bureaucracies more responsive to "the people." At the same time, reforming leaders in both mainline church and federal government institutions focused their energies on reshaping symbols and language to meet the demands of what many considered a radically new and unprecedented age.

For both the mainline churches and the federal government, attempts to adjust to a very different Canada in the 1960s were, however, controversial. Those enchanted with reform quickly discovered that Canadians were by no means agreed on the character of their country, its symbols, or the way in which religion should be publicly expressed. The country's symbols and the Canada they portrayed involved powerful ethnic and religious identities, and the attempt to change those symbols and identities was a complicated and often contested task.

To better understand how all these themes were publicly represented in the Centennial celebrations and Expo 67, I turn first to the broader context of the affairs of both national religious and state institutions in the 1960s.

The precarious situation of the old religiously and racially exclusive characterizations of Canada, the federal state's response to that situation, and the sensitivity of Canadians to changes in their national symbols and national identities were boldly displayed in the creation of a new official Canadian flag in 1964. Unofficially, the British Union Jack and the Red Ensign had long served as symbols of the country. As vivid reflections of its colonial past, however, they had been slated for retirement by some already in the 1920s. In those days devotion to Britain had remained too strong, and the discussions were scuttled due to their divisiveness.[1] As the one hundredth anniversary of Confederation in 1967 approached, however, things had changed. By 1964, in fact, the national symbols of British colonial rule were seen as a very visible declaration of the neglected position of the French in Canada.[2] In that context, more distinctly Canadian symbols seemed to make sense.[3] With Quebec well into its Quiet Revolution, Prime Minister Lester B. Pearson hoped that "in the race against national division, a new flag might be a rallying symbol."[4] The time had come for more inclusive and less British public representations of the country.

At least so he thought. When Pearson proposed the creation of a new Canadian flag to Parliament in the summer of 1964, one of the most emotional and divisive political debates in the history of the country began. "All hell broke loose," was how one MP described the House's reaction to the proposal.[5] For over two and a half months, Parliament immersed itself in a fierce discussion of how best to represent the nation. Outside its doors, the same debate raged in the media, provoking thousands of citizens to write to the prime minister.[6] What kind of country was Canada? And how could it best be symbolically represented? The attempt to answer those questions was so divisive and bitter within and outside Parliament, J.L. Granatstein has argued, that it "led many to despair of the future of the country."[7]

Throughout the debate, two very passionate camps made their positions clear. On the one side were those endorsing the idea of a new national flag based on both the need for independent national symbols and the need to accommodate Quebec. On the other side were those who vigorously opposed the more inclusive re-creation of Canada's public symbols and public image. For them, the idea of replacing the Red Ensign and the Union Jack seemed to suggest treason.[8]

It was not only the British nature of Canada that seemed to some Canadians to be at risk in the flag debate but also Canada's religious character. The lead architect of the Liberal plans for a new flag, John Ross Matheson, recalled that he and his colleagues "knew that the flag issue would evoke racial and religious overtones." In fact, those overtones were significant enough to shape how the government approached the issue. To avoid charges of "disloyalty to our British tradition," a tradition that clearly included Protestant Christianity, the Liberals had selected Matheson, one of their MPs, to lead the push for the new flag. Like Pearson, Matheson had served the country in war. And, as he would later recall, "Like Pearson, I was of British background and the son and grandson of a Protestant manse."[9]

Parliamentary speeches on the issue revealed the same concern about the flag's religious, as well as its racial, implications. John Diefenbaker, leader of the Opposition, passionately criticized the proposed new flag for ignoring the old symbols of Canada's "sacred heritage."[10] In an address recalled by Matheson as "one of the great speeches of the flag debate," Paul Martineau (MP for Pontiac-Temiscamingue) responded that the "maple leaf design that is being proposed is not a renunciation or a betrayal of our past, of our Christian principles ... After this debate has ended and this flag has been adopted," he continued, "we, as a Canadian and Christian nation, will continue to adhere to all those things that make our country great, that make the British heritage great, that make the French heritage great, and which, indeed, make our civilization worth living and fighting for."[11]

Nor were parliamentarians alone in discussing the religious significance of the new flag. The primate of the Anglican Church, the Right
Reverend H.H. Clark, claimed it to be "significant that when Canada
got a new flag there was no cross upon it."[12] An unnamed Presbyterian
minister from Montreal thought so, too. In a letter to Prime Minister
Pearson he wrote, "As citizen and churchman I earnestly deplore design of projected new flag [sic] as pagan and a flat rejection of Canada's
Christian heritage. The glory of the Union Jack is the union of three
Christian Crosses. How unworthy, how unfeeling to replace so inspiring a symbol with one reminiscent of a hockey team or an Indian tribe.
How can the Canadian Government expect priests and clergy to bless a
national flag which utterly ignores our holy heritage?"[13]

The long and passionate flag debate indicated that the times were
changing in Canada and that those changes were throwing into confusion Canadian national public identities. Debate about public symbols and representations of Canada invariably had religious
implications. Such debate was also bound to be emotional.

The flag debate also revealed the Canadian federal state's reaction
to the change and confusion of the 1950s and 1960s. Pearson and his
government were committed enough to the task of providing Canada
with a new image through a new national flag that they were willing
to endure the fierce political storm of the fall of 1964 to reach their
goal. Only by bringing in parliamentary closure, in fact, were the Liberals able to end the debate and bring the House to a successful vote
just before Christmas. Significantly, the new flag contained no reference to any particular ethnicity or to any particular faith. It was a
broad, inclusive symbol for an increasingly diverse and tolerant
country: a red maple leaf on white, with red borders.

The creation of a new flag was one part of a much larger reconstruction
of Canada's "symbolic order" engineered by reform-minded governments and encouraged by reform-minded citizens in the late 1950s and
in the 1960s.[14] The year 1957, in fact, seemed a sort of turning point
away from the status quo in Canada. Prime Minister John Diefenbaker
swept to power in an election in that year by criticizing the Liberal Party
for being arrogant and elitist. Picking up on the themes of an age so sensitive about democracy and equality, that point stuck. Under Diefenbaker, efforts to tone down racism in immigration laws were followed
in 1960 by the federal enactment of the Canadian Bill of Rights, a piece
of legislation that, among other things, recognized the equality of all Canadians with regard to race and religion.[15] In 1962, Ellen Fairclough, the
federal minister responsible for immigration, announced a new policy
that downplayed race as an explicit factor of evaluation.

Humiliated by the Diefenbaker victory, the Liberal Party indicated that it had learned its lesson. It quickly transformed itself into a much more progressive and democratic body, organizing a "thinkers' conference" to plan policy and selecting the former international diplomat and reform-minded Pearson as its leader and, eventually, Canada's prime minister. Imbued with a "cosmopolitanism that accepted progress, relativism, and liberalism," Pearson has been described as a person "eager to break with the past" in his effort to create a strong, modern Canada.[16] As the new flag demonstrated, when the Liberal Party under Pearson took back the reigns of government from the Conservatives in 1963, it responded to an increasingly diverse and demanding population and to the themes of participatory democracy and equality, not by maintaining a British and Christian Canada, but by dismantling its parts. The federal government under Pearson moved to change an old symbolic order that seemed increasingly out of touch with contemporary realities.

From Pearson's perspective, it had little choice. In historian Michael Behiels's words, the Liberals had come to office just as "Canadian society was embarking upon an era of great social, economic, and political transformation – similar to, but perhaps more intense than, the experience of Canadians during the boom years of the early twentieth century."[17] Negotiating through that rocky period was no easy task, but it was made particularly difficult by what Pearson recognized early on as the fragility of Confederation in the face of an increasingly dissatisfied Quebec. Not surprisingly, Pearson's biographer, John English, has noted that "what mattered most to Mike Pearson was 'whether Confederation satisfied' French Canada ... And so his programs, from the flag to the pension plan, from bilingualism to equalization, gained their shape in large part from his belief that in the mid-1960s, national unity mattered most."[18] Anything getting in the way of national unity, in other words, would have to go.

Pearson himself made that belief abundantly clear. "First among our national goals, the prerequisite to all others, economic, social, or cultural, is national unity," he argued at a federal-provincial conference in 1964. "That does not mean and cannot mean uniformity. It does mean Canadian identity, with the symbols and even more the spirit and pride to foster such an identity." That striking statement, in turn, reflected well a dominant trend within his government. The Pearson Liberals were directly interested in shaping Canadian identity through the orchestration of public symbols and national pride, and they engaged vigorously in what others have termed "the politics of culture."[19] Bolstered by the affluence of the 1960s, which mitigated economic concerns, they turned their attention to what an American historian has called "the social sphere of human action."[20] Within that sphere, Pearson worked out the key progressive themes of his day. Convinced that "tolerance and a respect for diversity were essential bonds of a civil society," in the words of one historian, he set out to transform Canada's "official" national identity by turning Canada's exclusive public symbols into new symbols of inclusive pluralism.[21] "If we are to achieve great things ... every Canadian must become involved – personally, individually involved," he argued at a Winnipeg Liberal dinner in 1964. "What we need today across Canada is participation by more people in determining the course Canadians will take to fulfill their hopes and aspirations for our national destiny."[22]

To those ends, in addition to giving Canada a new flag, Pearson also established the Royal Commission on Bilingualism and Biculturalism in 1963 to "recommend what steps should be taken to develop the Canadian Confederation on the basis of an equal partnership between the two founding races, taking into account the contribution made by the other ethnic groups to the cultural enrichment of Canada and the measures that should be taken to safeguard that contribution."[23] From the beginning, the goal of the commission was clear. It was to argue against the idea of a British Canada with a French minority and to argue instead for a bicultural and bilingual Canada in which the French and English were equals.[24] The B&B Commission, as it came to be called, reflected an impulse towards inclusivity and diversity that would mark many of the policies of the Pearson era.

That impulse would be interpreted well beyond French-English dualisms. Beginning with the clear goal of creating a bilingual and bicultural Canada, Pearson's royal commissioners soon became aware that their plan was unworkable. Canadians not of British or French origin were shaken by the commission's proposal of a *bi*cultural and *bi*lingual Canada, a plan that, they felt, relegated them to some kind of sub-Canadian status.[25] At least partly as a result of the protests of Canadians of non-French and non-British origin, the B&B Commission's original plan of pushing for a bilingual and bicultural vision of Canada was modified and broadened. A policy of official bilingualism was enacted by the Liberal government in 1969, but a policy dealing with the commission's study of biculturalism had to wait until 1971.

Caught between Canadians demanding that their country remain grounded in its British and French origins and Canadians who argued otherwise, Prime Minister Pierre Trudeau and his government, who had been elected in 1968, offered a compromise: a policy of "multiculturalism". In Trudeau's words, multiculturalism recognized that "other cultural communities ... too, are essential elements in Canada and deserve government assistance in order to contribute to regional and national life in ways that derive from their heritage yet are distinctively Canadian."[26] Through the new policy, Trudeau explained, the federal government would seek to do four things. First, it would provide resources to ethnic minorities to help them maintain their cultures. Second, it would help Canadians of ethnic minorities to overcome cultural barriers to participate fully in Canadian society and public life. Third, it would promote creative cultural exchange between ethnic groups in Canada, in order to build mutual respect and to strengthen national unity. Fourth, it would help ethnic minorities acquire one of the two official languages.[27] Linguistically, Canada remained English and French. Culturally, however, it now seemed wide open. Trudeau's words and his policy indicated just how far the drive for inclusion and national unity had taken the Canadian federal state from its racially and religiously exclusive days.

The general discontent of the 1960s had a clear impact not just on the laws and programs the federal government enacted but also on the very way it attempted to govern. In order to maintain a sense of legitimacy in a tumultuous social and political atmosphere, the federal government not only made the symbols and rituals of Canadian public life more inclusive of all Canadians, it also initiated wide-ranging changes to make the actual functioning of government a more inclusive and open process.[28] In the mid-1960s, the push to get everyone involved in the shaping of public policy led the government to make decision making appear more democratic and less restricted to elites, with consultation of citizen groups an increasingly popular tactic in everything from immigration policy to language policy.[29] Between 1963 and 1976 one of the most striking features of the development of federal policy was "the democratization of the process of policy formulation," as one scholar has noted.[30]

To the particular point of this study, changing policies and styles of governance played a vital role in changing state-sponsored representations of Canada, including its religious components, in a more inclusive and pluralistic direction. In obvious ways, a new Canadian flag, changing immigration laws, the Royal Commission on Bilingualism and Biculturalism and a program of multiculturalism each weakened or removed old ethnically exclusive representations of Canada's dominant culture. In doing so, they also had a striking, if subtler, impact on the old privileging of Christianity in Canadian public life. The Liberal Party's attempt to remove symbols of British dominance in the Canadian flag had religious implications. Given the close ties between religion and ethnicity in the period, changes to immigration policies also had profoundly practical implications for the public expressions of religion in Canada's dominant culture. The decision to proclaim Canada multicultural, for its part, effectively declared the official privileging of Christianity in national public life dead.

The dismantling of the old understandings of Canada, however, did not stop there. In the 1960s Canada's legislation of morality was also revamped in a way that left conservative Christian markings behind. In the 1950s, legislation restricting Sunday activities was weakened by the legalization of Sunday sports.[31] More significantly, after several years of consultation and discussion and with the approval of Canada's mainline denominations, divorce laws were liberalized in 1968. The legalization of contraception and homosexual activity was announced in December 1967 and passed into law in 1969.[32] Not by coincidence, that was the issue on which Pierre Trudeau, now prime minister, declared that the "state has no place in the bedrooms of the nation."[33] It was to become one of the best-known statements of a decade that demonstrated the clear discomfort of the federal government with any legislative endorsement of conservative Christian morality.

Furthermore, the shifting of emphasis onto citizen participation and participatory democracy in the 1960s had significant implications for the public presence of religion. The leaders of the mainline churches had rarely been able to dictate government policy before that decade, but they had influenced it. The transformation of Canada in a more inclusivist and pluralist direction in the 1960s meant that the public sphere became a more competitive place and that wielding influence within it became more difficult. Though the largest Christian churches in Canada continued to be significant public institutions, they were having an increasingly difficult time claiming that they alone constituted the conscience of the nation. Many more groups and institutions would now join them in public life.

The federal government's response to its changing Canadian context was to remove many of the visible barriers that kept national public life religiously and ethnically exclusive. Governments devalued exclusivity and dominant conformity and increasingly valued inclusivity and diversity. That shift was exemplified in the flag debate, changes to immigration law, and the redevelopment of Canada's linguistic and cultural policy. It was also reflected in changes to the legislation of divorce, contraception, and homosexuality and in changes in the way governments tried to govern. All those changes led to the considerable weakening of the historic foundations of the privileging of Christianity in Canada's dominant culture. Gradually and often implicitly, the ability of the Christian religion and of the mainline Christian churches alone, to legitimize and sacralize the state was increasingly questioned and dismissed. As a result, the old relationship between Christianity and Canada was finding itself on ever thinning ice.

The federal state, of course, was only one institutional complex that had historically stood behind the public privileging of Christianity in Canada. The mainline Protestant and Roman Catholic churches formed another. In the years after 1945, those churches, too, had taken note of the impact on their society of state development, the faith in scientific management and technology that partly fueled it, consumerism, and more inclusive and tolerant attitudes towards diversity. In 1950s Montreal, the very city Cardinal Léger had so confidently declared his bride, attendance at Sunday mass and observance of the church's teachings were in noticeable decline.[34] In that same decade, the Roman Catholic Church in Quebec had come to rely so heavily on government funds to manage the provincial programs of education, health care, and welfare that the premier, Maurice Duplessis, boasted, "The bishops eat from my hand."[35] Leaders of the United Church responded with shock and dismay when in 1951 the moderator of the church failed to receive an invitation to a reception for the Queen.[36] The Presbyterian Church, a major player in the creation and defense of Sabbath legislation, watched provincial governments dismiss its advice and legalize Sunday sports in the 1950s.[37]

For the first ten to fifteen years after World War II, Protestant and Roman Catholic leaders did respond to the growing challenges at hand, but in a manner that suggested those challenges could be overcome without fundamentally reconsidering the status quo. To be sure, historic relationships between Christianity, the mainline churches, Canadian culture, and the Canadian state did not go unquestioned. In the late 1940s and early 1950s, important voices in the churches criticized the historic attitudes, programs, and patterns of a Christian Canada. Eager for renewal and rejuvenation in institutions that they felt had become too conservative and complacent, some individuals had argued that reform was necessary for the survival of the religious institutions they loved.[38] That said, while some correctly noted the weakening influence of Christianity and the churches in Canada's dominant culture, few contemporaries saw the historic privileging of public expressions of Christianity as on the verge of collapse. In those years, John Webster Grant has argued, the Protestant and Roman Catholic churches "looked forward to a period of quiet consolidation."[39]

In the 1940s and 1950s, then, the churches responded to their cultural context with the usual blend of quiet accommodation and confident resistance, reflecting the desire to meet the changes of postwar Canada by adapting old patterns and methods to new situations, without fundamentally questioning the old framework. Such adaptations were often ambiguous and sometimes contradictory. In Quebec, for example, while the Roman Catholic Church quietly accepted

its own inability to fund the province's health and education systems and relied increasingly on government largesse to do so, at the
same time it vigorously defended its control of those institutions. In
English Canada, the churches perceived the growth of the welfare
state as a long-awaited positive response to their own demands for
state action in the social sphere.[40] Some voices did call for caution in
the early 1940s, fearing state domination of society and the diminish-
ing of individual initiative and personal responsibility, but their impact was generally limited.[41]

The high valuation of science and technology behind the growth of
the welfare state, along with the growth of consumerism in the postwar years, concerned the mainline churches more than the growth of
the welfare state itself. Ecclesiastical leaders worried about the de-
creasing willingness of Canadians to listen to them on matters that
were perceived to be better handled by experts in the social sciences.
Voices within the United and Roman Catholic Churches warned that
Canadians were interested far more in material consumption than in
spiritual reflection or in building a Christian social order.[42] Here, too,
however, their response was ambiguous and conflicted. Although
their official reports questioned materialism, the churches themselves
seemed to dive into it. In Protestant circles, fundraising and new
church buildings dominated the late 1950s and early 1960s, and the
appearance and size of church facilities seemed to become the primary criterion for judging the health of a congregation.[43]

Programs and projects developed by the mainline churches in the
late 1940s and 1950s further demonstrate both their accommodation
with and resistance to the new and increasingly unprecedented challenges of the liberalizing, egalitarian, and diversifying cultural context of the postwar period. Already in 1948, for example, plans for the
creation of a new, more critical and theologically liberal Sunday
school curriculum to match the changing times were discussed in the
United Church. A number of controversial theological studies and articles published in the late 1950s and early 1960s by the United
Church were informed by a pedagogical desire to unsettle and challenge churchgoers in order to renew their faith.[44] Meanwhile, concerns about the state of the church and the nation were met more
often than not by the old form of national missions, attempts to renew
the spiritual vigour of Canadians through inspirational meetings and
small group studies, as well as through advertisements in the mainstream media. The United Church, for example, ran its Christ in
Christmas campaign in the late 1950s and early 1960s, which tried to
counter the growing consumerism – and excessive consumption of
alcohol – of the Christmas season. Aimed at all Canadians, in 1960

the campaign involved press releases, advertisements on 100 lighted billboards, film clips on the CBC, and eight-second "flashettes" on 165 radio stations across Canada.[45]

The responses of the Protestant mainlines to issues of diversity and racism in the postwar period also indicated their attempt to fit that diversity into their old Christian Canada framework, rather than to acknowledge the decline of that framework altogether. Again, a sense of responsibility for the nation within Canada's mainline churches led them to comment directly on issues of national public policy. Both the United and the Anglican Churches, for example, were leaders in the push against racial and religious discrimination in the postwar period. At the same time, however, both showed hints of continuing to harbour some of that discrimination themselves. Hugh Dobson, the most powerful leader of the United Church in the Western provinces during the Second World War, publicly urged his radio and newspaper audiences to be tolerant of "minorities" while in private correspondence with his superior, he expressed concern about the fact that "Anglo-Saxons are the minority now in some provinces" and admitted that he did not "like Jews."[46] In the 1950s the Anglican Council for Social Service advocated a more open immigration policy and tried, in its own words, "to soften up public opinion regarding the reception of other races." In 1952, however, it had also asked the government to increase the percentage of immigrants of British origin. That request had been called racist, but the council argued in 1955 that it had never said no to any other race coming to Canada. It simply wanted British citizens because of the need "to establish a sufficient 'cushion' of British people to maintain the stability of our democratic way of life, our parliamentary and economic systems, and our political institutions."[47]

The Roman Catholic Church, for its part, took a stronger position against change than its Protestant counterparts. Particularly in Quebec, it stood firmly against modernity and "the materialism of the human sciences" and sent the clear message that "L'heure n'est pas au compromis."[48] With temperance crusades, a renewed campaign for public morality, and a Family Rosary Crusade – all assuming that the boundaries of the province of Quebec equalled that of the Roman Catholic Church in Quebec – the church attempted to meet the constant threat of "paganisme."[49] At the same time, however, it responded with at least lukewarm enthusiasm to the progressive emphasis of the 1950s and 1960s on citizen participation, tolerance, equality, and the responsible democratic individual. Those principles found themselves embodied in growing demands by laypersons for more significant roles in their denominations.[50] Partly due to lay activism and partly due to the church's shortage of qualified clergy, lay people began to become more prominent in the fields of education and social welfare in Quebec and in the direction of Catholic trade unions.[51]

The conflicted response of the Roman Catholic Church to its changing times was particularly seen in sharp divisions amongst the bishops of Quebec. Long involved in the project to draw Quebec's social institutions under its influence, the Roman Catholic hierarchy was deeply concerned in the 1940s and 1950s about signs that its influence was waning. The trend was visible when the Confédération des Travailleurs Catholiques du Canada (CTCC), a Roman Catholic trade union, opened up its membership to non-Roman Catholics in 1943.[52] The same trend revealed itself in a growing number of voices that demanded that the Roman Catholic Church give up its dominance of Quebec society, admit difference, and demonstrate tolerance of those outside of the fold.[53] The bishops themselves were divided on the issue, with Cardinal Léger being willing to take a more flexible approach to dissent and a majority of others arguing, into 1959, that Catholic participation in "religiously neutral" or Protestant social and charitable organizations, for example, was unacceptable, and that the church should fight the growth of Protestant "sects."[54] The cultural dominance of such a conservative Roman Catholicism was graphically revealed when in 1953 Quebec's censorship board banned the film *Martin Luther*.[55]

In the 1950s, then, the mainline churches responded to the challenges to their privileged position in a Christian Canada with a combination of resistance and accommodation – a combination that reflected their general desire to maintain their historic positions of privilege and public influence that the past century had accorded them. In the early 1960s, however, the situation changed dramatically.

The broad factors behind that change, as reviewed in the last chapter, are reasonably clear. The Quiet Revolution in Quebec, the end of the religious revival, a significant decline in church attendance and involvement beginning in the 1950s, and the increasingly vocal and vigorous critique of the mainline churches from within and outside went far beyond the challenges of the immediate postwar period, forcing the leadership in those churches to change their response and to fundamentally and explicitly rethink their assumptions in a way that had not been possible in the previous decade. When the challenges they faced escalated from warnings of caution to cries for change, many church leaders were compelled to wonder if the old ways of being the religious establishment in Canada were being weakened beyond repair.

If the challenges were not daunting enough at home, the churches were also encouraged to look critically at themselves and their relationship to their society by international events that coincided neatly with their own struggles in the 1960s. The Second Vatican Council, an international gathering of Roman Catholic bishops in Rome, began three years into the Quiet Revolution and ran until 1965. That was fortuitous timing for the church in Quebec.[56] With its influence and privilege in that province rapidly weakening, that church's establishment mentality was increasingly out of touch with the times. An institution historically renowned for its clear claim to be the "true church" and its stark refusal to acknowledge religious pluralism was now facing a society determined to squeeze out from under its shadow and to celebrate tolerance and diversity. It was precisely that dilemma, faced also by the Roman Catholic Church around the world, that Vatican II would confront.

Other world-wide changes in the Christian church also had an impact. A major influence on the Christian churches of Canada in the 1960s was the rise of liberation theologies in the tumultuous "third world." Emerging from beneath European colonialism in the postwar period, churches in African and central American countries, in particular, felt in their faith as much as in their politics the impact of independence movements and calls for justice. Struck with the discrepancy in wealth and opportunity between developed and developing nations, those churches of newly independent and struggling nations took their concerns to such gatherings of church leaders as the Anglican World Congress in Toronto, the Faith and Order Conference of the World Council of Churches in Montreal, and the Second Vatican Council, all of which took place or began in 1963. There those third world churches questioned the establishment mentality of churches in the West and called them to activism on behalf of the poor.[57] To churches already feeling ample pressure to change their historic relationship with state and society within a disintegrating Christian Canada, that message struck home.[58]

Combined with changes within Canadian society and culture, international affairs helped push the mainline Protestant and Roman Catholic churches to look beyond the old relationships between Christianity, the churches, Canadian culture, and the Canadian state. While voices critical of those churches had been rare in the 1950s, in the mid-1960s, they moved from the periphery to the core of their institutions and gained a wide hearing.[59] The publication of *The Comfortable Pew* illustrates that point well. That attack on the mainline churches was, after all, commissioned, paid for, and published by the Anglican Church of Canada. More to the point, when Anglican Church officials commissioned Pierre Berton to write the book, they were well aware that he was a known agnostic critical of the mainline churches and that he had recently left *Maclean's* magazine after creating a great deal of controversy with an article in favour of the sexual revolution. In other

words, Anglican officials asked for his withering attack and knew very
well what they were up to when they did so. They shared with him the
sense that something had to change. Quite significantly, many other
clergymen did, too, and Berton received not a few accolades for his criticisms from within the Anglican Church itself.[60]

As the commissioning of *The Comfortable Pew* illustrates, religious
leaders were not just reluctantly responding to their changing culture.
As important members of Canada's cultural elites, they were active participants in that culture and continued, in many ways, to lead it. The
growing mood of iconoclasm and reform was propelled by the same
optimism towards the future that Canadians more generally shared, as
well as by a concern that change was the only way to keep church institutions relevant in what was considered by some an entirely new and
unprecedented age.

By the mid-1960s, the prevalence of such attitudes within church
hierarchies was nowhere better demonstrated than in the Most Reverend H.H. Clark's president's address to the Anglican Church's tri-
yearly General Synod in 1965. The primate of that church for six years
and a respected and able interpreter of his day, Clark challenged the
gathering of clergy, laypersons, and administrators from across Canada to face and overcome their predicament as leaders of an estab-
lishmentarian institution in an increasingly pluralist and democratic
age. The primate took his church back to the Anglican Congress of
1963, a gathering of the world leaders of the church in Toronto that
had argued that the church must be reborn in loving service to the
world. "That was the vision and the challenge," he recalled of that
congress, "a Church renewed so that it can serve God in the world,
where He is leading men to responsible freedom in a community of
love." "The sacrificial character of action," he argued, provided the
only way that the church could meet modern realities. "Do we realize," he went on, "that a world community is being achieved, despite
all the checks and disappointments, and that only the devastation of
an all out atomic war could frustrate this development? And do we
understand that this means the end of Christendom as we have
known it, and the end, therefore, of the privileges and favoured position that the church once enjoyed? Now the Christian confronts the
Hindu, the Buddhist, the Moslem, the Communist, and the Humanist, with no prior advantages. Are we prepared to be a Servant
Church, neither demanding nor expecting those advantages?" In his
opinion, the church had little choice. "Gradually the customs, symbols, institutions, and even the laws which once supported our society and molded it into the likeness of a Christian society – one by one
they disappear, or else linger on as quaint relics."[61]

Even the briefest survey of some of Canada's other mainline churches indicates that Clark could have been speaking for them as well. The United Church of Canada was experiencing its own crisis of identity, a fact revealed in its seemingly unceasing effort to find efficient bureaucratic structures, as well as in the numerous committees with sweeping mandates that it commissioned to review the life of the church. In January 1965, for example, the Commission on the Church's Ministry in the Twentieth Century was appointed to answer such fundamental questions as "What is the Church For?"[62] "The meetings of the Commission have been intense," it reported three years later. "The call of the Church for radical change came through 'loud and clear.' It is the conviction of this Commission that there is a deep and anguished cry from all levels and areas of the Church for reform and that the Church must hear this cry."[63] The fervour for reevaluation and sweeping reconsideration reached such a level that in 1967 when the General Assembly tried to appoint a Commission on the Church and Society, the Executive Committee of the church said no. Though the church was apparently anxious for more information, the executive argued, there was little left that had not already been scrutinized by other church commissions.[64] Like the Anglicans, United Church leaders began to realize that their former privileges in Canada's dominant culture were slipping away and that an attitude of service and humility would serve them well in the new context. "Listen to the World" was the apt title for the Board of Evangelism and Social Service's 1965 report.[65] In 1964 and 1965, respectively, the United and Anglican Churches also released new curricula – revised church education programs that had been in the making in the United Church for twelve years and in the Anglican Church for four. They, too, reflected the reforming mood of their day. Both used the latest in pedagogical techniques, giving up the older Sunday school methods of the authoritative teacher imparting authoritative answers. An official behind the Anglican program described it as a response to "the need for much more openness in terms of the kinds of answers which are provided to people. Young people and adults must be encouraged to challenge and to question." In the new church education programs, the teacher was no longer the authority. "Instead, the role of the leader or teacher will be to encourage the sharing of experiences, the raising of questions and the exploration of resources and information ... There will be much more openness and fewer 'absolute' answers."[66] To that end, the United Church's New Curriculum encouraged students to think carefully and critically about the biblical record by challenging them with "difficult problems of biblical authorship and authority that most ministers had long evaded."[67]

Bureaucratic restructuring, commissions with sweeping mandates, and attitudes of egalitarianism and criticism were common aspects of other denominations, too. The Roman Catholic Church, for its part, emerged from Vatican II much more open to the fresh winds of change. Some leaders in that church in Quebec had played a leading role in Vatican II's reworking of structures and attitudes forged in the sixteenth-century Council of Trent into those more suited to a modern, pluralistic age.[68] Plurality, the Roman Catholic Church now conceded, was the stuff of modern life, and the church would no longer lay sole claim to the privilege to shape the society and culture of any nation. What the church thought best, it now recognized, was not always best for everyone else.[69] Returning from Rome, Quebec's clerical elites now had official sanction to accept the Quiet Revolution, to call an end to the exclusive privileging of the Roman Catholic Church in Quebec and of a broader Christianity in Canada, and to find a more modest and less exclusive position from which they might influence their society. While the episcopate was by no means unified in its approach to the changing social and political context, the changes made to the liturgy and architecture of Roman Catholic churches across the country in response to Vatican II were aimed at bringing the church more into line with the present age.[70]

Within the Presbyterian Church of Canada, the mood of reform was best illustrated by the appointment of the Committee on Life and Mission by the General Assembly in 1965. That committee was to "undertake a thorough study of the vocation, work and mission of the Presbyterian Church in Canada in the changing life of Canada and other nations, and a study of the resources of the Presbyterian Church in Canada in persons, finances, and institutions."[71] In the April 1967 *Presbyterian Record*, William E. Hume noted that "society is undergoing a process called secularization. God was once considered indigenous to our culture. Today he is being moved out of the culture. He is a sectarian symbol in a pluralistic society. This church, therefore, is feeling the pinch of being just one institution among others attempting to justify its existence."[72]

The reform impulse within Canada's mainline churches was further demonstrated by a sudden rush of interest towards ecumenical dialogue and church union in the 1960s. Ecumenical cooperation and talks of union were hardly something new in that decade. From 1960 to 1965, however, what had been a trickle of interest in ecumenism in the 1950s turned into a large wave.[73] Urged on by the palpable changes of the 1960s within and around their churches, growing numbers of church leaders became convinced that in a changing Canada, separate denominational structures were an unaffordable luxury.

Within and among the Christian churches of Canada, the ecumenical movement also sent the clear message that old exclusive denominational structures and religious identities were no longer suited for the new age. The two largest Protestant denominations in the country, the Anglican and United Churches, suddenly began to make significant progress towards a merger after fifteen years of on-again, off-again, discussions. By 1965, a major milestone was reached when committees of the two churches agreed on the Principles of Union. By the Centennial year, the dissolution of the Anglican and United Churches into a new United Church holding the affiliation of over six million Canadians seemed a tangible reality. By that time, too, the ecumenical spirit was affecting others as well. In 1967, the Evangelical Lutheran Church of Canada collaborated with the Lutheran Church of America to form the Lutheran Council in Canada, and the eastern conference of the Evangelical United Brethren Church in Canada joined with the United Church.[74]

Much more significant than either of the latter two developments, however, was the movement of the Roman Catholic Church into ecumenical discussions. In Canada, that movement had begun quietly and at the diocesan level already in the early 1950s. Prompted by Pope Pius XII's cautious authorization in 1950 of dialogue with "separated brothers" (as non-Catholic Christians were then called), Father Irénée Beaubien formed a Catholic Inquiry Forum in Montreal in 1952. That forum was more missionary in flavour than ecumenical, but by 1958 Beaubien continued to be on the cutting edge of Protestant-Catholic interaction in Canada and had moved further into the ecumenical waters. With the permission of Cardinal Léger, he began a truly ecumenical centre in Montreal that quietly welcomed a growing number of Protestants and Catholics into dialogue. At that point, it should be noted, many in the Roman Catholic hierarchy still considered such dialogue dangerous for the average parishioner, and it was carefully restricted to those deemed capable and stable enough in their faith to sustain it.[75]

All that changed dramatically in the early 1960s. Vatican II threw the Roman Catholic Church into a process of *aggiornamento*, or "updating," as Pope John XXIII called it, and prompted dramatic changes in liturgy and worship, a greater degree of collegiality and consultation in the hierarchy of the church, and a growing role for lay-persons in local programs.[76] Along with internal reform, the council led to what has been called "the most exciting ecumenical development"[77] of the 1960s: by accepting religious pluralism and passing statements favourable to the ecumenical movement, Vatican II broke down thick ecclesiastical walls that had stood firm for over four hundred years.

"Fortress Catholicism" was dead,[78] and suddenly the Roman Catholic Church was a leader in initiating ecumenical dialogue. It was the most stunning religious reform of the 1960s – a very visible "opening up" of a religious institution previously known as one of Christendom's most exclusive and authoritative denominations.

Notably, changes within the churches included theology as much as church organization. Leaders of the mainline churches, and of other faith groups as well, were sensitive to the latest trends in theology, trends which incorporated the larger cultural concerns of individual responsibility, participatory democracy, and tolerance of difference. Some influential leaders combined an awareness of their changing social context with a Christian existentialism much in vogue in the 1960s.[79] Enchanted by the rapid technological and social changes in recent years, they also carefully considered the argument of others that their age was a secular one in which "modern man" could no longer accept the old supernatural and mythical elements of the Christian faith.[80] Both the existentialist critique and the related contention that old ways of being Christian were doomed in the contemporary world were popularly expressed in two of the most influential and best-selling works of theology of the mid-1960s, John A.T. Robinson's *Honest to God* (1963) and Harvey Cox's *The Secular City* (1965). Building on the work of Dietrich Bonhoeffer, Cox, in particular, argued that in the new modern age, the individual could no longer accept the comforting supernatural myths of "religion." Shorn of those myths, Christianity would have to be translated into a new language better suited for a modern, scientific age. Christians, for their part, would have to face a harsher, down-to-earth reality and accept responsibility for making it better.[81]

A good number of theologians, church educators, and church officials, mostly from the mainline churches, reflected the latest "new theology" propounded by Harvey Cox and others and called for a "new language" of faith that would speak to the "modern man." Theologians of the God is Dead school took that argument to a radical new place and created a great deal of controversy in the early 1960s with their contention that the traditional Christian faith with its supernatural trappings was finished in Canada and around the world and should be buried.[82] The impact of such thought in the mainline Canadian Protestant churches was vividly demonstrated by the Reverend Ernest Harrison, an employee of the Anglican Church's Board of Education. After writing in 1965 a very controversial book described as "an urgent plea for the updating of traditional concepts in theology and ethics,"[83] Harrison went on to declare in an interview in early 1966 that the Christian concept of God as a trinity or a person was "no longer reasonable."[84] The accommodating mood of the Anglican Church was demonstrated in the response of the head of that church, Primate Clark, to the predictable calls for formal action against Harrison. Clark appealed for "more charity, more patience, and more understanding" and argued that though he did not agree with Harrison, there was room enough in the denomination for everyone.[85] Formal action was taken against him only when he wrote a third book, *A Church without God*, in 1967, but Harrison ended up resigning his position in the Anglican office on his own accord.[86]

To progressive clerical elites of many stripes, a new tolerant, inclusive, and pluralistic Canada called for new structures and new relationships, new ways of being the church in society, and new ways of thinking about Christianity. When they got the ball of reevaluation and criticism rolling in their churches, however, it was not easily stopped. With questions such as "What is the Church for?" on the table by the mid-1960s, all previous assumptions now seemed complicated, mysterious, and uncertain. By 1965, the breadth and pace of criticisms of the mainline churches was intense, even overwhelming.[87]

Not surprisingly, all of that change and reform called forth a range of reactions. On one side of the issues of the day were men like Clark and even Harrison, men who staked their future on catching the wave of change. On the other side were those who did not see the need for all of this turmoil and transformation and who argued that it all be quickly put to an end. In their opinion, in advocating a new language of faith, some of their fellow churchmen and churchwomen were actually advocating a new faith. Opposition was most vocal in the Anglican and the United Churches. The latter's New Curriculum, its revised church education program, was considered too liberal in theology by some within the denomination but also by many Presbyterians and by the Baptist Convention of Ontario and Quebec.[88] At Easter of 1965, the moderator of the United Church, Ernest Marshall Howse, further threw the credibility of his church into doubt for some when he publicly questioned the Christian doctrine of the resurrection of the body, a traditional tenet of that Christian holiday.[89] The publication of *The Comfortable Pew* by the Anglican Church raised similar questions about the leadership of that institution and crystallized opposition. Letters to Anglican periodicals feared that "Pierre Berton will finish us off," while the Anglican Diocese of Toronto, the executive committee of the Calgary diocese, and others "protested emphatically" the commissioning of Berton in the first place to write the book.[90] Resistance to change only deepened with the publication of the opinions of the Reverend Ernest Harrison. Was this, many asked, where the "progressives" were leading?

If so, some in the mainline churches decided that they would do their best not to allow their churches to follow. That decision was demonstrated by the formation within the United and Anglican denominations in the middle years of the 1960s of new conservative groups that attempted to slow and even reverse the pace of change. The Canadian Anglican Evangelical Fellowship was formed in the spring of 1966 in response to what its members described as "confusion within our own Anglican Church," while the Renewal Fellowship was formed in the United Church in that same year.[91] By the late 1960s, a considerable sense of alienation and misunderstanding between the leadership and conservatives in the Anglican and United Churches had developed.[92] Differences in opinion ran from the top ranks of the church hierarchies down to the people sitting in the pew.[93]

Some Canadians refused to accept the end of the historic privileges, influence, and authority of their churches in the 1960s. Regarding the turmoil of that decade as a phase, they believed the best way to survive the unrest was to change very little and to wait for it to end. "I am weary of our rebels – rebels in every line – rebels in art, in music, in literature, rebels in religion and in morals," wrote one Presbyterian to the *Record* in 1966. "They have served whatever strange purpose they were intended to serve and should now retire into decent obscurity."[94] Some of the Canadians who filled the pews on Sundays thought the whole shift confusing and unnecessary. As the church tries to "express the Gospel in the thought forms of today," Primate Clark of the Anglican Church had noted in 1965, "we find that, while some only seek to change the language, others are convinced we must change the content of the Gospel." Some did not want to change at all. In Clark's words, "This naturally has aroused a strenuous debate."[95]

Despite such criticisms and confusion from within the churches, however, by the mid-1960s, the dominant reaction amongst mainline church leaders was towards change. In each denomination, of course, change took different forms. The United Church seemed the most progressive, the Anglican Church less so, while the Presbyterians seemed most cautious of the three. Together, however, those three Protestant churches not only reconsidered their privileged positions but also changed their stances on several important moral and social issues. From the late 1950s and into the 1960s, all three liberalized their positions on such things as the consumption of alcohol, divorce, contraception, and abortion.[96] To keep in touch with the changing times, the Anglicans and the Presbyterians gave women the right to be ordained, something the United Church had done thirty years before. The Roman Catholic Church, on the other hand, continued to take a firm stand against divorce, contraception, and abortion, while it also continued to demand the celibacy of its priests and restricted women from joining clerical ranks.

Notwithstanding those differences, however, the leadership of the mainline churches did arrive at very similar conclusions about how they should behave now that their Christian Canada seemed gone. For one, they all agreed that some structural changes were necessary if they were to continue to serve a society that was demanding the democratization of decision-making processes and a greater acceptance of diversity. Faced with the same sustained critique of hierarchical authoritative structures that plagued many institutions of the period, the churches responded by removing some of those structures from their institutions and by granting laymen, laywomen, and youth a much more significant role in the governance of their congregations and denominations. In the Anglican Diocese of Quebec, women delegates to church courts were welcomed in 1968, and youth in 1969.[97] In 1964 the Canadian Conference of Catholic Bishops began using parliamentary rules of order and restructured its meeting space. Cardinals and archbishops were removed from a raised head table, where they faced the rest of the body of bishops, and placed on an equal level, facing forward, just like everyone else.[98] In 1966, Roman Catholic dioceses began establishing diocesan councils made up of lay people to advise and aid the bishop on pastoral issues.[99] In 1969, the Life and Missions Project (LAMP) of the Presbyterian Church concluded four years of comprehensive study with a report that emphasized two essential themes: greater participation of the laity in the life of the church and "institutional reform to promote participation and efficiency."[100] Those changes to church structures were the ecclesiastical equivalent of the federal state's shift to more democratic decision making and an emphasis on citizen participation.

More importantly – and the point needs to be emphasized – those churches all agreed that giving up on the historic privileging of Christianity in Canadian public life did not mean giving up on their attempt to shape their country, nor did it mean a retreat into the private sphere. The United Church's *Report of the Commission on the Ministry in the Twentieth Century* captured that crucial point well in 1968. Quoting a BBC radio program, it repeated the argument that though "'pluralism means that no church, no philosophy, can run the show … [t]hat does not mean a withdrawal from society, but it means a different form of presence in society.'"[101] Letting Christian Canada and its respective privileges go, the mainline churches would continue to try to influence Canadians and their politicians, as they had done for more than a century. The Roman Catholic Bishops' Labour Day tradition of publishing their perspectives on current issues persisted. The well-established tradition of presenting reports to royal commissions did too. At the prayer service on Parliament Hill on 1 July 1967 and in the Centennial celebrations and Expo 67, in general, the clergy of those churches continued to play important roles.

It was not in their commitment to Canada and in their shaping of its public life that those churches changed. As the United Church's report indicated, it was *how* they worked out that commitment that did. Echoing Primate Clark's words three years earlier, the *Report of the Commission on the Ministry in the Twentieth Century* went on to note that the United Church would no longer enter public life as "the establishment," with all the privileges, respect, and power that suggested. Instead, it would enter it as "a servant church."[102] Such a move was driven by the "secular theology" of the 1960s, as well as by the growth of "liberation theology" in developing countries, but it was also simply strategic. In the 1960s the traditional association of the mainline churches with hierarchy, authority, and privilege had come to be seen as a millstone around their neck. Disassociating themselves from their privileged past was as much a strategy for church survival as anything else. To survive in a pluralistic, modern culture, many believed, Canada's mainline churches needed to accept their position as one among many and to find new ways of using that position to continue to influence their communities and their country.

They did so in two particularly important ways. First, as a recent survey of the period has noted, the churches gave up on any notion that they could "define a set of dominant beliefs for society as a whole."[103] They accepted that what was right for their denomination was not necessarily right for the country – that church law did not necessarily make good civil or criminal law. In this regard, their response to the decriminalization of contraception in Canada was telling. Until the mid-1950s, Canadians had largely assumed that individual morality could be legislated appropriately by governments under criminal law. In the late 1950s, however, more Canadians began to contend that "criminal law was not to be used to intervene in the private lives of citizens or to enforce particular patterns of moral behaviour unless such behaviour caused an offense or injury to the common good of society."[104] Could Christian moral perspectives be enshrined in law and forced upon all Canadians, Christian or not? Significantly, the mainline churches said no. In what was then the most striking example of this change of mind, when the Canadian Conference of Catholic Bishops submitted a report to a government committee investigating the liberalization of divorce law in 1966, it noted that in principle "there was a recognized distinction between what the Church forbade or approved and what contributed to the common welfare," though the church hoped that the two "would most often be closely aligned."[105]

If Canada's most historically influential churches no longer considered it appropriate to impose beliefs particular to Christians on all Canadians, however, they continued to be strong public proponents of those things that they believed would benefit all Canadians, Christians or not. They continued to emphasize broad humanitarian ideals like justice, compassion, and tolerance. "Accepting their pluralistic character of Canadian society," one historian has noted, "the churches have redefined their role in public life, raising their voices, alongside others, to speak out on issues ranging from economic justice through aboriginal rights to responsible use of natural resources, world peace, and reform of the criminal justice system."[106] The churches had long been concerned about such things as justice and peace, of course. In the mid-1960s, however, they began to advocate humanitarian ideals, not as authoritative interpreters of the Christian faith (as they had done in the era of the social gospel, for example), but as "servant" churches concerned for the welfare of all Canadians.

And that led them to a second important aspect of their new approach to public life. In the 1960s the re-formation of the mainline churches away from establishment institutions and towards "servant churches" resulted in a much more critical perspective towards the economic, social, and political status quo.[107] It was in the 1960s that the mainline churches in Canada stepped very visibly away from their privileges (but not from public life) to become advocates for the dispossessed and to assume the sharp critical edge that that position required. According to a study of the Anglican Diocese of Toronto in the tenth decade of Confederation, "Christian organizations more than ever tended to see themselves as pressure groups standing up for the rights of the voiceless or dispossessed."[108] As one historian has succinctly written, in the 1960s the mainline churches "exchanged their former function, in which they defined and legitimated prevailing norms, for a prophetic role, in which they challenged the status quo."[109]

In the 1950s and 1960s, the embedded nature of Christianity in the country's dominant culture faced growing challenges that put dramatic pressure for change on both the federal government and the mainline Christian churches. As the key institutions responsible for the creation and maintenance of the historic privileging of Christianity in Canadian public life, the Canadian state and the mainline churches had little choice but to respond. The federal government, in particular, moved to slowly dismantle racially and religiously discriminatory legislation, to liberalize legislation reflecting conservative Christian moral values, and to remodel both its symbols and its structures with the participation of all Canadian citizens in public life as its goal. The mainline churches also eventually relinquished the establishment ideal of a Christian Canada for a more pluralistic and open image of their country. Not just responding to the changes of the postwar period, both church and state institutions also shaped the way those changes unfolded.

The transition from a Christian to a religiously plural Canada did not satisfy everyone. The clash between those advocating change and those demanding continuity resulted in much of the religious turmoil of the 1960s. The tension between the two could also be seen, however, in much more subtle and quiet acts of resistance, as well as in other particularly symbolic national events. The prayer service on Parliament Hill was one. As we will now see, the 1967 Centennial celebrations, the Canadian Interfaith Conference, and Expo 67 were others.

Those events would capture the remaking of a more inclusive, pluralist Canada with remarkable clarity. Partly recognizing the social trends of the postwar period, partly shaping those trends on behalf of the federal state and religious institutions, the celebrations and Expo 67 would boldly reveal the response to the new inclusive and pluralistic Canada by religious groups from the Roman Catholic Church to Canadian B'ahais. As will be noted, the shift away from the historic privileging of Christianity in national public life was not without complexity, ambiguity, and mixed motives. In the light of the previous 350 years of Canadian history, however, the mid-1960s, as seen through the Centennial and Expo 67, involved dramatic and very significant alterations to the religious component of Canada's symbolic order.

4

The 1967 Centennial Celebrations, the Canadian Interfaith Conference, and the Building of an Inclusive, Pluralistic Canada

Into the early 1960s, the privileged nature of the Christian religion in Canadian public life continued to reinforce Christianity as an important element of Canadian national identities. Legislation regulating divorce, birth control, adoption and immigration, school curriculums, public rhetoric, and public radio all pointed to that conclusion. At the same time, however, abundant evidence in the postwar years indicated that in fact the historic privileging of Christianity was not as strong as it used to be. In the post-1945 period, in particular, Canada was rapidly changing from a country still secure in a racially and religiously exclusive national identity to a country officially defined by the embrace of plurality. Christian understandings of Canada continued to find expression in the rhetoric of the Cold War and in the midst of the apparent religious revival of the 1950s, but by the early 1960s other forces were rendering them increasingly problematic.

In the midst of that fundamental transformation in religious understandings of Canada came 1967 and the commemoration of the one hundredth anniversary of Canadian Confederation. Caught in the political and cultural turmoil of the 1960s, the celebrations vividly reflected in symbol and ritual the federal state's nation-building effort to reinterpret Canada to Canadians. They threw into bold relief the effort to move Canadians away from what was seen to have been a divisive and exclusive understanding of themselves and their country and towards a pluralistic vision perceived to be more inclusive and supportive of national unity. That effort involved a strong emphasis on citizen participation – an attempt to strengthen commitment and loyalty to the country by getting every citizen involved in public life. Significantly, it also involved public religion in forms explicitly sponsored by the state and aimed at satisfying the goals of the state.

One organization involved in the planning of the Centennial, the Canadian Interfaith Conference (CIC), demonstrates these themes particularly well. In the CIC, the historic involvement of religion in public life continued unabated, complete with the familiar tension inherent in church and state relations. At the same time, however, the CIC represented a decided shift away from historic, dominant forms of public religion in this country. In the Canadian Interfaith Conference, federal state planners found an ideal institution to forward their goal of recreating Canada, religion and all.

It was dark and fifteen degrees below zero, with a bitter wind coming in from the Gatineau Hills.[1] Still, on the evening of 31 December 1966, two thousand brave Canadians huddled together on the snow-covered lawns before the Parliament Buildings, while thousands more watched on black and white television across the country. Canada's Centennial Flame was about to be lit, but first the spectators had to shiver through the prerequisite ceremony. Prime Minister Lester Pearson and Opposition Leader John Diefenbaker sat on a podium facing a nine-by-fifteen-foot television screen. To their side was a warmly dressed Centennial choir, to their rear, more officials, including the mayors and reeves of the surrounding municipalities. A prerecorded address from the Queen to Canadians was played on the screen, though, regrettably, CBC technicians forgot to pipe in the sound to the throngs on Parliament Hill. Following the mute royal address, the Centennial Commission chairman John Fisher rose to recite the Centennial Prayer. "Almighty God, who has called us out of many nations and has set our feet on this broad land, establishing us as one people from sea to sea," the prayer began, "gratefully we remember all the way that thou hast led us through one hundred years, to humble us, and to prove us, and to know what was in our hearts ... Grant thy blessing upon the joyous celebrations of our Centennial Year, and a deeper worthiness of the dreams that gave us birth; that ' ... with flame of freedom in our souls and light of knowledge in our eyes' we may magnify thy name among men, one nation, serving thee. *Amen*."[2]

Next came the Centennial Choir and the singing of the Centennial Hymn. Their breath crystallizing in the cold air, the choristers sang the final verse with vigour.

> Lead us to walk the ways that love has always taken.
> Guide us, O God of Love, and we will shape a spirit
> Worthy a nation reaching for her destiny.
> So may we show the world a vision of Thy goodness,

Our dream of Man to which all men may yet awaken,
And share glory still with Thee.[3]

Finally, Prime Minister Pearson, "swaddled in a black cashmere overcoat, red wool scarf, and fur-lined gloves"[4] rose to give his address. "Tonight ... with the lighting of this flame, with pride in our present and faith in our future, we open officially our centennial celebration," he said.

As this flame burns, so let pride in our country burn in the hearts of all Canadians, where the real meaning of Canada must ever be found ... Out of our experience in nation-building we are forging a new principle of democracy, the principle of political and economic unity in racial and cultural diversity. History and geography, man and the map, have made Canada a particular kind of community where we can show this unity in diversity that all mankind must find if we are to survive the perils of a nuclear age ... Tonight, we begin a new chapter in our country's story. Let the record of that chapter be one of cooperation and not conflict; of dedication and not division; of service, not self; of what we can give, not what we can get. Let us work together as Canadians to make our country worthy of its honoured past and certain of its proud future. God bless Canada.[5]

All rose, and while the assembled throng burst into a rousing rendition of the national anthem, the prime minister walked down to the concrete fountain, reached into its centre with a long torch, and lit the natural gas bubbling up from its centre. After more than a few seconds of embarrassing hesitation, it burst into flame. The crowd cheered, the Peace Tower carillon began the first strains of "Auld Lang Syne," and the crowd and choir joined in. Then, far above the singing crowds, the sky burst into light. Fired off from behind the Parliament Buildings, fireworks blasted Canadians into their Centennial year.

And what a year it was. "Happy Centennial!" boomed a full-spread advertisement in the country's newspapers in the first days of January.[6] "Let's have a wonderful year." It then went on to lay out the key events of the coming celebrations. The Centennial train, it declared, "the most exciting train you've ever seen," was at that moment on its way from Ottawa to Victoria, where it would begin its cross-country tour back again. Painted bright, vibrant colours and covered from engine to caboose with the large text Canada Confederation 1867-1967, it was pulling train cars converted into a travelling road show of the history and glories of the country. It would visit no less than 63 cities, while Confederation caravans of over-sized transport trucks would visit another 657 communities unreachable by rail. "Festival Canada," declared by the ad to be "the largest entertainment package ever offered to Canadians," would bring "virtually all of our most important entertainers plus attractions from outside our country" to communities throughout Canada, with travel expenses paid by the government. A military tattoo would travel to 40 communities. Winnipeg would host the Pan-American games. Montreal would host Expo 67, "one of the most outstanding projects for the centennial year" and "the first official world exhibition ever to be held in the Americas." A voyageur cross-country canoe pageant, an extravagant, colourful and grueling affair, would see a number of canoe teams follow a historic fur-trading route from Rocky Mountain House in Alberta to Expo 67 in Montreal. The publicly funded Youth Travel Program, already in existence since 1964, would allow young people to visit and spend time in various regions of the country. The Community Involvement Project had already involved "cities, towns, villages, and farm areas from coast to coast in an ambitious clean-up and beauty campaign." The Interfaith Program had been set up "to foster a greater awareness across Canada of [the] common objectives and beliefs" of all Canadians, "whatever [their] place of worship." With the help of federal tax dollars offered through the Confederation Memorial Program or the Centennial Grants Program, an Arts and Cultural Centre had been constructed in St John's, Newfoundland, the Ontario Science Centre in Toronto, and a Regional Library in Hay River, Northwest Territories, to name only a few of many such projects.[7] New museums, art centres, concert halls, and parks were built across the country, and everything from the new National Archives building in Ottawa to new sidewalks were emblazoned with the Centennial symbol. "It is this kind of participation," the ad concluded, "that can help you and every living Canadian to realize one very solid truth: 'Canada is a great country. And I'm very proud to be Canadian.'"[8] Massive in scope and daunting in size, the Centennial celebrations were without doubt the most comprehensive, expensive, and extravagant nationalist project ever undertaken by the Canadian state.[9] Not surprisingly, they gave Canadians a wonderful year, one described by *Time* magazine as "the world's longest, biggest and costliest birthday party."[10]

But the Centennial celebrations did far more. They both reflected their cultural and political context and also served as tools to shape it. Planned in a country historically and publicly identified as religious, they carried within them a distinctly religious note. Planned by the Centennial Commission, a federal state body established in 1961 as the National Centennial Administration and designed with clear connections to government, they embodied a philosophy and message that closely reflected that of the Pearson Liberals, the political party in power at the height of Centennial planning from 1963 through 1967. The celebrations vividly captured the effort of the federal government to unite the country by presenting it to Canadians in a new way. Canada, they implicitly argued, was no longer primarily a British and Christian country with a French minority. Now it was a pluralistic and inclusive country, a new nation leading the world into the global future by celebrating its diversity, not its homogeneity. As a result, the celebrations worked hard to build national unity by portraying a Canada in which all Canadians, regardless of their cultural and religious differences, would be welcome.

That goal had been readily apparent already in September 1964, a full two and a half years before the Centennial year began. In that month Prime Minister Pearson and the leaders of the various provinces met at a federal-provincial conference held in the Confederation Chamber, Charlottetown, on the one-hundredth anniversary of the first Confederation conference. The 1964 meeting was one in a series dedicated to working out financial issues between the two levels of government, particularly with respect to the development of federal social security programs. Quebec was determined to prevent what it deemed to be the intrusion of the federal government into provincial affairs and had demanded that it be able to receive federal funding for its own social programs. Tensions ran high.[11]

Politically sensitive, the Charlottetown meeting was also an important symbolic event, and, as Pearson himself later recognized, an important precursor to the celebrations to come.[12] In his brief opening speech, the prime minister appealed to both history and religion to drive home his inclusive vision for the nation. "It is a great honour to speak in this chamber on this centennial anniversary of Canada's first confederation conference; to meet with the premiers of all the provinces around the same table where those men of vision conceived a great new nation a hundred years ago," Pearson began. "I think today of the words of the sixtieth chapter of Isaiah: 'A little one shall become a thousand and a small one a strong nation. The Lord will hasten it in his time.' The Lord has hastened it in our time." A few minutes later, he described the focus of his government and the focus, he hoped, of the days of meetings to come. "First among our national goals, the prerequisite to all others, economic, social, or cultural, is national unity. This does not mean and cannot mean uniformity. It does mean Canadian identity, with the symbols and even more the spirit and pride to foster such identity." Calling for careful adaptation of the Canadian constitution in order to meet the need of a new and different day, Pearson went on to attempt to rally the premiers to the task in the name of God and country. "Gathered here in Confederation Chamber on this the first day of September 1964," he continued, "let us vow to do our part in lifting our country beyond the jeopardy of forces or factions which would divide it ... let us ask God's help and His blessing in our task. In this spirit, Canadians will never betray the faith of those we honour today, or the heritage and the hope of those into whose keeping we pass our trust tomorrow."[13]

It was a passionate address, heavily laden with the powerful rhetoric of both religion and nationalism and driven by a desire to remake Canada into a more inclusive, pluralistic nation, better suited to its times. As such, it summarized well what the Centennial Commission would endeavour to do with the coming Centennial year. Two months after the federal-provincial meeting in Charlottetown, Secretary of State Maurice Lamontagne, the public official most responsible for the celebrations, explicitly linked plans for the Centennial year to "the overall plan of the Government to foster unity in this country."[14] *The Centennial Handbook*, published by the commission in 1964, implicitly did the same. Running through that publication was the drive for national unity, which was to be achieved by welcoming as many Canadians as possible into the actual celebrations. In his brief introduction, the chairman of the Centennial Commission, John Fisher, emphasized the opportunity the celebrations gave "to add to the spirit of Canadian unity. If each and every one of us is determined to build a stronger and more harmonious Canada, this could be the most lasting and worthwhile project of the Centennial year."[15] In case the point was missed, the concluding paragraphs of the handbook drove it home again. "The aim of the Centennial year is to strengthen the unity of Canada and to build a better Canada," it bluntly stated. The success of the Centennial project, however, depended "almost entirely on getting all Canadians ... enthusiastically involved in the enterprise."[16] In the spring of 1965, Fisher argued that the Centennial year "is our never-to-be-seen-again chance to achieve unity in diversity, to reach a collective faith in the greatness and future of this Canada of ours ... This has been the philosophy underlying centennial preparations from the very beginning."[17] "As a cardinal principle," the minutes of the commission's board of directors read, "the Commission should endeavour to promote ... projects to enhance inter-cultural cooperation and national unity" and "should consciously seek to bring about a high degree of involvement and participation in centennial activities by as many people as possible throughout Canada."[18] While some have argued that a strong focus on citizen participation and federal state intervention in the voluntary sector really came into vogue with only Trudeau's election to the post of prime minister in 1968,[19] the story of the Centennial celebrations suggests a slightly different interpretation. Though the commission quite logically took upon itself the planning of major events of national scope, it very self-consciously emphasized its role as a catalyst to spark Canadians to plan their own celebrations and to build national unity themselves.[20]

Alongside the rhetoric of national unity through citizen participation and a renewed sense of national identity were words that directly connected the nation with the divine. The two had blended easily, for example, in the prayer read by Fisher, in the final verse of the Centennial Hymn, and in Pearson's address before the Centennial flame burst into light. That kind of public religiosity surrounded many of the other key events of the Centennial year too. When the Centennial train was sent on its way from Ottawa on New Year's Day, 1967, Madame Vanier, in the absence of the ailing governor general, Georges Vanier, presided over a short ceremony that was heavily religious in its symbolism. After singing "God Save the Queen" and the Centennial Hymn, the crowd gathered on the snowy platform heard the prayers of Reverend E.S. Reed, the Anglican bishop of Ottawa, and the Most Reverend René Audet, the Roman Catholic Auxiliary Bishop of Ottawa.[21] When the voyageur canoe pageant was launched, clergy were there to give their blessing.[22] At the inauguration of countless other Centennial projects throughout the country, clergymen did the same.[23] Religion was also a primary element in 1 July celebrations across the country, just as it was in the prayer service on Parliament Hill.[24] In case Canadians still missed the point, the Centennial Commission also published full-page advertisements in several of the country's major church periodicals. The ads were dominated by the familiar words of Psalm 72: "The psalmist wrote, 'In his days shall the righteous flourish; and abundance of peace so long as the moon endureth. He shall have dominion also from sea to sea, and from the river to the ends of the earth'… and so we should give thanks." In smaller text, it went on, "Over the years, hundreds of thousands of people have come to Canada for the precious freedom to worship as they wish. Because of this, Centennial should have a special spiritual significance for Canadians. In 1967, we must not forget to thank God for our country's long history of religious freedom."[25] When it came to celebrating one hundred years of "nationhood" and looking another one hundred years into the future, Canadians were asked to look to their God.

It was the Canadian Interfaith Conference (CIC) that best revealed the importance of public religion to the celebrations, as well as the Centennial's

part in building a more participatory, inclusive, pluralistic, and united
Canada. Begun in July of 1965 at the invitation of the Centennial Commission, by 1967 the CIC consisted of a membership of no less than thirty-
three Canadian religious groups.[26] Its purpose was to encourage those
faith groups to get involved in the Centennial celebrations, to add to
those celebrations a religious element desired by Centennial planners,
and to do so cooperatively, demonstrating harmony and unity in the
Centennial year.

   To achieve all this, the faith groups sent representatives to two conferences, one in 1965 and one in 1966, where delegates worked together
to come up with suitable plans for their cooperative involvement in the
Centennial year. Between and after those conferences, an executive,
board of governors, and secretariat worked on their behalf to translate
those plans into workable programs. Lavy Becker, the chairman of the
CIC, Eveline Gilstorf, the executive director, and several part-time sec-
retaries worked under considerable pressure to manage an institution
of unprecedented religious breadth.

   Trained as a rabbi and social worker, Becker had entered the family
business, Rubinstein Brothers, while at the same time serving a reconstructionist Jewish synagogue in Montreal that he had helped establish in 1960. A dynamic man of generous spirit, he would later receive
the Bronfman medal, Canadian Jewry's highest honour.[27] Gilstorf, an
energetic and capable administrator and communicator, came to the
CIC from the Canadian Centenary Council, a voluntary national organization that had done much in the early 1960s to encourage planning
for celebrations. A representative of the Centenary Council directly
involved in the early days of the CIC and appointed to its first board,
then to its executive, Gilstorf took over as executive director when
that position became available in January of 1966.[28] As chair, Becker
led the CIC, and represented it publicly. Behind the lines, Gilstorf handled virtually everything else.

   That entailed keeping in touch with the various faith groups involved and with the individuals heading up specific project plans on
their behalf. It also increasingly involved responding to requests from
the Centennial Commission, the Department of External Affairs, and
other government bodies for advice on religious matters and for help
in planning religious events in Canada and overseas. In the spring of
1966 Gilstorf travelled from Vancouver to Nova Scotia, organizing
meetings with local and provincial religious representatives to encourage the formation of Interfaith Committees at local and provincial levels. In April of that year, a second conference was held to
review and approve the work that the secretariat had done on the
various projects decided upon by the member faiths. Correspondence

flowed into the CIC as the Centennial commission advanced to it all inquiries involving religion, as word of the CIC's projects filtered out to interested Canadians, and as various government bodies continued to use the CIC as a central agency, or coordinating office, for religious involvement in the Centennial. In the end, through the coordinating efforts of Becker and Gilstorf, representatives of faiths varying from Pentecostal to Roman Catholic to Buddhist together planned such country-wide Centennial projects as interfaith library shelves, interfaith worship services, community demonstrations, and open houses. The CIC was also responsible for the Centennial prayer, which John Fisher read at the flame-lighting ceremony, the Centennial anthem and hymn (sung at the flame-lighting ceremony, the send-off for the Confederation Train, and the July 1 prayer service), a religious declaration (printed in full in the *Globe and Mail* on 17 December 1966), and a bilingual anthology of prayer. Pamphlets and copies of all of those projects were mailed to over nineteen thousand ministers of every known organized religion in Canada in January 1967. Those projects were intended to inspire Canadians from across the country to visit one another's churches, to learn about their different religious traditions, to organize interfaith, community-wide religious services, and to march in their streets – all to celebrate the Centennial in a spirit of unity and thankfulness to God.[29]

Dedicated to instilling a religious presence in the Centennial celebrations and closely linked to the federal government through the Centennial Commission, the CIC demonstrated that even in the tumultuous 1960s, religion continued to play an important role in national public life. The Interfaith Conference continued to embody familiar sensitivities in church-state relations and also took on a familiar mediating structure. At the same time, however, it left historic patterns of dominant forms of public religion in Canada far behind and graphically illustrated the impact of the Pearson government's reconstruction of Canada on the way religion would be welcomed into national public life.

Religious identities, the CIC boldly declared, remained a significant part of dominant understandings of Canada in the 1960s, a point well illustrated by the very close interest and involvement of government officials in the organization. The CIC, in fact, owed much of its very conception to Centennial Commission personnel. It was Robbins Elliot, director of the commission's Planning Branch, who in October 1964 first introduced the possibility of incorporating churches into planning for the centennial.[30] After seeking the advice of a panel of three clergymen on how to approach the issue, commission personnel invited Canadian faith groups (and not just churches) to a conference in July 1965, in order to "arouse interest and enthusiasm amongst Church groups relative to centennial celebrations," as well as to encourage religious organizations to exchange Centennial information, plan some interfaith projects, and establish a continuing committee and secretariat.[31] When the conference took place, all costs were completely underwritten by the commission, and John Fisher, chairman of the commission, gave the opening address. After the conference, commission personnel and office space were dedicated to the administrative tasks of the fledgling organization. Government employees prepared agendas for CIC board meetings, corresponded with participating religious groups, and handled all publicity through their own public relations team. When the Steering Committee chose to set up a board of directors and, within that body, an executive for the CIC, it appointed André LeBlanc, director of the Historical Division of the Centennial Commission, to an executive position. Along with Lavy Becker, then a representative of the Canadian Jewish Congress, LeBlanc was given full powers to appoint a further three persons to the executive.[32]

As we will see, as the CIC built up its own administrative capabilities, the influence of the commission in its affairs declined, but less explicit means of state influence and support continued. Throughout the life of the CIC, the organization of Canadian religions relied completely on the public relations department of the Centennial Commission for all its publicity needs. Furthermore, though the original plan of the Centennial Commission was to give just over a total of sixty thousand dollars to the CIC over three years to cover only administrative costs, by the end of the CIC's existence it had been granted a total of close to double that amount to cover all costs of the organization, including all publications, conferences, and promotional materials.[33] The member faiths, it turned out, did not contribute any funds over the entire two and a half years of the CIC's operations. All that the CIC did, it should be emphasized, it did at public expense.

That kind of involvement of the commission in the beginnings of the Canadian Interfaith Conference suggests that the participation of religious groups was indeed important to Centennial planners. The records of the Canadian Interfaith Conference note some reasons why. A closer look at Robbins Elliot's early interest in church Centennial participation in 1964, for example, suggests that involvement of Canada's faith groups meshed with two cardinal principles of the commission: complete coordination of all aspects of centennial planning, both public and private, and the involvement of as many Canadians as possible in the celebrations. Elliot's attention was turned to Canada's faith groups by a number of newspaper articles dealing with church plans for Centennial activities, as well as by "a few isolated inquiries to the Commission" about such matters. Those tips prompted him to try to bring these religious groups under the umbrella of the government body. "Because the Commission should either be cognizant of activities planned for 1967 by large organizations or should be fostering activities where none exist," he wrote, "it is considered that some form of liaison with the churches should be established as soon as possible." Besides, Elliot continued, "it is distinctly to our advantage to endeavour to enlist the support of organizations so well prepared in every way to do a fine effort on any undertaking they can be persuaded to accept."[34] That recommendation was directly in line with the official guidelines of the commission, laid out in 1964, which argued that it should look to "engage the services of organizations or agencies already established in specific fields to ... conduct programs under grant or subsidy, on behalf of the commission."[35] It also prefigured the formal agreement between the commission and the CIC, signed in December 1965, which requested that the CIC "co-ordinate the Inter-Faith Centennial activities of its member organizations" and cooperate with the Centennial Commission and provincial centennial committees to "co-ordinate and implement Inter-Faith Centennial activities" in the National Capital Area and in "the Provincial Capitals and the major population centres across the land."[36] With well-established national denominational bureaucracies able to influence individual congregations in nearly every sizable community in the country, faith groups and churches cooperating together seemed well-positioned to meet this challenge.

The interest of Centennial planners in the involvement of religious groups in the celebrations did not stop there, however. John Fisher's speech to the CIC's first meeting in 1965 made a similar point to Elliot's: "[C]ertainly there is no sounder approach to the 20 millions living in this vast land than through their places of worship," he stated. Unlike Elliot, however, Fisher appealed directly to more than the institutional capacity of the faith groups of Canada; he was also interested in their "spirit." "The enthusiasm you see created in building a new house of worship, paying off a mortgage, building a school or helping the less fortunate is the same excitement that can make centennial year one to be remembered by Canadians forever," Fisher noted to the assembled faith groups. "You can help us make this a grand year and add pride to our national spirit in laying proper emphasis on giving thanks for the many blessings this country of Canada enjoys."[37]

Other spokesmen for the Centennial Commission were more specific. It was not just the apparent ambition and energy of church-goers that drew attention to their institutions. The particularly religious nature of faith groups seemed also to enhance their appeal. They were the institutional representations of Canadian religion, some pointed

out, organizations that, due to their direct concern with the relationship between humanity and divinity, possessed a unique degree of
moral and spiritual authority within the nation. That moral and spiritual authority was coveted by Centennial planners who were working
hard to present the Canadian nation as something worthy of its citizen's loyalty and admiration.

Peter Aykroyd, the Centennial Commission's director of public relations, explicitly recognized this in an address delivered to the CIC in
1966. "This group here today is in a position of influence ... of power
and of responsibility, of a kind not represented by any other centennial group ... and potentially exercisable to a degree not possible by
secular oriented organizations."[38] Other speeches heard by the Canadian Interfaith Conference over its three years of existence also made
a direct connection between the CIC's religious representation and its
power to influence the country. At the 1965 conference, Secretary of
State Maurice Lamontagne spoke – in language that only thinly
veiled his government's concern with the growth of separatism in
Quebec – of the nationalist goals that the federal planners hoped the
CIC would serve. With dramatic rhetoric, Lamontagne expressed the
hope that the religions of Canada would help to "find a new spiritual
plateau ... from which the refining graces of love, tolerance and understanding can permeate our country, purging what is willful, self-
ish and destructive and so re-invigorating our national life that what
remains is selfless, devoted and united."[39] The following day, the
Ottawa Citizen paraphrased Lamontagne's appeal to religious groups
in Canada to provide together "a vast reservoir of goodwill and understanding in Canada's Centennial year to withstand the arid and
desiccating forces which seek to fragment and divide the nation."[40]
Georges Gauthier, associate commissioner and second in command at
the Centennial Commission, spoke at the 1966 conference. He was
even more direct, going so far as to name some of those forces that he
hoped the CIC could help to calm: "1967 is ... the moment when
French and English speaking Canadians arrive at the point in the century when they decide ... to unite their destiny," he argued. The religions of Canada were to play a key role in this decision. "To achieve
political, social and economic union – the kind of union we hoped to
achieve in 1867 – we will need the force of spiritual unity among the
Canadian people."[41] For both Gauthier and Lamontagne, the involvement of the religions of Canada was central to the success of the federal government's quest for national wholeness, stability, and peace.

The involvement of religious organizations was important to the Centennial Commission, then, because they possessed the ability to do what
few other institutions could – to reach out to millions of Canadians and

to inspire them to exercise their faith for the benefit of the nation. Citizen participation was a key goal of the commission, and the faith groups involved in the CIC could help in making the Centennial a truly grass-roots event. Just as importantly, those faith groups could offer a sense of national purpose rooted in a relationship with the divine. They could help raise the country out of its turmoil and instability by placing the nation in the realm of the communal, the sacred, and the incontrovertible. As commission officials and the prime minister himself had demonstrated, that relation between the divine and the nation was important to many in the Centennial year. It expressed something important about love of and commitment to one's country. It seemed to give Canada a depth of meaning that only the language of religiosity and spirituality could address. "Centennial year is, in its totality, a religious observance," a gathering of Centennial Commission and church officials agreed in 1965. "This means that each and every project is, by its nature, religious and, in its spirit, ecumenical."[42]

The CIC, then, demonstrates the strong interest Centennial organizers had in getting the faith groups of Canada involved in planning the celebrations and in getting them to lend to the celebrations the tone that some forms of public religion could so capably provide. More specifically, it demonstrates the willingness of public officials to explicitly draw on religion as a resource in accomplishing nationalist and political goals. Here in 1967 was an attempt to draw on a lowest common religious denominator – one that emphasized such state-friendly ideals as loyalty, love of neighbour, and generosity of spirit – in order to stabilize and legitimize the Canadian nation.

The CIC also demonstrated much more. Just as much as the CIC was shaped by the desire to include public religion in the Centennial celebrations, the actual structure of the CIC reflected the historic fear of what could happen if the involvement of religion in national public life went wrong. The positive qualities of state-friendly public religion – its ability to sacralize and legitimize the nation while uniting the populace in its defense – had long been held in tension in Canada with public religion's negative qualities – the threat of state control over religious organizations or of political instability caused by public expressions of religion hostile to the purposes of the state. The constant fear of such conflict had, as recently as 1955, prompted the premiers of Alberta and Saskatchewan to refuse to allow the CBC to include a religious service in the celebrations of each province's fiftieth anniversary.[43] In the context of Canada's Centennial celebrations, religion made it in, but that tension remained. From its very beginnings the structure of the CIC offered hints that Canadians in the institutions of both church and state were cautious of standing too closely together.

The panel of clergymen to which the Centennial commission turned for advice in 1964 was the first to articulate that caution. Evidently relishing an opportunity for influence in public life, while at the same time cherishing their independence from the state, that panel included in its report the caveats that religious leaders "should decide for themselves" what they would do for the Centennial and argued that the commission "should simply act as a catalyst" to get those leaders thinking.[44] After the first 1965 conference, that note of caution virtually disappeared from the minds of CIC officials, who seemed more than happy to benefit from state largesse. Federal officials, however, kept it alive. In the early days of the CIC, the commission offered to pay for its administrative costs but argued that the faith groups should pay for the religious programs themselves.[45] That was inconsistent with broader patterns of government grants at the time, which offered funding for programs, not operating costs.[46] It was also inconsistent with the Centennial Commission's treatment of other groups. The commission was happy enough, for example, to provide funds to private organizations like the Canadian Conference of Christians and Jews to sponsor youth travel and exchange programs that "would make a positive contribution to the celebration of the Centennial of Confederation."[47] Nor was the CIC asking for an unreasonable sum of money. What it eventually needed to pay for both its administration and its programs was considerably less than what the Commission spent on historical reenactments or on "participation by Indians."[48]

Meanwhile, the commission made it clear that its early involvement in the CIC would last only until the organization got on its own two feet. Already in October of 1964, Robbins Elliot was suggesting that the CIC should have its office space outside of the commission's doors because it should "be independent of the Centennial Commission."[49] Lest any of the members of the executive had begun to consider their close relations with the commission permanent, CIC executive member and Centennial commission officer André LeBlanc served notice in July 1965 that "the Commission foresaw itself gradually withdrawing from the picture, leaving the Inter-faith Conference and its executive on its own, with the commission maintaining a liaison."[50] When the CIC established its own secretariat in December of 1965, the commission ceased to serve as headquarters to the CIC. Finally, André LeBlanc's position on the executive of the CIC, perhaps the most obvious token of the Centennial Commission's involvement, ended in May 1966. LeBlanc resigned, listing "the pressure of work" as his first reason and then explaining that his resignation was necessary because it was "preferable that the Centennial Commission be represented by an observer rather than a member of the board."[51]

Thus, in the CIC the combination of a desire for the benefits of public religion and a wariness of too close relations between church and state institutions channelled religious expression into avenues where it could best serve both church and state institutions. Direct and formal links between the two bodies lessened as the CIC established its own administrative capabilities, and by 1966 it was largely running its own affairs. At the same time, it continued to benefit from close relations with the commission, which continued to pay all its bills and publicize its activities. The CIC received government funds and expertise that allowed it to inject a religious element into the celebrations and to proclaim the value of religion to the nation. Centennial commissioners, on the other hand, ended up with an institution with the expertise to handle the potentially divisive aspect of religion in the Centennial year, without directly involving themselves in the murky area of religious affairs.

The CIC, then, became an institution not unlike the National Religious Advisory Council of the CBC, an organization established in 1938 to mediate between religion and a federal state corporation in an earlier time and place.[52] Like that council, it became an arm's-length body to which the Centennial Commission could defer on religious issues. Though administratively independent, the CIC directed its energies to the fulfillment of the mandate assigned to it by the Centennial Commission. That mandate, not coincidentally, asked the CIC to assist the Centennial Commission and other Centennial planning bodies in the creation of Interfaith activities in the national and provincial capitals and in other major population centres across the country. In those important places, the CIC gave the commission the expertise and networks it required to create celebrations with religious depth and significance and with sensitivity to the diverse faiths of the population.

The commission drew on that expertise freely. The minutes of a board meeting in September of 1966 stated with some exaggeration that "the CIC has mushroomed into one of the most active planning branches of the Centennial Commission," but noted correctly that it had become "an info centre and clearing house for Provincial and National bodies."[53] Eve Gilstorf, executive director of the CIC, recognized the same point. In a summary of the CIC's activities written at the end of the Centennial year, she noted that in "all our efforts, we kept our parent body, the Centennial Commission, constantly informed, for it was our bridge to the government departments concerned."[54] On the other hand, she noted, the CIC had served as "the resource office both for the Centennial Commission and various other government agencies." When in late 1966, for example, the commission was asked for funding by three religious organizations, the Religion-Labour Council of Canada, the Toronto Institute for Pastoral Training, and the National Committee on the Church and Industrial Society, it forwarded those requests to the executive of the CIC for advice.[55] Similarly, the Department of External Affairs looked to the CIC for planning Centennial religious services in consulates and countries overseas. As Gilstorf accurately observed, by 1967 the CIC had become a kind of "coordinating agency, a central office" for guidance in religious matters.[56]

In the CIC, then, religion took public forms that suggested a great deal of continuity with its historic Canadian roots. It was important to public officials, sometimes for purely practical reasons (citizen participation), but often for much more. It helped bring a notion of "spirit" to the nation, and it might potentially have helped to raise the country out of the mire of political and cultural turmoil by connecting it with something sacred. Combined with a desire for a religious element in the celebrations, old concerns about too close relations between religion and the state helped shape the CIC into the familiar role of an arm's-length advisory body. From that position, the CIC could serve the needs of both the religious bodies and the Centennial Commission, without implicating the commission too much in religious affairs and without giving too much control over the churches to state officials.

There, however, the pattern of historical continuity ended abruptly. The CIC was part, after all, of larger celebrations designed to strengthen national unity by encouraging Canadians to replace old exclusive concepts of Canada with a new inclusive and pluralistic one. The Centennial celebrations and the Pearson government indicated that Canada was being restructured so that all Canadians, and not just a privileged few, would feel welcome and comfortable in Canadian public life. That restructuring, the CIC vividly declared, also had very considerable implications for the way religion would be welcome in Canadian public life.

Canadian anthropologist Raymond Breton has argued that in the late 1960s and in the 1970s, the Canadian state reworked its aging symbols, rituals, and values, formerly based on British symbols and ideals, to include those outside the British tradition in Canada.[57] The Bilingualism and Biculturalism Commission, as we have already seen, was one step in that restructuring, the new Canadian flag another. As a result, Breton argues, Canadians who formerly held a privileged place in the symbolic order of Canada were relegated to a position of equality with all others. The restructuring of the ethnic component of Canada's symbolic order necessarily involved the demotion of those who had been overrepresented in that order, to make room for those who had formerly been underrepresented.

The CIC, it can be argued, is an illustration of the demotion of formerly powerful religious groups and the promotion of formerly underrepresented groups in Canada's symbolic order. In this sense, the CIC demonstrates that religion, like ethnicity and language, was also acted upon and influenced by the adaptation of public symbols and rituals by the federal state.[58] At an official, symbolic level, while those of British ancestry slipped in status in Canadian public life in the 1960s and 1970s, they also lost some of their privileged status in dominant forms of Canadian public religion.

Established in the midst of the changes and challenges to the old Christian Canada, examined in the two previous chapters, the CIC, like the Centennial celebrations as a whole, reflected its time. It offers a unique glimpse, therefore, not only of the importance of public religion to the celebrations but also of the way public religion was officially reconfigured in the attempt to unify the country around a new inclusive and pluralistic image of Canada. All Canadians should feel welcome and involved in Canadian public life, the Pearson government and the Centennial Commission had declared. Not surprisingly, then, citizen participation and symbolic inclusiveness, not proportional representation, were key principles behind the CIC's formation. To draw every citizen into the religious celebration of his or her country, the CIC necessarily had to move beyond the historically tight and exclusive relationship between the mainline Christian churches and Canadian public life. Logically, it had to include citizens of as many religious persuasions as existed in the country.

It attempted to do just that. When the Centennial Commission sent out invitations for the first gathering of the Canadian Interfaith Conference, it sent them to far more institutions than the mainline Protestant and Roman Catholic churches. Already at that early date, twenty-four faith groups were welcomed to take part in Centennial plans. By the end of 1967, thirty-three different faith groups participated on what appeared to be an equal basis in the organization. At the two conferences, two delegates from each member faith sat side by side with others to listen to speeches, then broke into smaller groups to discuss specific projects. Beside the Roman Catholics were Buddhists, and beside the Anglicans were Pentecostals. While expressions of state-sponsored public religion earlier in the century had certainly made efforts to include Canadian Jews and some smaller Christian denominations, the CIC was a gathering of religious organizations featuring a breadth of diversity previously unheard of in Canadian public life.

On the surface, the symbolism of the CIC was clear. It testified to the attempt to include as many faith groups as possible in the public life of Canada and signified the demotion of the larger Christian churches from places of privilege, creating instead a tapestry of religious organizations that symbolically redefined Canada not as a Christian nation, but as a country inclusive of many religions.[59]

Viewed historically, the recognition of religious diversity embedded in the very nature of the CIC was an act of creative innovation. The National Religious Advisory Council of the CBC, as we have already noted, had been similar in its arm's-length structure. That council, however, reflected the Christian Canada of its own day, enshrining Canada's largest and most "respectable" churches in places of dominance and public privilege from which they could choose who else to favour.[60] The CIC, on the other hand, used public funds to gather as many of Canada's faith groups as possible into one organization, all for the purpose of strengthening the impact of the Centennial celebrations. There had been no precedent for that great a degree of religious pluralism in state-sponsored expressions of public religion. Instead of choosing to encourage faith groups individually to initiate or continue their Centennial plans, the commission took the bold step of forming the first organization in Canadian history, if not North American history, to include nearly every known organized religion within the nation's borders.

That kind of intermingling of faith groups could have been disastrous, if not impossible, if it had not matched the mood of its times. As the next chapter reveals, Canadian faith groups agreed to participate in the CIC because it seemed to meet their own needs. While their needs differed,[61] all groups were engaged in what Raymond Breton has called "the search for institutional recognition and the competition for status."[62] To the religions of Canada, the CIC offered government recognition in the Centennial year and a chance to proclaim the existence and significance of their specific religious group to the development of Canada and its peoples.

The CIC can be seen as a religious counterpart of the Royal Commission on Bilingualism and Biculturalism and the new Canadian flag, other projects that transformed Canada's public symbols in a more pluralistic direction. That, in fact, seemed to be one of the very important reasons why the Centennial Commission was willing to push for the creation of such a unique and unprecedented interfaith Centennial organization in the first place. Unlike local Christian ministerial associations or even separate denominational organizations, the CIC could serve the commission in two important ways. First, according to a commission advertisement, it could "foster a greater awareness across Canada of [the] common objectives and beliefs" of all Canadians, "whatever [their] place of worship."[63] Reflecting on the work of the Centennial Commission over twenty-five years later, the former public relations director made the same point. The CIC was "subsidized" by his organization, he wrote, because it was "a way of encouraging unity among the country's different faith communities."[64] Working for the Centennial Commission, the CIC was to promote national unity by convincing Canadians, regardless of their particular religious affiliation, that they shared universal ideals and aspirations and a common love of nation.

Second, the CIC could work to make sure that religious elements of the Centennial celebrations were not strictly Christian but represented the faiths of all of the relevant religious groups in Canada. That organization was asked in its formal contract with the commission to "plan and implement a number of Inter-Faith activities on the occasion of the Centennial," not Christian ones.[65] By doing so, it could help to create an inclusive, pluralistic Canada by placing the nation in a universal religious context to which all Canadians could ascribe. As a "tentative agenda" for the 1966 conference stated, the "basic purpose of the Canadian Interfaith Conference is to develop mutual respect and cordiality between the leaders and members of various faith groups and, on the basis of this mutual respect, to encourage a common front for Centennial celebrations."[66] In short, it was to promote the kind of national image and the sense of "unity in diversity" that the Pearson government and the Centennial Commission both desired.

The CIC, then, demonstrated the attempt to symbolically reconstruct Canada on a more inclusive and pluralistic model through state-sponsored forms of public religion. It also demonstrated how complex redefining national identity could be. In the 1960s, I have argued, the shift away from a Christian Canada was in process, but it was still very much in its early stages. Caught in the midst of that change, in fact, official forms of public religion, like the prayer service on Parliament Hill, were riddled with ambiguity. Some elements of the CIC, like the large number of member faiths, pointed to a tolerant, pluralistic Canada. Paradoxically, however, others continued to point to a Christian country.

Although the CIC eventually represented thirty-three different religious faiths on an apparently equal level, the religious representatives on the board of directors consisted of four Roman Catholics, one United Church representative, one Presbyterian, one Anglican, one Baptist, one representative of the Canadian Jewish Congress, one Lutheran, one member of the Ukrainian Greek Orthodox Church, and one Mennonite. Lavy Becker, the Jewish representative, was also the chairman of the board and was therefore on the executive committee. Along with him, the executive consisted of the United Church representative, and two Roman Catholics. While the persons on the board and executive committee changed over the two and a half years of the CIC's existence, the religious representation on the board and executive did not.[67] Non-mainline Christian denominations, let alone Mormons, Baha'is, or Muslims, had at best minority voices in the hierarchy of the organization.

To be fair, their exclusion from inner circles may have been self-imposed or imposed by economic and institutional restraints. Though conservative evangelical Christian groups, for example, were willing to participate as members in the CIC, their distrust of ecumenism may have made them reluctant to become too closely involved in the obviously ecumenically minded organization.[68] For other member faiths, the small size of their groups, their possible lack of central administrations, and their relative lack of financial resources may have rendered the appointment of officials and their travel to board meetings difficult.[69] It is equally likely, however, that the sheer size, wealth, historical dominance, and national significance of the major Christian churches in Canada assured them of a distinctly louder voice than that of their less privileged religious brothers and sisters. While the mainline Christian churches, then, participated as equals on a symbolic level with all Canadian faith groups, practically speaking they maintained their hold on the levers of power in the CIC.

That same paradoxical display of inclusivity and exclusivity was reflected in most of the key religious moments of the Centennial year. Like the prayer service on Parliament Hill, many events were planned with the active help of the CIC. In the prayer service, in particular, the signs and symbols of both a Christian Canada and a more inclusive, pluralistic one were present. The readings and hymns of that service, it may be recalled, were strictly from the Christian tradition, with the prime minister himself reading from the Bible. Six of the eight religious representatives on the dais, too, were Christian. On the other hand, however, a Jewish rabbi and Lavy Becker, chairman of the CIC, also took part. While they, too, read and sang texts and hymns associated with the Christian tradition, those texts were carefully chosen to avoid specific references to Christ and to appeal, instead, to a presumably more interfaith concept of God. At the lighting of the Centennial flame on 31 December 1966, the context had seemed much more clearly interfaith, with John Fisher, representing the Centennial Commission, reading a nonsectarian Centennial prayer prepared by the CIC itself. A day later, however, the Centennial Train was sent on its way with blessings offered by representatives of two of Canada's historic denominations, the Roman Catholic Church and the Anglican Church of Canada.

It might be tempting, in the light of this ambiguity, to rule out the symbolic significance of the thirty-three member faiths of the CIC altogether. Was that organization inclusive at all? That same question has been asked by numerous scholars writing about the Royal Commission on Bilingualism and Biculturalism, the new Canadian Flag, and the move towards a program of multiculturalism – events all closely related in their broadening function to the CIC. Largely limited to the realm of cultural symbolism, those events have all been sharply criticized as half-hearted attempts by the dominant Anglo-Protestant group to accommodate difference in Canadian society without significant political or economic change. "The main objective of the [B&B] commission," one analyst has characteristically stated, "was to reassert the dominance of the two cultures and to justify and legitimize this dominance through appropriate symbols, assumptions and ideas."[70] Multiculturalism, others have argued, had become a "song and dance show," emphasizing cultural particularities without investing substantially in erasing the economic and political barriers to full participation in public life.[71] Himani Bannerji has contended that the shift from an exclusive to an inclusive image of Canada in the 1960s and 1970s has to be placed in the context of a country run largely by an elite of British extraction reluctant to let the reins of power go.[72] "However functional or not," another recent study has concluded, "the evolution from [biculturalism] to [multiculturalism] is in the logic of nation-building by a dominant ethnic group that rests its legitimacy, in part, on its ability to arbitrate the often divergent claims of the less powerful ethnic communities."[73] Others have argued more bluntly that the shift to more inclusive public symbols was no more than an "Anglophone device to minimize the valence of the French minority" or "a tactic of politicians to control the new ethnic and immigrant vote."[74]

Those critiques should make us cautious when analyzing the importance of the CIC. Without doubt, the impact of the CIC and the Centennial was largely symbolic in its attempt to build national unity by making all Canadians welcome in public life. Without doubt, too, the CIC reveals the ambiguity of those dominant groups who were willing to give greater recognition to diversity, as long as it did not substantially weaken their grip on the levers of political and cultural power. Difference was welcome, some have convincingly argued, as a way of pacifying dissatisfied minorities in a manner that would preserve as much as possible of the former status quo.[75] The difference between symbolic religious pluralism and the Canadian religious reality was graphically displayed, for example, when External Affairs rejected a suggestion of the CIC in 1967. Asked to recommend religious representatives of Canada for the Centennial celebrations in Westminster Abbey, the executive of the CIC suggested, among others, a Buddhist, but were surprised to learn that he had been quietly replaced at the event by a representative of the Christian faith.[76]

The tension between Christian dominance and religious inclusivity in the Centennial celebrations further revealed the apparently contradictory positions and approaches of the historically dominant churches to the changes at hand. In the CIC, they quietly welcomed members of other smaller and historically marginalized religious denominations and faith groups to join them on the public stage. Behind the scenes, however, they continued to seek the kind of influence to which they were accustomed.[77]

Those criticisms are justified, but they need not lead to the dismissal of the CIC's inclusive symbolism altogether. Instead, the obvious disjunction between the outward symbolism of the CIC and its inward power structures should point to the complexity of the way in which expressions of religion in Canada's dominant culture *were* changing in Canada in the 1960s. The ambiguity of the Canadian Interfaith Conference should underline the fact that the portrayal of an inclusive and tolerant pluralistic Canada, though based on key trends of the postwar period and of the 1960s, was still *prescriptive* as much as it was *descriptive*. Canadian society was becoming increasingly diverse, to be sure, but with over 80 percent of Canadians still affiliating themselves with either the United, Anglican, Presbyterian, Baptist, or Roman Catholic Churches in the 1960s, Christianity remained by far the religion of the majority in the country.[78] For many, therefore, it remained the appropriate religion of the country itself. The ambiguity and paradox of state-sponsored forms of public religion in the Centennial year qualifies the significance of the CIC's outward inclusivity and plurality, but it should also indicate the clear innovation involved in building a religiously plural Canada and the complexity of changing deeply embedded national characteristics.

The complex and even confusing nature of state-sponsored public religion in the Centennial and the CIC tells us that the decline of a Christian Canada did not begin or end in the 1960s. What the CIC captured was not a completely religiously plural Canada but a Christian Canada in the midst of change. Though legally enshrined church establishments had been dissolved by the mid-nineteenth century in much of Canada, historian John Webster Grant has astutely argued that the 1960s saw a more complete "second disestablishment" of religion in the country. By the end of that "decade of ferment" he contends, the mainline church "was no longer the keeper of the nation's conscience, and few Canadians seemed to regret its dethronement."[79]

Members of the larger Christian churches in Canada must have noted their very visible dethronement in the two conferences of the CIC as they sat beside representatives of the Buddhist churches of Canada, the Byelorussian Authocephalic Orthodox Church, the Canadian Jewish Congress, the Canadian Unitarian Council, the Canadian Yearly Meeting of the Religious Society of Friends, the Christian and Missionary Alliance in Canada, Christian Science, the Churches of Christ (Disciples), the Church of Jesus Christ of Latter-Day Saints, the Church of the Nazarene, the Islamic Community, and the National Spiritual Assembly of the Baha'is of Canada, to name only a few.

Since the Centennial Commission was the sole provider of the CIC funding, it held the fate of that organization completely within its hands. As the year 1967 was drawing to a close and the work for the Centennial neared completion, it became ever more apparent to the board of directors of the CIC that government funding would be removed and its existence ended. That was an eventuality against which, not surprisingly, it fought. Already in the spring of 1966, voices from within the CIC had suggested the possibility of its continued existence beyond the Centennial year. Speaking of the value of the interfaith dialogue that had been facilitated by the CIC at its second major gathering, an After Conference Planning Committee recommended that "continuing such dialogue beyond the centennial year 1967 should be given considerable study."[80] Though national unity was a clear concern of the CIC, the ecumenical movement was for many of its participants an equally important motivating factor in their involvement that led them to look beyond the Centennial year. Towards the end of 1966, the CIC was also beginning to find opportunities for involvement in other events distinctly unrelated to the Centennial. Gilstorf and others thought that the CIC could play a major role in planning for the Year of Human Rights in Canada (1968), and an organization responsible for planning that year, the National Consultation for International Year on Human Rights, agreed. "The Canadian Interfaith Conference has proven to be an effective vehicle in furthering human rights in the religious field and should be extended beyond 1967," that body proclaimed.[81] Gilstorf also argued that the CIC should continue as "a clearing house and info centre in convening conferences in the religious field and in co-ordinating religious programs whenever necessary."[82] Not surprisingly, Lavy Becker stated in February of 1967 that "there is definitely a need for the existence of the Conference beyond centennial year, judging from various requests from different Ministries, especially the Secretary of State and External Affairs, who have used our address for guidance."[83]

If the CIC was enthusiastic about the continuing role it could play in the religious and public life of Canada, the Centennial Commission was considerably less interested. Hence, when the CIC requested continued financial support beyond the Centennial year, it was bluntly turned down. At its 13 March 1967 meeting, the executive committee of the Centennial Commission had instructed the CIC to terminate its existence by 1 December 1967. A push by the CIC for its continued survival resulted in a reappraisal of the issue in August, but the outcome did not change. The minutes of an executive committee meeting recorded its decision: "It is suggested that while it was justifiable for the government on the occasion of the Centennial of Confederation to be directly involved in Church Activities, no such justification will exist after 1967 ... It is recommended that no action be taken to perpetuate the Canadian Interfaith Conference."[84] The executive of the CIC took the final news quietly, but its members were deeply disappointed that an institution in which they had seen so much potential would not continue.

The commission, of course, had created the CIC with clear goals in mind. It was to be an arm's-length Centennial planning body responsible for adding a religious element to and involving religious communities in the celebrations. Citizen participation was an important goal of the commission, a goal that it hoped the CIC would help it to reach. Ultimately, however, the Centennial was about building national unity. Citizen participation was a means towards that end, and so was the CIC, which, it was hoped, would build unity between Canada's various faith groups and which would strengthen Canada by raising the nation above the realm of human-self interest and placing it in the realm of things most worthy of devotion, sacrifice, and praise.

Despite the ambiguities and differing agendas analyzed in the preceding pages, the CIC is a testimony to the importance of religion to understandings of Canada in the 1960s. It also illustrates how the nature of state-sponsored forms of public religion in those understandings was changing. On the surface, that change looked drastic. Created in the context of a Liberal government focused on building Canadian unity around a new inclusive and pluralistic image of Canada, the CIC bore the emphasis and intent of key Liberal innovations, including the B&B commission and the new Canadian flag. Symbolically, it included all Canadians. Underneath the surface, however, it revealed an inconsistent mix of old and new: the old signs of Christian dominance and a new religious pluralism.

In 1967, that made sense. The image of an inclusive, pluralistic Canada, after all, was imposed by planners on Canadian society, as much as it reflected trends in its development. Older understandings of a Christian Canada sometimes showed through the pluralistic set of symbols pasted on top of them. In fact, as we will see in the following chapter, the success or failure of the CIC depended heavily on what faith groups and local communities across the country thought of its reconstruction of Canada, religion and all.

5

"The National Interfaith Conference Has Been Lost Sight of in This Area":

Public Religion as Contested Ground in the 1967 Centennial Celebrations

In 1967 even the energetic and optimistic directors of the Canadian Interfaith Conference had to admit that promoting an inclusive, pluralistic interfaith Canada was no easy task. According to their parent body, the Centennial Commission, religion in the Centennial was to serve the purpose of building national unity by encouraging Canadians to celebrate their Canada together, regardless of their faith differences. The wishes of the commission, however, were only one side of the CIC coin. On the other were the sometimes very different plans and purposes of religious groups and individual Canadians whom the CIC hoped to reach. In the centennial celebrations, the CIC presented one version of a religious Canada. Other institutions and individuals sometimes cooperated with that vision and sometimes challenged it with their own. The Centennial Celebrations became contested ground where official and unofficial religious understandings of Canada competed for public expression.

That point was made clear to Eve Gilstorf, the CIC's executive director, in several episodes over the life of her organization. Throughout 1967, she had been doing her best to keep clergymen and religious leaders in Canada up to date on the CIC's program proposals and activities. Much to Gilstorf's frustration, however, the Reverend Lloyd Leadbeater, a Convention Baptist, kept returning the CIC's mail unopened. Finally, in October 1967 a puzzled Gilstorf decided to get to the bottom of the issue. In an attempt to pin down the problem, she sent a letter to the national organization of which Leadbeater was a part, the Baptist Federation of Canada. The general secretary of the denomination, the Reverend Fred Bullen, carefully explained in his reply that "we have a native reluctance for involvement in anything which savors of a state church or movement towards structural unity."[1] Although his denomination continued to participate in the CIC, Reverend Leadbeater refused to do so, evidently feeling that such involvement would compromise his firm belief in the need for the separation of the churches and the state and his disagreement with the ecumenical movement.

At least Leadbeater's denomination stayed in. Another Baptist denomination, the Fellowship of Evangelical Baptist Churches of Canada, was involved in the CIC in its early days but did a rapid about-face in December 1966. It was a move that blind-sided Gilstorf and Becker, all the more because they were accused of causing it. In a letter to Gilstorf, the Reverend C.A. Tipps, the general secretary of the fellowship, pointed out that in a recent Centennial Commission press release the CIC was said to represent a "coming together" of the different faiths involved. According to Tipps, that was "not only misleading but untrue to the facts."[2] Upset by the insinuation of movement towards unity amongst the member faiths of the CIC, the fellowship asked to be removed from the list of participating religions and denominations.

Fortunately, the Fellowship Baptists were not large in number. Unfortunately, the population of Quebec was. Gilstorf's frustration with Leadbeater and disappointment with the Fellowship Baptists was nothing compared to the bitterness with which she referred to the CIC's problems in that province. While attempting to inspire provincial interfaith committees throughout the country in 1966, the CIC had had no success in Quebec. An exploratory meeting in Montreal in June 1966 suggested that a series of small conferences held throughout Quebec might be a good alternative to the provincial committee, so the CIC set itself to organizing them.[3] The first was to be in Montreal on October 3. Given the tense English-French relations in Quebec at the time, the CIC was advised to put great effort into making the conference thoroughly and convincingly bilingual.[4] That warning was heard, over six hundred names were gathered, and the invitations were sent. As a later report of the meeting noted, however, "it was obvious at the secretariat that it would not be well attended, and impossible to obtain the co-operation of the French speaking religious leaders in Quebec, for whatever reason."[5] On 3 October, just over one hundred Quebeckers turned out. The program went as planned, with the CIC taking the morning to present its plans and projects and with the afternoon committed to getting feedback, but the response was disheartening, to say the least.[6] Press coverage was pitiful, with only one article, and that unfavourable, appearing in the French-language press.[7] The gathering "was doomed from the start," an angry Eve Gil-storf reported. "The whole conference down there reeked of separat-ism, and there is no other way of saying it."[8]

Convincing faith groups and individual Canadians to sign on to the state project of the Centennial was sometimes impossible, as the response of the Fellowship Baptists made clear. Straight-out rejec-tions of the CIC, however, were rare. Instead, the norm for religious groups was to join the organization, but to do so with particular goals and hopes in mind. The Canadian faith groups involved in the CIC were not simply coopted by the Centennial Commission to help shape the nation. They freely joined or rejected that organization in response to their own needs and dreams, sometimes for reasons that seemed to have little to do at all with the celebration of a pluralistic Canada. The Centennial Commission hoped for public expressions of religion that would be dedicated primarily to the stabilization and le-gitimation of society and the state. Canadians from a wide variety of faith groups sometimes agreed. Sometimes they chose instead to use the Centennial as a platform to express their own particular religious concerns, which, at bottom, had no real connection to the celebration of Canada at all.

Involving faith groups in the CIC was only the first stage of the or-ganization's task. The second was to convince individual Canadians in local communities across the country to pick up the idea of an in-terfaith Canada and to celebrate the country through it. As the cases of the Reverend Leadbeater and the province of Quebec aptly sug-gest, here, too, the goal of building Canadian unity around a new, in-clusive image of Canada sometimes ran into trouble. The rejection of the CIC by Leadbeater and many Quebeckers signalled that not all agreed with the picture of an inclusive, tolerant, and united Canada it presented. Local responses to the work of the CIC revealed that other ways of understanding Canada remained more convincing for many Canadians in their country's Centennial year.

The Canadian Interfaith Conference, like the Centennial celebrations as a whole, was fundamentally based on negotiation, compromise, and cooperation. The CIC and the Centennial Commission were involved in what was essentially a public relations program – a state effort in the midst of turbulent times to convince Canadians to love and celebrate a Canada united in its diversity. The success of that program, as CIC and commission officials had long made clear, depended on voluntary citi-zen participation. That was nowhere more clear than in the CIC itself, a voluntary organization that relied completely on the interest and good-will of faith groups who made up its membership.

The need to persuade and convince Canadians to participate in the Centennial celebrations in general and in the CIC in particular made both entities much more fluid and flexible than their clear mandates implied. The Centennial Commission's goals of citizen participation, national unity, and interfaith cooperation were clearly articulated in the early days of the CIC. It was also apparent, however, that the religious organizations of Canada had their own reasons for joining the organization and were shaping their own involvement in the CIC to meet their own needs as much as those of the Centennial Commission. How religious organizations wished to publicly celebrate the Centennial was closely linked to what was happening within those religious organizations themselves.

That point was exemplified well in the development of Centennial projects within the Anglican Church of Canada. Already in 1961, four years before the CIC was formed and in the year that the Centennial Commission was established, the denomination had appointed the Proposals Committee on the Church's Observance of Canada's Centennial and had carefully chosen a number of influential churchmen and churchwomen to fill its seats.[9] Significantly, the idea for that committee had come out of an assessment of the needs of the church and a recommendation that a Missionary Advance Crusade be launched in 1962, to culminate five years later in the Centennial year. The crusade, it had been proposed, was not to be about fundraising. Instead, it would be about "education, stimulation and cultivation focusing the attention of Anglicans on the past, present and future contribution of the Anglican Church of Canada in the development of the Canadian nation and in pointing up the urgent need of greater Canadian Anglican participation in the work of the world-wide Anglican Communion."[10]

Those goals were clearly shaped by the particularities of the denomination. The committee's early suggestions for Anglican observances of the Centennial were too. Proud of its past significance to the country, the church had placed the Centennial in the context of a "crusade" to further its public influence in the present and future. The committee emphasized the themes of thanksgiving and reaffirmation as it urged Anglicans to "witness to their contribution to Canada's Christian life."[11] Celebrating Canada publicly and religiously, for the Anglicans, could serve to strengthen both the church and the nation.

In 1961, plans for the upcoming Anglican World Congress were also shaping the Centennial committee. To be held in Toronto in 1963, that congress had already awakened the church to the themes of the "worldwide Anglican Communion" and service to the underprivileged.[12] To that end, the committee recommended an 8:00 A.M. communion service in every parish on 1 July 1967. Collection money from the service, it suggested, could go towards the Centennial Fund, which would be used to build community halls for native communities, to provide travel money for Canadians to go abroad and for others to come here, to provide scholarships to cultivate leadership in developing countries in Africa and Asia, and to build a school or hospital in a "new dominion." Reflecting the importance of the ecumenical movement, the committee also pushed for cooperation with other churches and with the Canadian Council of Churches in celebrating the Centennial.[13]

By 1965, times had changed for the Anglican Church, and so had its plans for the Centennial. The Proposals Committee had been replaced by the Committee on the Observance of Canada's Centennial.[14] More importantly, a significant decline in patterns of financial giving since 1961 had the church pinching pennies and dipping into its accumulated reserves to fund its regular programs adequately in 1965.[15] Most of those programs, including the World Mission Fund, were deemed more important than the proposed Centennial Fund and the service projects and youth travel it was to finance. As a result, that fund and those projects were dropped.[16]

Reflecting the larger trends of the 1960s, what had remained and grown in significance since 1961 was an ecumenical spirit. In 1965 the committee recommended that the Anglican Church use a Centennial order of service created by the Canadian Council of Churches. It also advised that the two primary Centennial activities of the church be support for a Christian Pavilion at Expo 67 and a summer of service and Christian Youth Assembly in 1967,[17] both projects of an ecumenical nature.[18] The committee also continued to highlight its close association with the welfare of the nation, producing a 1967 edition of the *Prayer Book* (with a Centennial symbol on its cover), and recommending that metropolitans of provinces use the Centennial to call all Christian people "to explore national issues during the year 1967."[19] Recommendations to mark and preserve the oldest church building in each diocese and to launch a general campaign of beautification for all church premises demonstrated that the Centennial also brought with it a chance to celebrate the history of the church and to serve its own aesthetic and structural needs. In its religious celebrations of the nation in 1967, the Anglican Church of Canada would blend particular denominational interests with concerns for the wider national community of Canada. Such things as Centennial symbols on prayer books served to legitimize the Centennial celebrations and their goals, while at the same time they reinforced the national importance of the church. Even such particular projects as planned efforts to beautify church properties had the effect of beautifying the communities of which they were a part.

The Anglican Church's Centennial plans demonstrate the importance of the particular situations and perspectives of Canada's faith groups in shaping their approaches to the Centennial. By comparison, the Centennial goals of the Pentecostal Assemblies of Canada (PAOC) reflect how different those approaches could be. A much smaller Christian denomination with a much less prominent history in Canada, the Pentecostal Assemblies of Canada first struck a Centennial committee in 1964.[20] Perhaps reflecting its humbler sense of connection to the country and its more modest interest in public affairs, that denomination did not begin planning in earnest until June 1966. At that point, with six months to go before the Centennial year, it took only several meetings to come up with three major Pentecostal Centennial projects, each of which reflected the denomination's ethos: a week of prayer, an effort to bring an evangelistic Canada for Christ crusade team into every church district with the hope of starting a new church in each, and the production of Christian programs for radio and television.[21]

The driving force behind Pentecostal involvement in the Centennial was the driving force behind the denomination itself: evangelistic outreach. All Centennial projects in one way or form contributed to that end. A meeting in July 1966 agreed that the major goal for the Centennial year would be the opening of one hundred new churches in 1967, in overseas missions and in Canada.[22] The Centennial radio and television productions were designed to promote the "history of our movement and the important place, both present and future, of our Pentecostal message in the light of world events and Biblical prophecy."[23] In August 1966 a booklet on the "place of the evangelical message in the growth and development of Canada" was placed on the Pentecostal Centennial list,[24] but significant revisions in late 1966, made on behalf of the General Conference of the Church, changed that booklet into pamphlets on "our position as to the Holy Scriptures and evangelism."[25] Calling the pamphlet a "Home Missions Centennial Project," the conference passed a resolution arguing that since the mainline Christian denominations were responding to the changes of the 1960s by abandoning the historic Christian faith now was the time to reach out to Canadians in those churches to beckon them to become Pentecostals.[26] Set against the Anglican Church's emphasis on cooperation with other denominations in the Centennial year, the PAOC viewed the Centennial as an opportunity to draw more Canadians into the Christian faith and – specifically – into its own fold. Furthermore, the PAOC's planned religious celebrations of the Centennial were only loosely connected to the Centennial, the nation, or the state. They had far more to do with its own particular preoccupation with individual conversion and church expansion.

With that kind of denominational particularity and variation in approaches to religious celebrations of the Centennial, the CIC had its work cut out for it. Neither in the plans of the Anglican Church of Canada nor in the plans of the PAOC, after all, was there any discussion of interfaith activities. The Anglican Church's emphasis on cooperation with other Christian denominations was close, to be sure. The PAOC's emphasis on evangelistic outreach, however, represented an approach to public religion that seemed to fly in the face of that of the CIC. The latter's plea for religious tolerance and inclusivity was to lend support to national unity and the stability of the federal state. The Pentecostal approach had the potential to divide Canadians into particular and exclusive religious groups, each seeking its own growth. If the CIC was to fulfill its mandate, however – if it was to add an interfaith religious component to the celebrations and if it was to forward national unity by publicly symbolizing the common bonds of all Canadians, no matter their religious background – it needed somehow to bring both those organizations, along with many others far more diverse in religious belief and perspective, together in the same organization.

It managed to do so for a number of reasons, not the least of which was its appeal to a shared sense of Canadian identity. A genuine love and commitment to the nation wove its way through the CIC from beginning to end and no doubt helped to pull the various faith groups together in their common quest to celebrate Canada's hundredth anniversary. Most faith groups in the CIC were there out of a sense of attachment to the country they had come to celebrate. That, the rhetoric of the CIC made clear, was what would allow them to work together. "Our religious pluralism will place boundaries," Father John Keating, a priest at the Catholic Information Centre in Toronto, said to the assembled religious delegates at the first gathering of the CIC, "but a common desire to manifest national solidarity will find a way within any limitations. Without compromise, without loss of integrity, without uneasiness in conscience, we can show forth the unity we possess as those who dwell in one country."[27] A genuine nationalism, Keating suggested, was the tie that could bind together the diverse interests embodied in the CIC.

The fact that many of the member faiths cherished their Canadian identity was exemplified by the projects they supported. When faith groups like the Anglicans or Lutherans chose to celebrate their history in 1967, they did so as explicitly Canadian institutions and testified to the importance of that aspect of their identities. Their history was significant, they claimed, because it was intimately wrapped up with the history of their country. Even evangelistic campaigns, when placed in the context of the Centennial, could point to the importance of national identities and serve nationalist ends. The term "crusade," which was used by the Anglican Church, carried the historic weight of political, national, and religious allegiances. When the PAOC called their evangelistic campaign in 1967 Canada for Christ, they also explicitly linked the desire to save souls with the desire to save their country. Not only would individuals be brought to Christ, but the nation itself would declare itself Christian. As much as those crusades oriented their adherents to religious concerns, they also drew them into a concern for the nation.

Keating's "desire to manifest national solidarity," of course, was not necessarily the simple unifying principle that he suggested it to be. His appeal to nationalist sentiments fell short on two counts. First, underlying the assumption that a common citizenship and a common love of country could unite all Canadians was the deeper assumption that loyalty to nation could somehow transcend loyalty to religious particularity. In the minds of some mainstream churchmen heavily influenced by the ecumenical movement, that assumption evidently made sense. In the minds of others, like the Reverend Leadbeater and the Fellowship Baptists, nationalism did not always overcome religious conviction. Just as importantly, an appeal for national solidarity could be deeply problematic for some. As the indifference to the Centennial and the CIC in Quebec demonstrated, there was in fact more than one meaning to the term "nation" in the country.[28]

Nonetheless, if nationalism was not always the strong uniting force Keating thought it to be, it still served the CIC for the better. Religious and national concerns, the CIC ably demonstrated, were not necessarily discrete categories. That point was made obvious in the way concerns for national unity and religious unity blurred together in the CIC. Faith groups lured to the organization through the ecumenical movement or interfaith dialogue, in particular, shared with Centennial Commission planners a mutual desire for better understanding and unity. That was an important point of agreement, and one on which faith groups and the Centennial Commission could work together to forward both the faith groups' desire for better relations among themselves and the federal government's desire for national wholeness.

The link between religious and national unity was explicitly noted and celebrated across institutional lines. "Never, perhaps, have so many diverse religious beliefs come together to plan joint worship," suggested John Fisher. "It augurs well for our centennial celebrations."[29] Claude Ryan, a Roman Catholic, editor of Le Devoir, and keynote speaker at the first gathering of the CIC, asked the member faiths to take the opportunity provided by the Centennial to bring religion once again to a society so desperately in need of its unifying touch.[30] A Canada that prayed together would stay together, Lavy Becker argued in the foreword to the CIC's *Anthology of Prayer*.[31] "The more we know and respect each other's traditions and beliefs," Father Keating noted, "the more effectively religion can play its part to weld Canada into ever greater unity."[32] The link between national and religious unity was one that could inspire public expressions of religion that served the purposes of both the faith groups and the Centennial Commission very well.

A closer look at the CIC suggests, however, that its success was due to more than a genuine sense of loyalty and commitment to Canada. The championing of national solidarity in the CIC implied that faith groups would check their differences at the door for the sake of the nation. In reality, they brought their differences with them. The success of the CIC, in fact, was partially due to its ability to accommodate difference, and not simply to overcome it.

The reasons for faith group involvement, offered by the faith groups themselves, help prove the point. Ecumenism, many argued, was a primary motivator for their participation in the CIC, which was conceived as an idea and as an institution in 1964 and 1965, years that coincided with the height of union talks between the Anglican and United Churches, as well as with the Second Vatican Council in the Roman Catholic Church. It was predictable, then, that in his keynote address to the first gathering of the CIC in the summer of 1965, Father Keating recognized the role of the Protestant ecumenical movement and the opening of the Roman Catholic Church through Vatican II as essential factors in the success of the CIC. In the opinion of those involved in the ecumenical movement, in fact, the CIC was more than just a result of better interchurch relations. Keating and others were interested in the CIC because it seemed to offer another avenue to forward that movement. In his words, the CIC presented the assembled faith groups "with an opportunity for intensifying our contacts and for translating our growing goodwill into action more quickly than the ordinary process of dialogue might present."[33] Others agreed. "Ecumenical and centennial [sic] comes at a providential time when the ecumenical spirit is beginning to be felt in the community," one participant in the first gathering of the CIC said, "and we are blessed indeed when the Canadian Government is assisting our efforts."[34] In words that were considered the best summation of the feeling of the CIC's first gathering, Bernard Daly, also a Roman Catholic, suggested that, "Important as all our centennial projects are, perhaps the most important thing to emerge will be the spirit of openness to each other in our various religious persuasions, a spirit learned from our unprecedented working together."[35]

According to historian John Webster Grant, the desire for dialogue fostered by the ecumenical movement not only "affected all [Christian] cooperative ventures and union negotiations of the 1960's. It could also be applied more broadly to conversations between Christians and Jews ... [and] members of other religious communities."[36] Such was the case in the CIC. The goal of dialogue and discussions among Christians sometimes seemed to slip easily into the goal of wider dialogue towards better understanding among those of all religions. Strictly speaking, the former was referred to as the ecumenical movement, the latter, interfaith dialogue. Throughout the life of the conference, however, the terms "ecumenical" and "interfaith" were used loosely, sometimes meaning the same thing.

The blending of ecumenical into interfaith interests, in fact, seemed to be what was most important to some groups about the CIC. In its report to the CIC at the end of 1967, the Reformed Episcopal Church detailed the hosting of weekly discussions entitled One God and Father of All, interfaith services and a televised panel discussion on the topic of interfaith and peace.[37] In a letter to the CIC dated 1 November 1967, the bishop primus of that denomination wrote with fervour of the hope that "the cooperation and unity of spirit which is now evident among all faiths will continue to grow and expand in the years ahead."[38]

Not surprisingly, that was the wish of members of the Baha'i faith, too. Emphasizing a universalistic approach to world religions, the Baha'i faith encouraged the spirit of cooperation and goodwill that the CIC sought to inspire. For that reason, an article in the June 1966 Canadian Baha'i News noted that the interfaith projects of the CIC "were of special interest to Baha'is, because they are so much in the spirit of Baha'u'llah's injunction to 'consort with men of all religions with joy and fragrance.'"[39] The article went on to praise the work of the CIC, strongly recommending all its proposed programs to the local Baha'i communities across Canada.

A number of other faith communities, on the other hand, demonstrated that cooperation among Christian faiths, and not interfaith cooperation, was their desire. If the language of ecumenism could blur into that of interfaith, it was also apparent that interfaith in the 1960s was sometimes understood to mean cooperation between strictly Christian faiths or denominations. To solve the confusion, the tentative agenda for the 1966 conference took pains to distinguish between the goals of the CIC ("to develop mutual respect and cordiality between the leaders and members of various faith groups and on the basis of this mutual respect, to encourage a common front for centennial celebrations") and those of the ecumenical movement ("a movement among Christian denominations towards a greater understanding of their doctrinal positions and a discovery of their areas of doctrinal agreement").[40] That distinction, however, did not always seem to sink in.

The insistence that the term interfaith did, indeed, mean cooperation between strictly Christian groups was most clearly displayed in disputes across the country between members of the Baha'i faith and local Christian ministerial associations. In a letter to the CIC in May 1967, the National Spiritual Assembly (NSA) of the Baha'i faith in Canada complained that its local members were being shut out of interfaith services and activities across the country.[41] "It would seem that the lovely Canadian spirit projecting from the National Interfaith Conference has been lost sight of in this area,"[42] wrote a member of the Baha'i faith from Saint John. The situation was grave enough to be reported on in *The Canadian Baha'i News* in July of 1967. Quoting from a letter sent to the CIC by the NSA, the article read, "Unhappily, we are continuing to find the doors closing in our faces." The members of the Baha'i faith had found a "general unwillingness on the part of the Christian Clergy, both Protestant and Roman Catholic, to extend the privilege of interfaith membership to Baha'i communities."[43]

For still other groups, ecumenical or interfaith dialogue was less important than using the CIC to infuse an increasingly secular society with practical demonstrations of the continuing importance of religion. This, it may be recalled, seems to have been the case for the Pentecostal Assemblies of Canada, which shared the Fellowship Baptists' distrust of ecumenism and their focus on evangelism but which remained a member of the CIC. That perspective was shared by others from an apparently broad range of religious groups, as well. "[T]he centennial gives us an opportunity to prove to [Canadians] that religion is viable," argued the minutes of an early meeting of faith groups in 1965.[44] In the 1960s, an age of rapid change and cultural and religious turmoil, that goal could be of importance to every religious group, Christian or non-Christian, large or small.

The promise of national and very public recognition was equally alluring. The larger Christian churches, which had traditionally represented religion in Canada's symbolic and public life, had long assumed a sense of historical value to the country and an honoured place in it. Throughout their history, organizations like the United, Anglican, Presbyterian, and Roman Catholic Churches had actively pursued opportunities to serve and shape their society or to declare their importance to its health and welfare. The CIC fit neatly into that pattern, offering those churches such opportunities in the Centennial year and offering recognition of services past. That they were interested in such public recognition was demonstrated by some of the Centennial projects they selected. The Anglicans, for example, placed historical plaques on their churches, claiming the attention, respect, and dignity that long institutional histories could apparently offer.[45] The Canadian Council of Churches, for its part, published a history of the Christian church in Canada (particularly of the mainline churches) as a Centennial project.[46] Appropriately, its dominant theme was the development of a truly Canadian and ecumenical Christian church in Canada.

For those religious groups who had never enjoyed the level of recognition given to the larger Christian churches, the opportunity for public recognition provided by the CIC was particularly alluring and a very welcome change. Symbolically integrating Canadians of all religious persuasions into the public life of the country, the CIC suggested, on the surface at least, that whatever religious creeds or beliefs divided citizens in the 1960s, all were Canadians, and all were equally welcome in Canadian public life. The Zoroastrians, a tiny faith group and the smallest in the CIC, caught the message. In a letter requesting membership in the CIC in September 1966, their representative stated that "the purpose would be mainly to make the Canadian Nation aware of the very existence of a religious group that has survived as a minority for the last 2500 years."[47] Judging from the rush for membership of other faiths on the peripheries of Canadian religion, which increased the CIC's number of participating faiths from twenty-four to thirty-three in little more than a year, few desired to be left out of the national celebration.

Far from being a simple tool of the state, then, the CIC embodied the varying interests of a wide range of faith groups. The real accomplishment of the CIC, however, was to find a place for all those interests inside a negotiated and cooperative whole. In the CIC, faith groups were to find ways of working together towards common goals – goals that intertwined their own interests with the search for national unity in the midst of diversity.

How the diverse faith groups managed to meet both their own needs and those of the CIC itself was best revealed in the programs and events that they planned cooperatively under the latter's auspices. As a coordinating and planning body, the CIC's primary task was to come up with suggestions for interfaith Centennial activities. It then mailed those suggestions, in the form of clearly laid out pamphlets and folders, to local churches or faith groups, hoping they would then translate those ideas into interfaith celebrations in their own communities. Unlike the projects of particular faith groups organized by each group alone, the programs of the CIC were planned communally in the year and a half preceding the Centennial.

Specific CIC projects aimed at different goals. As such, they reflected various kinds of public religion. The Community Demonstrations

Program, for example, clearly reflected the desire of some in the CIC to evangelize the nation, to make, in the closing words of Chairman Lavy Becker at the April conference, "religion viable in the lives of the Canadian people."[48] Through the program, the CIC encouraged local faith groups to plan a parade or public gathering that would explicitly demonstrate the importance of religion to their community. A pamphlet describing the project provided two "guiding questions" behind the demonstrations, each of which focused directly on religion, not on the Centennial or Canadian unity: "How do we bring to remembrance the role of religion in Canadian life to date?" and "How do we alert citizens of all faiths, and of no faiths, to religion's continuing presence and power for good?"[49] Contained within those questions was the desire to testify publicly to the power of religion in the past and the present. Expressions of unity in diversity were only a tangential side effect of bringing faith groups together to make their common point.

Other projects and publications more successfully combined within them the interests of faith groups and the CIC's parent body, the Centennial Commission. Open Houses, in this context, displayed how the religious goal of ecumenism could combine with the state's goal of national unity to strengthen and legitimate the nation. Each local religious organization was encouraged to open its doors to members of the community and members of other faiths, who could come, at designated times, to learn more about its religious beliefs and style of worship. "An ecumenical open house," read a promotional flyer, "is basically a friendly gesture to promote better understanding among those of different convictions."[50] By promoting better understanding, its aim was to unify, not to proselytize. "When others visit us and we visit them," the flyer continued, "there is no thought of winning someone over." "A continuous series of such social and educational exchanges between Canada's many faith groups," read a press release devoted to the project, "will light the fires of ecumenism across the country during the 1967 centennial."[51] According to Becker, the Open House project "could be one of the most effective means of promoting unity ... if local groups will take it up."[52] That unity, he implied, was both national and religious.

Interfaith services, a third project of the CIC, also met the many interests of the faith groups and state planners. This project managed to merge within it the desire for national recognition and the desire for religious and national unity. Essentially, the interfaith service was a worship service that, relying on an interfaith spirit, would, it was hoped, involve all religious groups in a specific community. Aware of member faiths uninterested in ecumenism, let alone interfaith activity, the CIC committee responsible for the interfaith services stressed that they did not reflect an assumed doctrinal unity of the participating religious groups. Still, the committee hoped, interfaith services could "express some degree of unity in our diversity."[53] In addition, while guarding the specific identity of each religious group, they allowed them to "reflect the role we have all had in varying degrees in the history of Canada"[54] and to give witness to the fact that "we in all our diversity also have something to say to those for whom religion is not a vital part of life."[55]

Finally, the *Canadian Centennial Anthology of Prayer*, published by the CIC and distributed widely throughout the Centennial year, demonstrates the conference's ability to articulate a wide range of interests. Consisting of 124 "devotions and acts of worship distinctive of many differing religious faiths,"[56] the *Anthology* was compiled from a vast number of items submitted by individuals and religious organizations from across the nation. Its purpose, wrote Becker in the foreword, was "to achieve ... the sense of unity of all Canadians praying together."[57] More than that, the *Anthology* deftly wove religious and national unity into a seamless whole. "We take pride in our Canada," Becker continued, "whose centennial brought us so closely together, to learn to respect each other and otherness itself, and taught us unity in diversity."[58]

The first section of the *Anthology*, for example, was comprised of numerous prayers of a nationalist nature, including the "Centennial Prayer for the Parliament of Canada," "A Prayer for Canada," and "A Prayer for Our Country." "LORD of the universe," the latter began, "we invoke thy blessing upon our Country and upon all who exercise just and rightful authority." "Unite in loyal and loving accord all the inhabitants of our Country," it went on, "so that men of all races and creeds may find in their common citizenship the bond of true brotherhood. Banish all hatred and bigotry, and safeguard the ideals and free institutions which are our country's pride and glory. May this land, under thy providence, be an influence for good throughout the world, uniting men in peace and freedom, and helping to fulfill the vision of thine inspired seers, 'Nation shall not lift up sword against nation, neither shall men learn war any more.' *Amen*."[59] All the key themes of the Centennial and the CIC were present in that prayer. Representing the leaders of the nation as possessing "just and rightful authority" and lauding "the ideals and free institutions which are our country's pride and glory," the prayer boldly sacralized the nation, raising it above the turmoil of the day. In the language of "loyal and loving accord," "common citizenship," and "the bond of true brotherhood," it called, in the gendered language of the day, for the unity of all Canadians, regardless of "race" or "creed." The final paragraph of the prayer even gave to Canada the distinctively messianic role of godly peacemaker in the world.

If the prayers sacralized the nation, however, they also explicitly called it to God. Here the faith groups of Canada declared their own message. "O LORD, may our leaders imitate your wisdom," a prayer entitled "For Our Leaders" began. "May they be just in dealing with others. May they inspire confidence in those under their jurisdiction. May they imitate your kindness and generosity in anticipating the needs of others. May they remain loyal and steadfast, true to their country. But above all, LORD," it concluded, "may they realize that you are the Eternal Judge, the Omnipotent Ruler, the Supreme Authority, and, the Humble Servant. *Amen*."[60] The leaders of the country may possess "just and rightful authority," the prayer declared, but they were also human beings in need of God, and under God. Alongside the requests for loyalty and wisdom for "our leaders" was, again, the desire of the religious groups of Canada to reinfuse religion into an increasingly secular society.

The programs of the CIC, then, reflected expressions both of particular religious concerns more closely connected to the faith groups involved and of the larger Centennial goal of uniting the nation around the image of an inclusive, pluralistic Canada. They expressed on paper the general success of the first round of the program of bringing as many faith groups as possible into the planning phase of the interfaith organization. They also indicated, however, that the attempt to build an interfaith, and not simply a Christian, understanding of Canada necessarily involved careful negotiation of a vast range of diverse religious convictions and goals. The CIC remained a voluntary organization that had to cater not only to the Centennial Commission but also to the interests of the religious groups who would do its work.

The successful merging of the particular interests of the state and the faith groups in the CIC was, in fact, only the first round of negotiation in the life of that organization. It took place at the organizational level in the CIC, between representatives of faith groups themselves, and between those representatives and the interests of the Centennial Commission. Another challenge for the CIC came when the second round of negotiation began – when the CIC took its programs and proposals to communities and individuals across the country. As the Centennial and CIC organizers well understood, they could succeed only if they were able to reach down to the grass roots and spread their nationalist and interfaith message effectively among the citizens of Canada.

Over its two-and-a-half-year life span, the CIC attempted to do so in several ways. Using Centennial Commission public relations personnel to coordinate press releases as well as advertising, the CIC tried to use the media to its full advantage. Realizing that that would not be enough, however, it also tried to put a human face on its efforts by sending its director, Eve Gilstorf, across the country on a speaking tour in 1966.[61] Gilstorf visited major population centres in every province but Newfoundland (bad weather made the trip there impossible), with the goal of inspiring the creation of provincial and municipal interfaith committees. In the early months of 1967 the CIC sent a package containing a whole range of promotional material to every known local leader or clergy of their member faiths. That package included separate pamphlets promoting each of the CIC's recommended programs, a copy of its "Declaration," and a promotional placemat. Finally, the CIC offered for sale copies of all its promotional literature, including its *Canadian Centennial Anthology of Prayer.*

The end result of all that effort is not easy to define. As the CIC itself came to realize, evaluating the effectiveness of what was essentially an ideological campaign was a difficult task. Gilstorf herself wrote in her final report to the board of directors "that the degree to which our materials and suggestions were helpful, is hardly known to us ... there is an uneasy feeling that this report is incomplete in this respect."[62] As Gilstorf's extraordinarily detailed report suggests, however, some tools of evaluation were at hand. Though by no means offering a definitive answer on the impact of the CIC, Gilstorf had gathered an impressive amount of information that sheds some light on the ability of the CIC to reach Canadian citizens from coast to coast. More importantly, it says a great deal about how Canadian citizens responded to the CIC's interfaith and nationalist message.

The barest of facts are themselves impressive. By the end of November 1967, an estimated 23,000 to 25,000 *Anthologies of Prayer* had been sold.[63] A total of 332,200 interfaith placemats had been sold in Ontario alone. More significantly, as of 30 March 1967 provincial interfaith committees had been formed in Prince Edward Island, Nova Scotia, New Brunswick, Ontario, Manitoba, Saskatchewan, Alberta, and the Yukon. (Though it was not able to establish a provincial interfaith committee in the province of Quebec, the CIC did have an interfaith steering committee there.) Local communities had also climbed aboard the interfaith bandwagon. Municipal committees existed in the Halifax-Dartmouth metropolitan area, in Sydney, Antigonish, Edmonton, Calgary, and Vancouver, to name a few of the largest centres.[64]

Asked to report on their activities to the national office of the CIC, those provincial and municipal committees gave a good indication of the level of activity that they had managed to plan and inspire. Ontario, it appeared, had run the hardest with interfaith activities, and

Ottawa had played a big part in that effort. Apart from the prayer service held on Parliament Hill on 1 July, the Ottawa area committee had also organized an interfaith service geared specifically for youth on the evening of 2 July. In the latter service, hymns and Sunday-best clothes had been replaced by folk songs and more casual dress. Other religious services in that area had been held on 31 December 1966, 1 January 1967, Thanksgiving Day, and 31 December 1967. A national prayer breakfast took place on 7 June 1967. Lavy Becker was a guest at the ceremony in the Ottawa train station in which Madame Vanier launched the first Centennial Train. A CBC hymn sing program included the Centennial hymn and the CIC's declaration. Governor General Vanier had greatly honoured the CIC by using its declaration in his New Year's Day message to the nation.[65]

Outside the national capital, too, local interfaith committees dotted the province, and planned such events as open houses and interfaith worship services from Kingston to St Thomas and Elgin to St Catharines. Alex Maurice, the chairman of the provincial committee, reported that a Centennial Town Talk event was "one of the outstanding activities" in November of the Centennial year.[66] Focusing on discussion of community problems, Town Talks used CIC material and incorporated religious activities. In Toronto, a well-attended Provincial Interfaith Service was held in Queen's Park on 25 June and involved in its liturgy the lieutenant governor as well as members of the Christian, Baha'i, Moslem, Buddhist, and Jewish faiths.[67] That service appears to have been the most inclusive interfaith and multicultural event of its kind in Canada.

If Ontario seemed to lead the nation in CIC-inspired national religious fervour, the Maritimes and the Prairie provinces were not far behind. In Nova Scotia, for example, seventy-eight communities were reported to have either started or ended their Centennial celebrations with interdenominational church services. In the Dartmouth-Halifax area, in particular, "most congregations of the principal denominations made some use of the Anthem and the Hymn," while excerpts from the *Anthology* were also reported to have been widely used. On Sunday, 2 July, an interfaith service of Thanksgiving sponsored by the Halifax-Dartmouth Council of Churches had attracted around eight thousand people, while a civic service in Halifax's Grand Parade on 31 December 1967 used prayers from the *Anthology*.[68] In New Brunswick, the Centennial year began with the ringing of church bells and a flame ceremony in Fredericton that included interfaith prayers, hymns, and a proclamation. Such prayers and hymns were also used, according to the provincial committee's report, in many other centres in the province. "People were encouraged at every ceremony connected with the Opening of centennial Projects to include something of a religious element of invocation and dedication," it said. "In most cases, reps. of the clergy were present to give a religious aspect to all ceremonies."[69]

In Manitoba, the provincial committee reported that it had inspired interfaith programs "in rural communities all over the province" and, among other things, arranged to have the CIC's declaration given to every family at every Manitoba church service on 1 January 1967. In metropolitan Winnipeg, Salvation Army, Anglican, Presbyterian, and Roman Catholic churches held open houses, events also held in "most communities in Manitoba."[70] Among the activities of the Saskatchewan Interfaith Committee was a marriage and counselling course offered as a Centennial social action project and the placement in churches of seventy-five thousand pew leaflets that encouraged citizens to plan and attend interfaith services on Sunday, 25 June, the last Sunday before 1 July.[71] In Alberta, Calgary held an interfaith service of thanksgiving on 2 July, Lethbridge an interfaith weekend attended by four thousand.

Last on the provincial list rating reported interfaith Centennial fervour was British Columbia, followed by Quebec. In both provinces, activities were not altogether absent. In New Westminster, for example, an interfaith service was co-sponsored by the local Centennial committee and the New Westminster Ministerial Association, and Burnaby and Comox had interfaith committees.[72] In Quebec, an interfaith service held in the Pointe Claire Arena on 20 September 1967 also suggested that some communities in that province had been reached.[73] British Columbia and Quebec also managed to place a very distant second behind Ontario in sales of CIC materials. Nonetheless, it was clear from Gilstorf's summary that neither province had caught the interfaith flame to the extent of the others. Regarding Quebec, in particular, Gilstorf noted that "there was little involvement as such from that Province, other than personal contacts made by the Chairman and Exec. Director."[74]

Gilstorf's Canada-wide summary of Centennial religious activities stretched to over fifty pages. As she recognized, however, listing those events raised some important questions, and was not alone a justification of the CIC. Even though a significant amount of Centennial religious activity had taken place over the past year, there was no way of knowing how much of it would have happened without the CIC. Many Canadians, after all, did not need the CIC to suggest that religion should play a part in their celebrations. As the early existence of the Centennial committees in some churches suggested, plans for religious celebrations were around long before the CIC.

The uncertainty surrounding the impact of the CIC was made worse by a significant body of evidence suggesting that, in fact, many local planners were not convinced by the CIC's interfaith message at all. In their effort to persuade Canadians to celebrate a religiously inclusive, pluralistic (and not a particularly Christian) Canada, CIC officials knew very well that many Canadians had very different understandings of their country. Tensions between the celebration of a particularly Christian Canada and that of an interfaith, religiously plural one ran through public expressions of religion in local Centennial celebrations throughout the country. Inside Quebec, many objected to connecting religion with the Centennial at all.

Three events, one in Nova Scotia, one in Quebec, and one in Alberta, ably demonstrate this point. On 2 July 1967, Haligonians filed into their streets and watched from their windows and doors as a religious procession made its way towards Citadel Hill. Hours before, participants had begun to gather in the tree-lined streets surrounding the Anglican Cathedral of All Saints. When all was in place, the procession began to weave its way towards the citadel and clock tower, which had come to symbolize the city. Gathered along the roadside, spectators looking down the street were greeted first by sunlight reflected off a crucifix moving above the crowd. Slowly the bright robes of choirs appeared behind it. Then came the clergy, followed by "the open Bible flanked by tapers, the preacher (Dr. Chalmers of the United Church) and the Anglican and Roman Catholic Bishops walking side by side and accompanied by their Chaplains." By the time the procession had reached Citadel Hill, eight thousand Haligonians had joined it. A Christian ecumenical service, without representation of any non-Christian faiths, followed. Led by a Presbyterian and a Baptist minister, congregants also heard music provided by a Salvation Army band. Reflecting on the event afterwards, the Reverend Gordon W. Philpotts, chairman of the Halifax-Dartmouth Interfaith Committee, noted that the crowd was receptive, and all had gone well.[75]

Things did not go so smoothly in the largely francophone industrial towns of Noranda and Rouyn in Northwestern Quebec.[76] Four months earlier, the pages of the local newspaper, the *Rouyn-Noranda Press*, were alive with scandal. At the centre of it all were the local churches and the Centennial. According to one account, the churches had made plans for a week of religious thanksgiving in connection with the Centennial, to be followed by an interfaith service held in May.[77] At the end of March, however, those celebrations were suddenly called into question. In recent days, each of the clergy had received "roughly stenciled" pamphlets "stamped with the standard separatist description of the 100 years of Confederation, '100 ans d'injustice.'" One pamphlet bore the image of clergymen blessing the Union Jack. Inside, it described Confederation in apparently "obscene terms," and denounced "any 'hiding of a hypocritical government' behind churchmen." Fearing disrespect to their churches and even damage to their facilities, a number of clergy had expressed a desire to withdraw from the planned thanksgiving services.[78] "Did the Church Chicken Out?" an article in the local paper asked.[79] The local Centennial committee apparently did. In an attempt to salvage the event, they excised any reference to the Centennial from the billing of the services, instead describing them as "a way of thanking God for 'the farms, the mines, the petroleum, the forests, for all the products which have given Canada today one of the highest standards of living.'"[80]

Nestled on the edge of the prairies and in the shadows of the Rocky Mountains, Lethbridge, Alberta, was worlds away from Northwestern Quebec. Unlike in Noranda and Rouyn, that city's religiously focused Centennial efforts were getting nothing but good press.[81] The weekend of 10–11 June 1967, dubbed the Lethbridge Inter-faith Centennial Weekend, had begun with a Saturday night dinner featuring entertainment by the Mennonite Male Choir of Coaldale. That event's considerable attendance of eight hundred, however, was small in comparison to the big event of the next day: the Massed Family Service of Thanksgiving and Re-dedication at the Lethbridge exhibition grounds attracted four thousand. Under the bright sun, men in dark suits and women in light dresses were edified and entertained by the Salvation Army Citadel Band of Calgary for thirty minutes before the service began. After a brief pause, the band struck up the hymn "All People That On Earth Do Dwell," and as the crowd sang, a total of thirteen clergy and religious representatives dressed in everything from plain suits to the colourful robes of bishops proceeded to the podium and took their seats. The Reverend L.D. Hankinson of St Andrew's Presbyterian Church and president of the Ministerial Association offered words of welcome and introduction. An invocational prayer was followed by the hymn "O God Our Help in Ages Past," a General Confession, and then the singing of "O Canada" and "God Save the Queen."

What followed were addresses by prominent religious officials from out of town, spaced out by readings from the Old and New Testaments, litanies, and hymns. Dressed in a simple suit and tie, Elder Thomas S. Monson, representing the Mormon Member Council of the Twelve Apostles in Salt Lake City, Utah, urged the assembled crowds to make "more room for Christ in the home." Following "A Litany of Thanksgiving for Canada's Centennial" and the singing of the CIC Centennial hymn, the Venerable Archdeacon Cecil Swanson of Calgary, an Anglican, spoke about recruiting people for the work of the Christian church in Canada, there, on that day. Following another reading from the Bible and the offertory hymn "Faith of our Fathers," the Roman Catholic bishop of Calgary, F.J. Klein, extolled the blessings God had given Canada and urged more sharing, helping, and love of neighbour. Another reading from the Gospel of St John, another hymn, and the Right Reverend W.C. Lockhart, moderator of the United Church of Canada, took his turn to speak. A benediction, followed by the hymn "Now Thank We All Our God," concluded the service. As the *Lethbridge Herald* noted, it had been the largest religious assembly in the history of the city.[82]

What do these three episodes reveal? First, that the inclusive, pluralistic, interfaith expressions of public religion encouraged by the CIC directly challenged Christian understandings of Canada deeply embedded in the minds of many of its citizens. It was therefore either not understood or directly opposed in significant celebrations across the country. In their explicitly Christian character, the services of Halifax and Lethbridge represent the replacement of interfaith services with Christian ecumenical services, to the exclusion of non-Christian faiths.

In part, the exclusively Christian nature of such Centennial worship services was due to demographics. In Lethbridge, for example, the 1961 census listed over 94 percent of the population as affiliated with a Christian church or a faith group, like the Jehovah's Witnesses, that was close to the Christian tradition.[83] Even assuming that all of those categorized by the census as "other" were non-Christian (and that is a generous assumption), those completely outside the Christian tradition made up only 5 percent of the population.[84] The crux of the matter was that in many towns and communities across the country – like Lethbridge – Christian Canada was alive and well. Adherents of other religions either did not live in the area or were so few in number as to be virtually invisible and easily ignored in their overwhelmingly Protestant and Roman Catholic environments. In Lethbridge, where the vast majority of citizens were members of a Protestant, Roman Catholic, or Mormon Church, a Christian service including Mormons was the result, not a service celebrating a Canada inclusive of all world religions.

In Halifax, however, something different seemed to be going on. There, in a provincial capital with a much larger population and greater degree of religious diversity than Lethbridge and other smaller communities, the major worship service connected with the Centennial was exclusively Christian – and apparently explicitly planned by the Dartmouth-Halifax Council of Churches to be that way. Adherents of non-Christian faiths were citizens of Dartmouth, Halifax, and the surrounding area, and they were interested in the Centennial. Registrants at an interfaith meeting in Halifax on 18 March 1966 included Jews and Baha'is.[85] The CIC made sure that Centennial planners in the city were

also aware that a Centennial worship service might be interfaith, and
not just exclusively Christian. Hearing in early May of plans to hold the
combined Protestant and Roman Catholic worship service in the city,
Lavy Becker wrote a letter to the chairman of Halifax's Interfaith Committee, Rev. Gordon Philpott, in which he delicately asked that an
explicitly interfaith celebration of the Centennial be kept in mind. Tell-
ingly, Becker felt it necessary to include a justification for such a gathering. "All of us have much in common in the religious interpretation of
our twentieth century life in Canada," he wrote. "Together we have the
problem of facing indifference even antagonism to the basic philosophy of a religious interpretation and practice of life. But the combined
strength of Christians and non-Christians should be co-ordinated towards this purpose."[86] The idea of an interfaith religious service, however, was clearly rejected in Halifax and replaced by a Christian
ecumenical one.[87]

Episodes in other parts of the country confirm that in local communities, the CIC's presentation of an interfaith Canada met resistance from
those still imbued with a Christian vision of their country. At a meeting
of the Ontario Interfaith Committee held on 27 April 1966, two complaints by a Rabbi Liman and by Mrs Betty Frost, a Baha'i, forced the
committee to reevaluate its plans for the provincial interfaith service to
be held in Queen's Park on 25 June. According to both Liman and Frost,
the service was too Christian, and not truly interfaith. The "Prayer for
the Commonwealth," for example, had an explicitly Christian ending,
and Liman wanted it revised. Two other members, Mr Roblin and
Mr Kulbeck "protested that [as Christians] their only real approach to
God was through Jesus Christ, his son, and so felt that the prayer ending should remain in."[88] A stalemate ensued until Mr Leslie Tufts, of the
Christian Science organization, suggested cutting out the end of prayer
and leaving in its place a moment of silence.[89]

Disagreement with the basic concept of "interfaith" through the
country was best exemplified in reports that members of the Baha'i
faith had found, in the words of an article in the *Canadian Baha'i News*, a
"general unwillingness on the part of the Christian Clergy, both Protestant and Roman Catholic, to extend the privilege of interfaith membership to Baha'i communities."[90] Daphne Clayton's letter to Gilstorf in
January 1967 is particularly descriptive in this regard. Clayton was a
Baha'i who had recently moved to North Bay, Ontario, from Ottawa,
where she had been involved in interfaith activities and had become familiar with the CIC. In North Bay, she wrote, the chairman of the interfaith committee knew "practically nothing at all about the Interfaith
Commission [sic]." Clayton also disclosed the results of a very informa-
tive but "rather embarrassing interview" she had had with the mayor

and council of her new city. When she asked the mayor to proclaim the third Sunday in January World Religion Day, she was bluntly turned down. "The Deputy Mayor was rather rude about the whole thing, and had never heard of the Canadian Government setting up an Inter-Faith Centennial Project and he could not understand why the Government would do such a thing." Clayton was mortified.[91]

According to other Baha'i sources, she was not alone in her predicament. The year-end report of the National Spiritual Assembly of the Baha'is of Canada to the CIC noted, with strong evidence, that "no CIC member organization more enthusiastically welcomed the establishment of a national interfaith program than did the Canadian Baha'i Community." Open houses had been held in an estimated seventy-five cities and towns in the spring, and two hundred more meetings like these were planned for November and December. In response to the Library Shelves Program, subscriptions to the Baha'i magazine *World Order* were given to one hundred libraries. Nonetheless, the report went on, "we were dismayed to discover how little of this spirit of understanding had penetrated to the clergy at the local level, particularly to the clergy of the five or six major Christian denominations." They were more often than not excluded from interfaith services, but found that those including Jews usually included them.[92]

The executive director and chairman of the CIC, though obviously distraught by a situation that demonstrated division, not unity, could do little to change it. Clearly, in several local communities, Centennial planners, including local clergymen, were not allowing the interfaith concept to reach the masses. In a letter to the Ministerial Association of Yellowknife, Lavy Becker pointed out that "the financial support for our work comes from a grant from the Centennial Commission whose money is governmental, out of taxes." Because everyone paid taxes, he implied, everyone should be included in interfaith activities. He continued to express hope that "imagination on the local level will find a way to bring together, for the sake of unity in Canada, all groups, no matter how they differ. Even if you do not believe the Baha'is to be Christian you could still find some program through which to cooperate with each other. It would not be ecumenical. It would be interfaith. It would be true Canadianism."[93]

If Centennial services in Lethbridge and Halifax and in a host of other Canadian communities revealed resistance to the replacement of a Christian with an interfaith Canada, the case of the threatening pamphlets in Noranda and Rouyn demonstrated an equally important point of contention: whether the CIC represented the use and abuse of religion for explicitly political purposes. That point was also demonstrated in Montreal, where the CIC's efforts to organize an interfaith

committee in 1966 were poorly rewarded and bitterly disappointing
for Eve Gilstorf. As any Canadian within reach of the news knew perfectly well in the mid-1960s, the province of Quebec was in a tenuous
relationship, at best, with the federal government and with the rest of
Canada. To Quebeckers who felt increasingly misunderstood and ill-
treated by the rest of Canada, the hundredth anniversary of Confederation was nothing to celebrate. That message was made loud and clear
in Quebec by the Société St-Jean Baptiste, a French Canadian nationalist organization with considerable influence in the province. In a letter
to Roman Catholic clergy, that society argued against clerical involvement in the Centennial. "The spirit of Christian ecumenicalism and especially the Catholic Church in western Quebec should not be
employed 'to celebrate the virtues, benefits and merits of a political
system legitimately brought into question, the system of Confederation,'" the society argued.[94]

Many of the Quebec clergy, much to Gilstorf's dismay, were as
much affected by the cultural context as anyone else in the province.
As one contemporary author argued, the CIC was seen by many in
Quebec "as an unjustified utilization of ecumenism for political
aims."[95] It represented not an opportunity for ecumenism but another federal government program aimed at maintaining the very
flawed status quo. Gilstorf wrote to Becker: "Even people who have
been welcome in Quebec in the past no longer enjoy this relationship,
regardless of how fluent their French is, if they do not consent with
the thinking that Confederation is not a happy occasion and Quebeckers have no reason to feel grateful to those who shaped our country ... Many great men in Quebec have fallen at the hands of the
separatists. Some of the most prominent religious leaders have also
suffered and the hate propaganda is building all the time."[96]

If Quebec was, at best, unwelcoming to the CIC, due to its relations
with the federal government and the CIC's evident role as a propo-
nent of an "official nationalism," the province's own religious climate
after Vatican II and in the midst of the Quiet Revolution also played a
role in shaping the cool reception of the CIC. In her letter to Becker,
Gilstorf had suggested that "the reorganization of the Roman Catholic Church and, in fact, all Churches at the present time, coupled with
the unrest in the province, is something we will just have to live
with."[97] Certainly, the Quiet Revolution had not been a purely political phenomena. Its rapid program of modernization had included a
rapid process of secularization, leaving the Roman Catholic Church
of Quebec reeling from falling church attendance, a rise in the number of resignations of priests, and the secularization of social services
in the province.[98] An apparently sizable portion of Roman Catholic

clergymen in Quebec may have been unwilling to risk alienating their parishoners further by endorsing the Centennial celebrations. They may also have been simply too overwhelmed by more important things to pay attention to the Centennial or to the CIC.

Events in Halifax, Lethbridge, and Noranda/Rouyn made at least one point clear. Trying to build national unity by reshaping the religious identity of the nation was no easy or simple task. CIC officials could say what they liked about "true Canadianism." Many Canadians simply chose to work with much older and much more deeply ingrained, self- and communal understandings of their religious national identities.

The Canadian Interfaith Conference worked hard to spread the message of interfaith cooperation and the vision of an inclusive and tolerant Canada from 1965 through 1967. Negotiation, compromise, and cooperation made it possible for an impressive number of faith groups eventually to find a place in the CIC, and that alone was a sign of that organization's success. Gaining the cooperation of local clergymen and Centennial planners, however, was much more difficult than gaining the cooperation of their denominational and institutional representatives. While some towns and cities with a large degree of religious diversity caught the vision of an inclusive, pluralistic, and interfaith Canada and translated it into forms of public religion, others did not. As the non-Christian citizens in Halifax, Lethbridge, North Bay, and across the country found out, a significant number of communities and individuals simply were not able to think of celebrating their Canada in anything other than Christian terms. Much to the dismay of the CIC and non-Christian faith groups, many Canadians simply chose to interpret "interfaith" as ecumenical or interdenominational. Others, specifically in Quebec, rejected the CIC as an attempt to use religion to legitimize the federal state. As a result, in their final meeting in November 1967, the CIC's directors recognized that they could not be "sure that a closer understanding of each other's faith was brought about on the local level."[99]

In 1967, celebrating Canada was a potentially controversial affair. The Centennial celebrations took on very different meanings as official presentations of an inclusive, pluralistic, and interfaith Canada struggled for public dominance with older Christian understandings of the country. As the following chapters will explore, that struggle played itself out on the site of Expo 67, as well. Federal planners had no monopoly on defining "true Canadianism." In 1967, as a result, the construction of a diverse, religiously inclusive Canada was challenged by those who brought other understandings of their country to their local public squares.

6

Changing the Meaning
of the Word "Canada":

State-Sponsored Public Religion at Expo 67

If you hold on to my hand
You'll step into a dream
Onto a magic island
Like a painted summer scene.[1]

If the centennial celebrations were Canada's birthday party, Expo 67 was its birthday cake.[2] Held in Montreal in the summer of 1967, the Universal and International Exposition was an astounding project, not unlike the staging of an Olympics in size, complexity, and international prestige. It involved the municipal government of Montreal, the provincial government of Quebec, and the federal government of Canada in a joint venture that eventually transformed the middle of the St Lawrence River into a dream-land of national cultures, cutting-edge technology, and thrilling entertainment that would captivate citizens of Canada and the world.[3]

Officially linked to the Centennial celebrations, Expo 67 tried to both reflect and shape its cultural context in similar ways. Expo planners, like their Centennial Commission counterparts, viewed their project in the light of Canada's struggle for national unity and sought to do their part to further the nationalist cause. They did so, too, by presenting to Canadians and to the world an image of a Canada that emphasized inclusion, not exclusion; impartiality, not ethnic or religious prejudice; unity and cooperation, not separation and division. In Expo 67, Canada was reconstructed to emphasize what Canadians held in common, not what held them apart. And at Expo 67, as in the Centennial celebrations, religion was to play a significant role.

Although Expo 67 and the Centennial had much in common, Expo 67 was a much more complicated entity than the anniversary celebrations. Planned by a state corporation structurally distinct from the Centennial Commission, it was an international exposition planned according to international rules and on a global scale. It was also initiated and funded by three levels of government, two of which (the province of Quebec and the municipality of Montreal) were at least ambivalent about the national anniversary it was to commemorate. Those complications placed the message of "unity in diversity" on a global stage and gave it a sophistication and depth beyond what the Centennial celebrations had to offer.

When the gates of Expo 67 opened on 28 April 1967, the first visitors poured into a wonderland. A small peninsula, Île Ste-Hélène and Île Notre Dame had been a small island and some mud flats only four years earlier. Since that time, Montrealers had watched them slowly rise from the river. The islands, growing in beauty, had become adorned with the splendour of canals, broad pathways, and, best of all, the stunning wealth and glory of the assembled nations of the world.

A place of astonishment, wonder, and enchantment, the Expo islands worked their magic on nearly all who entered. "There has never been any other show of its kind that has come near it," claimed Jonathan Aitken of the London *Evening Standard*.[4] Some called it a "utopia,"[5] others a "revelation," a "happy place to be; a totally new planned environment."[6] Ron Haggart asked in his *Toronto Star* column, "After we have all seen Expo, how can any of us, ever again, be content with the cities in which we live?"[7] For Pierre Berton, the exposition was a "miracle," "one of the shining moments in our history, up there with the building of the Pacific Railway or the victory at Vimy Ridge."[8]

The closest thing to Expo 67 ever witnessed in Canada into the 1960s was perhaps the Canadian National Exhibition (CNE) in Toronto, but Expo organizers rightfully scoffed at the comparison.[9] While Expo 67 included some of the basic elements of the CNE, such as cultural displays and an amusement park, it did so on a much larger scale and in a much more sophisticated manner. The CNE might attempt to display one foreign nation in one of its buildings, while at Expo 67 over sixty nations had come to Montreal to showcase themselves, spending millions of dollars constructing their own striking and unique pavilions and then filling them with their own theatres, restaurants, and treasures. The CNE's midway was an impermanent and notoriously questionable affair. Expo 67's La Ronde amusement park was built to rival the best of its kind in Europe.[10] More importantly, while the CNE was really a large agricultural and trade fair offering space to innumerable sales booths, Expo 67 was nothing of the kind. Though numerous corporations chose to build pavilions and fill them with displays at Expo, neither they nor the national pavilions were permitted to sell any merchandise. It was an exposition of the best in culture and technology that every nation and corporation had to offer. And it was designed to be beautiful.

By all accounts, it *was* beautiful. Emerging from the subway on Île Ste-Hélène, the visitor entered a completely manicured, clean, and enchanting world, a world designed first and foremost for people. Dirt, crime, and discomfort were banished from the scene, to the best of the organizers' abilities. So were automobiles. The exposition was a pedestrian's paradise, a place of broad pathways, open vistas along beautifully landscaped grounds, and quiet, blue canals. Strict rules and careful planning ensured that everything felt in its place, that line and colour contributed to a pleasing "total environment," and that each pavilion, uniquely and often extravagantly designed with unheard of materials and brilliant colour, was displayed to its best potential. It was a world apart, a sense encouraged even by the smallest details. Uniform signage, garbage cans, benches, and light posts designed only for this site distanced Expo 67 from the cluttered reality of daily life. Along with carefully placed statues and art installations, attention to such things helped make the Expo islands feel like a wonderland, a separate world where the troubles of life were left behind and where the mind could be set free to dream.

The many outlandish structures housing brilliant national and technological displays were, of course, the real attraction of Expo 67, and they did not disappoint.[11] High above the trees and other roof tops and glimmering in the brilliant sun was Buckminster Fuller's geodesic dome of the United States, its translucent material offering glimpses of the yellow NASA parachutes, space equipment, and pop-culture tributes suspended within. Across a channel of water, directly and symbolically opposite the American pavilion, stood the massive, ramp-like roof line of the pavilion of the USSR, seemingly supported by nothing but glass. The Soviet pavilion offered visitors a very rare chance indeed to see what those communists were really all about and rivalled the United States with its display of space technology and tangible proof of the USSR's advanced application of technology to industry and agriculture.[12] At the end of Île Notre Dame stood the twenty-four-million-dollar Canada Pavilion, a conglomeration of white tent-like structures housing exhibits, a massive upside-down pyramid called Katimavik, and a huge People Tree with pictures of Canadians as leaves. Labyrinth, another Canadian contribution, was a massive, cathedral-like concrete maze of movies on ceilings, floors, and walls. Constructed by the National Film Board, it astounded many with its cavernous spaces and multiple screens. Indeed, new film technology was one of the major crowd-pleasers of Expo 67. The Czechoslovakian Pavilion drew huge crowds with its film presentation, which allowed the audience to choose the plot line. And the Telephone Pavilion awed many with its 360-degree theatre, which caused the crowds to duck under the hooves of charging Mounties, then turn to see them riding off beside and behind them. Off in the distance, beyond the monorail whisking visitors around the park and over the canals where gondolas quietly glided, was Habitat, the very ambitious and very expensive modular housing complex that modelled for all the urban apartment complex of the future.

From its opening day to its closing day six months later, Expo 67 was deemed a popular and critical success. Already on its third day it had broken the world fair record for daily attendance, welcoming over 550,000 people to the site.[13] It pushed on from there to outpace even the great Paris Fair of 1900 in overall attendance, and it far outshone its most recent rival, the Brussels Exposition of 1958.[14] Journalists and editors from around the world heaped praise on the Canadian event. "The fair bids to be one of the great international shows of the century ... The sophisticated standard of excellence ... almost defies description," wrote the *New York Times*.[15] According to *Time*, it was "the greatest international exposition ever."[16]

As several studies of exhibitions and world fairs have ably demonstrated, "World's fairs are among the best sites for interrogating cultures about the social construction of meaning."[17] Like public celebrations in general, expositions, too, highlight key points of agreement and disagreement in their host societies, throwing into bold relief important struggles of citizens and planners to make sense of their time and place, and of themselves. For that reason, anthropologist Burton Benedict has insightfully argued, a "world's fair can be seen as one of a series of mammoth rituals in which all sorts of power relations, both existing and wished for, are being expressed. It is a contest in which the contestants are jockeying for advantage in the worlds of both commerce and politics. In this contest all sorts of symbols are employed, and there are blatant efforts to manufacture tradition, to impose legitimacy."[18] In her recent study of Canadian exhibitions in the nineteenth century, Elsbeth Heaman has reinforced that point. Early agricultural fairs in Canada, she argues, "were developed by social elites and supported by the state as instruments of indoctrination."[19] Likewise, the apt description of Quebec's tercentenary celebrations by Vive Nelles applies equally well to both the Centennial celebrations and Expo 67. "[I]t was entertainment," Nelles notes, "but it was entertainment with an intent, or rather intentions."[20]

What the intentions of Expo 67 were was at least partly revealed in the origins and nature of the exposition itself. Expo 67 was the centrepiece of Canada's centennial celebrations and had been originally conceived in that regard. Quebec senator Mark Drouin, former director of the National School of Theatre and speaker of the Senate from 1957–62, first suggested publicly that Canada host a World's Fair in 1967 with the hope that the exposition could help Canadians celebrate their country's one hundredth birthday.[21] His hope was translated into reality in the act of Parliament that established the Canadian Corporation for the 1967 World Exposition (CCWE) in 1962, one year before his death. The exposition, the act declared, was to be planned "in connection with the celebration of the Centennial of Confederation in Canada in a manner in keeping with its national and historical significance."[22] That connection, furthermore, was popularly understood. Commentators such as Peter Newman called Expo 67 "the focus of the celebrations."[23] Robert Fulford called it "the greatest birthday party in history."[24] Judy LaMarsh, Canada's secretary of state, noted in Expo 67's official guide that the exposition was "the largest single item" of the Centennial celebrations.[25] Directly connecting the Centennial and the exposition, that guide included a sixty-page Centennial celebrations insert.

Planned in connection with Canada's Centennial, Expo 67 was shaped by the same context and moulded by some of the same intentions. That fact was made clear by the man who was most responsible for making Expo 67 work: Pierre Dupuy. Dupuy had been named commissioner general of the CCWE in 1963, shortly after the corporation's first chief executive, Paul Bienvenue, had resigned.[26] The organization Dupuy inherited was not in particularly good shape and had accomplished little over the previous year. Skeptical voices were already being raised to suggest that the international exposition would not be ready on time – that it would be a monumental failure and a global embarrassment for Canada.[27] Dupuy was determined to make sure that would not happen.

At the age of 67, he brought a life-time of experience in international and diplomatic affairs to the job. Born into a Roman Catholic family in Montreal, he had practised law, then entered the Department of External Affairs in 1922. From there, he came to represent Canada in various missions abroad, becoming Canadian ambassador in more than a few.[28] He left the position of Canadian ambassador to France to become commissioner general of the CCWE in 1963. That wealth of international and diplomatic experience served Dupuy well as he set out to convince as many nations of the world as possible to be exhibitors at Expo 67. One month after Dupuy's appointment, he had gathered a very capable management team to aid him in his task, and Expo 67 was finally on its way.[29] Over the next three years, he would visit 125 countries, spending at least three days in each to request their presence at Expo 67. The result would be 61 nations at Expo 67, the largest number in the history of such exhibitions.

That was no small accomplishment for a man his age. What drove him to such efforts, his memoirs suggest, was a passion to serve his country in an hour of particular need. Fired by the Quiet Revolution, the "crise de croissance que traverse mon pays" had had a profound influence on the shape and form of his exhibition.[30] A fiery federalist and Canadian nationalist who had committed his life to the service of his country, Dupuy had accepted the position of commissioner general for Expo 67 because he saw the great potential it could have for strengthening his nation. Expo 67 "pourrait être un facteur d'unité entre tous les Canadiens," he wrote. "En travaillant ensemble à une grande entreprise de portée nationale et internationale, les Canadiens prouveraient que la collaboration, la compréhension, l'entente étaient possibles entre eux et que cela pourrait être la vraie façon de célébrer le Centenaire de la Confédération canadienne."[31] It was with full sincerity, one gathers, that in appealing to others to join the staff of the CCWE, Dupuy used the familiar refrain, "Votre pays a besoin de vous."[32] Nor was he alone in his nationalist interpretation of the world's fair. According to Dupuy, his Expo team shared the conviction that this was Canada's chance to pull itself together and show its coming of age to the world.[33] Andrew Kniewasser, Expo's general manager, certainly felt that way. "Please keep praying for the success of the Exhibition," he wrote to a Roman Catholic priest, "and, therefore, [for] the success of our country."[34]

Shaped by the same cultural context as the broader Centennial celebrations, Expo 67 also reflected the same response to the challenges of the 1960s. A drive to strengthen national unity by forwarding an inclusive, pluralist image of Canada found its way onto Expo's two enchanted isles. It was particularly apparent in the explicit, extensive, and very expensive construction of "Canada" offered to fairgoers in the Centennial summer.[35] Among the national pavilions on the Expo isles, of course, was the Canada Pavilion, replete with its own commissioner general, H. Leslie Brown, and its own team of designers and builders.[36] "The Pavilion of Canada tells a story of a people and their country," Brown wrote in a small foreword to a number of souvenir booklets of his pavilion. "Canada has different meanings for different people," he recognized, but that did not keep him and his team from coming up with their own interpretation.[37] The end result was the largest and most diverse national display on the Expo islands.[38] The Canada Pavilion is worthy of close description.

The pavilion, in fact, was an amalgam of structures, rather than a unified structural whole. The Katimavik, or "meeting place," was at its visual and geographic centre. A nine-storey-high, thousand-ton, hollow-steel inverted pyramid with translucent sides, the Katimavik was open to the sky with a promenade around its edges. On the four large sloping inner surfaces of the pyramid, larger-than-life sculptures of a sun-dial, hour glass, compass, and Kyogen and Haida masks helped present what Expo's information manual called "things universal to all men": Time, Navigation, Nature and Man.[39]

Below the Katimavik's southeast edge and standing at the entrance to the pavilion was the People Tree, a structure aptly described by Mordecai Richler as a "multi-coloured, illuminated magazine cover tree."[40] Sixty-six feet high, the tree consisted of over a thousand "leaves" made of nylon panels suspended by a system of steel cables from all around the trunk. Five hundred of those leaves carried silk-screen photographs of Canadians "at work or at leisure," tinted in the colours of autumn.[41] A staircase spiraling up around the massive wood trunk made the leaves accessible to the public. At the base of the tree were the "roots" of the Canadian population: presentations, through massive three dimensional maps, of Our Work Pattern, Our Urban Growth, and Our Ethnic Diversity.[42]

On the northeasterly edge of the pavilion grounds stood the Arts Centre, a large, nearly flat-roofed building enclosed by bronze glass that housed a five-hundred-seat theatre, a display of Canadian art, handicrafts, photographic portraits, and a reference library "containing over 3000 Canadian volumes in English and French and in 26 other languages spoken and written in Canada."[43] Also on the site was the Children's Creative Centre (emphasizing the education of tomorrow's citizens and featuring an operational nursery school, playground area, and art, drama and music studios) and La Toundra, a "deluxe restaurant with a High Arctic atmosphere created by Eskimo murals, carvings, tapestries, as well as Eskimo prints on the menu covers."[44] In the open-air bandshell on the grounds, crowds heard free concerts from, among others, Vancouver's Cassenti Players, Toronto's Hart House Orchestra, Montreal's L'Ensemble Couperin le Grand, and the Halifax Trio.[45]

The Canadian display proper was housed under fourteen white pyramidal roofs clustered like a three-leaf clover under and around the Katimavik. Visitors began their tour in the Growth of Canada section, where film was used to introduce visitors to Canadian history from the time of exploration to the present. Moving out of the theatre, those visitors then entered the Resources and Energy area, a space "crammed with things to see and touch." A simulated coal mine, a "monster map of Canada" and a "mosaic of geological specimens," among many other things, introduced Canada's raw materials.[46] Moving into the Transportation and Communications area, visitors encountered the computerized control centre of the pavilion and a film on the development of transportation and communications technology. The final area of the display was entitled Changing Times. Here, according to Expo's memorial album, "graphics, films and the printed word involve you in abstract problems – learning, coping with change, handling rights and duties, and understanding the world around us."[47]

How was the visitor to interpret this complicated and diverse array of structures and displays? What, in fact, was the Canada Pavilion trying to say? Visitors walking through the Growth of Canada section and exiting through Changing Times might have had the clearest answer. Canadians, through cooperation and the application of their intelligence, had used technology to master their environment and had created a thriving and prosperous nation where wilderness had once stood. According to an official summary of the pavilion, the story of Canada presented was, in fact, about unity.[48] A brilliant example of consensus history, it mentioned conflict between the British and French only in pre-Confederation days. After 1867, those two groups vanished into a united Canada and were further bonded by such nation-building events as the construction of the railway and the two world wars. (The writers evidently forgot, among other things like the Manitoba schools crisis and the Jesuit's Estates Act, that the world wars had plunged Canada into tensions between English and French Canadians that had threatened to divide the country.) Canada was not presented as a bilingual or bicultural entity but as "a land of compromise" in which "the many worlds of our people ... are held together by the tenuous bonds of nationhood and a common love of liberty."[49] With that positive message behind it, the Changing Times section was far more an enthusiastic call to arms than a foreboding warning of transition. Indicative of the turmoil faced by Canadians in the 1960s, that section noted that Canada was still developing. It asserted, however, that Canadians had the power to solve their problems. A rapid pace of change demanded ongoing education, even while it brought more leisure time. How would Canadians react? "We show you a glimpse of possibilities," another Pavilion publication stated. "But the real possibilities are in you."[50]

The message of Canada's "still-in-development" status dovetailed nicely with the image of youth and education that it presented in its

Children's Creative Centre. The emphasis there was on leaders of the future, not figures from the past. In Canada, the Creative Centre argued, young minds were set free to dream. It was the energy and imagination of youth that would lead the country forward.[51]

Altogether, however, the Canada Pavilion said something more important than any one of its sections alone could imply. Throughout all its varied exhibits, Canada stood before the world as a country filled with the people of many nations and cultures. It did so in sharp contrast to the United States, for example, a country equally diverse in the cultural and ethnic roots of its people. While the United States presented a unified cultural front to the world through its massive installations of pop-art and Americana collectibles, Canada celebrated its now famous "mosaic." [52] In its high-class restaurant, an Inuit theme was joined by "arctic specialties such as iklaluk (Arctic char), Canadian specialties such as buffalo steak, and international cuisine prepared with Canadian foods."[53] The library in the Arts Centre offered books to readers in over twenty-six languages. Canada, in fact, was something of an oddity at Expo 67. It was an international nation.

That explanation of Canada was also prominently displayed in the People Tree. Ascending and descending the internal spiral stairs, the visitor was symbolically introduced to a Canada filled with a diversity of people united by their common roots in Canadian soil. Explaining the tree on behalf of the organizers of the Canada Pavilion, Norbert Lacoste noted that it "represents both our diversity and our unity."[54] The trunk, holding all the diverse pictures together, symbolized how "We link our human communities, our regional groups, our industrial enterprises, our cultural and religious associations." According to Lacoste, the purpose of those organizations and groups was nothing more than "to help establish ties among us in endeavoring to respect our differences."[55] When he went on to describe what the tree highlighted as the four basic problems facing Canada, Lacoste got even more explicit about the planners' desire to see a pluralistic Canada. A "bilingual, free, understanding and tolerant Canada" was, in his mind, "an aim that all men who love Canada have at heart." The "pluralist character of the Canadian culture" was its novelty, he argued.[56] The roots of the People Tree themselves could not have made that message more clear. At the base of the tree, the presentation of Canadian demographics titled Our Ethnic Diversity was significantly translated into French as "pas seulement britannique ou français."[57]

The now quintessential message of Canadian identity, that of unity in diversity, was captured particularly well in the architectural design of the entire forty-five thousand square metres of Canadian space. Though diverse in both form and content, all Canada's displays seemed to huddle around the Katimavik, the "meeting place." There, visitors found themselves rising above their particularities and differences to stand side by side before the world. They did so both figuratively and literally in what was perhaps one of the cleverest architectural metaphors of the fair. Rusted brown, massive, and primitive, the upside-down pyramid beckoned visitors to explore its hidden inner space. One of four flights of stairs on the inside of the structure's corners led them away from the cacophony of faces and voices, colour and line below. Ascending, they spread out, accompanied on the inner surface of the pyramid only by "eerie electronic music," by moving sculptural representations of Time, Navigation, Nature, and Man, and by one another.[58] In that rarefied world adorned only with strange symbols of universal elements of human life, each step up was like a cleansing of particularities, the gradual removal of a mantle of nationality to reveal a universal humanity. On the edge of the meeting place, at the very top, universal human beings, not British or French or Ukrainian ones, stood side by side to survey the dazzling clusters of national pavilions and crowded pathways that constituted the Expo world. From the vantage point of Canada, perhaps, it all melted into one beautiful, diverse, but unified whole.

Canada, its official government pavilion argued, was to be a nation of nations: a community of diverse peoples united by its openness to all cultures, and by its commitment to plurality. Britishness and Frenchness, for all intents and purposes, were gone, replaced by a type of internationalism that proclaimed multiculturalism before Prime Minister Pierre Trudeau did. Exclusivity was out, inclusivity in. Sanitized and sterilized for the world, all Canada's ugly ghosts of disunity and dissent were deeply buried in the closet.

With them went the old Canada that had reserved a privileged public place for Christianity. In the representation of Canada at Expo 67, as in the broader Centennial celebrations, religion was present in an interfaith form. In the shadows of the Katimavik stood one other Canadian display, a structure called the Sanctuary. Officially described as "a simple place for meditation," that structure was decorated in an interfaith, and not a particularly Christian, style; it was simple, with no recognizable symbols of any particular religion. Stained glass windows of abstract designs and a nonfigurative bronze statue, the room's only embellishments, ensured a sense of sacred space, while maintaining its intended universal appeal.[59] That religious chapel in the Canada Pavilion said two important things. First, the Sanctuary joined in with the rest of the Canadian Pavilion to display Canada to Canadians and the world as a country where people of all ethnic and religious backgrounds were equally and fully welcomed into national public life. Canada was interfaith, the religious equivalent of "multicultural." The particular privileging of Christianity in Canadian public life was a thing of the past.

However, the Sanctuary also proclaimed that a *religious* Canada was quite alive. According to Expo's official information manual, it and other Canadian exhibits illustrated "some typical aspects of Canadian life."[60] The planners felt religion to be important enough to Canada and to Canadians to build it directly and very visibly into the structure of their pavilion. They did not have to do so. Designers could have worked religion more quietly into their display of Canadian history, relegating it to a force of the past. They could have worked it into the section Changing Times, relating it to the Christian churches and the tumult of the 1960s. Or they could have ignored it alltogether, as the Soviet pavilion did. Underneath its long sloping roof and within its towering walls of glass, that pavilion was a graphic demonstration of how countries might not portray religion at all. The Soviet pavilion was a monument to the technological and scientific achievements of human life in a communist world without God. Oriented thematically around the concepts of earth, sky and sea, the pavilion demonstrated what the Soviet people had done to use the raw resources of the world "all in the name of man, for the good of man."[61]

The Sanctuary of the Canadian Pavilion stood in stark contrast to the secularism of its Cold War rival. Canadians chose to build a house of worship, a place were citizens could express their faith in the present.[62] The fact that they did so said something important about themselves and their country, just as much as the Soviet pavilion said a great deal about its planners' ideals. Religion, the Sanctuary would imply, was still a recognized element of Canadians' lives, not just privately, in the context of their own homes, but publicly, in the context of a world's fair. Canada, the Sanctuary declared, was not Christian, but neither was it completely secular.

The Canada Pavilion at Expo 67, then, offered the same interpretation of Canada to Canadians as the Centennial celebrations themselves tried to portray. Canada was a country that welcomed everyone into full participation in its national life. That image of Canada stood in stark contrast to one much more familiar to many Canadians: the older conception of a Christian, British Canada with a French minority. Like the Centennial celebrations of which it was a part, the Canada Pavilion looked far beyond the old religiously and racially exclusive public symbols and rituals of the country to view a Canada wide-open to the peoples of the world, and united in its diversity.

Intended as an important part of Canada's Centennial year, Expo 67 also had an international purpose and a global perspective that looked far beyond Canada's own borders. Like other such Universal and International Exhibitions, it welcomed the world to its show and was strictly controlled and regulated by the International Bureau of Exhibitions (IBE). Expo 67 was assigned by that body the daunting task of distilling the previous ten years of world history into a powerful and clear theme. The exposition was to be an educational event, a timely chance for people from all over the globe, and not just from Canada, to pause and reflect on where they had come from and where they might be going.

Given Expo 67's uniquely international perspective and specific purpose, it is significant that not only the Canada Pavilion but the entire fair sought to promote greater human harmony and cooperation and promoted interfaith public expressions of religion towards that end. Demonstrating just how important the themes of inclusiveness, national unity, citizen participation, and cooperation were to Canada's cultural and political elites, Expo did not abandon them to fit its international context. Instead, it translated the nation-building and religious themes of the Centennial into language that continued to push away from exclusively Christian Canadian identities and towards the celebration of unity in diversity, though in terms appropriate for a global stage.

That was most evident in the theme around which Expo 67 was built. According to Jean Drapeau, the mayor of Montreal in the Expo years and a key figure in bringing the exposition to Canada, Expo's theme was chosen by representatives from the three levels of government involved in the project. They had gathered on the third Sunday of September 1962 to complete their common application to the IBE for the right to hold the exhibition. Under the pressure of deadlines, they had the afternoon to choose a theme. As Drapeau recalled, all present wished for an idea of universal proportions that would emphasize the centrality of humanity. It was Claude Robillard, then director of planning for the city of Montreal, who coined what would be Expo 67's famous title. "In effect," he suggested, "the theme we are trying to express resembles the title of the St-Exupéry work: *Terre des Hommes*."[63] It was translated into English as Man and His World.

The way that theme was developed into the more specific ideas, structures, and displays of a world's fair confirmed not only the importance of political and cultural elites in the process but also the key concerns and trends of the 1960s themselves. Terre des Hommes/Man and His World was vague, to say the least. That fact no doubt appealed to the government officials, who were desperate for a theme that would give future planners and designers the widest scope for their activity. Expo officials, however, evidently felt the need to give Man and His World more symbolic and descriptive power. As they

considered how to translate the theme into actual structures and exhibits in a world's fair, they gathered some of Canada's most respected
and prestigious intellectuals at the Seigneurry Club at Montebello,
Quebec, in May 1963 and asked them to put flesh on Expo 67's the-
matic skeleton. That meeting included, among others, Alan Jarvis, director of the National Gallery, novelists Hugh MacLennan and
Gabrielle Roy, the geophysicist, J. Tuzo Wilson, and the man who
coined the theme, Montreal city planner Claude Robillard.[64]

Judging by Gabrielle Roy's recollections of the Montebello Conference, that gathering set in place an ideological plan for Expo 67 that
highlighted much that was definitive of that decade: a liberal and
even utopian progressivism and a profoundly social, or human-
centred, worldview. Recalling that event four years later, Gabrielle
Roy indicated that she and her colleagues recognized the intentions
of the IBE for their exposition. Expo 67, they noted, was to be "a kind
of balance sheet of the evolution of the world's peoples at a given moment."[65] She and her colleagues agreed that in the 1960s that balance
sheet amounted to one fundamental idea: human progress through
interdependence and cooperation. In the midst of the discussions of
that weekend, she recalled, it became clear that the first and fundamental point of agreement between those gathered was a faith in
progress. The goal of humanity, they decided together, was "well-
being, progress, evolution, universality, or brotherhood."[66] The theme
Man and His World captured that goal well. In Roy's words, the
theme was the "expression of the merging of efforts coming from
thousands of sources and uniting in the creation of a single vision:
Earth, the creation of man."[67] Roy and her colleagues agreed that
Expo 67's main idea could be boiled down to one phrase, another
from the pen of St Exupéry: "To be a man is to be responsible, to feel
that by placing one's own stone, one contributes to building the
World."[68] What the theme of Man and His World captured for them
were the ideals of the responsible individual working together with
others for the betterment of humanity.

Roy's description of the thoughts of her colleagues at the Montebello
Conference was loaded with the key intellectual themes of the decade.
Progress and reform, again, were first on the list. In the minds of those
gathered on that May weekend, the most powerful point of agreement
about the previous ten years was that it had been a time of development and change – a time of pushing beyond the status quo to "contribute to the building of the world." Their vision for Expo was fueled
by an almost utopian sense of optimism, an optimism well-grounded
in the affluence and rapid technological development of the 1950s and
1960s. In those years, Canadians watched their roads being paved,

more of their neighbours driving cars, and modern new schools being built.[69] In their homes, many in more prosperous areas watched the recent invention of the television, washed their clothes in new automatic clothes washers, and enjoyed new central heating and flush toilets.[70] Fears of hard times were relieved by plentiful jobs, not to mention the development of a government-funded social safety net, including old-age pensions and medicare. Progress and change were the themes of years that seemed to many to be ushering in a new age of efficiency, leisure time, and social security. Able to send rockets into space, human beings could also change their world.

Roy and her colleagues captured the atmosphere of Canada's more prosperous areas well by looking beyond economics to human development – to such things as "brotherhood," "universality," and "human progress." Buried within those terms were the same liberal ideals of inclusivity and tolerance that fueled much of the reformist energy of their day. Howard Brick has recently argued in the American context that if affluence gave people a "faith in progress," it also refocused their attention away from economic concerns to social ones. It did so for both positive and negative reasons. On the one hand, as John Kenneth Galbraith argued in his landmark book, *The Affluent Society* (1958), if North Americans no longer had to worry about having enough, they could now focus their attention on building a better society.[71] Social reformers in the 1960s, Brick has argued, set out to "redefine and enrich democracy, eliminate poverty, enhance popular participation in government, expand opportunities for self-fulfillment, put reason at the helm of public policy, and make flexibility and variation keys to a new order of social roles."[72] In the United States, Lyndon Johnson announced his plans for the Great Society, which would serve "not only the needs of the body … but the desire for beauty and hunger for community."[73] In Canada, Prime Minister Pearson was leading his own social and cultural crusade, not only creating new social programs but paying a great deal of attention to such things as national flags, national identities, and, above all, a spirit of national unity. In North America, grand projects of social engineering such as slum clearance and the building of planned communities were still at their height.[74] Such projects, of which Expo could be seen as a type, have been called by one scholar a 1960s response to "the drive to create a homogeneous environment, a totally modernized space"[75] that could clear away all the tensions of modern life. It was only in that optimistic, affluent, and progressive atmosphere of the 1960s, perhaps, that the idea of building a pristine social environment on a peninsula and two artificial islands in the St Lawrence River could actually become reality.

Although the affluence and rapid institutional and economic growth of the 1950s and 1960s seemed to set people free to recreate their societies, in the eyes of some those trends were also threatening. As big governments, big corporations, and technological innovations like the computer became ever more influential in the affairs of everyday life, some Canadians and Americans began to fear the bureaucratization, automation, and dehumanization of society.[76] The result, in the end, was the same turn to a focus on social needs. Dominated by a note of liberal progressivism and a positive vision of making society more humane, the 1960s were also characterized by more anxious, existential concerns for the autonomy and authenticity of the individual.[77] "Man," in the gendered language of the day, was urged to break out of established moulds, to rethink the status quo, to make society a place where, first and foremost, people could make real choices for themselves and work with others for a better, more humane world.

Here, too, Expo's planners threw their age into bold relief. Building on the writings of St Exupéry, they reflected that author's profound attachment to existentialist thought – to the plight of the individual in the modern "mass age." The vision of the responsible, authentic individual was portrayed well by St Exupéry's stories of lonely pilots heroically facing danger and tragedy high above the earth, all in the name of the common good.[78] "To be a man is to be responsible," he had written, and Roy and her colleagues had seized on the phrase. Translating that vision into the terms of Expo 67, they had created a profoundly humanistic theme; a vision in which "man" would be the centre of attention and in which the creation of a global human community was the end. That meant that the visitor was not to be "just a passive spectator ... but an active participant, in charge of his own destiny amid constant change."[79]

Expo's theme of human cooperation and global unity became corporate law in the CCWE's *General Rules and Regulations*. "One of the prime objects of the Exhibition," those rules declared, "will be to endeavour to attain among men, unity with regard to the human personality."[80] That goal resonated with Pierre Dupuy, a man who had dedicated his life to international diplomacy. The philosophical implications of Man and His World were immediately grasped and celebrated by the new commissioner general when he joined the CCWE in the fall of 1963. Dupuy trumpeted the "growing interdependence of all men and all nations" as "one of the most important developments of our age."[81] "The Montreal Universal and International Exhibition's aim is to provide an explanation of the world we live in to each and every one of its visitors," Dupuy wrote in the exhibition's official guide, "so that they may realize that we are all jointly and severally answerable for and to each other and that what divides men is infinitely less important than that which links them together."[82]

Over thirty years later, when the term "globalization" has become commonplace, Expo 67's emphasis on human interdependence seems somewhat trite, if not boring. In the context of its own day, however, it was quite avant garde and unique in the history of world fairs, its originators claimed with some justification.[83] Other fairs, they argued, had focused not on the human person but on his or her inventions. They celebrated and discussed and popularized what humanity had created, not the essence of humanity itself. The central symbol of the Brussels exhibition of 1958 demonstrated the point. At the centre of that fair was atomic energy, a topic of particular interest in the most chilling period of the Cold War. Accordingly, the symbol of the fair was an atom.[84]

In contrast, the symbol of Expo 67 was a ring of stylized human beings holding hands, a design based on the oldest-known image of a human being.[85] To be sure, Expo 67, like other world fairs, also sought to "embrace the achievements of man, irrespective of his frontiers, and ... show his accomplishments."[86] According to the official memorial album of the exhibition, however, Expo 67 addressed humanity's achievements not in technological isolation, but in a human context.[87] The role of technology was defined by how it served to satisfy the needs of humanity.[88] As Burton Benedict, a scholar of world fairs, has noted, "The Montreal exhibition, perhaps more than any other, injected the social element into virtually every exhibit."[89] The exposition's symbol, explained the minister responsible for Expo 67 to the House of Commons, "gave priority to man over earth, contrary to what is usually done."[90]

With all of the attention of Expo 67 focused on human problems and social concerns, one might wonder if there would be any place for a transcendent or religious element on the Expo grounds. A turn on biblical language, Roy's own description of the Expo theme captured its humanism well: "Earth, the creation of man." In that magic total environment in the middle of the St Lawrence, the world clearly belonged to "Man," not a deity. The individual human being was the active agent on whom the making of a better world relied. Divine beings seemed clearly written out of the picture.

In fact, to the contrary, reflecting the religious elements both of the Centennial celebrations and of the Canada Pavilion, Expo officials explicitly included religion in their plans for the Expo isles. If the *General Rules and Regulations* of the exhibition proclaimed that the theme Man and His World would forward the cause of uniting humanity into a global community, it also declared that it would "embrace the achievements of man, irrespective of his frontiers, and [would] show his accomplishments in the fields of Intellect, Economics, Science, Engineering, Culture and Religion. This Exhibition," it went on, "intends also to show the spiritual and material aspirations of a world in evolution and the general characteristics of the human genius."[91]

As the chief executive officer in charge of Expo 67, in fact, Pierre Dupuy, a Roman Catholic, argued for the value of religion to the fair as vigorously as he argued for Expo's larger theme of human interdependence. He did so because for him the two were inextricably intertwined. Describing himself as a "believer" on one occasion, Dupuy looked upon religion as one of three crucial avenues through which the human race could establish tighter bonds of understanding and a larger sense of togetherness.[92] In a conversation with a fellow Roman Catholic in 1964, Dupuy confided that in his opinion the "forces unificatrices de l'avenir" could be found in religion, political forces for international unification, and the youth of the world.[93] These three forces would play a crucial role in the creation of a more tolerant, peace-filled, and prosperous world. He was determined to have them all clearly represented at Expo 67.

How Dupuy wished religion to be presented on the Expo grounds indicated that religion would be there not to challenge Expo's human focus but to reinforce it. Religion was to be present, not on its own, but as a force for human unity. To that end, Dupuy and his Expo officials knew what they did *not* want to see on Expo's opening day. The previous Universal and International Exhibition, held in Brussels in 1958, had represented religion through a Vatican Pavilion for the Roman Catholic Church and a Protestant pavilion that had housed separate booths for several Protestant denominations. At the New York World's Fair (1964–65) a similar approach had reflected the American reality of denominational pluralism. Alongside the Vatican and Protestant pavilions there had been a separate pavilion presenting the Mormon faith, an evangelical Sermons from Science pavilion, a Billy Graham pavilion hosting ongoing revival services, and displays by the Russian Orthodox Church, the Wycliffe Bible Society, and Christian Science.[94] At both Brussels and New York, religion had not been incorporated into any theme of the fair but had instead come to the fairs simply to present itself. In some cases, such as the Billy Graham pavilion, religion came seeking converts.

Dupuy was determined that this would not be true of religion at Expo 67. Devoted to presenting to the world the most thorough, focused, and extravagant world exposition in history, Dupuy wanted every aspect of Expo 67, including religion, to point to the interdependence and commonality of every human being. The point of religious participation in Expo 67 would be not to advertise one's particular faith over and against that of others but to present the theme of Expo 67 through religious means and through symbolic unity. Religion would not be at Expo for its own sake; it would be at Expo for Expo's sake.

Given the purpose of the world exposition as defined by the International Bureau of Exhibitions, that was as it should have been. The job of such expositions was to present a grand overview of life on the planet in their particular period. They were to provide a metareflection on the state of the world, a perspective from which to stand back and assess all that had happened, was happening, and would happen. In essence, the organizers of Expo 67 were fully within their rights to do everything in their power to ensure that *their* perspective on the world was not challenged on the Expo grounds by any others.

That said, the fact that their rights directly contradicted the historical character of religious systems of belief was an obvious problem. The religions of the world, of course, commonly offered their own grand narrative of humanity – an all-encompassing perspective on and interpretation of the past, present, and future, just as Expo 67 hoped to present. On the Expo site, however, Dupuy determined that the global perspective of the exposition would be the definitive one and would trump that of any religious groups or any nonreligious groups, for that matter, that would be involved. The role of religion would be to stand as a unifying force among human beings. To that end, just as in the Canadian Interfaith Conference and in the Sanctuary, public expressions of religion at Expo were to emphasize things held in common, not things that divided. The historic privileging of Christianity, not just in Canada, but throughout the Western world, was not to be reflected on the magic, modern islands of Expo 67.

How did all these ideas translate into structures and displays that would be visited by some fifty million people over the summer of 1967? How was the goal of furthering a tolerant, inclusive, and unified global community, complete with a presentation of religion, to be imposed on an exposition that would involve over eighty corporations and nations in building their own pavilions and displays?

Past expositions had depended on the building of a central symbol, often massive in size, to dominate the fair physically and to reflect its theme.[95] The Eiffel Tower was the result of the Paris World's Fair in 1889. The Atomium, a massive stainless steel model of an atom with a restaurant in its molecules and conveyor belts in its bonds, was Brussels' central symbol in 1958.[96] Expo 67, however, would be different. The Montebello gathering argued for a number of theme pavilions that would serve as the central point of the fair, both physically and symbolically, and that would serve as the lens through which the private and national exhibitions would be viewed. On the final Expo site, five such pavilions dedicated themselves to one of five subthemes: Man the Explorer, Man the Creator, Man the Producer, Man the Provider, and Man in the Community. At Expo 67, recalled Roy, the theme pavilions, "with consistent emphasis on the idea of human interdependence, would ... form the hub of the great wheel of men and nations."[97]

Expo 67's theme pavilions, unique themselves in the history of world fairs, deftly illustrated their planners' dreams of human progress through greater global interdependence. They also demonstrated an existentialist concern that both progress and development be controlled by individuals empowered to take responsibility for themselves and their world. The Man the Producer pavilion, located in the centre of Île Notre Dame, did this particularly well.[98] An odd, distinctive building composed of massive six-sided, honey-comb-like structures leaning against one another, the pavilion was divided into three sections. The first, entitled Resources for Man, was starkly scientific, displaying and discussing through interactive exhibits such things as coal, the chemical table, and the percentages of various chemicals in various compounds. As the title suggested, however, all the items under discussion were placed in the context of their usefulness to humanity. The second section of the pavilion, Progress, was introduced by the text, "Animals accept their world, Man changes his through machines. Different Machines – a different world. This is progress."[99]

Progress, however, was not presented as something inherently good. For perhaps the first time in a world's fair, Expo's "human centredness" resulted in the explicit questioning of technology in a number of theme pavilions.[100] In a time of rapid social and technological change in which development encouraged both hopes for a better society and fears of a dehumanized one, progress was ambiguous. "The value of progress is relative," the display went on to argue, "and the price you pay for progress is change. Some men feel they pay too much – others feel it's cheap at the price."[101] The automobile, film projectors, the camera, aircraft, industrial machines installed in factories, computers – all were then examined in this ambiguous light. Noting the misuse of machines in ways that had been destructive for people, the pavilion argued that a "machine in itself is not progress. The application of Man's Dreams to human problems is." In keeping with the theme of human interdependence, it also argued that "the benefits of progress are more apparent collectively: As a group, we live more securely – more productively. The ills of progress are more apparent individually: Some of us suffer because of change."[102]

The final section in the pavilion, Man in Control? continued the evaluation of technology based on its usefulness to humanity, as well as the emphasis on the need for human communication and cooperation if humanity was to better itself. In a day of growing automation, the question mark in the title was ominous, but the answer to the question was distinctly positive. "To control his environment, man must understand it," the textual account of the exhibit went on. "To understand, man must observe and find new ways to see, measure and learn the nature of things." None of this could be accomplished, however, without a total human effort. "Man needs all the world's resources, and all his ability to progress in order to control his environment," one aspect of the display argued. "Man's greatest need is the ability to communicate with others, to understand their problems, to exchange information. To control, man must communicate."[103]

As a whole, the Man the Producer pavilion could be seen to carry on a debate on the relationship between technology and humankind. In the end, however, the debate was resolved in a message that was empowering, encouraging, and optimistic. Humanity *was* in control, it argued between the lines. With all the other theme pavilions, Man the Producer showed that the resources for human progress were all at our finger tips. In the end, it was only responsible individuals themselves who could choose to make that progress a reality by guiding technological development in ways beneficial for all. "The impression the visitor receives is that the resources available to man are still abundantly adequate if he will use them with intelligence and understanding. The mood of Man the Producer is therefore of confidence,"[104] stated Expo's official guide. "How we use our power," Man the Producer concluded, "is up to us."[105]

Where did religion fit into that empowering message of cooperation and individual responsibility for a better future? What place did it have in Expo's profoundly humanistic theme? Inside the theme pavilions themselves, religion was nowhere to be found. Elsewhere on the Expo grounds, however, it was to take a prominent place indeed. One of Dupuy's first visits on the day after his appointment as commissioner general was to Cardinal Léger of Montreal. Dupuy wanted to discuss his "désir de voir à l'occasion de l'Expo un immense autel érigé … où à certains moments les catholiques pouvaient avoir une messe un soir à minuit, à d'autres moments les protestants auraient leur culte, à d'autres moments les juifs, etc."[106] In Dupuy's mind, all the religions of the world would be gathered in one religious pavilion on the Expo site, not in individual pavilions of their own. In their common devotion to the divine and in their common call for love of God and neighbour, the religions of the world would testify together to the oneness of humanity. Dupuy hoped that such a pavilion would be placed among the United Nations Pavilion and a Pavilion of Youth. The three primary themes that would unify the world, in Dupuy's opinion, would be clustered together: religion, political forces for international unification, and the youth of the world.

As will be elaborated in the next chapter, it became clear in 1964 that an interfaith pavilion would be impossible in the Canadian context and that an ecumenical Christian pavilion would be the best the CCWE could hope for. Even then, however, Dupuy continued to be an active promoter of religion at the fair, becoming himself the primary negotiator with the Vatican for its involvement in the first Christian pavilion to be built cooperatively by Roman Catholics and Protestants in the history of world's fairs. In those negotiations, Dupuy argued that the ecumenical movement was a key representation of the globalizing trend of the postwar period and an effective means of uniting the Christian churches of the West against a common divisive foe: atheistic communism. Since Expo 67's task was to illustrate the trends of its time, an ecumenical pavilion would be a necessary fixture on the Expo site. The presentation of a strong, united Christianity would be imperative in the face of the communist threat.[107] "Ma récente tournée en divers pays m'a fait sentir que le mode actuel attend beaucoup de l'Occident Chrétien," Dupuy wrote in a draft letter to Cardinal Léger in 1964. "Je sens que l'Expo peut poser des gestes de grande conséquence pour l'avenir. En tant qui commissaire général, je considère le Pavillon de l'Unité comme celui qui répond le mieux au thème général de l'Expo."[108] If one pavilion for all world religions would not work at Expo, Dupuy argued that a unified Christian presence at Expo would still be an important element of the fair. Expo 67, according to Pierre Dupuy, would tell visitors "that what united them was much more fundamental than what divided them."[109] A Christian presence at Expo, he hoped, would say the same.

Significantly, "official" public religion at Expo 67 would therefore serve the same role as it would in the Centennial or in the Canada Pavilion. Leaving its particularities behind, it would work for the benefit of the larger whole. Legitimation, not proselytization, was its raison d'être. At Expo, as in the Centennial, inclusivity and universality, not Christian exclusivity, would be public religion's desired character.

Visitors to Expo 67 invariably connected the exhibition itself with the nation that had given it birth. When they did so, they recognized what Expo 67 and the Canada Pavilion both worked hard to communicate. The concept of Canada itself was being dramatically changed. For international observers, that change represented the transformation of Canada from a drab and colourless nation of the North to a nation full of vitality, dancing on the cutting edge of modernity. Expo 67's "very existence," wrote *Time*, "is a symbol of the vigor and enthusiasm of the Canadians who conceived an impossible idea and made it come true."[110] "The Canadians whose ego, individualism, and sense of personal worth have long suffered in the shadow of the colossus of the south will take a prideful look in the mirror and exclaim: 'We did it!'" wrote the *Washington Post*. On 1 July 1967, *The Economist* of London argued that "the acclaim won by the show on the man-made islands in the St Lawrence may have done more for Canadians' confidence than any other recent event."[111]

For Canada's own, however, Expo 67 was more than an ego boost. "How ... can we ever be the same again?" Peter Newman wrote in the *Toronto Star* on opening day. "This is the greatest thing we have ever done as a nation (including the building of the CPR), and surely the modernization of Canada – of its skyline, of its tastes, its style, its institutions will be dated from this occasion and from the fair ... The more you see of it, the more you're overwhelmed by a feeling that if this is possible, that if this sub-Arctic, self-obsessed country of 20 million people can put on this kind of show, then it can do almost anything."[112] Enraptured by the same spirit after spending four months at the fair, Robert Fulford could only agree. "[F]or Canada and the world," he rhapsodized, "Expo 67 was a revelation," "the greatest birthday party in history," and "for those willing to learn ... an education."[113] Expo 67 seemed to him "to mark the end of Little Canada, a country afraid of its own future, frightened of great plans." "The jewel in Canada's Centennial crown, [it] earned so much publicity that our national image changed." "Expo," Fulford proclaimed, even "changed the meaning of the word 'Canada.'"[114]

In the 1960s, Expo 67's apparent ability to transform Canada's national image was connected with a larger effort to do the same. In the message of the Canada Pavilion, the concerns of the Centennial celebrations found obvious duplication. The theme of Expo 67 as a whole, however, also bore a striking resemblance to the message of "unity in diversity" offered elsewhere in the Centennial year. Planned by the country's cultural and political elites, both the Centennial and Expo appealed for a new united human community based on the toleration of difference and the inclusion of all. To be sure, in its attempt to shift the contemporary focus "from rivalries between nations to the interdependence of men of all nations" and to place emphasis on "the common bonds uniting the peoples of the world rather than on the differences, real or artificial, that tend to separate them," Expo's theme of international cooperation differed from the national focus of the Centennial.[115] That said, however, its emphasis on things held in common was essentially in line with such efforts towards national unity as the B&B Commission, the creation of a new and inclusive national flag, and the Centennial celebrations.

Looking back from a much more disillusioned day, the enthusiasm and vision of Expo planners for a united global humanity unmarked by racial, religious, economic, or political tensions seems hopelessly utopian. Obviously presenting a prescriptive view of the world, it overlooked or downplayed in its own day riots on university campuses, assassinations of key political figures south of the Canadian border, bombs in mailboxes in Quebec, and the Cold War and the Vietnam War. Just as significantly, one could argue, the message of Expo 67 dismissed differences of race, ethnicity, religion, nationality, and class as relatively insignificant aspects of individual identity – aspects that could be celebrated as curiosities but that could not be allowed to stand in the way of the formation of a global human community. It dismissed other metanarratives in order to offer its own.

For that reason, if Expo 67 was transforming understandings of Canada, it would not have an entirely easy time doing so. The public role of religion in that transformation, in particular, was far more complicated and controversial than Dupuy had hoped. As we will see in the following chapter, planners' prescriptive dreams changed when they met Canadian reality. How religion *actually* showed up at Expo 67 can tell us a great deal about how that fair, too, became "contested ground" in its effort to reshape the way religion informed understandings of Canada in the turbulent years of the 1960s.

7

"Should the Government of Canada ...
Decide That All Denominations Must
Cooperate or Unite Before They Can
Be Present at Expo 67?"

Negotiating a Religious Presence
on the Expo Isles

Expo 67 was a dreamland, a magical paradise planned to the smallest detail by organizers anxious to announce to Canadians and to the world a new era of progress and global cooperation. When the gates of Expo 67 opened in April of the Centennial year, however, the Expo reality did not always reflect official plans. The actual presentation of religion on the Expo site, in particular, did not at all seem to resemble the dreams of Expo's CEO, Pierre Dupuy. Instead of one pavilion displaying the common unifying force of world religions, Expo had three pavilions devoted entirely to religion, as well as two less comprehensive displays. Not even the Christians seemed to have been able to get their act together. While the Christian Pavilion attempted to portray a united Christianity to the world at Expo, the presence of another Christian pavilion, Sermons from Science, seemed to suggest that Christian unity was not yet attainable. Furthermore, while Dupuy had hoped to have all world religions together at his exposition, the Pavilion of Judaism offered the only in-depth presentation of a non-Christian religion.[1]

The incongruity between Dupuy's ideal and the final Expo reality suggests something important about what was happening at Expo and, as this study has argued, in Expo's Canadian context: public religion was "contested ground." At Expo 67 a carefully planned attempt to define and shape a particular understanding of "man and his world" was evaluated and sometimes challenged by visitors and participants.

On the one hand, Expo's celebration of a cooperative, pluralistic humanity meshed well with the basic philosophy of the ecumenical movement within some of the mainline churches in the mid-1960s. On the other, dreams of one religious pavilion expressing unity in diversity met significant opposition in a Canadian religious environment marked by Christian dominance and conservative resurgence and by a significant amount of diversity, even within and among Christian churches. Because representatives of world faiths outside Canada were reluctant to build religious pavilions at Expo 67, officials ended up with only one non-Christian religious pavilion: the Pavilion of Judaism, built by the largest non-Christian faith group in Canada.

In order to have their "official" vision presented at all in the uncertain and confusing context of Canada in 1967, Expo officials were forced to improvise, negotiate, and compromise. They worked hard to impose their own message on the religious groups wishing to be involved in Expo 67, all in an effort to ensure that religious presentations would complement, not challenge, the message of Expo 67 as a whole. In the process they had some success. They also met their religious match. If some forms of public religious expression were much more welcome than others at Expo, some were determined to be there, welcome or not.

This chapter will again look through Expo 67 to its larger Canadian context. It will argue that the way religion was publicly represented on the Expo islands sheds light on the way state-sponsored forms of public religion were changing in the mid-1960s and on how Canadians of various religious persuasions responded to the transformation of official public religion from representations of a broad Christianity to those of religious universality.

The problem of translating grandiose dreams into reality was nothing new to Expo 67 or to the history of such expositions.[2] As noted, Expo's planners wanted first and foremost to use the world's fair as an opportunity for education and reflection – a chance to encourage the concept of human interdependence in a global community. To do so, however, they needed to attract attention: ideas had to be translated into entertaining displays. "The first challenge" for Expo planners, Expo's official memorial album rather condescendingly noted, "was to bring [the exposition's] ambitious program to the level of the man in the street."[3]

Translating Dupuy's dreams for a religious presence at Expo into actual buildings and displays was a massive challenge indeed. It began with the first communications between possible exhibitors and the CCWE in early 1963 and quickly dissolved into uncertainty and confusion. Almost immediately after Montreal was declared the home of Expo 67, enthusiastic Canadians of various religious persuasions began to request exhibit space on the New York model for their organizations. Confident that their religious convictions belonged in the public square on the Expo grounds, a group of evangelical businessmen was the first religious body to contact the CCWE in April 1963.[4] A committee from First Church of Christ Scientist in Montreal followed them a month later.[5] A few days after them, the president of the Synagogue Council of Greater Montreal wrote to the CCWE to request a Jewish "chapel" for religious observances at Expo.[6] All requests were well received but were delayed by CCWE personnel. Although Pierre Dupuy had come on board in August of that year, in November, six months after they had received their first request, Expo officials were still apparently without clear direction. They continued to put the Christian Scientists on hold, claiming that the general plan for Expo was still in formation and religion's role in it was still uncertain.[7]

That uncertainty was understandable. The hope for a message of religious unity in diversity put forward by Dupuy after his appointment in August had few contact points with the actual religious situation in Canada, if not around the world. The difficulty Expo officials faced, of course, was that in many respects the faith groups of Canada were far more divided than they were united. It was significant, after all, that the Jewish community and the evangelical businessmen, among others, requested space to present their own particular message to the Expo crowds, not space in a common religious pavilion. Outside the magic Expo isles, as well, diversity and particularity, not unity, were often apparent. At the same time that an endless stream of trucks dumped landfill into the St Lawrence River, Jewish citizens were struggling alongside others, and against significant opposition, to make public education in Ontario "religiously neutral." In the early 1960s, some conservative evangelicals within and outside the mainline denominations criticized the apparent drift of those denominations away from traditional Christian orthodoxy to more liberal points of view. Some of those more comfortable in the "respectable" mainlines dismissed conservative evangelical denominations as insignificant "sects." Tensions between Protestants and Roman Catholics, too, remained palpable in church periodicals and denominational yearbooks, let alone in the effort of some conservative Christian denominations to send missionaries to Roman Catholic Quebec.[8]

Faced with a wide variety of faith groups requesting separate exhibition space at Expo, officials found unexpected salvation in one important religious movement of the 1960s that *did* mesh with their plans: the ecumenical movement towards Christian unity. Planning for Expo began in a period of profound ecumenical fervour in Canada's largest denominations, Protestant and Roman Catholic. In 1963 the Anglican and United Churches were only two years away from issuing a statement of principles on which the organic union of the two churches might be based, while the Roman Catholic Church was one year into its meetings in the Second Vatican Council in Rome. Roman Catholic openness to ecumenical discussion, a result of that council, was of particular importance to Expo 67, being constructed, as it was, in Roman Catholic Quebec. And it was particularly fortunate for the CCWE that the Roman Catholic church in Quebec had influential leaders on the progressive side of the world-wide church in the early 1960s.[9] The church in Canada was making its own steps to develop dialogue with its "separated brethren," steps made particularly visible by Cardinal Léger's appearance at the Protestant and Orthodox World Council of Church's Faith and Order Conference in Montreal in 1963.

The passion for building Christian unity gave Expo officials the break they desperately needed. As in the Canadian Interfaith Conference and the Centennial celebrations, the ecumenical movement had already been laying a foundation of institutional cooperation and raising concern for Christian unity long before the Expo corporation had shown up on the scene. More than that, priests and clergy involved in ecumenical discussions were directly responsible for presenting to Expo what was a radical proposal for their time: the idea of a common Protestant-Roman Catholic pavilion. On 19 November 1963, Irénée Beaubien, a Jesuit priest serving at the newly established Diocesan Ecumenical Centre of Montreal, requested a meeting with the CCWE to discuss the possibility of forming an ecumenical pavilion at Expo 67.[10] Two weeks later, at the meeting, Expo officer Robert Letendre learned that a plan for a cooperative religious pavilion at Expo was farther along than anyone at Expo, including Dupuy, had thought possible.

One of the leading Roman Catholic figures in the ecumenical movement in Canada, Beaubien informed Letendre that since 1958 he and a small number of other Christians from both Protestant denominations and the Roman Catholic Church had been meeting in ecumenical dialogue. They had been ahead of their time in doing so and had therefore proceeded discreetly, even secretly. Their work had born fruit, however, and Beaubien had managed to build an understanding between a small number of Protestants and Roman Catholics in the city of Montreal. After hearing about Expo 67, he had challenged this group with the task of building *one* Christian pavilion for the exhibition that would testify to the unity of the Christian Church and to the "scandal," in his terms, of Christian division. A month before his meeting with Letendre, he had formed a "research committee" with his Protestant and Roman Catholic colleagues. It had met weekly to define a workable concept for an ecumenical pavilion, appropriately named the Pavillon de l'Unité, which it hoped to present to the churches of Canada for their approval. First, however, the committee had informed the CCWE about the idea to get a better sense of what would be involved.[11]

The response of the CCWE was swift and positive. The official report of the meeting argued that the "magnificent" Pavilion of Unity would include Roman Catholics and Protestants under one roof for the first time at a world exposition. It would "become one of the achievements of Expo 67."[12] The day after the meeting, Pierre Dupuy himself expressed his "great pleasure in this important project" and offered to provide the research committee with all of the rights of foreign exhibitors, the most important being free land, to keep their costs low.[13]

The Pavilion of Unity offered Expo officials a way to organize religious participation at the world's fair, but it did so only partially. In the afterglow of the news of the possible Pavilion of Unity at Expo, CCWE personnel, including Dupuy, seemed willing to overlook a key discrepancy between the research committee's vision and their own: the pavilion was to be exclusively Christian in representation. A few months later, however, it became clear that Dupuy's dream of one interfaith pavilion had not vanished. Concern over the solely Christian nature of the Pavilion of Unity seemed to arise after the first formal meeting between the CCWE and officials of the churches involved in the pavilion. The next step in planning the pavilion (until now conceived by local clergymen) involved inviting high-ranking representatives of several Canadian denominations to meet in the Expo offices to discuss their official participation in a common pavilion. Quietly, and with care taken to keep their gathering private, Cardinal Léger of the Roman Catholic Church, an Anglican bishop, an Orthodox bishop, a Baptist representative, a Lutheran representative, a Council of Canadian Churches representative, and the moderator of the United Church met with CCWE officials.[14] Judging from the high rank of the religious representatives, it was an important meeting. It also demonstrated conclusively to the CCWE that no non-Christian groups were involved.[15]

Roughly a month later, Pierre Dupuy himself met with Father Beaubien to discuss the pavilion. While this meeting indicates once again the high level at which religious participation in Expo was being discussed and the personal importance of that participation to the commissioner general, it also left no doubt in Beaubien's mind that Dupuy was not entirely satisfied with the research committee's work. After Beaubien had given him the background to the pavilion and brought him up to date, Dupuy proceeded to lay out his hopes for an interfaith

pavilion that would be able to provide a place of worship and meditation for persons of all religions, not just those of the Christian faith. Indeed, it was important enough to him that he offered to go to the Pope
himself to convince him of the necessity of such a project.[16]

Caught between their dream of a truly interfaith religious pavilion
and the achievable reality of a strictly Christian one, CCWE officials
then sent very confusing messages to the Christian pavilion organizers.
A week after Dupuy's meeting with Beaubien, Pierre de Bellefeuille,
the director of exhibitions, was still sure that Dupuy wanted a "pavillon reunissant toutes les confessions" and not just a Christian pavilion.[17] Dupuy himself, however, had accepted the idea of a strictly
Christian, ecumenical pavilion and even went to Rome on behalf of the
Christian churches of Canada to convince the Vatican to forego its own
pavilion (a tradition of world's fairs) and allow the Canadian churches
to build a Christian pavilion in common.[18] Nearly two months after
that trip to Rome, de Bellefeuille was still fighting the exclusively
Christian nature of the pavilion, and he asked the Pavilion of Unity
board of directors, point blank, if it would consider allowing room for
other religions within their pavilion, because "the religious dimension
of the Fair should be as universal as possible."[19]

The board of directors put an end to the confusion by stating with
some finality that including non-Christian religions was out of the
question. The pavilion would be exclusively Christian and would be
cooperatively built by eight Christian churches: the Roman Catholic
Church, the United Church, the Anglican Church, the Presbyterian
Church, the Canadian Lutheran Council, the Eastern Association of
Churches of the Baptist Convention of Ontario and Quebec, the
Greek Orthodox Church and the Ukrainian Greek Orthodox Church.
The Reverend Paul Gibson, on behalf of the board, offered a two-page
written response that was a concise and gracious apology for the exclusively Christian character of the Pavilion of Unity and that boldly
indicated the limits of the participating churches in their accommodation to a more inclusive, pluralistic presentation of Canadian religion
at Expo. Four points, in particular, were significant. Christian ecumenism, let alone interfaith dialogue, was still too young in Canada,
Gibson argued on behalf of the directors of the Christian pavilion. In
fact, he went on, "Although many Christian leaders are committed to
the ecumenical struggle, there are still large sections of the Christian
population which need to be convinced of its importance."[20] If Canadian Christians were having a hard time accepting greater cooperation between Christian denominations, the argument continued, they
were certainly not ready for such a radical idea as one pavilion for all
religions. The whole ecumenical movement could be jeopardized if it

was "confused by the introduction of extraneous factors, even in the form of other classical religious traditions."

Second, Gibson went on, Christians in Canada still thought of their country in *Christian* terms. While the board of directors of the Christian pavilion assured the CCWE that it respected "your desire for universality in the Exposition," they could only conclude "that the Christian Pavilion must reflect the shape of the Canadian scene to a large degree." And that shape was Christian.

Two of the remaining reasons for Christian exclusivity carried those arguments into the realm of theology. If the members of the Canadian churches still thought of Canada as a Christian nation, they also thought of religious truth as an exclusively Christian possession. Gibson wrote, "we are forced to recognize that Christianity is irrevocably missionary in foundation and in essence ... While we are anxious to cooperate in any meaningful way with men of good will of any religious tradition, we would be less than honest if we gave them the impression that we believe all religious postures to be equal and interchangeable." Besides, Gibson went on, Christians were not the only ones who might be unwilling to express universality in religion. Noting the "radical differences among various religious traditions," the letter suggested that "It is quite possible that some Moslems and Jews would be even more scandalized than Christians" by a common religious pavilion. On the other hand, Gibson expressed the concern that other religious groups such as "some Hindus and Buddhists might misunderstand a premature invitation to cooperation," thinking that the Christians involved were giving up on the exclusive claims of Christ and were now in favour of a more universalist form of religion.[21]

Dupuy's desire for one religious pavilion, Gibson's letter made clear, was simply not realistic for an exposition in Montreal in 1967. The ecumenical movement was too young and too fragile and Canadians remained too exclusively Christian to support such an interfaith venture. De Bellefeuille, perhaps embarrassed by his earlier audacity, accepted that response a month later.[22] Dupuy himself responded to the board's decision much more quickly. Within a few days, he wrote Father Beaubien to confirm, among other things, the board's decision for exclusivity. "Il n'y a pas lieu de devancer l'oeuvre des siécles. Nous nous en tiendrons donc à l'oecuménisme entre chrétiens," he wrote.[23] While reconciled to the Christian nature of the Pavilion of Unity, however, Dupuy made it clear that he was still not giving up on the participation of other religions outside that pavilion.

Attempting to impose a universalistic and inclusive presentation of religion on the Canadian scene, the CCWE, like the Centennial Commission and the CIC, came face to face with a very different cultural and religious reality. The hope of seeing the religions of the world gathered together in one pavilion in a symbolic display of human solidarity matched closely the more national goal of the Centennial's Canadian Interfaith Conference. However, it too was severely restricted and re-structured by the fact that many Christian Canadians were unwilling to view their country in any but a Christian religious context. As a re-sult, the vision of Expo officials, fueled by prescriptive dreams of progress, unity, and harmony, came tumbling down to a much more complicated world of religious difference and particularity.

If an ecumenical Christian pavilion had not been exactly what Dupuy and his Expo officials had wanted, however, they quickly came to terms with the need to compromise. In fact, they did far more than that. From their first meeting with Beaubien in late 1963, they had seen in the priest's proposal something of real significance for their exposition. After it became clear that the Pavilion of Unity, renamed the Christian Pavilion, would be exclusively Christian, their excite-ment and support did not seem to change significantly.

Though the Christian Pavilion was private, sponsored like others by institutions and/or interest groups, the CCWE made sure to set it apart and highlight it whenever it had the chance. The *Expo Digest*, one of several promotional newsletters published by the CCWE, de-voted an entire issue to the Christian Pavilion's official announce-ment of participation and paid a great deal of attention to it thereafter.[24] Thanks to the lobbying of the CCWE on its behalf, the Christian Pavilion was given the status of a national state pavilion by an order-in-council passed by the federal Cabinet. That national sta-tus gave the pavilion organizers exemption from all taxes and a na-tional day, later called Christian Pavilion Day, on 13 May, Pentecost Sunday.[25] In the Expo 67 Edu-Kit, a promotional package offered to teachers in Canadian schools, the Christian Pavilion was the only nonstate or nontheme pavilion profiled.[26] Expo officials spoke of it as "our" pavilion.[27] They gave it the best location, "on one of the busiest thoroughfares of Île Notre-Dame, close to the Expo Express Sta-tion."[28] The favoured pavilion was set next to the United Nations Pa-vilion, on the way to the Canada Pavilion.

The CCWE was so happy with the Christian Pavilion, in fact, that in the fall of 1964, the commissioner general recommended that the board of directors of the CCWE make the board of the Christian Pavilion an of-ficial body within the CCWE itself. Significantly, the recommendation was turned down because of the specifically Christian nature of the pa-vilion, among other things.[29] That decision, however, did not prevent Dupuy and his colleagues from unofficially endowing the organizers of the Christian Pavilion with considerable power and influence well before the pavilion was even a certainty.

After January 1964 – a full two months before national representatives of the Christian churches had even been asked their opinion of a possible Pavilion of Unity – religious organizations inquiring at the CCWE about exhibit space were steered by Expo Corporation personnel in the direction of those planning the pavilion. Not yet more than a small group of local clergymen with an intriguing idea, the research committee was called by Expo personnel the "Christian faith society"[30] and was eventually referred to more consistently as the "Ecumenical Committee."[31] First the Salvation Army, then the Canadian Lutheran Council, then a line of others were asked to contact Father Beaubien and his colleagues to discuss participation in Expo 67.[32] In February 1965, CCWE officials recommended to their board of directors that the now denominationally approved Christian Pavilion be recognized as the only pavilion presenting Christianity on the Expo site. The board agreed, and the Christian Pavilion was given an official monopoly over Christian expression on the pristine Expo isles.

Those favours demonstrated a number of important things about state-sponsored forms of public religion at Expo 67. To be sure, some privileges were heaped upon the Christian Pavilion simply because it was an astounding first for a world exposition – "one of the achievements of Expo 67."[33] Never before had a pavilion been built cooperatively by Protestants and Roman Catholics, and that fact put the exposition on the cutting edge of its time. The historically unique character of the Christian Pavilion offered the CCWE a chance to distinguish its exhibition from others and a chance to acquire always coveted publicity.

Just as importantly, the message of the pavilion itself promised to forward the theme of the fair in a way that excited Expo planners a great deal. When Expo officials finally came to terms with the fact that Dupuy's ideal of one religious pavilion was simply not tenable in Expo 67's Canadian context, they quickly celebrated the Christian Pavilion as the next best thing. Though not uniting all world religions under one roof, the pavilion would unite all Christian groups and would therefore fit well into Expo's emphasis on commonality, not division. The Christian Pavilion became for Expo officials the best expression of religious solidarity possible, given the circumstances. For that reason, Dupuy considered that pavilion "essential to the success of the World Exhibition in order to give its full meaning to the theme: Man and His World."[34]

Since the full power of the Christian Pavilion's message of cooperation and goodwill depended on it being the *one* united representative of Christianity at the exposition, the CCWE eventually granted the pavilion a monopoly on Christian expression. All requests for Christian participation were channelled through the Christian Pavilion, allowing it to absorb as many faith groups as possible and to avoid having competing Christian voices on the Expo site. The CCWE did its best to discourage those religious groups refusing to join the Christian Pavilion from having a separate presence at Expo 67. For the Christian Pavilion and for the CCWE, a monopoly on Christian religious expression at the fair was deemed fundamental to their success.

Something more subtle and less altruistic was also going on here, however. Much to the relief of Expo officials, the Christian Pavilion gave them a convenient way of dealing with the thorny issue of religious diversity on the Expo isles. Faced with a diverse number of religious groups seeking the chance to present their own public message at Expo, the CCWE saw the Christian Pavilion as an effective way of ensuring that only those Christian groups willing to endorse the Expo theme would be allowed on the site. It was the same Canadian dilemma that CBC officials had faced years earlier when regulating religion on public radio and that the Centennial Commission had faced in trying to inspire religious celebrations in 1967.

Expo officials solved the dilemma the same way. From day one, in fact, the Christian Pavilion became for them an arm's-length regulatory body to which they could refer all requests by Christian groups for representation at Expo 67. When faith groups applied for participation, they were first asked to enter negotiations with the organizers of the Christian Pavilion. If groups did not want to join the Christian Pavilion, it was hoped, they would give up and go away. Their inability to participate in Expo would then be their own choice. Using the Christian Pavilion as a screen, the Expo corporation could sift out unwanted religious presentations while avoiding charges of religious discrimination.

For the most part, that approach worked. Sent to talk with the organizers of the Christian Pavilion, some groups joined them, others did not.[35] The Salvation Army said no to the Christian Pavilion and was delayed and stalled for two and a half years before being squeezed by the Expo Corporation into funding medical stations.[36] The Prairie Bible Institute, a conservative evangelical school focused on missions and evangelism, wanted a booth of its own, did not want to join the Christian Pavilion, and gave up.[37] The Mormons, after being referred to the Christian Pavilion twice, also apparently decided to just throw in the towel.[38] So too did the Seventh Day Adventists.[39]

And so too did Billy Graham. Graham's story, in fact, demonstrates particularly well the importance of the Christian Pavilion to the

CCWE and bears a closer look. When it first approached the CCWE in August 1964 to ask for exhibition space at Expo 67, the Billy Graham Association did not get very clear answers. The Expo Corporation was looking into a possible "Ecumenical Pavilion," it was told, but no decision had yet been made on an official policy for religious participation in the exposition. Pierre Dupuy would be deciding the issue in December of that year, and at that point, the CCWE would provide more information.[40]

Shortly after that meeting, however, a number of hand-written internal memos revealed a very different response to the Graham Association's request. A Billy Graham pavilion at Expo 67? No, said Pierre de Bellefeuille, director of exhibitions.[41] Within a week (and not exactly the four months the CCWE had predicted) the final message came down in the negative from Dupuy, the commissioner general himself.[42]

Why the quick and negative response? Though the protection of the ecumenical Pavilion of Unity was obviously a factor, a clear note of religious discrimination was revealed in the internal memos that were passed between the highest rungs of the Expo Corporation. The day after first contact, the director of exhibitions set the tone. He categorically opposed a Billy Graham pavilion because the CCWE had already accepted "le projet d'un pavillon de l'unité chrétienne qui sera préparé par des représentants sérieux de religion sérieuse."[43] The latter words were suggestive. By indicating a respect for the "serious" religion of the Christian Pavilion, he clearly placed Graham's more evangelical brand of faith on a lower level of religious sophistication. For that reason, among others, he heartily approved of using "une tactique dilatoire" with the Graham association.[44] Furthermore, when the time would come to say no to Graham, he thought that "nous n'avons rien à perdre même si Graham veut faire des histoires. Nous pourrons lui répondre que grâce à notre Comité Oecuménique nous avons déjà choisi le Christ."[45] Among other things, de Bellefeuille's tongue-in-cheek remark indicated just how useful the Christian Pavilion could be to the CCWE.

In the months that followed, de Bellefeuille's sarcastic suggestion that the Christian Pavilion gave them an easy way out of the Graham dilemma became prophetic. Though the CCWE kept trying to stall the Graham Association, the association was persistent. At the next meeting of the two organizations in November of 1964, Robert Letendre, in the words of his own report, "made it quite clear ... that all churches and sects would be grouped together in the same pavilion and that there was no question of any separate pavilion dealing with Christianity being entertained. This was corporation policy, and he saw no reason why it should be changed."[46] He then suggested that the Graham

Association might try to work through the Christian Pavilion, but Graham's representatives insisted that they wished to apply for their own space, in spite of the CCWE's apparent religious policy.

Sure enough, in January of 1965, Leighton Ford of the Graham Association wrote a letter to the CCWE in which he explained that the association would not join the Christian Pavilion and that it was now formally applying for its own exhibition space. "I believe that the literally hundreds of thousands of our Canadian friends and supporters, both inside and outside the churches, would be deeply grateful to have this exhibit as part of Expo 67," Ford wrote, obviously well aware of the weight his organization carried.[47] Following the now well-established pattern, the Graham Association application went straight to the top of the CCWE. Robert Shaw, the deputy commissioner general and second in command at Expo, was given the very sensitive task of writing the letter containing the negative response to the Graham Association.[48]

All of this changed, however, when Expo's general manager, Andrew Kniewasser, suggested in early March that they stall a little more.[49] Obviously wanting to avoid the possible public relations disaster of a straight "no" directly from the CCWE, Kniewasser fell back again on the Christian Pavilion line of defense. Calculating that the CCWE's policy on favouring the Christian Pavilion had never been formally approved by its board of directors, he now recommended seeking that board approval. "If the Board agrees," Kniewasser concluded, "we then direct Billy Graham to get in touch with the Christian Pavilion, and wish him luck."[50]

In the end, Kniewasser's plan worked. In a letter dated 11 May 1965, Robert Shaw informed the Billy Graham Association that the board of directors of the CCWE had passed the following resolution: "That the Christian Pavilion be and is hereby officially recognized by the Board of Directors of the Corporation as the only pavilion where the Christian Churches may be represented ... That the participation of the Billy Graham Evangelistic Association, be within the general framework of the Christian Pavilion in accordance with the criteria established by the Director's Committee of the Christian Pavilion and with the rules and regulations decreed by the said Committee."[51] The Billy Graham Association finally gave up.

The association's illuminating story, however, did not end there. After reading in an issue of the CCWE publication *Expo Digest*, that the Christian Pavilion would be the only Christian presence allowed on the Expo grounds and that the "corporation would decline [any other] offer because it would destroy the very purpose of the Christian Pavilion," the executive secretary of the Mennonite Central Committee (mcc), J.M. Klassen, wrote directly to the Honourable Mitchell Sharp, minister of trade and commerce and the federal cabinet minister responsible for Expo 67. To his well-tuned ears, this decision of the ccwe sounded like nothing less than religious discrimination within a government corporation. With carefully chosen words and in a conciliatory style typical of his denomination, Klassen recognized the appeal of "a single Christian voice at Expo 67," and expressed appreciation for the fact that the Christian Pavilion was open to newcomers.[52] Nonetheless, he went on,

Our concern is the exclusion from Expo 67 of those denominations who do not wish to participate in the Christian Pavilion. Should the government of Canada, or any of its agencies, take it upon themselves to decide that all denominations must cooperate or unite before they can be present at Expo 67? In other words, we feel that our freedom of religion may be threatened if it becomes the prerogative of the government or one of its agencies to decide that only one united church body can be present at Expo 67 and in that way force denominations into relationships or associations which they may not seek voluntary [sic] as a result of their desire to relate, but only as a way of gaining entrance to the Fair.[53]

The Graham Association's story raised others' eyebrows, too. In November 1965, an article in the *Toronto Star* noted that although Billy Graham had a revival pavilion at the New York World's Fair, he would not be present at Expo 67, "because asking for decisions for Christ has been prohibited."[54] One Canadian, Earl Hawkey of Bancroft, Ontario, read that article and was so concerned that he wrote directly to Prime Minister Lester B. Pearson himself. In full, the letter read, "With the millions of dollars being spent in Quebec re-worlds fair I as a Canadian born and raised in the Province of Ontario in a Christian home would like to ask these two questions: 1) Is it true that Billy Graham was refused the privilege to ask for Decisions for Christ as he did at New York World's Fair and therefore will not be participating in Expo 67? 2) If this is true, why?"[55]

The official responses to both men were telling. The response to Klassen, in particular, was a classic example of the politics of damage control. In a letter co-written by the ccwe's general manager, the Honourable Mitchell Sharp simply denied what the *Expo Digest* had clearly said. Christian groups wanting to participate in Expo 67 outside the Christian Pavilion would be given serious and fair consideration by the ccwe, he wrote.[56] The response to Hawkey, on the other hand, simply re-emphasized the importance of the Christian Pavilion as an arm's-length regulatory body of the Expo corporation. The prime minister's office sent Hawkey's letter to the minister of trade and commerce, who passed it on to the general manager of the Expo Corporation, who in turn passed it on to Abbé Martucci of the Christian Pavilion. Eventually, it was the Honourable Robert H. Winters, the new Cabinet minister responsible for Expo 67, who replied. Quoting from the new policy of the CCWE Board of Directors, he indicated that Billy Graham had never applied to be in the Christian Pavilion and therefore had not been rejected.[57]

Regardless of official attempts to sidetrack the issue, Klassen and Hawkey were on to something important. In order to have a presentation of the Christian religion at Expo 67 that fit into the fair's universalistic theme, the Expo corporation had to say no to many Christian organizations and churches who wanted to bring their own particular message to the world's fair. Unwilling to say no to such faith groups itself, the CCWE adopted the practice of stalling, delaying, and continually referring groups back to the Christian Pavilion organization until, it was hoped, frustrated applicants went away. It took time to plan and build a pavilion at Expo, and if delayed long enough, most participants simply had none of that precious commodity left. Christian groups that were not willing to accept a place in the ecumenical Christian Pavilion faced a long, hard road of delay and resistance if they insisted on being at Expo 67. The Christian Pavilion served as a front-line regulating body, and even when groups refused it, it maintained its monopoly, thanks to the hard work and support of the CCWE.

The Christian Pavilion maintained its monopoly on representations of the Christian religion at Expo 67, with the important exception of one other Christian pavilion. Called Sermons from Science, that pavilion boldly called its visitors to conversion to an active, theologically conservative Christian faith – precisely the kind of religious expression that Graham had wished to bring to Expo. While apparently contradicting Expo religious policy, however, the story of the Sermons from Science Pavilion only further demonstrates the point of this chapter: that Expo officials' dreams of religious participation at the fair were out of touch with Canadian religious realities, that the CCWE was therefore forced to discriminate against some forms of religious expression to maintain its goals for Expo, and that the Christian Pavilion helped it do so. Negotiation and compromise, in fact, were at the heart of the relationship between the Expo corporation and the band of conservative Christians who, in the end, managed to outwit them. More than any other, the story of the Sermons from Science pavilion demonstrates just how difficult it was to limit public expressions of religion at Expo 67 to voices willing to endorse a message of inclusive pluralism.

In the 1960s conservative, evangelisticly minded Christians both within and outside the mainline denominations were attempting to gain a more visible place in Canadian public life. Discouraged and frustrated by the accommodating stance of the mainline churches to the challenges of 1960s, they were stepping into what they felt was a vacuum of orthodox Christianity created by that accommodation. Determined to proclaim and defend a conservative and evangelistic Christian faith that made few adjustments to inclusive and pluralistic ideals, they moved on to the Expo site, too.

The story of the Sermons from Science organization's relations with Expo began in late 1962 with the small group of English Protestant businessmen in Montreal already mentioned earlier. Led by two determined and energetic men, Stan Mackey and Malcolm Spankie, that group had been formed mostly through contacts made in the local chapter of the Christian Businessman's Association, an organization bringing theologically conservative and conversionistic Christians together at regular lunch hour meetings for prayer and Bible study and to hear speakers.[58] Mackey, Spankie, and their colleagues were committed to sharing with others their passionate conviction that Jesus Christ was the only saviour of humanity, and the idea of presenting that message to the millions expected at Expo seemed a once-in-a-lifetime opportunity too significant to ignore.[59]

Besides, they also had a ready-made program close at hand. The Moody Bible Institute of Chicago had been producing and distributing scientific films with a Christian message for some years. At the upcoming New York World's Fair, those films were going to be presented and then followed by an invitation to Christian conversion. If it could be done there, Spankie and Mackey agreed, it could be done at Expo 67. The concept of the Sermons from Science Pavilion was born, and the Sermons from Science group became the first religious organization to contact the CCWE in April 1963. By June 1964, months before the Christian Pavilion had received a similar reservation, Robert Letendre of the CCWE had reserved lot 4248 for a Sermons from Science pavilion.[60]

As an evangelistic Christian group that had secured a site at Expo 67 without having to join the Christian Pavilion, the Sermons from Science group was the exception that proved the rule. Its quick success, it turned out, was something of a mistake. Three months after Letendre had given the group a lot, his superiors began to question his decision and to put the Sermons from Science group under a very critical light. Interestingly enough, that critical examination was not touched off until the Billy Graham Association raised the possibility of evangelistic Christians seeking conversions on the Expo grounds. After Andrew

Kniewasser, the general manager of the CCWE, had responded in the negative to the Graham Association, he apparently had a closer look at some other possible exhibitors, including the now suspicious-sounding Sermons from Science organization. "What is 'Sermons from Science', lot 4248?," he inquired of Letendre's superior, Pierre de Bellefeuille.[61] If his questioning was not enough, the man at the very top added his own concern. If we are saying no to Graham, Dupuy asked, why have we said yes to Sermons from Science?[62]

Forced to defend his department's decision to grant a lot to the group of evangelical businessmen, de Bellefeuille tried to explain. We have all agreed not to accept as exhibitors "Billy Graham et les autres groupes évangélistes et farfelus," he wrote. The question, then, was whether or not "Sermons from Science appartenait à la même catégorie." In de Bellefeuille's eyes, the answer to that question was yes and no. Although he recognized that the Sermons from Science group was attached to the Moody Bible Institute, an institute that was "patronné par un certain nombre de groupes religieux y compris des organizations évangélistes et farfelus," de Bellefeuille argued that "le travail principal de Sermons from Science consiste à faire réaliser des films et autres présentations de vulgarisation scientifique." He continued, "C'est donc la qualité des films et autres présentations de vulgarisation scientifique de Sermons from Science qui est à mon avis le critère qui en fait un exposant accepta-ble. Il n'est pas question, dans le pavillon de Sermons from Science, de diffuser des sermons évangélistes dans le style de Billy Graham."[63] Ap-parently aware only of the scientific films and not of the evangelistic pitch that was to follow them, Bellefeuille recommended the Sermons from Science Pavilion on scientific grounds.

Bellefeuille's explanation helps clarify the Sermons from Science group's early acceptance at Expo. That group's head start on other re-ligious groups in applying for space at Expo certainly stood in its favour, allowing it unknowingly to take advantage of the early confu-sion over how to include religion at the exhibition. As an organiza-tion of businessmen, not a church or a group of clergy, the Sermons from Science group may also have been more difficult than its ecclesi-astical partners to pin down as religious. Most importantly, however, and as Bellefeuille's recommendation indicated, the group had used the scientific aspect of its program to full advantage.

At ground level, the English-speaking Montreal businessmen who formed the core of the Sermons from Science organization wanted to be present at Expo 67 for one reason only: to convince others that Jesus Christ was their personal saviour, too. Realizing that such prose-lytization was increasingly unpopular outside conservative Christian circles, however, the group had chosen a two-stage program that placed their appeals for conversions behind a legitimately scientific facade. The first stage of the pavilion, a series of accurate and award-winning scientific films and live presentations, was intended to attract visitors who might otherwise avoid an explicitly religious pavilion. At the conclusion of the scientific films, the second stage began.[64] Visitors to the pavilion would hear a brief reference to how the natural order of the universe pointed to God and would then be offered the chance to see another film in the next room that, it was suggested, might change their lives. The pavilion was deliberately designed so that everyone had to exit through this second room, where organizers clearly hoped that some would decide to stay out of curiosity.[65] Ironically for Expo officials, the second film featured Leighton Ford of the Billy Graham Association and a presentation of "four spiritual laws" that, he suggested, could help one to find a personal relationship with Jesus Christ. Religious counselors were available after the second presentation to offer help to anyone who wanted to follow his advice.

In hindsight, then, de Bellefeuille and Letendre had been taken in by one of the oldest and most well-worn strategies of North American conservative evangelical Protestants. As Kevin Kee has recently argued in the Canadian context, conservative evangelicals have long been adept at updating their means of communication in order to present what they consider to be an unchanging and timeless message.[66] Sometimes carefully picking up on key aspects of their cultural context, at other times quite unconciously adopting them, evangelicals have been quick to use everything from Broadway musicals to radio to television to attract a listening crowd. The Sermons from Science group, too, effectively accommodated its medium to fit the contemporary culture. Playing on one of the most powerful themes of the exposition and of their day, the Sermons from Science group brilliantly packaged its evangelistic message in a sophisticated scientific box.

It did so because it was well aware that its evangelistic approach to faith was not the best way to sell its bid for participation in Expo. By the 1960s conservative evangelicals had learned through long experience that traditional calls for individual conversion to Jesus Christ were not always looked upon favourably among political and cultural elites, including many in Canada's mainline Protestant and Roman Catholic denominations. Their focus on individual conversion and their conservative beliefs had had them derogatively labelled as sects and dismissed to the corners of public life and culture, particularly in Quebec. Roman Catholics had resented the efforts of conservative denominations to convert them to evangelical Protestantism – efforts that bluntly declared that Roman Catholicism was a false faith. Quite predictably, in

the overwhelmingly Roman Catholic province of Quebec, conservative
evangelical Protestants had traditionally been given a hard time. They
had faced restrictions on their public activities in some communities.[67]
French Protestants, largely evangelicals, had been restricted from airtime
on the French-language CBC network.[68] In the 1950s, Jean Hamelin has
argued, the Roman Catholic Church in Quebec continued to view Protestantism as "un 'péril constant.'"[69] Placed in that light, the peculiar silence of Sermons from Science planners about the second portion of
their program and the highlighting of the scientific films was a natural
and astute response to what was potentially a hostile situation.

As de Bellefeuille argued, the scientific aspect of the Sermons from
Science Pavilion was the key to its acceptance at Expo 67.[70] When the
CCWE had a closer look inside that box in the wake of Billy Graham's
application, however, the real nature of the evangelical businessmen's
plans became more apparent. Not surprisingly, given their response to
the Graham Association, CCWE officials did not like what they saw.
Even though the Sermons from Science group had already been formally approved and given a lot number on the site, Expo officials fell
back on their usual plan: they sent the pavilion organizers to discuss
cooperation with the Christian Pavilion board of directors.[71] The Sermons from Science group had already done so, however, and the process had been futile. Almost three months earlier, after nearly five
months of discussions, the representatives of the Christian Pavilion
had reluctantly agreed that the two programs could not be merged,
had wished the Sermons from Science group well, and had expressed
their desire to at least maintain the appearance of Christian unity by
continual close contact between the two pavilions.[72] The Sermons from
Science group was determined to reach non-Christians with their message and feared that only Christians would visit the Christian Pavilion.
They wished to attract the fairgoer who might have little interest in the
church, but who might be very interested in scientific entertainment.
Furthermore, their desire to voice a traditional, revivalistic call to conversion to faith in Jesus Christ at Expo grated with some organizers of
the Christian Pavilion, and tensions between conservative, evangelistic
Protestants and Roman Catholics in Quebec no doubt also contributed
to the mutual desire of the two pavilions to remain apart. Sent back to
the Christian Pavilion a second time, the organizers of the Sermons
from Science Pavilion and the Christian Pavilion again agreed that they
should go their separate ways. [73]

Significantly, the CCWE disregarded the approval of the Christian
Pavilion directors and continued to resist the evangelistic group. The
organizers of the Sermons from Science pavilion, however, seemed to
know their opposition all too well. Spreading the message through

the press that they had already received a lot at Expo, the Sermons from Science committee also arranged an impressive meeting of approximately 125 clergy and 50 Christian laymen in Montreal on 17 November 1964.[74] Both moves were designed to rally broad public support for the Sermons from Science Pavilion, not coincidentally making it more controversial for the CCWE to reject it. The use of the press and of public meetings also indicated that the organizers of the pavilion knew that ecumenism and religious inclusivity were the way to the CCWE's heart. Stan Mackey, president of the board of directors of the Sermons from Science Pavilion, made sure to pass on to Robert Letendre a very favourable report of the meeting in which he noted, in particular, that William Bothwell, dean of the Anglican Church in Montreal and a member of the Christian pavilion's board of directors, opened the rally. He also referred to the comments of Dr Stewart Johnson, secretary of the Canadian Bible Society. Johnson "commented on the excellent composition of the meeting noting that nearly every denomination, both Protestant and Roman Catholic, was responsibly present."[75] The more general and inclusive one's religious message and the more popular one's presentation, the Sermons from Science organization evidently understood, the more likely one was to receive the CCWE's favour.

As with the Billy Graham Association's application, the Sermons from Science issue went to the top of the Expo organization in December 1964. Internal memos had made it clear that the "Commissaire général n'est pas du tout convaincu qu'il serait désirable d'accorder un pavillon à cette organisation."[76] After an intense personal interview with the businessmen behind the pavilion, however, Dupuy himself concluded that the group would keep their own separate pavilion. The decision was apparently not to his liking. A report of the meeting noted in frustration "that these people took for granted that his approval had already been obtained."[77] That made it very difficult for Dupuy to take it away. As a later document noted, the CCWE had decided to accept the participation of the Sermons from Science group because it had "committed itself to them prior to the creation of the Christian Pavilion."[78] According to the report of the meeting, it was "now a matter of pacific co-existence until 1968."[79]

That conclusion was optimistic. Expo officials were working hard to present a message of religious universality and human solidarity – trying to focus attention on what people held in common, not what divided them – and they had no qualms about discouraging groups who they feared would undo their dreams. In a letter to Stan Mackey in March 1965, de Bellefeuille laid out what he considered to be the CCWE's official position with regard to expressions of Christian faith at Expo. The letter had been carefully crafted with critical comment from several CCWE staff, and various drafts revealed its intention to place "a condition" on the participation of the Sermons from Science organization: that it focus on science and leave its efforts to evangelize at the Expo gates. "May I … stress a very important point," de Bellefeuille wrote. "In view of the importance to us of a project with which you are familiar, the Christian Pavilion, we have formulated a policy whereby we will not allow the separate participation of Christian churches and organizations in pavilions of their own. We feel that such separate participation would not be in keeping with the spirit of unity which inspired the decision to proceed with the Christian Pavilion." It followed that the agreement to allow a Sermons from Science Pavilion at Expo 67, he went on, "presupposes an undertaking on your part that there will be no proselytizing in your pavilion and that your presentation will be restricted to exhibits on science."[80] He asked the Sermons from Science organizers, rather naively, to keep their religion to themselves.

Earl Hawkey and the *Toronto Star* were both right, but to the Sermons from Science group, that did not much matter. Bellefeuille's ban on proselytization was completely ignored, and official plans for the public expression of religion on the Expo isles were visibly contradicted. Faced with a wide range of Christian groups with particular Christian visions, Expo officials simply made the best of the situation. Celebrating the Christian Pavilion as an able religious expression of the Expo theme, they also used it to screen out religious expressions that they deemed inappropriate for Expo's public space. Compromise, negotiation, and confusion were the predictable result when noble dreams of unity and cooperation met a more conflicted Canadian reality.

The presence of three non-Christian religions at Expo 67 is a further reminder that Dupuy's original plans for religious universality were negotiated, compromised, and modified to fit their much less utopian Canadian context. Though Dupuy and the CCWE were willing to let their hopes for a single religious pavilion die in the summer of 1964, it was obvious before, during, and after that summer that they continued to work towards having all the major world religions represented at Expo. Wanting Expo 67 to display to the world the growth of a truly global community and the increasing commonality of human experience, the officials of the CCWE considered it of great importance to have more than just Christianity represented on the Expo grounds.

That concern went well beyond even the commissioner general himself. In July 1964, Michael McCabe, executive assistant to the minister of trade and commerce responsible for Expo 67, wrote to the CCWE to express his minister's concern about the need to have religious representation beyond the Christian faith at Expo 67.[81] Coming so quickly after the CCWE's acceptance of the Christian Pavilion, that concern suggests that the minister, Mitchell Sharp, had heard of that acceptance and was not entirely pleased.[82] Andrew Kniewasser tried to assure him that things were under control in a response that succinctly highlighted the importance of religious participation to the CCWE, the usefulness of the Christian Pavilion as an arm's-length body, and the continued importance of a message of religious universality. "This project is being handled personally by our Commissioner General, Pierre Dupuy," he wrote, "as it is by its very nature an extremely delicate and complex project." He went on to distance the CCWE from the Christian Pavilion by explaining that it was being organized by an unofficial committee (true in 1964). Finally, he reproduced for the minister the pavilion's own reasons for its exclusively Christian character. "However," he assured McCabe, "Mr Dupuy is very concerned for these other denominations to hold religious services on the exhibition site and elsewhere in the Montreal area. As an indication of Mr Dupuy's concern, he intends to visit the King of Morocco, one of the Moslem spiritual leaders, sometime this coming Fall."[83] McCabe's confidential reply only two weeks later indicated the depth of the minister's concern by pushing again for a Jewish presence on the Expo site.[84] Not only was Dupuy personally convinced of the necessity of a broad representation of religions at Expo 67, the CCWE now also had the federal minister responsible for Expo 67 forcefully declaring his own desire for the same.

In the end, Judaism did find representation at Expo 67. The Pavilion of Judaism, positioned close to the Sermons from Science building, housed a Jewish Chapel, a collection of Judaica, and a lower level reserved for lectures and art exhibits. And Dupuy did in fact consult the Sultan of Morocco that fall. Using Moroccan friends and acquaintances from his years in foreign diplomacy, Dupuy invested himself heavily in twisting the Sultan's arm, specifically requesting that he build not just a Moroccan national pavilion, but an Islamic mosque. For the mosque Morocco substituted a minaret at its pavilion's door.[85] Dupuy also went after a representation of Buddhism, first trying to convince Buddhist authorities in Colombo to find a way of being present at Expo and then, when rejected there, going after Thailand for the same. Thailand responded well, building an exact replica of an eighteenth-century Buddhist temple outside its national pavilion.[86]

Like the Christian Pavilion, none of these contributions was exactly what Dupuy had wanted. Instead of one religious building he now had two Christian exhibits and three exhibits of other world religions. Furthermore, while the Pavilion of Judaism managed to present the Jewish faith on a scale that made it a noted addition to the exposition, the Islamic and Buddhist presentations were both small and relatively low in profile, both more sidelines to national pavilions than presentations of a world religion in their own right. The Buddhist temple was more of an historic exhibit than an account of Buddhism's vitality in the present, while the minaret was more an architectural symbol than an in-depth account of the Islamic faith.[87]

For these reasons, perhaps, commentators on religion at Expo often noted the two Christian pavilions and the Pavilion of Judaism but overlooked the Buddhist temple and the minaret. Nonetheless, Dupuy wrote, the three presentations of other world religions made him "very happy." "Car il ne me suffirait pas d'avoir obtenu le pavillon chrétien," he argued, "il fallait que les autres religions puissent, elles aussi, faire connaître le rôle qu'elles jouaient dans la solidarité spirituelle entre les hommes."[88] The Moroccan minaret was considered the addition of "une autre religion au dénominateur commun des forces spirituelles."[89]

Though any details of the conversations between Dupuy and representatives of non-Christian religions remain unknown, the absence of such faiths as Hinduism and the development of the presentations of Judaism, Islam, and Buddhism is important to note. They indicate that having the major religions of the world present at the exposition was perhaps more important to Dupuy than to the representatives of the religions themselves. The three representations of non-Christian faiths at Expo also confirm how unrealistic dreams of one religious pavilion were. While Jews, Muslims, and Buddhists could have joined together in one pavilion even without the Christians, they too rejected Dupuy's hoped-for symbol of religious unity.

Just as importantly, the presence or absence of non-Christian faiths at Expo 67 says something significant about the Canadian religious context in the 1960s. While the Christian Pavilion was presented at Expo 67 entirely by Canadians, Dupuy had to go outside the country to seek representation of Islam and Buddhism. Canadian Muslims and Buddhists were just not present in the early 1960s in enough numbers and were not laden with enough wealth to make sure that their faiths were represented. The Christians in Canada were quite right, of course, in arguing that Canada was still overwhelmingly populated and led by those at least associated with the Christian faith.[90]

In the same vein, a look at the Pavilion of Judaism tells us something about the Canadian Jewish community and, more specifically, the Jewish community in Montreal. If the presentation of the religious aspect of Judaism had been left up to interests outside of Canada, the story of the Pavilion of Judaism shows, the Jewish religion would not have been represented at Expo 67 to the same degree. Israel, it became clear already in 1964, was going to be present at the exposition with a national pavilion. That pavilion, however, would emphasize the development of the state of Israel, and focus on the historic struggle of Jews to reclaim their Holy Land.[91] A specific presentation of the Jewish religion would not find a place within it.

With the federal cabinet minister responsible for the CCWE urging that the Jewish religion be represented at Expo 67 and with Israel itself unwilling to help, Robert Shaw, the deputy commissioner general and second in command at Expo, wrote to the Canadian Jewish Congress in July 1965 to ask that they head up a Jewish pavilion on the Expo site.[92] The congress had already been negotiating since 1964 with the Israeli government to gain the concession of a kosher restaurant in the bottom of the state pavilion. By November 1965 (with little more than a year and a half to go before the gates of Expo 67 opened for its first visitors), the congress pledged nonfinancial support for the building of a separate pavilion dedicated to the Jewish faith. By the summer of 1966, an arm's-length body, the Foundation of Judaism, had been organized to plan and implement the project.[93]

The presence of the Pavilion of Judaism at Expo, then, says as much about the Jewish community in Canada as the foreign backing of a minaret says about the Canadian Muslim community. On a basic level, the pavilion was a testimony to the size, strength, and confidence of the Jewish population in Canada and, more particularly, in Montreal, by the early 1960s.[94] Comprising only 1.4 percent of the population in 1961, the Jewish community was nonetheless the largest by far of any non-Christian religious group in Canada.[95] It had also become well-enough established to afford the three-hundred-thousand-dollar cost of the pavilion.[96] While the pavilion organizers claimed that the Pavilion of Judaism was "a contribution of the Jewish communities in Canada made possible through voluntary gifts gathered from across the country,"[97] a significant portion of that money came from Montreal and, more specifically, from a number of very wealthy individuals, such as Montreal Jewish businessman, Sam Steinberg.[98] Still, unlike the other major religions of the world, Judaism was presented at Expo 67 by Canadians because Jews in Canada had the resources, financial and otherwise, to make sure that it was not forgotten.

The final religious scene at Expo 67, then, appeared to be a far cry from Dupuy's original hope for one religious pavilion. In spite of the CCWE's best efforts to translate that dream into reality, it had no choice but to settle instead for two Christian pavilions, a Pavilion of Judaism, a reproduction of a Buddhist temple, and an Islamic minaret. Faced with the diversity of Christian belief in Canada and the determination of evangelistic Christians to present their gospel to the world, the Expo corporation had stalled and delayed while it sought a way to forward its own religious message without being charged with religious discrimination. Other world religions, on the other hand, were sought-after entities in that pluralistic and inclusive world on the Expo isles.

Ironically, in fact, the quest of Dupuy and his colleagues for an inclusive presentation of religion at Expo 67 was itself exclusive of faith groups, like the Billy Graham Association, who chose to emphasize the particularities of their own religious perspectives, not what they held in common with others. The CCWE welcomed one particular religious message to the public square on the Expo grounds: the urging of goodwill and cooperation among human beings world-wide. As in the Centennial and the Canadian Interfaith Conference, that perspective was not shared by all Canadians. Many remained immersed in a much more varied, distinctive and potentially exclusive Canadian religious reality – a reality not entirely welcome at Expo 67.

8

The Christian Pavilion, the Sermons from Science Pavilion, and the Pavilion of Judaism:

Varying Constructions of Public Religion in 1967

In the summer of 1967, Expo 67 proclaimed to Canadians and the world a message of hope for a better future. For Canadians, the people who claimed the exhibition as the centre piece of their birthday celebrations, that message was intended to bear particular symbolic power. The magic islands offered to them a sense of pride in their national accomplishment, a sense of coming-of-age in their sophistication, and the hope for a better world in the shape of a country equally welcoming of all ethnic groups and religious creeds. Canada, Expo 67 argued, was a nation of nations, a state that asked its citizens to conform to no more than the ideal of unity in diversity, to emphasize what they held in common, not what held them apart, and to work together to overcome all odds.

Like the broader Centennial celebrations, Expo 67 and its vision of the present and the future had significant implications for religion. In a new inclusive, pluralistic society, the Centennial and Expo implicitly argued, public expressions of religion were officially welcome if they helped to forge unity in diversity by emphasizing things held in common, not things held apart. Like the Centennial celebrations, however, Expo 67 also offered an opportunity for faith groups themselves to present their own expressions of religion to Canadians and to the world.

Having negotiated with the CCWE and having won the chance to be present on the Expo islands, organizers behind the Christian Pavilion, the Sermons from Science Pavilion, and the Pavilion of Judaism went on to bring quite distinct messages to the public, pluralistic world of the Universal and International Exhibition. As public expressions of religion, they necessarily reflected the particular religious and cultural perspectives of their creators, and they can give us another window into the shifting shape of religion in Canada in the 1960s. Understanding their creators, in turn, will help us better understand what the pavilions had to say about unofficial understandings of the way religion should inform Canadian identities and Canadian public life. As we have already seen, Expo officials were not alone in their desire to tell a grand tale that could make sense of the past, present, and future. The pavilions built by faith groups at Expo 67 made it clear that religious messages would not be simply subsumed by the Expo story. The religion they brought to the public in the summer of 1967 would be their own, at times supporting and at times challenging the official perspective of the world's fair.

It was 15 April 1967. A mere two weeks before Expo 67 would open its gates, the finishing touches were being added to the many pavilions and to the landscaping around them. With anticipation close to a fevered pitch, today was the Christian Pavilion's turn for detailed exposure. The planners had arranged a press preview of their shiny new project on the Expo Isles.

Most Canadians with access to a newspaper had seen pictures of the outside of the pavilion before.[1] Compared to most other pavilions, the white stucco and wood structure was small and quite plain. Its only flair was in its dramatic roofline. Shaped like a gigantic checkmark, it began about twenty feet off the ground at the front, angled sharply down into the middle, and then shot high into the air at the rear. A five-feet-high white stucco wall emerged out of the sides of the pavilion and enclosed a front courtyard. The only descriptors on the outside of the pavilion were the simple, rather modest-sized letters Christian Pavilion and a tau cross.[2]

Most Canadians had not, however, seen the interior of the pavilion. Earlier press releases had described it, of course, but their words had done more to raise interest than answer questions. It was clear from the beginning, for example, that the Christian Pavilion would not be what most Canadians might have expected from a group dominated by the mainline Christian churches. It was going to use photographs and film to try to reach the "modern man" with the message of Christianity. Exactly what that would look like, however, remained largely unknown and a matter of some curiosity for many within and outside the supporting churches.

What the reporters gathered together at the white stucco wall experienced that day was something even they were unprepared for. Inside the wall they found themselves in a small garden area where trees grew, where flowers would bloom, and where small spouts of water sent ripples over a tranquil pond.[3] They then left that natural world, entered into the pavilion proper, and were surrounded by blown-up photographs. Photographs of ordinary people in everyday life were everywhere, from floor to ceiling, hung on jungle gyms of steel bars that allowed the reporters to walk in, under, and among them, gazing. The rest of the building, as far as they could tell, was concrete and wood. There was no narrator, no guide, no interpretive signs. The only sound was the regular thump of a human heart.

A sign indicating Zone 2 drew the scattered press people back into a group and down a flight of stairs out of the room of photographs. Above the stairs on the wall, a large collage of more photos rose above them, but this piece was disturbing. Mixed among the images was the larger-than-life upper torso of a woman, her head replaced by an upside-down padlock, an arm emerging from between her breasts. A huge eye stared out from the top middle of the piece, flanked by a body builder's torso in a woman's skirt and a woman with the bodybuilder's legs.

The stairs turned into a ramp, and the reporters continued to descend. By now, the impact of what they were witnessing was beginning to sink in. Still no interpreter. Still no narrative. And most surprising of all, no indication whatsoever that this was a *Christian* pavilion. Nowhere had they yet seen the names of the eight churches involved.[4] Nowhere had they yet even seen a recognizable image of Christianity, heaven, the church, or Jesus.

The tunnel they were now in was completely made of unpainted concrete. More photographs lined the cold and dark gray walls, but like the collage, those photographs, too, were disturbing. Scenes of struggle and pain now began to dominate: children fighting, a darkly shrouded woman walking down a war-torn street, a beggar. The ceiling seemed to get lower, and in this more contracted, hard place, the constant drum of the heart beat seemed to penetrate everything.

At the end of the tunnel was a sparse, bare room furnished with backless benches and a small film screen. The room was dark, still all concrete, and felt tight even with the relatively small group of reporters. When everyone was seated, the film began.[5] The first few scenes were of an amusement park and clips of comedic violence from a Charlie Chaplin film. Following the cue of the silent movies, music and noise replaced narration and voice. The pace of the film slowly sped up, and the combination of image and sound crescendoed to a level that was almost unbearable. The comedy clips turned into real footage of death and destruction from the two world wars, then horrible close-ups of the carnage of the Holocaust. The soundtrack followed with little more than screeching that pierced the ear and wailing notes that pierced the soul. As the images sped up, shots of cars and Barbie dolls and consumer goods sped by. Then, in silence, a flower bloomed in elapsed time, a nuclear mushroom cloud slowly flared, and the flower shrunk back into a shrivelled stalk.

Rising from their seats, the reporters exited the theatre up a flight of stairs and found themselves in Zone 3. A brightly lit, large and spacious room that ran the length of the back half of the pavilion, it was a pleasant change from the horror of Zone 2. Here, too, however, the churches were invisible. Instead of displays of Bibles, of the story of the missionary, or of the churches' impact on Canadian life, the reporters found high cathedral ceilings supported by soaring beams of wood, a few stools to sit on, and five huge twenty-by-fifteen-foot photographs covering the back wall of the pavilion. The soft, soothing sounds of classical music, Charles Ives's *The Unanswered Question*, filled the air. The photographs at first seemed much like those in the first room: a close-up of upturned faces in a crowd, a small white dove descending into an expanse of black, a little girl in a white dress holding a bouquet of flowers and running to a small old cabin in a clearing in the woods. But here, at last, was at least some kind of religious message. Under each photograph was a biblical text. Under the little girl, for example, were the words "Why do you look for me among the dead? I am with you always."[6] Above the exit were the words "The Light still shines in the darkness, and the darkness shall never put it out. He who loves his brother dwells in the Light." And then the reporters were outside, looking across the water at the skyline of Montreal.

In the days after that visit, newspaper headlines said it all. "Christian Pavilion Surprises," said the *Montreal Star*. "SHOCKING: Frankness of Christian Pavilion Astounds Newsmen," shouted the *Ottawa Journal*. The *Toronto Telegram* declared in large, bold print, "Expo's 'Shock' Pavilion."[7] After Expo's opening day, that reaction was affirmed by dozens of other headlines, editorials, and letters to the editor in an impressive array of newspapers and periodicals across the country. Some, of course, were more colourful and interpretive than others. "Blasphemy," read a letter to the editor from a couple in Nova Scotia, while a headline in the *Victoria Colonist* proclaimed that the "Christian Pavilion at Expo Shows All Life As It Is."[8] But the theme of shock and surprise was a consistent one in the life of the Christian Pavilion.

It was entirely appropriate. What the eight churches behind the pavilion had done at Expo was very much out of character. Christians and non-Christians agreed on that point. Instead of displays declaring the influence and importance of the church to Canada and the world, there were photographs of people. Instead of the comfortably status quo, middle-class environment of a mainline church, the Christian Pavilion's bare concrete and wood housed a display of the horrors of humanity. And instead of an explicit declaration that in Jesus the world's problems could be solved, there was only *The Unanswered Question* and some elusive biblical texts loosely associated with photographs.

The most controversial aspects of the pavilion seemed to be the ones for which visitors were most unprepared. The designers had included among the photographs such images as the naked breasts of a go-go dancer and four-letter words on tenement walls.[9] Among others, those two examples of what one church official called "uncensored pornography, obscenities, nudity and blatant vulgarity" offended many.[10] Furthermore, in a culture still unaccustomed to the levels of graphic violence commonly presented in television and film today, the awful images of human death on a mass scale often completely overwhelmed. One reviewer called the film thirteen minutes of "unrelieved horror."[11] Another called the pavilion a "trip to hell and back."[12] "You bet it's depressing," said a pavilion attendant working in Zone 2. "But I don't watch the film anymore. I watch the people ... this show really hits people. This is the pit down here."[13] Reporters and pavilion officials themselves noted that people often emerged from the film dazed, almost stumbling up the stairs. The negative effect was so strong that when some saw the exit sign at the end of Zone 3, they headed straight for the fresh air and space outside.[14]

If the frank and at times brutal reality of the pavilion surprised and shocked many, the shock was magnified by the pavilion's soft sell of its more positive message. The major issue, it turned out, was not only the graphic presentation of an ugly human reality but the refusal to wrap up that reality neatly into a clear Christian solution. It was not that the pavilion intended to leave the visitor in despair. Zone 3, the large, open, brightly lit space under the soaring lines of the rear roof of the pavilion, was intended to be the positive antidote to the despair of Zone 2. The real issue of the pavilion, however, was the means it employed to communicate its message of hope. Again, there were no voice-overs in the pavilion, no narrators or guides to interpret what was being said. Even in Zone 3, where the message of hope was intended to be given, organizers and designers were careful to be as unintrusive in their instruction as possible. The name of Jesus, or even of God, appeared nowhere. The "answers" were there, said the pavilion planners, but the visitor had to be willing to spend time looking for them.

A powerful representation of religion on the Expo grounds, the Christian Pavilion and the controversy it created made very clear the difficult and contested nature of the relationship between Christianity and Canadian public life in the 1960s. The pavilion itself, of course, said a great deal about the churches that built it, and any attempt to understand it will need to start there. On the one hand, the pavilion was another graphic demonstration that in that decade the principles of reform and innovation heavily influenced the eight supporting denominations. It attempted to accommodate the message of Canada's most "respectable" churches to a new modern age, and to do so in a manner that would help place those churches on the intellectual cutting edge of their culture. On the other hand, as will be discussed, it also demonstrated the important divisions within and among the Christian churches of Canada. If it was dominated by a reform-minded mentality, it also revealed that as the historic privileging of Christianity in Canada was increasingly challenged, Canadian Christians were by no means agreed on the way their faith should be expressed in the public life of their nation.

The Christian Pavilion's attempt to reach the Expo visitor reflected the both vigorous and anxious response of Canada's leading denominations to their rapidly changing cultural context. The details of the program and design were planned from the second half of 1965 on, after the organizers had hired a young Montreal artist, Charles Gagnon, to help them. The pavilion's formative months coincided with a period in which the mainline churches of Canada dropped into an unprecedented swirl of controversy and disruption. It was in 1964 and 1965 that the churches were first confronted with an unmistakable decline in everything from finances to membership numbers.[15] Total membership, the number of ordinations and of lay readers, Sunday school attendance, the size of the men's and women's organizations, the number of congregations and the number of clergy serving parishes – all had been rising in the Anglican Church through the 1950s but began to fall for the first time around 1964.[16] The United, Presbyterian, and Roman Catholic Churches did not fare any better.[17] Combined with those disturbing numbers, the mainline denominations faced a wave of open dissent within and outside the churches, a wave epitomized – as we have seen – by Pierre Berton's 1965 publication of *The Comfortable Pew*. As the title of the United Church take-off of the book put it, Berton got the religious sea "boiling hot"[18] with accusations that the mainline denominations were conservative, paternalistic, and authoritarian.[19]

Planned in the midst of the tumult of the mid-1960s, the Christian Pavilion responded to it by drawing on the most current theology and cultural theory of its day. In good existentialist form, the pavilion provoked the individual to confront a harsh reality and then called for a response. Standing between, under, and among the photos in Zone 1, visitors found themselves drawn into a sea of humanity. In Zone 2, that human community was qualified and questioned with devastating impact. Images of violent horror and empty consumption attacked the comfortable status quo, leaving ultimate questions of meaning and purpose in their wake. How was the visitor to respond? Zone 3 provided suggestions, not clear authoritative answers. As Abbé Martucci, the first chairperson of the Christian pavilion claimed, "The aim of our project is to bring about a certain amount of introspection."[20] In response to criticisms of the churches as irrelevant defenders of the status quo, the pavilion offered visitors the church of Pierre Berton's dreams – a church starkly facing reality and a church determined not to preach. Irénée Beaubien proudly argued that the visitor to the pavilion "will be subjected to a sort of infernal experience after which it is totally impossible for anyone to accuse the Christians of ignoring so many sad situations in our time."[21] The whole pavilion, in fact, was a sustained argument in photography and film that the churches *were* relevant. More than that, it declared that the churches were intimately in touch with the deepest questions of life – in the language of those years, that they were "real."

Existential themes, in fact, were woven through another body of contemporary thought that also marked the pavilion: the "new theology," or the thought of the "secular theologians," of the early 1960s. One of the most successful popularizers of the new theology was American theologian Harvey Cox, author of the influential bestseller, *The Secular City* (1965).[22] "The age of the secular city, the epoch whose ethos is quickly spreading into every corner of the globe, is an age of 'no religion at all,'" Cox wrote. Enraptured by modernization in the postwar era, he and others believed that the changes of the previous fifteen to twenty-five years had ushered in nothing less than a new age in which the secularization of daily life was the most important principle. In that new age, Cox approvingly declared, "the gods of traditional religions" no longer had meaning to "modern man."[23] Wrapped up in ancient "supernatural myths and symbols," traditional religions were considered what existentialists called "bad faith" – belief systems that served to protect individuals from reality and to reinforce the status quo. The "death" of those traditional religions meant, in the existentialist language of German war-time theologian Dietrich Bonhoeffer, "man's coming of age."[24] No longer able to put hope and faith in an "other world," individuals would finally have to take responsibility for themselves and focus on improving their own world. What this entailed was not the end of religion. Instead, the religious principles of the past would have to be translated into the secular present. "If we are to understand and communicate with the present age we must learn to love it in its unremitting secularity," Cox argued. "We must learn, as Bonhoeffer said, to speak of God in a secular fashion and find a nonreligious interpretation of biblical concepts. It will do no good to cling to our religious and metaphysical versions of Christianity in the hope that one day religion or metaphysics will once again be back. They are disappearing forever and that means we can now let go and immerse ourselves in the new world of the secular city."[25]

It was in the context of that new theology that the Reverend John O'Brien, chairman of the pavilion's Programme Committee after 1965, noted, on behalf of his colleagues, "We believe that modern man sees himself as self-sufficient; we believe that he is a pragmatist; that he is able to put aside problems which he cannot handle ... in a word he feels he can get along quite well without God."[26] It was in that context, too, that Abbé Martucci agreed. "To speak in a true manner to modern society, the Pavilion must give positive answers to the unbelief and atheism which reject God as being in conflict with research by man," he argued to a meeting of the board of directors. "The pavilion must make clear to all that God is among us and with us, from the beginning of the world to the end, and that man's mission ever is to render more manifest this presence of the living God."[27] The irrelevance of religion and unbelief were the key marks of their age, the pavilion organizers declared. Harbingers of a post-Christian day, those marks were the most important challenges to the Christian churches and to Christian faith.

The attempt of the pavilion to translate the Christian message into the language of "modern man" also reflected Cox's conviction that "modern man" could not be reached in the old ways or by the old expressions of faith. Notably, the language of modern man included a shying away from hierarchical patterns of authority and tried to speak to its culture on what the planners of the pavilion believed to be that culture's own terms. "The Christian Pavilion must be the 'Word of God' for the contemporary world."[28] This was a new secular age, unlike anything the churches had experienced before, and it called for the translation of the Christian faith into the nonreligious language of the "secular city."

The Christian pavilion was a response to that call. Art and film were the secular mediums, and the scarcity of religious texts in the pavilion displayed an aversion to old religious methods of communication. Experimentation with the latest theories and methods of communication, in fact, were at the heart of the pavilion's design, again displaying its organizers' drive to be current and relevant to what they believed was a new modern man and a new age. Charles Gagnon, the young up-and-coming artist in Montreal who designed the pavilion, explicitly connected the project to the work of 1960s communications theorist Marshal McLuhan. "This pavilion is what Marshall McLuhan talks about – total communication," he told reporters. "There is no new technique but, for one of the first times in public, you will see what everyone has been trying to do, or talking about." Making specific reference to the film in Zone 2, he went on to declare, "Like McLuhan... [we] will implant psychological intonations that will make [the visitor] discover what the film is about and what Christianity is about. You will be amazed by its effectiveness."[29] In its use of film, photography, and atmospheric sound, the pavilion attempted to demonstrate the power of visual and audio communication. In the theory of McLuhan, such forms of communication had been lost in the age of the text but rediscovered in the age of television. In the Christian pavilion, the medium was the message, however vague and ill-defined that might be.

All this attention to philosophy, theology, and communications theory indicated a number of important points about the dominant mentality behind the planning of the Christian Pavilion. Most importantly, reform and innovation were the watchwords of the day, not just in religion, and the pavilion made their power clear. That said, understanding better how the pavilion reflected the particular perspectives of its creators can help us better understand how it reflected their view of the public place of religion in Canada's dominant culture. With the public privileging of Christianity on the wane and with the leading cultural trends bearing down on the authoritative, hierarchical, and privileged institutions that had supported it, the most prevalent response in the offices of Canada's mainline Christian denominations was to let all those things go and to find new ways of maintaining influence in Canada's dominant culture. The "servant church" was the way of the future, the establishment church of a Christian Canada a thing of the past. In its nontraditional, nonauthoritative approach to publicly expressing the Christian faith, the pavilion made that clear.

What the Christian Pavilion demonstrated equally well, however, was that the way of the future did not imply an end to public expressions of the Christian faith or a complete renunciation of the historic position of Canada's largest churches among the country's leading cultural and intellectual institutions. Implicitly, the fact that the churches spent over one million dollars to build a pavilion at Expo made both points clear. More subtly, however, in its attention to the latest theologies and communications theory, the pavilion said something important about the goals of its planners and their perception of the visitors they wished to reach. It was constructed by representatives of churches that had had a tremendous influence on the development of the country. Though willing to tone down their preaching to the "modern man," they remained determined to reach that modern man with all the sophistication and intellect they could muster. Having long charged the "sects" with irrelevance in their broader society, Canada's mainline churches were clearly determined not to fall into that same category. They were determined to remain among the leaders of Canadian culture, not to join the followers.

That determination was revealed in the kind of person the Christian pavilion tried to reach. The "modern man" it implicitly appealed to was a thinker, a person who no longer respected hierarchical, authoritative voices and who no longer believed in the immediacy of God in the contemporary world. He was a man unlike men in the past, and to be reached he required new ways of communication. Those ways implicitly assumed a significant degree of education, perception, confident critical thinking, appreciation of the fine arts and, as the use of Charles Ives in Zone 3 suggested, appreciation of classical music. The visitor, the pavilion itself implicitly suggested, did not want to be entertained so much as challenged. Modern man was not into fluff or easy answers. He was a respectable citizen, and one very much in touch with the latest cultural and intellectual trends. In playing to him, the pavilion clearly declared that in becoming "servant churches," the mainline denominations still considered themselves worthy of sophisticated company.

The Christian Pavilion demonstrated a very clear approach to its changing religious and cultural context. Reflecting both the religious ferment and the latest intellectual and theological concepts of the early 1960s, it took it as given that Canada and Canadians no longer held to the Christian faith in the same way as their forbears had done. Just as importantly, it claimed that the secularism of the new age could not be met by the old Christian faith in its old guises and forms. A changing Canada required a changing church and a changing message. If Canada was no longer the Christian country it had once been, the pavilion declared, then the way in which the churches attempted to speak to that Canada had to be fundamentally reconfigured. Keeping in close touch with Canadian culture as they conceived it – remaining relevant – was the key.

If reform and innovation were the dominant notes in the planning of the Christian Pavilion, however, they were not the only ones. A closer look also demonstrates another key theme of this study: that the official shift away from the public privileging of Christianity and towards broader interfaith public expressions of religion left Canadian Christians divided and in conflict about how to respond. The pavilion was ecumenical, of course, and put on an admirable display of unity among the eight churches involved. Behind the scenes and in the press, however, the formation of the pavilion and the response it generated demonstrated that the mainline Christian churches themselves harboured a wide variety of opinions on how Christianity could best be presented in modern Canadian public life.

It is important to note, for example, that in the early years of planning the pavilion, the organizers representing their various Christian churches had found it very difficult to agree on a program. Father Irénée Beaubien's research committee, it may be recalled, had tentatively agreed on the concept of a Pavilion of Unity – a structure that would simply emphasize the growing unity within the Christian churches. When Beaubien's committee members had tried to get their respective denominations to sign on to the project, however, they had found that their concept needed to change. Members of the Roman Catholic hierarchy had insisted that the pavilion shift its attention from ecumenism to evangelism and had suggested that the churches could display their unity through a common expression of the gospel of Jesus Christ.[30] By July 1964, that had become the new thrust of the pavilion, but its organizers had struggled for another year over how to translate the Christian message into a presentation with which all of its eight and very diverse supporting churches could agree.[31] The best they could do was to plan a pavilion with an exhibit area where biblical texts would be illustrated; a chapel where the Bible would be publicly read, where prayers could be offered and where special days of each denomination could be celebrated; an auditorium for special meetings of visiting organizations and for showing films; and a bookroom in which the various denominations could provide information on their churches in the city.[32] Even that plan had not satisfied everyone, however. While some had insisted that the churches be presented as one and not have individual displays, others, like the Lutherans, had continued to push for a chance for each church to reflect its own particular theology and style of worship.[33]

As testimony to the lack of consensus within their ranks, the pavilion organizers had invited tenders in May 1965 from professionals to design the pavilion's interior. It was at this point that Charles Gagnon had come on the scene. Tying into two elements of the earlier plans of 1964, film and art, Gagnon had come up with an image-based program that gave the eight churches a way to avoid their liturgical, doctrinal, and language differences while still presenting a Christian message.[34] For that reason, and not just because of his avant garde style, Gagnon had been given the job.[35] Still, with Gagnon's views now thrown into the mix of opinions, negotiation and compromise had remained necessary. Gagnon's religious convictions were never clearly enunciated, but his plan for the pavilion leaned toward a broad, universalist message, the expression of the conviction, as he put it, that something had to be done about the problems of the world.[36] The church representatives had expressed concern that his plan was not Christian enough and had pushed him to add more explicitly Christian elements.[37] The struggle continued over how exclusively Christian and Christ-centred the pavilion would be.

That struggle was significant enough that in February 1966 the *Toronto Telegram* got wind of the internal tensions of the pavilion organizers and, in particular, the concerns of a priest that the message of Christian salvation was not clear enough in the pavilion.[38] In fact, differences of opinion among the pavilion organizers threatened to scuttle the whole project in March 1967. When the planners themselves had their first walk through the actual exhibit in that month, a number were taken aback by the vagueness of the message – so much so, in fact, that they feared that controversy over the pavilion might damage their denominations. As a result, according to the later reflections of one of the organizers, a number of representatives actually considered pulling their churches out of the project altogether.[39] Some strategic damage control kept everyone in, but the episode made it very clear that agreement among even the planners themselves on how to present a Christian message to a changing world was thin, to say the least.

The different opinions that had to be negotiated within the planning bodies of the pavilion themselves were evident in the way various planners chose to describe it. There were clear indications that the pavilion's vaguely Christian message was considered by some to be an appropriate way to bring religion to a pluralistic and inclusive world's fair. As part of the promotion of the pavilion its deputy commissioner, A.C. Roberts, offered speakers a list of answers to common questions about the pavilion, such as "What will be a visitor's feelings on leaving?" Roberts thought the pavilion would provoke visitors to ask, "Am I my brother's keeper? Does my brother live under these conditions? Is it my concern? If so, what am I doing, and what ought I to do about it?" Roberts went on, "The faithful non-Christian, Jew, Hindu, Buddhist, Mahomeddan should be able to recognize in our presentation of the Christian message the fundamentals of the teaching of his own faith, and ask himself the same questions."[40]

The Christian Pavilion's designer, Charles Gagnon, also thought of the project in broad, and not necessarily Christian, terms. A professional artist commissioned to create a work of art, he was willing to serve his patrons as best he could and arrived at his final plan only after much discussion with the pavilion organizers and only after their final approval.[41] Nonetheless, Gagnon had his own reasons for taking on the project. "I felt I was made to do this job," Gagnon said to a reporter, "because of my concern for the problem (broadly defined by him as the 'lack of seriousness in finding solutions to human problems.') – I'm not pointing my finger but we must begin to think – much more needs to be done in so many fields: housing for instance." As the reporter pointed out to readers, this was a humanist approach to the pavilion that had little to do with Christianity, in particular.[42] A year later, the *Ottawa Citizen* quoted Gagnon as saying that the "pavilion has a message common to all religious denominations, that God is involved in everyday living."[43]

Others involved in planning the pavilion clearly hoped that it would do more than appeal to everyone and encourage visitors to seek solutions to the ills of humanity. They wanted their pavilion to be a distinctly *Christian* pavilion. Roberts' comments above suggest an understanding of Christianity as a universal response to human concerns. Though he hoped members of all faiths could recognize their own principles in the pavilion, he also expressed hope that the "Atheist and Agnostic should be able to say – if that is what Christianity really means, if all that is the true concern of the Christian, then surely there is more in it than I have so far supposed."[44] An advertisement for the pavilion in the May 1967 issue of the national Anglican periodical, the *Canadian Churchman*, captured this perspective well. "Here you'll see how man and God blend in harmony through Christ," it began. "Although no solutions to all the problems of man are offered, an attempt is made to explain how Christ has supplied life's meaning and purpose for millions of people. Imaginative and provocative photography, light and sound are used to tell the majestic story. A story as old as time, told in a manner as new as tomorrow."[45] Horace Boivin, the commissioner general of the pavilion from mid-1966 on, noted the same sentiment in the spring of 1967. "It is our hope that for the Christian and non-Christian alike the experience will bring a realization that it is through Christianity that life takes on purpose and value."[46]

In the end, the Christian Pavilion represented a negotiated compromise between all these hopes and goals. Though experimentation and innovation were most dramatically revealed in the Christian Pavilion, in its final presentation it both affirmed and challenged Expo 67's Man and His World. It affirmed them by agreeing that a new language was needed to reach them, by agreeing that having all the answers was no longer a good thing, and by reflecting, at least on the surface, Expo officials' concern that public expressions of religion should put more emphasis on what was held in common than on doctrinal or religious differences. By doing so, the pavilion fit well into the world's fair. On the other hand, the pavilion explicitly questioned Expo 67's declaration of hope that with more cooperation and more technology, the progress of humanity was assured. Zone 2, especially, demonstrated with horrible impact that technology was not humanity's saviour and that human goodwill alone could not be trusted. The film's final moments, filled with blistering and rapid images of postwar material goods, unforgettably declared their meaninglessness, while the nuclear mushroom cloud declared their end. Human cooperation and technology were in themselves no guarantee of progress, the pavilion stated with blunt force. It was only with divine help that such progress would in fact be attainable, and as the biblical texts in Zone 3 suggested, that divine help was best provided by the Christian God. In the end, an evangelical component remained a part of the pavilion's message. It boldly challenged Expo 67's grand story of the past, future, and present, and trumped it with its own.[47]

After opening day, the many varied responses to the pavilion further captured the dissension and disagreement in Canada about how the churches could best be present in Canadian public life. Notes of controversy came from the very top of the denominations themselves. Bishop Timotheos, head of the Greek Orthodox Church in Canada and the United States, "condemned the absence of Christian symbolism" in the final pavilion, according to an article in the *Ottawa Journal*.[48] "Jesus Christ should be represented by a cross or at least a picture of the Mount of Olives," he stated. Roman Catholic cardinal Léger also noted the vagueness of the pavilion, but he did argue that a message was there. The Very Reverend W.C. Lockhart, moderator of the United Church, carefully stated that "the Christian link is not strongly emphasized."[49]

What did other Canadians, both inside and outside its sponsoring churches think? How visitors interpreted and responded to the Christian Pavilion demonstrated well their own thoughts on the place and role of Christianity in a pluralistic Expo and, beyond that, in a pluralistic Canada. Some, like the officials of the CCWE, read both the churches' refusal to adopt an authoritative, privileged voice and their attempt to speak through the avant garde language of art as an implicit acceptance of pluralism and as a willingness to focus on what all people presumably held in common. Ted Greenslade, of the *Cornwall Standard-Freeholder*, held this point of view. In reviewing the pavilion, he proposed a summation of the Christian faith that would have made traditional Christians squirm but that fit well into a pluralist culture. "If the aim of Christianity is to promote a better world through making man see for himself the error of his ways," he proposed, then the pavilion was "an outstanding success. The most amazing thing about the exhibit," he went on, "is that it does not attempt to cram religion down anyone's throat. Its appeal is universal to all men, no matter what colour, race or creed. A Hindu could go through it and come out a better Hindu, a rabid segregationist could go through and would most likely come out a little more tolerant. No religion or faith is belittled but man's inhumanity to man is vividly portrayed. In this age of Billy Grahams and other proponents of the 'hard sell' method of gaining converts, the Christian Pavilion is refreshing."[50]

Perhaps not coincidentally, the modern, pluralistic aspect of the pavilion's message appealed to those who were already quite comfortable in the new, pluralistic, and post-Christian interpretation of Canadian society. For them, the pavilion represented a big step ahead, a progressive move out of the dark ages of authoritative, moralistic statements and cultural privilege and into the new age of inclusive democracy, self-determination, and a humble, servant church. Church officials pushing for change had no problem seeing the Christian message of the pavilion. Keith Woollard, the director of broadcasting for the United Church of Canada and a director of the Canadian Interfaith Conference, described the pavilion as "a graphic, high-opening, realistic portrayal of a world God loved so much that He sent His Son that it might live, not perish."[51] According to informal surveys of visitors by pavilion staff, the young, those likely to be most in touch with modern trends, also appreciated the pavilion. People over forty-five years of age were confused and often critical of it, officials claimed, while "95–98% of the young people under 30 were positive."[52]

If the young, non-Christians, and sympathetic Christians praised the pavilion, many other Christian Canadians, however, found it a horrible mistake. One of those people, Canon Alvin J. Thomson, rector of St John's Anglican Church in Sudbury, considered the pavilion a "waste" and "the most disappointing thing at Expo" and declared that it had "no Christian message ... no image ... no challenge. The Canadian church has squandered over a million dollars."[53] In fact, many lashed out at the pavilion organizers and the churches in frustration and anger at what they had done with the Christian faith at Expo. The pavilion, they made perfectly clear, looked nothing like the Christian faith they knew and misrepresented what they considered to be the role of the church in Canadian society. "I am convinced that if the Pope should visit the exhibit there will be some TOTAL EXCOMMUNICATIONS for those who have led the Roman Catholic Church into compromise," argued one commentator in the *Toronto Telegram*. The "nondescript and vulgar displays" of the pavilion, in her opinion, were "the antithesis of the Christian message of hope and comfort."[54]

Some of these Canadians expressed contempt and disagreement for what others considered the highlight of the pavilion: its apparent accommodation to an increasingly pluralistic, modern Canada. The pavilion organizers, disgruntled Christians believed, had watered down the Christian faith in order to find a lowest common denominator that all the supporting Christians could support and to find a presentation acceptable at Expo. One unhappy visitor compared the pavilion to a camel, the proverbial result of a committee trying to design a horse. "The members of the committee leaned so far backwards in their efforts to avoid stepping on each other's toes that they all fell flat on their backsides," he charged.[55]

Why the different interpretations? For many, it seems, the pavilion was too difficult to understand. Its vagueness and ambiguity were a common source of concern and frustration. "In my experience," wrote one commentator, it "is the only pavilion that requires a degree in psychology and theology to understand." Unfortunately, that left most visitors in the dark. "Why the guesswork?" he argued. "The designers surely overestimated the public's intelligence, and underestimated their ability to appreciate the simple and beautiful."[56] Zone 3, which was intended to highlight the Christian response to the human condition, was just too abstract and too subtle for most visitors, others also concluded.[57] Its message was aimed high over their heads, and even the editor of the United Church *Observer*, A.C. Forrest, admitted that he did not understand the message of the third part of the pavilion until it was explained to him.[58]

Cardinal Léger of Montreal offered one explanation for the lack of understanding. He emphasized the varying ability of individuals to "read" the new medium of art and film, what Gagnon called "total communication." As Léger himself noted, "My generation visited the pavilion and came away with a deep sense of frustration. But many, many of the young generation, teen-agers, went though the pavilion two, three, five, 10 times."[59] In his opinion, it was the "language of pictures and symbols" that reached the young but that went completely over the heads of the old.

That explanation makes a good deal of sense, but it misses a closely related element that might also explain why the pavilion appealed to the young but frustrated the old. Not only was the lack of clarity in the pavilion's "language" an issue for its guests. The lack of an authoritative message and voice in the pavilion was equally disturbing. When visitors over the age of forty-five approached the pavilion, they anticipated seeing themselves and their churches reflected there.

What they found was not what they knew at all but something radically different. The clear structures, symbols, and beliefs of the churches of the past were traded for the ambiguity of the present. The authority and stability of the institutions they had grown up with were traded for open-ended questions and subtle hints. The world the pavilion was speaking to was, in brief, not their world but the world of the young, visitors more open to change, more flexible in their ideas, and more accustomed to the pluralist and tumultuous nature of urban Canadian life in the 1960s. Again, it was not the medium alone that confused some Canadians but the message as well. While some Canadians were willing to accept a more inclusive and universalistic version of public Christianity called for by the pluralistic world of Expo 67, others responded that such a version of public Christianity was a sell-out, that an authoritative and distinctive Christianity, even if it was exclusive in its claims, remained essential.

What the CCWE trumpeted as a key demonstration of the role religion could play in a new inclusive and pluralistic age, then, was not what many in the churches themselves had desired. The pavilion's message of "love one another," as summarized by Dupuy, or of "human love and the hope of mankind," as a good number of secular newspapers put it, was itself acceptable to many Canadians and Christians, but many wanted more. The *Canadian Mennonite* was closer to the position of more conservative Christians when it translated the words of pavilion officials into more traditional evangelical language in March 1966: "The Christian Pavilion intends to provoke a question mark in the conscience of its visitors and, without coercing them, it will attempt to attract them into the road leading to God through His beloved Son."[60] Christianity, both in public and private, many Canadians continued to implicitly argue, was nothing without a triumphant, positive, and authoritative declaration of the importance of Jesus Christ, whether that excluded somebody or not.

"It is a misnomer to call this pavilion 'Christian,'" declared Rev. Lindsay Howan, president of the Association of Regular Baptist Churches (Canada), after visiting the pavilion. It would be more appropriate, he thought, to name it the "Ecumenical Shock Pagoda." "From start to finish there is not the slightest reference to the Christian message: the gospel of Jesus Christ ... Many people from the denominations supposedly represented in this pavilion have been caused to weep at the apostate condition of churches which would pay for this shocker." If Howan was disgusted by the pavilion, he was relieved that Christianity, in his opinion, was represented elsewhere at Expo. "It was gratifying by contrast to visit the Moody Science Pavilion called 'Sermons

from Science,'" he went on. "The Sermons from Science pavilion does
not promote any particular church but emphasizes the amazing fact:
'The great Creator became my Saviour' – Christ the only answer to
man's sinful condition."[61]

In his perception of the sharp contrast between the Christian Pavilion and the Sermons from Science Pavilion, at least, Howan was
right. For the many Expo visitors who made sure to visit both, the
two pavilions graphically demonstrated that what it meant to be
Christian in Canada in the 1960s was clearly in dispute. Even though
the Sermons from Science Pavilion was only a short walk away from
the Christian Pavilion on Île Notre Dame, it was worlds away in everything from architecture to its medium and message. There was
nothing dramatic about the building. It was white but more industrial looking than the Christian Pavilion. Instead of a sweeping roofline, this one was flat, with a raised, square tower-like structure on
the front right corner bearing its name. Sermons from Science, too,
drew large crowds that blocked the walkway by its door.

Visitors joined the line of people weaving like a large snake through
railings constructed to control the crowd and keep them under an
overhang for protection against sun and rain. Beside the line-up by the
door was an oversized clock indicating the time and a description of
the next show. The wait was made to feel shorter, perhaps, by well-
dressed hosts and hostesses wearing Sermons from Science tags and
handing out literature on their pavilion and the various shows it offered. Visitors gladly left the heat when the doors opened. About three
hundred entered into a large, very modern, comfortable and cool auditorium. Finding a seat, they also found a small headset on the armrest
and a dial beside that. A young man or woman stepped onto the large
stage and informed the now-seated crowd that the show was to begin.
The headsets, they explained in a number of languages, were part of a
state-of-the-art translation system. With a twist of the dial, the fair-goer
could choose to listen to the performance in French, Spanish, or Japa-
nese. The performance would be in English, untranslated.

The shows varied widely. Four times a day, an exhilarating live show
that had rightly earned a good reputation on the Expo grounds would
be presented. Led by Dr George Speake, a scientist employed by the
Moody Institute of Science and an excellent showman, it combined a
sense of humour, folk wisdom, scientific experiments, and some words
from the Bible to argue that those who believed only what they could
hear, see, or touch were hardly being scientific. Science and faith, Speake
argued, were mutually supportive and not hostile. Science, in fact, could
be used to prove the existence of two worlds, one spiritual and one
physical, and to provide ways of understanding how two such worlds

could exist at the same time. His show tried to make his case. It was all about forces, he argued. A human being cannot walk through a wall simply because the forces around the matter in his or her body collide with the forces in the wall. The particles of matter that make up both a human being and the wall are so few and far between, he noted, that they would miss each other and pass through each other if it were not for the forces around them. If those forces could be changed so that they would not collide, a human being could indeed walk through a wall.

To demonstrate this scientifically, he used a number of eye-catching experiments. Forces of nature are already selective, he argued, working on some objects but not others. While some metals are magnetic, others are not. Over the course of his presentation, he had aluminum rings floating in air around a conductor, a glass shattered by sound, and an egg cooked on a plate that was cold to the touch. The grand finale, however, came when he removed his shoes, rings, and watch, took off his jacket, rolled up his shirt sleeves, and stepped onto a conductor. Raising his arms to the sky, he shouted "Lights!," and the room went dark; "Power!" and his muscles tensed as one million volts shot through his body and out of his finger tips in the form of lightning bolts. It was loud, awesome, and stunning. And the message at the end was clear. The electricity was selective; at the right frequency, it could pass through his body without harming him.

Switching now to Christian belief, in the light of all this evidence, Speake argued, the resurrection of Jesus Christ is based on scientific fact, not irrational belief. Jesus left his grave and walked through walls, because his spiritual body was untouched by the forces of our physical world. It was scientifically possible that there could indeed to be two worlds, one spiritual and one physical. If you would like to learn more, Speake suggested at the end, stay for the next film.[62]

When the live show was not on, films were shown. *The Red River of Life* explained how the human circulatory system worked and then used the lessons learned to demonstrate truths from the Bible. *The City of Bees* gave the crowd an inside view of a beehive, explaining the elaborate system of communication and how bees have known much longer than human beings how to maintain a constant temperature in their homes. Where did bees get this knowledge? Only from a master designer. *Dust or Destiny*, using other marvels of nature such as bird migration, pushed the same point. And on went the list. At the end of each film, just as at the end of the live presentation, visitors were welcomed into a second room where they could learn something that might change their lives.[63]

Most of the visitors had not realized there were two parts to this pavilion. The sign outside had only advertised one show. But as they exited through the doors at the front of the auditorium, they found themselves in another room, roughly one-third the size of the last. Some visitors took a seat. Others pushed on down the side of the room to the exit signs at the front, and left. Soon, the screen lit up, and Leighton Ford, brother-in-law of Billy Graham, addressed the crowd. There was no more science now. Ford smoothly launched into a presentation of the Billy Graham Evangelistic Association's "Steps to Peace with God." It was a classic call to conversion, laying out the cause of human pain and suffering (the lack of a close relationship between humanity and its creator, God, due to the Fall of human beings into sin with Adam and Eve in the Garden of Eden) and its solution (Jesus Christ as God-incarnate, who took the punishment for human sin upon himself in order to restore humanity's relationship with God). To be restored to God, Ford contended, one simply had to acknowledge one's sinful human nature, believe in Christ as the saviour of humanity, and accept his sacrifice for the forgiveness of one's sin. Inviting viewers to offer a short prayer for forgiveness of sin and acceptance of Christ's gift, Ford recited such a prayer and then the film was over.[64] Another person ascended the stage and asked all who had made a commitment or who were interested in learning more about Jesus Christ to talk to counsellors standing by in a final room. Some went, some made for the exits. A few minutes later, a new crowd filed in.

For the almost 850,000 Expo visitors who made it into the Sermons from Science Pavilion, it offered a clever and attractive combination of entertainment, showmanship, and religion. With their stunning visual demonstrations and clear popularization of scientific knowledge, the scientific films and program that had won over the CCWE won over the crowds, too. "This Pavilion could be a sleeper but ... NO ONE SLEEPS HERE!" declared a headline in *En Ville: The Business Family Paper*, a Montreal publication.[65] According to the religion editor of the *Toronto Telegram*, the pavilion was "a smash success."[66] "To meet the holiday mood and satisfy the curiosity of people at Expo 67," some of the pavilion's promotional material claimed, "Sermons from Sciences is accurate from a scientific point of view [and] exciting from an entertainment point of view."[67]

The Sermons from Science Pavilion, however, sought to do more than simply entertain. At the press conference announcing the participation of the pavilion in Expo 67, Robert Shaw captured its true intentions well. "It is a Christian lay organization dedicated to the principle that the order to be found in Science and Nature must be under Divine control. It is their objective, by demonstration of the wonders of science, to turn the thoughts of men to Christianity and thus encourage association with the Church."[68] As Keith Price, general manager of the pavilion, stated to Stan Turner of the CCWE, the main auditorium was to display the physical laws of nature, with the argument that they were divinely created. The second part of the pavilion was "designed to show how [those] physical laws ... have spiritual counterparts which we call 'Spiritual Laws.'" "We feel that the interest in the second auditorium will be created whilst the primary audience sits fascinated by the main presentation," he went on. There was no advertisement of the second aspect of the pavilion because "to publicize the nature of this before hand may well defeat our object by causing people to 'miss out' [on] a 'religious' pavilion."[69]

The differences between this pavilion and the Christian Pavilion were stark. The Reverend Howan's acidic judgment, noted above, that the former was Christian and the latter was not was echoed by many other individuals and organizations who held to a conservative and evangelistic interpretation of the Christian faith.[70] They were not the only persons, however, who distinguished between the "truly Christian pavilion" and the pavilion that distorted the Christian faith. As Jacques Quay, of Le Magazine Maclean demonstrated, those favourable to the presentation of the Christian Pavilion could be equally quick to dismiss the Sermons from Science Pavilion. Echoing the same opinions as the CCWE staff noted in the previous chapter, Quay found no comparison between the "magie stupide" of Sermons from Science and the "véritable présence religieuse" of the Christian Pavilion.[71]

Attempts to define the differences between the two pavilions in this manner tended to add more heat than light to the situation. Though conservative and evangelistically minded Christians were often quick to call the Christian Pavilion unchristian and hopeless, the organizers of the pavilion themselves made every effort to use it to communicate the same message as the Sermons from Science pavilion: that the only hope of humanity was in Jesus Christ. In intention, at least, both pavilions were "evangelical"; that is, both attempted to communicate the Christian message of hope in Christ within the context of "man and his world."[72]

The similarities between the goals of the two pavilions were demonstrated, among other things, by the fact that members of the Christian Pavilion's board of directors actually supported the Sermons from Science project. When the Sermons from Science group decided to establish a ministerial council in April 1964, they listed three Christian Pavilion directors,[73] Dr C. Ritchie Bell (Presbyterian), Rev. E.T. Bartch (Lutheran), and Rev. E. Jenkins (Baptist), among a number of ministers who, they hoped, would "strive towards broad involvement of their denominations."[74] The Reverend William Bothwell, dean of the Anglican Cathedral in Montreal and also a member of the Christian Pavilion's board, was a key figure in convincing his colleagues that the Sermons from Science project deserved to be at Expo 67.[75] In late 1964, the Anglican bishop and Dean Bothwell were open to committing themselves and their denomination to the Sermons from Science project but seem to have been limited by their denomination's promise of support for the Christian Pavilion.[76] The Presbyterian Church, too, expressed sympathy for both projects.[77] So did the Baptist Federation of Canada.[78]

That the two pavilions shared a common goal and even common supporters testifies, again, to the diversity within the mainline Christian churches in the 1960s and suggests that the two Christian Pavilions were not either/or options. Some Canadian Christians supported both. The commonalities between the two pavilions, however, do not weaken the fact that they were dramatically different. While the Christian Pavilion was subtle, ambiguous, and even open-ended, the Sermons from Science Pavilion was captivating, then quite blunt and unequivocal. While the Christian Pavilion offered a message that to some was as universally acceptable as "love one another," Sermons from Science made it clear that loving one another was useless in terms of people's eternal destiny if they had not accepted Jesus Christ as their personal saviour. And while the Christian Pavilion used the modern and avant garde technique of "total communication" to reach its visitors, the Sermons from Science pavilion used scientific entertainment as a "hook," then drew on the old and very familiar language of sin and salvation, of making Jesus Christ, the saviour of the world, Lord of your life.

Underlying those differences in presentation, of course, was the artistry and design of Charles Gagnon in the Christian Pavilion and that of the Moody Institute of Science in the Sermons from Science Pavilion. But there were also major differences in cultural and theological interpretation between the two groups of organizers themselves. Again, to understand the religious pavilions at Expo, we need to try to understand the particular positions of the faith groups that built them. In their attempt to reach non-Christians with the Christian message, it seems, both pavilions noted what they saw as a lack of faith in the world around them. They arrived at that position, however, by different routes. Those leading the call for reform in the mainline churches did so in the midst of churches in apparent decline and in response to current intellectual and theological trends. Many of those supporting the Sermons from Science Pavilion came from a different place.

Their pavilion had no official sponsoring churches and received the bulk of its financial support from individuals from a wide array of

churches, including the mainline denominations. What all its supporters shared, however, was the evangelical conviction that many
Canadians, inside and outside their churches, needed to be converted
to Christ. That conviction may have been enhanced by the tumult of
the 1960s, but it by no means depended on it. The Christian Brethren,
the Pentecostal Assemblies of Canada, and the Fellowship of Evangelical Baptist Churches, among others, were strong supporters of the
evangelical pavilion, and those denominations were not in steep decline in the 1960s. The PAOC, as noted, was in fact the fastest-growing
denomination in Canada. Their decision to speak to atheism and unbelief at Expo did not come as much from the practical experience of
decline or from the latest theologies as from the belief that real, truly
converted Christians with true conviction were a minority in this
country. The job of true Christians was simply to save as many of
their neighbours as they could.

Coming from some different places to the conclusion that Canadians needed the Christian faith, the Christian Pavilion and the Sermons from Science Pavilion took that conclusion and ran in very
different directions. Echoing the ideas of the "secular theologians,"
the dominant voices behind the Christian Pavilion decreed that to
reach "modern man," the Christian faith itself would need to be over-
hauled and translated into the language of the secular city. The Sermons from Science Pavilion took a very different approach to the
problem. Throughout the history of the United States, Joel Carpenter
has noted, conservative evangelicals "eagerly assimilated the latest
techniques of mass communication – and beyond that, the idiom and
format of popular entertainment – in order to propogate their old-
time faith."[79] In Canada, they did the same. In the Sermons from Science Pavilion they adapted the means by which they attracted an audience, but they did not attempt to adapt the evangelical Christian
message itself. Whereas the Christian Pavilion looked at the religious
turmoil of the 1960s and decided that Christianity was out of touch –
that it needed a new language to communicate well – the Sermons
from Science Pavilion saw no significant disjunction between the
ideas of the present and the Christian language of the past. Leighton
Ford's appeal for "decisions for Christ" in the last section of the pavilion was scarcely different from the appeals Billy Graham had been
making since the late 1940s. Even more telling, the Bible used by the
Moody films was the King James Version, replete with "thees and
thous," and at times almost unintelligible to the untrained ear. What
the Sermons from Science Pavilion presented to its visitors was, in the
apt description of one reviewer, the "ABC's of Christianity ... through
an old-time evangelistic pitch."[80]

The way the Sermons from Science Pavilion employed science also sent the message that old forms of Christianity were not out of place in the modern world but were perfectly comfortable in it. To speak to its visitor, the pavilion bought into exactly what the Christian Pavilion questioned: the message of human progress through science and technology. It did so subtly, of course, but the message could not have been missed by many. Just the stage itself made the affirmation of science and technology clear. Like so many others at Expo, it awed visitors with its array of panels and switches and lab tables and transformers – all before the one million volts blasted through the room. More importantly, perhaps, the underlying values of Expo's scientific and technological culture were actually employed for the most worthy project of all: to prove the truth of Jesus Christ. While the Christian Pavilion highlighted the worst human applications of science and technology to point to the need for God, Sermons from Science appealed positively to scientific and reasonable fact and pointed through it to Christ. Christianity, it went great lengths to prove, was not out of place at all in our modern world. Christians could be as modern and entertaining as anyone else. Dr George Speake was the perfect example. An intelligent, witty, and entertaining scientist arrayed in a lab coat, he was also an evangelical Christian.

If the Christian Pavilion represented mainline churches determined to maintain their long history of influence and relevancy among Canada's political and cultural leaders, the Sermons from Science Pavilion represented evangelicals relegated since the early twentieth century to the fringes of Canadian culture and largely averse to accommodating their faith to the latest intellectual and theological developments.[81] Existentialism and "secular theology," for example, had no place in the evangelical businessmen's pavilion. In fact, the philosophy and theology that were represented there were not the latest trends, but relatively old ideas; science was used in the same way as it had been used by evangelicals in the 1860s.[82] The presentations used sophisticated machinery and very modern scientific concepts, to be sure. As John Stackhouse has perceptively argued, however, "the pavilion was an odd blend of Enlightenment 'evidences' and the common medieval practice of seeing biblical truths 'played out' in the natural world." It relied upon "the typical evangelical view of the world as being in clear harmony with God's revelation in the Bible."[83] Following long-established apologetic patterns, it used evidence from the natural world of science to attempt to prove the scientific accuracy of such central Christian concepts as the Resurrection of Christ.

If the Sermons from Science Pavilion eschewed the latest intellectual and theological insights, which the Christian Pavilion took very seriously, it also spoke to Canadians not as elites spoke to elites but as average Canadians spoke to their neighbours. Instead of trying to reach an intellectual who valued art as a medium and appreciated subtlety and sophistication, the Sermons from Science Pavilion reached out to someone who wanted a good show and who valued practical language and clear instruction. No new language was needed to send the message, and no university degree was needed to receive it. The Sermons from Science visitor, the pavilion suggested, was a fair-goer looking for fun. If the Christian Pavilion was elitist in its avant garde presentation, the Sermons from Science Pavilion, with its well-worn approach to science and its entertaining program, was far more popular.

Given its reflection of a conservative body of Protestant Christians eager to use the latest technology to present a very traditional Christian call to conversion, the Sermons from Science Pavilion said something important about how its supporters viewed the way religion should be presented publicly in Canada in 1967. While the Christian Pavilion represented the dominance in the mainline churches of reform-minded approaches to the transformation of their cultural context in the 1960s, the Sermons from Science Pavilion represented the belief of many others within and outside those churches that no reform was necessary and that the old evangelistic ways were entirely appropriate in the public life of a pluralistic country. It was the latter approach to public life, it seems, that led the planners of the Sermons from Science Pavilion to confront directly and to refute one of the key ideals of political and cultural elites in their day. Much to the frustration of Expo officials, as noted in the previous chapter, the pavilion refused to downplay the fact that it had *the* Truth, and refused to tone down its conviction that those who did not share its beliefs were wrong. It refused to affirm that in modern Canadian public life, such ideas were impolite, divisive, and best kept behind closed doors. The pavilion did not just challenge people with the message of the "old-time" gospel. It challenged the whole concept held by those planning the Centennial celebrations and Expo 67 of what was considered appropriate in a religiously plural public sphere. Not surprisingly, given the generally dismissive reaction of many in Canada's cultural elite to conservative evangelicals, the Sermons from Science Pavilion got far less media attention than did the more "respectable" Christian Pavilion.[84]

How Expo visitors responded to the Sermons from Science Pavilion can tell us something about how others viewed this conservative, evangelistic expression of religion in such a prominent public location. Often, the same people who rejected the Christian Pavilion's harsh presentation of reality admired the Sermons from Science Pavilion for its clean, modern, and comfortable buildings, for its positive message of the good relationship between science and religion, and for its clear and concise conviction that Christ was the only answer. Compared to the "uncensored pornography, obscenities, nudity and blatant vulgarity" of the Christian Pavilion, the Reverend Lindsay Howan, our earlier commentator, found the Sermons from Science Pavilion "gratifying," because, in his opinion, it declared that Christ was "the only answer to man's sinful condition." But Howan perhaps unwittingly highlighted another aspect of the pavilion. "Inside this 300 padded-seat, air conditioned theatre," he noted, "earphones provide narration for those who do not understand English."[85] While the Christian Pavilion shook its visitors out of their complacency through cold concrete and photographs that denied middle-class standards of decency, the Sermons from Science Pavilion, with its comfortably decorated and air-conditioned auditorium and impressive use of technology, confirmed that life in one of the wealthiest nations of the world was good and put Expo's "modern man" at ease.

Sermons from Science officials, in fact, were overwhelmed by the positive response to their pavilion. Their original projection for total attendance of 900,000 was close to the mark, but what really impressed them was that far more visitors stayed for the Leighton Ford film and counselling than they had expected. Original projections of 90,000 for the second room soared to 260,700 by the end of the six-month run, while a projection of 10,000 for counselling soared to 26,700.[86] Visitors waited for up to five hours to get in, with reports of one woman stealing a wheel-chair in order to bypass the lineups. "Most have expressed amazement at the enthusiastic reception to their presentation," an Expo publication noted after one hundred days of the fair. Pavilion designers were wishing they had made the second auditorium bigger to handle the larger-than-expected crowds.[87]

What made the pavilion so positive for some, however, was also what made it so controversial for others. At the press conference announcing the official participation of the pavilion in May 1965, reporters had raised the question of whether the pavilion "might not be offensive to non-Christians, and even atheists and agnostics, because of what might be interpreted as missionary programming?" Stan Mackey had said no, arguing that the pavilion's films were open to all, and that they were trying to "outreach to millions who might have lost contact with Christianity."[88] Skeptics, however, were not appeased. Charles Lazarus, a person of Jewish faith on the editorial board of the *Montreal Star*, wrote a number of insightful articles that reflected a clear dislike for the evangelistic nature of the pavilion. After hearing in November 1966 that the pavilion would have "counsellors," he again publicly raised the issue of proselytizing, pointing out that it was not desired by Expo officials.[89]

That the pavilion *was* exclusive, drawing lines even between those within the various Christian churches themselves, became obvious outside the pavilion's display itself. For example, in its search for an executive secretary for its pavilion, the board of directors of Sermons from Science rejected a promising candidate simply because he had shown interest in the ecumenical movement.[90] Exclusive boundaries between those on the inside of the pavilion and those outside were also clear in the way the evangelical supporters of the Sermons from Science project related to Roman Catholics. As a board meeting in 1965 noted, an emphasis on witnessing to Roman Catholics was, in fact, a particularly effective way to gain the support of Protestant evangelicals for the project, especially in Western Canada.[91] It was a perfect way to appeal to those in such denominations as the Pentecostal Assemblies of Canada and the Fellowship of Evangelical Baptist Churches in Canada, two denominations among others who explicitly viewed Quebec as a "mission field."[92] The apparent conversions of priests and nuns were particularly powerful moments of triumph, and evangelical communities across Canada highlighted them.[93] Equally telling, members of the Sermons from Science board of directors expressed concern over how to follow up on converts from the Roman Catholic faith. One director asked of a colleague, "Is there any way in which converts, and others, can be placed in touch with a local minister who will be a spiritual help to them, in the cases where this will not be true in their home church, e.g. R.C.?"[94]

On the ground at Expo 67, some visitors to the pavilion reacted sharply to its exclusive and proselytizing nature. J. George Teplick, MD, wrote to the *Montreal Gazette* after visiting Expo in May to say that the Sermons from Science pavilion was the only "discordant and irritating note" at an otherwise wonderful Expo 67. The pavilion, he argued, was "a contrived bit of deception, a series of religious proselytizing talks, punctuated with crude and embarrassing attempts at humor all thinly disguised as science information." In this "great international exhibition," he argued, "a Christian revival movement is definitely out of place, in poor taste and is an affront to non-Christian believers who represent or come from any of the participating nations. Clear cut religious exhibitions, such as the Pavilion of Judaism and Christianity, are neither openly nor covertly proselytizing, and are important and relevant to the spirit of Expo 67."[95] For some Canadians, the revivalistic approach of the Sermons from Science Pavilion was simply inappropriate and unwelcome at Expo 67.[96]

In the midst of such objections, the Sermons from Science Pavilion demonstrated a refusal among conservative evangelical Canadians to downplay the exclusive aspects of an evangelical Christian faith in public life, even when they faced opposition. When told in a letter from the CCWE not to proselytize at Expo and to focus on their scientific demonstrations instead, Sermons from Science organizers ignored the request. Though they were also vaguely aware of Expo regulations forbidding handing out literature outside pavilions, they did so anyway.[97]

The refusal to water down their evangelistic efforts in the face of resistance was not simply the habit of a few evangelical businessmen in Montreal; it was a sentiment found among the supporters of the pavilion spread across Canada.[98] Using networks among Canada's evangelical churches and organizations to get support for the pavilion among those who shared their faith, the organizers ensured that it was clearly a national project. They pointed out that its bills had been paid not by a few wealthy Canadians and corporations but mostly by five- and ten-dollar donations from individual Canadians from across the country. Southern Ontario contributed about 25 percent of those donations, British Columbia about 15 percent, and the Montreal area about 10–12 percent. The rest was spread broadly across Canada. Denominationally, the small and conservative Christian Brethren contributed about 30–40 percent of the overall cost of the pavilion, but the Pentecostal Assemblies of Canada[99] and the Fellowship of Evangelical Baptist Churches, among others, also gave the pavilion their official support.[100] They did so because it *explicitly* declared an evangelical Christian message.

For some supporters the Sermons from Science Pavilion represented not just a refusal to tone down their proselytization efforts in a pluralistic environment but the rejection of the pluralistic environment itself. As the examination of the Centennial celebrations has noted, some Canadians simply refused to agree that in 1967 the privileged connection between Christianity and their country of Canada was in the past. That refusal was not articulated as explicitly in the Sermons from Science project, but a number of subtle clues pointed to that conclusion. In the pavilion's promotional literature itself, some phrases were suggestive. "Sermons from Science is based on the fact that Expo 67 presents an unparalleled opportunity for Canadians to reach today's untouchables – the unchurched, nonreligious masses," one booklet began. "Thousands of these spiritually needy people will be among those who are expected to make 30,000,000 visits to Expo 67."[101] The distinction between Canadians and unchurched, nonreligious untouchables suggested who was considered truly Canadian and who was not.

Outside the pavilion itself, the concept of a Christian Canada received even more explicit support. In advertising the presentation of a Sermons from Science promotional meeting at his Lambeth Bible Church in the spring of 1966, the Reverend D.L. Patterson wrote that the Montreal businessmen behind the project were "conscious of presenting the gospel of Jesus Christ, the message our country claims to uphold."[102] The 11 June 1966 edition of *En Ville* ran an article with the dramatic headline, "Thanks to sacrifice of Montreal businessmen, there'll be an Expo pavilion on *Canada's Ideology*." The article praised the "spirit of selflessness and sacrifice beyond the call of duty" demonstrated by the Sermons from Science organizers, but its real point soon followed: "While millions are being spent by the US and USSR and others to promote the communist and capitalist ideologies, Sermons from Science is probably the only Pavilion at Expo committed to advancing the simple Canadian ideology – 'that God shall have Dominion from sea to sea.'"[103]

Again, those phrases represented not the opinion of a few conservative Christians in the mid-1960s but the opinion of a growing number of Christians who had historically been relegated to the edges of Canadian public life. "That God shall have Dominion from sea to sea" was a phrase also claimed by Leslie K. Tarr, secretary of the Home Missions Board of the Fellowship of Evangelical Baptist Churches, in his triumphalist history of the denomination, published in 1968. Entitled *This Dominion, His Dominion: The Story of Evangelical Baptist Endeavour in Canada*, Tarr's book painted the relatively small Fellowship of Evangelical Churches in Canada as the most significant Christian organization in the country and concluded with the words, "Canadian evangelical Baptists should long for prophecy to be fact: 'And His dominion shall be from sea to sea and from the river even unto the end of the earth.'"[104]

In the early 1960s, the Pentecostal Assemblies of Canada had also taken a more active position in defense of the Christian character of Canada. "In laying the foundations of Canada the Fathers of Confederation did something unique in the area of Church and State," a 1961 "Dominion Day" editorial in the *Pentecostal Testimony* stated. They "adopted the premise of a practical co-operation between Church and State, recognizing the legitimate and separate areas of each, and that for the greatest public good, certain areas call for the co-operation of both."[105] More frequently than in the past, the paper had begun to call its readers' attention to national issues in a country that it had begun more vigorously to claim as its own.[106]

In doing so, Fellowship Baptists, Pentecostals, and other conservative evangelical Protestants were making it clear that in their opinion their national context should continue to be Christian. Echoing the thoughts of Leslie Tarr and the Fellowship Baptists, an editorial in the

Pentecostal Testimony explicitly rejected any argument that since Canada was a pluralist country, the Christian religion should be removed from legislation and education. To be fair to all in a religiously diverse context, it stated, "the majority in any given area will not use its legal power to impose or coerce its religious or cultural views upon those outside of its own faith. By the same token, the minorities will not use their status to deprive the majority of its right to indoctrinate those of its own persuasion. Such was the attitude of the Fathers of Confederation, the proposition is just as sound today as it was 94 years ago."[107] While the leaders of the largest Christian churches were questioning the assumptions of Christendom and attempting to accommodate to a new pluralistic Canada, many Canadians continued to insist that Canada be Christian and continued to push towards that goal. As historian John Webster Grant wrote in the early 1970s, conservative evangelicals both within and outside the mainline churches "now seem to constitute the only important segment of the church that seriously believes in the continued existence of Christendom."[108]

The Sermons from Science Pavilion captured one more important point about changes in Canadian public religion in the 1960s. If the mainline churches had had a stranglehold on representing religion in Canada when Christianity held a privileged position in Canadian public life, those days were coming to a close. Quietly ignored as "outsiders" in public life since the early twentieth century, Canadians with a conservative evangelical faith were now organizing and attempting to move inside amid the confusion and disarray surrounding the dismantling of the historic privileging of Christianity in Canadian public life. Whereas the story behind the Christian Pavilion revealed division and diversity within the mainline churches on how to be Christian in a "modern" Canada, the Sermons from Science Pavilion revealed growing unity and cooperation among evangelicals as they began to more earnestly attempt to make an impact in Canadian public life. John Stackhouse has argued precisely this point in his study of evangelicals in Canada in the twentieth century. The Sermons from Science Pavilion, in his interpretation, was an important part of the broader growth in the 1960s of "transdenominational alliances" among evangelicals in Canada, alliances that would later lead them deeper into Canadian public life.[109] In the United States, Joel Carpenter has noted, since the end of the Second World War evangelicals had begun to "put aside internal differences for the sake of successful mass evangelism and a unified voice in the public arena."[110] The list of organizations and denominations who lent their support to the pavilion proved the point for Canada, but evangelical ties, unlike those of the mainline churches, also drew on U.S. support. The Pentecostal Assemblies of Canada and the

Fellowship of Evangelical Baptist Churches, two organizations that explicitly denounced the ecumenical movement in the 1960s, lent their full support to the Sermons from Science project. In fact, the Sermons from Science organization was the first non-Pentecostal body to officially address a General Conference of the Pentecostal Assemblies.[111] Other supporters of the pavilion made up a who's who of evangelical institutions in Canada and in the United States. The Christian Businessman's Committee, of which the original organizers of the pavilion were a part, provided immediate links to evangelical businessmen across the country.[112] The Prairie Bible Institute in Three Hills, Alberta, sent and funded a couple to do full-time ministry at the pavilion.[113] InterVarsity Christian Fellowship raised money for the project, provided a bilingual staff member as one of two head counsellors, sent more than a dozen staff to counsel over the six-month period, and gave its substantial mailing list to the pavilion.[114] The Christian Medical Association offered two mailings to its list of members.[115] The Full Gospel Men's Fellowship agreed to recommend Sermons from Science to its members, and gave its four-thousand-name mailing list for Eastern Canada.[116] A Mr and Mrs Kurt Mackey of the budding Campus Crusade for Christ organization out of California were largely responsible for training all of the pavilion's volunteer counsellors.[117] Mrs A. J. Rawlins, a Salvation Army brigadier went across the country in the fall of 1966 to raise support and find volunteers.[118] The Billy Graham Evangelistic Association provided Leighton Ford to make the evangelistic film for the second half of the pavilion, and in both Halifax and Vancouver, where Graham crusades had recently been held, people who organized those crusades joined teams pushing for Sermons from Science.[119] The Canadian Bible Society provided copies of the Gospel of John for every person counselled.[120] Other organizations listed for their "close involvement" were the American Board of Missions to the Jews, Christian Life Convention, Emmaus Bible School, Gideon's International in Canada, and Youth for Christ.[121] By 1967 the Sermons from Science organizers had used all these contacts to raise dozens of local committees supporting the project in towns and cities from Vancouver to Halifax. It should also be remembered that the supporters of the pavilion ranged far beyond evangelical organizations and denominations, to include many in the mainline denominations, including high-ranking clergy.

As the mainline churches struggled through diversity and division to understand and respond to their changing context, Canadian evangelicals seemed more sure of themselves, less caught up in change, and more determined to work together to present a traditional Christian message at Expo 67. While the Christian Pavilion represented a re-evaluation of old ways of being Christian and of representing

Christianity in mainline churches, Sermons from Science indicated
that many Canadian evangelicals sensed a vacuum of religious truth
in Canadian public life and took it upon themselves to fill it. Those
evangelicals continued to insist that Canada needed to support Christianity, that in a pluralistic environment majority, as well as minority,
rights had to be observed. Evangelicals were becoming politicized.
They were insisting on continued public support of the Christian
faith *in public*.

Conservative evangelicals were not the only religious minority to
have a pavilion at Expo 67. Across the road and two doors down from
the Sermons from Science Pavilion, in fact, stood the Pavilion of Judaism, a testimony to the pride and determination of a significant number of Canadian Jewish leaders in the city of Montreal. Begun in
earnest only in the summer of 1966, those organizers had worked fe-
verishly to prepare a structure and a program that would open in less
than a year. The result was impressive, though more diverse, varied,
and complex than either of the two Christian pavilions.

Only slightly smaller than the Sermons from Science Pavilion, the
Pavilion of Judaism was an essentially rectangular, flat-roofed structure topped by a small golden dome in its centre. Adorned on all four
walls with Jewish sayings in Hebrew script, its front entrance was
graced with *The Procession*, a series of three bronze, life-size figures by
Elbert Weinberg. On the green grass before the pavilion, a rabbi holding aloft the Scroll of the Law was followed by a figure carrying a
prayer book and a third person carrying a menorah.

Inside, the pavilion was divided into two floors.[122] The lower floor
consisted of a small, 125-seat auditorium and exhibition space that was
home to an impressive array of changing events and programs. The auditorium hosted everything from the Reconstructionist Assembly on 28
May to interviews with "distinguished women leaders" on International Women's Day to Yiddish Culture week from 18–25 June, while
the exhibition space housed twelve three-week exhibitions of Jewish
Canadiana, as well as works of contemporary artists.[123] It was to be an
"international meeting place," a space where "Jewish organizations,
groups and individuals from all parts of the world convene meetings
and symposiums."[124]

A permanent, unchanging exhibit presenting the main theme of the
pavilion was housed in the top floor. "Man in his world needs guidelines," the pavilion declared to the visitor, and then set out to answer the
question, "What are some of the guidelines of Judaism?" The interior of
the pavilion had been designed around six basic principles taken from
the ancient Talmudic commentaries, "The Ethics of the Fathers." Each

of those principles was illustrated through attractive displays housed in small clusters of self-supporting booths spread throughout a spacious and comfortable room. A four-hundred-square-foot model of Solomon's temple, a display on the history of Canadian Jews, and a section declaring the importance of the state of Israel to Jews around the world filled up the remainder of the upper floor.

The first principle, torah (teaching or learning), was illustrated by displays of rare and ancient books and manuscripts from around the world. Then, as the story line noted, the principle of torah was made contemporary in "works of scholarship and in the very latest expression of 'belles lettres' and modern literary activity."[125] The second principle, the quest for truth made it clear that the "Torah was not only a letter but a spirit. That spirit has as its goal to bring man closer to the truth of life and to the truth of the world." Portraits and statements of twenty-one famous Jewish men and women, including Albert Einstein, Martin Buber, and Sigmund Freud, demonstrated the impact of Jewish scholars and thinkers on the world. The quest for justice, a third principle, was illustrated by a trio of works of art. A sculpture entitled *The Broken Man* and a painting entitled *Riot* drove home the horrors of justice gone wrong, while Micah 6:8 offered a better way: "What doth the Lord require of thee? Do justice, love mercy, and walk humbly with thy God."[126]

Out of a quest for justice, the pavilion suggested, had arisen the state of Israel. A display of Maimonides' *The Eight Degrees of Giving* proceeded to illustrate the importance of "Love of Man" while a small chapel at the centre of the pavilion and underneath the small dome declared that "Love of God," or worship, was also essential to the Jewish faith. At the heart of the pavilion, the chapel offered visitors a quiet, serene place to reflect, pray, and listen to recordings of ancient and contemporary liturgical music. Each evening, from 7:00 P.M. to 7:30 P.M., the chapel also housed a brief religious service led by an ongoing rotation of local Jewish congregations. It was used, as well, to celebrate Jewish holidays and special days throughout the six months of Expo 67.

The final principle illustrated on the top floor of the pavilion, shalom, or peace, was found in a text entitled "The Message of Shalom." "Judaism affirms the universal covenant of Man," it declared. "It acknowledges the validity of differences without violence; unity without uniformity." "The concept of Unity-in-Diversity," it went on, "teaches that among humans there can be no monopoly of truth, of justice or of wisdom; that the quest for peace is the great goal of history which free men everywhere can share as a common hope."[127]

The Pavilion of Judaism, in short, was made up of a collection of ancient and rare documents and items displaying the history of the faith, a celebration and demonstration of that faith's impact on Canada and the world, a declaration that the historical faith had relevance for the future, and a chapel to demonstrate the core of the faith's experience, corporate worship. Beautifully and intelligently designed, the Pavilion of Judaism was what some considered to be a rare place of rest and reflection on the busy islands of Expo.[128] In marked contrast to the two Christian pavilions, in fact, the Pavilion of Judaism did little to cause any significant controversy.[129] It was a quiet display, not a dramatic declaration. It offered beauty and rest, not shock and provocation. Whereas both the Christian Pavilion and Sermons from Science challenged some of the assumptions of Expo 67 in fairly dramatic ways, the Pavilion of Judaism announced a positive, inclusive message that fit very well with the exposition's larger theme.

Seen from one angle, the pavilion took aspects of both Christian pavilions and combined them into an appealing whole. Like the Sermons from Science Pavilion, it used spectacle and novelty to gain the attention of and to entertain fair-goers. The 440-square-foot model of the temple of Jerusalem, painstakingly and loving constructed over thirty years by Lazare Halberthal and Suzette Halberthal of Montreal,[130] had little to do with the six principles of the pavilion but was irresistible to pavilion planners (and to many fair-goers) because of its dramatic entertainment and educative value. For the fair-goer out for an interesting time, the temple and the many ancient scrolls and books, some protected by stunning cases of precious metals and jewels, were worth a look.[131]

While it attempted to entertain, however, the pavilion avoided the dramatic extremes of the Sermons from Science show. It provided a much more refined, reserved, and artistic display. In some ways, it managed to find a happy medium between the popular smoke and sparks of Sermons from Science and the somewhat esoteric and vague presentation of the Christian Pavilion. To get its core message across, it employed contemporary sculpture and art, but it surrounded that art with interpretive texts that made it easy to understand and follow. Whereas the Sermons from Science Pavilion was popular entertainment to the point of being a fireworks show, the Pavilion of Judaism was popular entertainment with grace and refinement. Whereas the Christian Pavilion was artistic and creative to the point of alienating the "average Canadian," the Pavilion of Judaism combined art and text in a way that welcomed, educated, and entertained.

Most importantly, the pavilion affirmed the very things that Expo officials and the vast majority of Expo pavilions sought to promote: the hope for progress through the combined application of human intelligence in a pluralistic and tolerant world. In the section, Quest for

Truth, the pavilion praised the Jews of past and present who had contributed to the development of human knowledge and praised the thirst for learning that lay at the basis of Judaism, as well as of Expo. It did the same on the lower floor when, over the course of Expo 67, it used its auditorium space to interview and acclaim "prominent personalities of world renown."[132] The "quest for truth", the pavilion declared, was a fundamental principle of the Jewish faith.

The second part of Expo's creed, the need for tolerance and cooperation in a pluralistic world, was also explicitly affirmed in the Pavilion of Judaism, which nearly shouted from the rooftops that difference in life-style and belief was to be not only accepted but also desired. As a public presentation of religion in a pluralistic environment, the pavilion did everything Expo organizers had hoped. It was not there to proselytize, its souvenir book explicitly argued: "Judaism is not a movement which seeks to convert." Instead, the pavilion offered to the world "concepts and values" by which Jews had lived for millennia and that might "strengthen and nourish the conscience of all mankind."[133] Instead of trying to draw people to itself, the book implied, the Judaism of the pavilion offered itself to the world.

The last principle of the pavilion, shalom, demonstrated this vividly and could admirably stand as a brilliant enunciation of the Expo theme itself. "Mankind faces the urgent problem of living together despite ideological, national or racial differences," the last panel of the top floor of the pavilion began. "Having the capacity to destroy one another, men and nations must learn to live together ... Judaism affirms the universal covenant of Man. It acknowledges the validity of differences without violence; unity without uniformity. The ideal of pluralism is something to be cherished as the unique birthright and flowering of the human spirit."[134] Quoting from the prophet Micah, it declared the quintessential pluralistic creed, live and let live: "For let all the peoples walk each one in the name of its God, but we will walk in the name of the Lord our God for ever and ever."[135]

What the Pavilion of Judaism said, and how it said it, made sense within the context of its supporting community. For Canadian Jews, the message of pluralism was entirely appropriate. A relatively tiny religious minority in an overwhelmingly Christian country, Canadian Jews had quietly worked for the acceptance of diversity and plurality since their first ancestors had set foot on Canadian soil over two hundred years earlier. Having long lived under what was sometimes the dark shadow of Christendom, they had in recent years more actively campaigned for its fall.[136] While the mainline Christian churches struggled to accommodate that fall – struggled to learn to live as one among many – the Canadian Jewish community, having long *been* one among many, took the changes in Canada in the fifties and sixties in stride and seized the opportunity to advance the concerns of a minority group. While conservative evangelical groups began to work to maintain what they perceived as Canada's Christian heritage, Canadian Jews at Expo 67 continued to argue for a pluralistic, tolerant, and inclusive Canada. That was what Saul Hayes, on behalf of the Canadian Jewish Congress, had done before the Massey Commission in 1949. Arguing for a form of what would later be dubbed "multiculturalism," Hayes had suggested that if Canada's public institutions could work to make Canadians aware of the contributions of their country's various ethnic groups, then democracy and the Canadian identity could be strengthened.[137] Their history, Canadian Jews proudly declared, was one of pluralism, of working towards full equality, religious and otherwise, for all human beings. Canadian Jews, then, were fully in tune with the message of Expo 67.

In the 1950s and 1960s, in fact, they were finally beginning to reap the rewards of a pluralistic Canada and were moving from the shadows into the light of public life. "The post-war era ... demonstrates that Canadian Jews as a collective were seeking accommodation and integration into the mainstream and enjoying economic and social advancement at unprecedented levels," Gerald Tulchinsky has recently argued.[138] The Pavilion of Judaism came in the midst of several key developments that affirmed the Jewish quest for equality in a predominantly Christian population and in a country that had historically privileged Christianity in its public life. Ontario had led the way for other provinces with the Racial Discrimination Act in 1944 and the Fair Employment Practices Act in 1951, which outlawed discrimination and the dissemination of hate literature.[139] Throughout the 1960s in Ontario, Jews had heavily invested themselves in a largely successful attack on the religiously discriminatory nature of public education in that province. In August 1966, after twelve years of lobbying by the Canadian Jewish Congress for legislation to curb hate propaganda, Prime Minister Lester B. Pearson had declared that federal legislation was on the way.[140] Anti-Semitism clearly remained across Canada, but by the mid-1960s, the horrors of the Holocaust and a liberalizing culture had limited its public support to a small, if sometimes vocal, minority.[141] Strong immigration and a strong economy bolstered Jewish congregations and led to a move to the suburbs and a synagogue building spree not unlike that in the Christian churches of the time.[142] Demand for professors in Canada's burgeoning universities led to an impressive increase in Jews in university faculties, while a growing number of Jewish businessmen entered the class of Canada's wealthiest men.[143] All these developments had further boosted the confidence already manifest in the celebration of the two hundredth anniversary of the Jewish faith in Canada in 1959. "From many lands our people have come to these hospitable shores in search of religious and political freedom and economic opportunity," read the "Proclamation of Faith and Thanksgiving on the Occasion of the National Bicentenary of Canadian Jewry," written and distributed by the Canadian Jewish Congress. "Thanks to these advantages we have taken our place with our fellow citizens in the promotion of the economic, political, religious, social and cultural life of our country."[144] The proclamation read like a Jewish declaration of full and equal Canadian citizenship.

In this context, the Pavilion of Judaism represented a kind of coming of age of Judaism in Canada. That, at least, was the perspective of Sam Steinberg.[145] President of the organization behind the pavilion and the wealthy owner of a chain of 170 supermarkets and 15 department stores in Quebec, New Brunswick and Ontario, it was Steinberg who had, as mentioned, been most responsible for the Jewish presence at Expo.[146] By his wealth and age, he was a member of the older professional and business male elite who filled the seats of Canada's leading Jewish organizations such as the Canadian Jewish Congress. He shared their desire to work their way into the mainstream of Canadian public life, not through radical action and protest, but through quiet diplomacy and the demonstration of their ability to work in the Canadian cultural, economic, and political circles of power.[147]

Though the Canadian Jewish Congress had been ready to content itself with some sort of presence in the Canadian and provincial pavilions, Steinberg had taken up Expo's request for a Jewish pavilion and had charged ahead with it. When finances grew slim, he had bolstered them with his own funds, insisting that if a pavilion was to be built, it would have to be done right or not at all.[148] What had driven Steinberg to invest himself so heavily in the project, it seems, had been a desire to have Canadian Jewry move from the "outsider" status it had so long held in Canadian society to a place of prominence and public importance. That was the sentiment he had drawn on to convince others to contribute to the project. The Pavilion of Judaism was "one of the most exciting and important events to offer itself to our people in this country," he had written to a fellow Jewish businessmen in Toronto in 1966. "We stand before a great challenge which goes beyond charity, beyond self-defense, beyond the traditional Jewish concern for 'taking care of our own.' We have here an opportunity to be counted proudly among our fellow-Canadians of other faiths and origins, and to express, in a context that is truly world-wide, the significance of the Jewish presence in Canada."[149]

That message was clearly expressed in the pavilion itself. Not only did the displays emphasize the long and dramatic history of the Jewish people, they also explicitly drew attention to the history of Jews in Canada. While the section Quest for Truth highlighted the contributions of Jewish people to the knowledge of humanity and its world, the auditorium and exhibition space in the basement were used to highlight Canadian Jewish writers such as A.M Klein and Canadian Jewish artists, alongside the work of famous Jewish writers, artists, and scholars from around the world. The pavilion was not just an offering of Jewish principles to a pluralist world but also an attempt to declare the importance of the Jewish faith and the Jewish people to Canada.

The pavilion did not explicitly proselytize, but it did go after something other than converts: it went after respect. Unlike the Christian Pavilion, it did not aim itself at convincing agnostics and atheists of the need for God. Unlike the Sermons from Science Pavilion, it did not try overtly to convince fair-goers to believe in its religious truth. But it did try to convince its visitors that Judaism was a historically, culturally, and artistically rich faith. And it did try to present Judaism as a faith perspective that could offer a distinctive and valuable set of guidelines appropriate to "man and his world." Jews were not an insignificant minority on the fringes of society, culture, and public life, the pavilion declared. With the names of prominent Canadian artists and writers on their roster and men of astounding intelligence and significance like Albert Einstein to back them up, Sam Steinberg and his organization placed Canadian Jews directly into the mainstream of Western, and Canadian, civilization. Choosing to emphasize principles of their faith that they deemed universally shared by all men and women and that could provide valuable answers to the questions of "modern man," the organizers of the Pavilion of Judaism applauded and declared their importance to Expo 67's pluralist theme.

In a pluralistic society, with the historic public privileging of Christianity on the wane, what form should public religion take? In the Centennial celebrations and in Expo 67, state planners had their "official" say, but other Canadians did too. Some prominent Montreal Jews had eagerly responded to Robert Shaw's request for a Jewish presence at Expo. Breaking out from the shadows of Christendom into the light of an emerging pluralistic and inclusive Canada, they were eager to lend their voices to the celebration of unity in diversity and the tolerance of difference. The Christian majority, however, was divided over whether they should help usher in a pluralistic, multifaith Canada or work to defend the Christian Canada that seemed to be passing.

Influential voices in the mainline Christian churches argued that the way ahead for those institutions was one of accommodation and change, that a "servant church" in touch with the language of "modern man" and the "secular city" was the best hope for continued influence in shaping Canadian society. Leaving behind the burdens of tradition and institutional dominance, the churches might become vital again, able to influence and shape their society and work for its betterment through the diffusion of Christian love. For men and women with such a perspective, the Christian Pavilion, with its fresh and unusual "secular" language, was a triumph; Sermons from Science, with its outdated language, an embarrassing anomaly.

For many other Christians, however, the very opposite was true. In their minds, the push for a tolerant, inclusive pluralism in the 1960s was not a positive or even exciting thing. It was troubling. Whether within or outside the mainline churches, those Christians reacted with concern to the sweeping changes of the 1960s, changes that to them reflected a drift from the historical Christian faith – which reflected loss, not gain. What mattered most to them was that non-Christians would hear the gospel message and be saved. The Sermons from Science Pavilion, not the Christian Pavilion, served that goal best.

As with the Centennial celebrations, Expo 67 offered an opportunity for faith groups to present *their* version of public religion to Canadians and to the world. The pavilions they created captured well how Canadians outside of state elites wished to express their faith prominently in public life and also hinted at how they felt about the waning of a Christian and the rise of a modern, broader, interfaith Canada.

Conclusion

In the 1960s Canadians and their social, cultural, and political institutions struggled through a period of dramatic and intense change. Reevaluating old patterns and norms of daily life, Canadians also found themselves immersed in a broader reconsideration of the very character of their country, their institutions, and themselves. That reconsideration, in turn, involved public religion. In the 1960s, in a process that had begun long before and continued long after, the religious component of Canadian public identities was being officially redefined.

The 1967 Centennial celebrations of Canadian Confederation and Expo 67, the Universal and International Exposition in Montreal in that same year, caught that process in mid-step and threw it into bold relief. Welcoming Canadians to cheer and sing on Parliament Hill, to offer thanks for their country in their own local communities, or to explore the "magic" islands in the St Lawrence river, those two events gave Canadians the opportunity to celebrate themselves and Canada as they had never done before. They also did much more. "Expo 67 was the greatest birthday party in history," an insightful reporter wrote, "but for those willing to learn it was also an education."[1] Carefully planned and orchestrated events, the centennial celebrations and Expo 67 were powerful symbolic statements that both reflected their sociopolitical context and became in turn important tools in efforts to shape it. They were nation-building moments, events devised by government corporations and commissions to instill in Canadian hearts an understanding of their country and of themselves, religion and all. "By one of those accidental miracles of history that sometimes quite suddenly crystallize a country's character," Prime Minister Pearson noted during a visit to the Expo grounds, "we have achieved in Montreal through Expo and in Canada through our Centennial, the portrayal of a developing Canadian personality, both for the present and I hope for the future."[2]

The Centennial and Expo were created in the context of a country in turmoil, and both responded to that context in the hope of stabilizing and uniting Canada. By the 1960s, the understanding of Canada as a Christian country dominated by citizens of British descent had been under duress for some time. In the postwar period, racial and religious exclusivity in Canadian public life increasingly became untenable. As a result, driven by a desire for reform and enabled by the affluence of the post-1945 period, the Pearson Liberals moved to bind together their fragmenting country by offering Canadians a different understanding of themselves and their nation. They presented to Canadians a vision of a developing Canadian personality – a decidedly more inclusive, pluralistic country that would be united in its diversity. Under Pearson, the federal government began in earnest to remove the exclusive public rituals and symbols of the past, replacing them with more indeterminate ones for the present and future.

The reformist impulse that was alive in the Canadian federal state was also alive and well elsewhere, too. Growing in size and self-confidence, those groups that been historically relegated to the sidelines of public life when Christianity (and the mainline Christian churches, in particular) was privileged grew more effective in their criticism of that privilege and made their presence increasingly felt in public life. At the same time, Canada's historic mainline Protestant and Roman Catholic churches themselves began to reconsider the cultural and political status quo. Long imbued with an establishment mentality, those churches found themselves suddenly looking for new ways to be Christian in Canadian public life – ways that would allow them to maintain their historic identification with Canadian culture in the midst of the turmoil of the decade. As in the culture at large, their churchly past was put into a critical light, and attention was focused on the potential of the present and future.

That sharing of the reformist impulse of the 1960s by Canada's elites in religious and state institutions helped define the decade. While the mainline Protestant and Roman Catholic churches could have bitterly fought the removal of their exclusive and historic public privileges, they did not. In Quebec, as David Seljak has pointed out, the willingness of the Roman Catholic Church to accommodate the secularization of the province was particularly significant. Across the country, that kind of cooperation spared communities from divisive and costly battles. Put more positively, the shared reformist mindset of leaders of key churches and the state enabled the relatively smooth reimagining of the official religious understanding of Canada.

The Centennial celebrations and Expo 67 captured that reconstruction of Canada and defined the country not as racially or religiously exclusive but as united in its diversity. Within that newer version of Canada, both events boldly declared, religion remained an important aspect of Canadian nationality. The celebrations and Expo also declared, however, that official expressions of public religion were changing. In the Canadian Interfaith Conference (CIC), the Canada Pavilion, and Expo 67 at large, every effort was made to present Canada as a country where all faiths were equally welcome and given equal recognition in Canadian public life. The leading voices within the Canadian mainline churches joined those within the federal state to agree that the privileging of their Christian voices was a thing of the past and that the way of the future was a pluralistic, inclusive Canada guided by broad humanitarian principles shared by, but not exclusive to, Christianity.

As popular conceptions of the 1960s often suggest, the changes of that period seemed revolutionary in size and scope. They were. As in any historical period, however, change in the 1960s was a complicated mixture of old and new, a process as evolutionary as it was revolutionary. Continuity between the past and present was apparent, for example, in the usefulness of arm's-length religious organizations to Expo and Centennial officials, as they attempted to manage the delicate and sometimes volatile matter of public religion. Given that a wide variety of religious institutions and individuals were eager to represent their faith in national public life, how could state officials make sure that religion in their events would be unifying, and not divisive? Notably, both Centennial and Expo planners responded by encouraging the formation of the CIC and the Christian Pavilion organizations – arm's-length religious institutions that could regulate public religion *for* the state, but at a safe distance *from* the state. In adopting such regulatory tactics, state officials shaped public religion in a manner that had been effective in the past and that would serve them well in 1967.

Continuity between the past and the present was apparent not only in the structuring of religious bodies close to public institutions. It was also embedded in the very logic of state-sponsored public religion itself. In the 1960s, as in the previous century, such public religion was dedicated to the service of "the nation." It was concerned with nation-building and legitimation, not the salvation of souls. As a result, the Interfaith Conference was organized to convert Canadians to a love of neighbour and nation, not to any particular faith. At Expo, too, religion was a valuable tool for working towards "earthly" ends, a fact made particularly clear by the effort of the Canadian Corporation for the 1967 World Exposition (CCWE) to silence the quest for religious conversions on the Expo grounds. Federal state-sponsored public religion in the Centennial and at Expo was formed primarily by the need to forge an increasingly diverse society into a united and stable nation. To do so, it needed to have broad appeal. In the past, that need had led to a nonsectarian and humanitarian interpretation of Christianity in national public life – an interpretation intended to be inclusive of all Canadians. As Canada diversified both demographically and ideologically, however, the principle of inclusivity for the sake of national unity was taken to its next logical extension. If Christianity was no longer deemed useful as a "lowest common religious denominator" for Canadians, a broader, more indeterminate representation of religion might fit the bill. Not surprisingly, it was an interfaith Canada that was very visibly presented to Canadians both through the CIC and the Canada Pavilion at Expo 67.

It is noteworthy, of course, that in spite of the optimism and energy poured into the Centennial celebrations and Expo 67 by reformist elites, the idea of an interfaith Canada continued to be more a vision than a reality in the 1960s. Canada was changing, to be sure, but it was not changing as quickly as some leaders seemed to imagine or desire. As organizers of public exhibitions, celebrations, rituals, and symbols had done in the past, Centennial and Expo planners had constructed an image of Canada that was prescriptive as much as descriptive. It was *their* vision of Canada, and one that they hoped the public at large could be convinced to adopt. In Centennial events across the country and on the Expo isles, however, it became clear that the vision of an interfaith, inclusive, and pluralistic Canada was not receiving an overwhelmingly positive response. Clearly demonstrating how they imagined the religious element of their national identity, many local planners organized and participated in Christian Centennial services, not interfaith ones. Conservative Protestants, in particular, seemed determined to defend the historic privileging of Christianity in Canada. Differences of opinion over how to imagine Canada religiously also contributed to significant controversy and discussion within the mainline churches themselves. Reform-minded leaders may have had the most influence within those institutions, but not everyone agreed with their ideals and plans. The controversies surrounding the Christian Pavilion captured the deep division that engulfed the mainline churches as they struggled to respond to the waning of a Christian Canada.

Given the difficulties of convincing Canadians to rethink their country's religious identity, it should not surprise us that efforts to present a pluralistic Canada to Canadians were tinted with irony. Billed as a celebration of diversity, the new official and inclusive approach to public religion captured by the Centennial and Expo 67 did admirably answer

the pleas of minority faith groups for greater public recognition. Without doubt, it made more room than in the past for religious diversity in
Canadian public life. In the CIC, thirty-five different faith groups found
both recognition and symbolically equal representation to a degree
they had never known before. At Expo 67, too, a desire to have religious diversity represented at the world's fair gave Canadian Jews a
chance to put themselves and their faith tradition on the Canadian map
and to declare their value to Canada as a whole.

The inclusive approach to public religion was ironic, however, because from the perspective of some faith groups, it was hardly inclusive at all. Apparently offering public representation to every
religious group in the country, federal state reformers were, in fact,
attempting to have a certain kind of religion present in public life. As
a nation-building tool, state-sponsored public religion was to celebrate what all Canadians held in common and to avoid what divided
them. As a result, particular religious beliefs and doctrines were to be
de-emphasized in public life, while such things as the cultivation of
love, self-sacrifice, and loyalty for the sake of the common good were
put to the fore. Difference was to be downplayed. Commonality was
to be celebrated.

That emphasis on things held in common, however, effectively excluded a number of faith groups from public life. Promoted as welcoming to all faiths, the attempt to make state-sponsored forms of public
religion inclusive of all religions continued to be intolerant of those who
refused to downplay their differences and who insisted, instead, on
bringing particular doctrines, beliefs, and religious emphases into public life. Again, the Centennial celebrations and Expo 67 provide examples to prove the more general point. Because the Fellowship Baptists
believed they had to compromise their distinctive beliefs to be members
in the CIC, they withdrew from that organization. Because of their determination to evangelize, the Sermons from Science group's participation
in Expo 67 was seriously reconsidered by the CCWE, while the participation of Billy Graham was not permitted at all. In fact, in trying to make
room for all religious faiths in Canadian public life, state planners found
themselves opposing a significant number of citizens who continued to
believe that as Canadians, they had the right and privilege to defend a
particularly Christian vision of Canada in prominent Canadian public
spaces. As they always had, public officials interpreted the inclusion of
religious diversity in public life to mean the inclusion of those religious
voices that would contribute to their vision of national unity, not endan-
ger it. Working to dismiss religious discrimination in national public life
for the betterment of the country, federal state officials in fact continued
to use religious discrimination as an essential tool for that task.

Given the continuities and contradictions of the restructuring of Canadian religious public identities in the 1960s, one cannot help but wonder what it all accomplished. What was the result of all of the progressive fervour – of all the talk of dramatic change and optimistic visions of the future?

Nearly forty years later, one is first struck by the fact that the elation of the centennial year was short-lived. So were the general optimism and the reformist drive of the years that surrounded it, for that matter. Affluence and forecasts of economic plenty in the 1960s turned into "stagflation," the oil crisis, and soaring government deficits in the 1970s. Dreams of national unity and global cooperation inspired in the Centennial year were eventually tainted by the FLQ crisis (1970), student revolt, and the escalation of the Vietnam War.[3] Ecumenical fervour slowly dissipated, leaving plans for the merger of the United and Anglican Churches to die on the negotiation table. Calls for dramatic change in church structures and the language of faith were stymied by a much more traditional and slowly changing Canadian – and still nominally Christian – reality. Pierre Berton's claim that 1967 was Canada's "last good year" is overstated, of course, but coming from one of Canada's most vocal 1960s reformers, its tragic tone of hope unfulfilled is telling.[4]

In retrospect, even if it did not entirely change Canada, the ability of political and cultural elites to harness the reformist optimism of the 1960s must be recognized as one of the most important features of that decade. Before the Centennial, for example, political scandals and the wranglings of minority government had done nothing to build confidence in the federal state.[5] Nonetheless, by putting themselves in step with the positive expressions of the 1960s through everything from a new Canadian flag to new social programs to the Centennial and Expo 67, federal state institutions managed not only to weather the turmoil of the sixties but to ride its wave. The phenomena of Trudeaumania, with its celebration of youth and the sixties' iconoclastic spirit, demonstrated this particularly well. In 1968, Canadians invested their optimism and hope for the future in a dashing young sophisticate – Prime Minister Pierre Elliot Trudeau. How much they were empowered to do so by the Centennial year and Expo 67 remains to be told.

If much of the optimism and hope waned in the late 1960s and early 1970s, it did so, perhaps, because Canadians hoped for too much, too fast. Though the 1960s brilliantly exemplified the reconstruction of understandings of Canada from a Christian to a religiously plural country, the decade did not begin or finish that change. The reconstruction of the religious element of Canadian national identity is better viewed not in the isolation of one decade but as a very visible manifestation of a much longer and slower process. The reimagining of Canada's public symbols in the 1960s was, in effect, one episode in a long and tiring struggle to define Canada, religiously and otherwise – a struggle that continues at the beginning of the twenty-first century, some forty years later.

That struggle did not go further in the 1960s, perhaps, because those pushing for a more pluralistic and inclusive Canada also placed boundaries around just how pluralistic and inclusive they wanted their Canada to become. While the symbol of a new Canada was championed by leaders in both religious and state institutions, the reality those leaders helped to maintain sometimes remained strikingly familiar. In the Canadian Interfaith Conference, we might be reminded, thirty-five faith groups achieved symbolic equality, but the mainline Protestant and Roman Catholic Churches continued to hold the levers of power in the organization's administrative bodies. At Expo, the CCWE encouraged all faith groups to be represented on their islands, while at the same time it heavily favoured the Christian Pavilion with publicity, resources, and eventually, official standing. While reformers in the mainline Protestant and Roman Catholic Churches conceded that a Christian Canada was no longer appropriate and rebilled themselves as critics of the status quo and defenders of the dispossessed, they also continued to seek influence among the country's cultural and political elites and continued to be the leading voices in Canadian organized religion. While government planners pushed for the recognition of diversity, they did so not for the sake of diversity itself but for the strengthening of national unity. The reform that was urged by Canada's political and cultural elites was often urged for the purpose of stabilizing their political and cultural context, not revolutionizing it.

The transition to a pluralistic and inclusive conception of Canada in the 1960s was limited, as well, because it was led primarily by elites more enchanted by change than were some of their fellow citizens. Reforming elites tried hard in those years to convince Canadians that a more open image of Canada was the only one capable of uniting the diverse elements of the country into a cohesive and dynamic whole. In doing so, however, they seemed to overestimate the desire for change of a significant number of others. Like the inclusive and pluralistic presentation of religion in the CIC and in the Christian Pavilion, the presentation of a pluralistic and inclusive Canada did not conclude the debate about the religious element of Canadian identities. Instead, it seemed only to open it up.

Efforts to redefine Canada in the 1960s, in fact, helped set the stage for the continuing reconstruction of public religion as a component of

Canadian identity, which continues today. Political and cultural elites in the 1960s, it might be argued, shaped a public religion better suited for 1997 than 1967. In the tenth decade of Confederation, the close connections between Christianity and Canada were still too strong to change easily. Thirty years later, on the other hand, the Charter of Rights and Freedoms had helped to dramatically reduce the privileging of Christianity in Canadian public life, while more tolerant immigration laws had had several decades to have a greater effect on the country's demographics.

Today, the presence of religion in public life continues to be hotly contested. As I write, religious controversy surrounding the redefinition of marriage to include same-sex couples has burst into the press, spurred on by a Roman Catholic bishop's suggestion that those supporting such a redefinition, including the prime minister, may find themselves eternally damned. Religious neutrality, even today, has its public limits.

That said, the argument for a religiously neutral pluralism in Canadian public life seems to have won much of the public ground at the beginning of the twenty-first century. For many of those raised since the official declaration of the policy of multiculturalism, such a position is a common sense assumption. The 1960s did not end up precisely as many overly eager reformers had hoped. Thus far, however, time seems to have been on their side.

Notes

INTRODUCTION

1 The order of service of the prayer service described below, including the
speech of the Queen and the various readings and hymns, was printed in
Hansard (4 July 1967), 2248–57. Descriptions of the event have otherwise
been drawn from Greg Connelley, "French, English Canadians Urged: Re-
solve Differences," *Ottawa Citizen*, 3 July 1967, 15, and "Disappointed:
Few Hear Monarch's Speech," *Ottawa Citizen*, 3 July 1967, 15; and Lewis
Seale, "Queen Urges Understanding and Goodwill," *Globe and Mail*, 3 July
1967, 8.

2 The first line is from Psalm 33:12, the second and third from Psalm 95: 6–7.

3 The anthem appeals to God, of course, to "keep our land." The official
French version, first performed in 1880, is even more distinctively Christian:

O Canada! terre de nos aïeux, ton front est ceint de fleurons glorieux!
Car ton bras sait porter l'épée, il sait porter la croix!
Ton histoire est une épopée, des plus brillants exploits.
Ch.
Et ta valeur, de foi trempée, Protégera nos foyers et nos droits.
Protégera nos foyers et nos droits.

Translated, it reads:

O Canada! Land of our forefathers
Thy brow is wreathed with a glorious garland of flowers.
As is thy arm ready to wield the sword,
So also is it ready to carry the cross.
Thy history is an epic of the most brilliant exploits.
Ch.
Thy valour steeped in faith
Will protect our homes and our rights
Will protect our homes and our rights.

Source of translation: http://www.pch.gc.ca/progs/cpsc-ccsp/sc-cs/
anthem_e.cfm.

4 Since the early 1940s, for example, rabbis had been allotted two or three
   Sunday service slots a year on the CBC's *Church of the Air* program.
   Miedema, "Preaching to the Nation."

5 The *Globe and Mail* was more generous, covering the service on page 8 as
   the first item of its 1 July Centennial story. The *Ottawa Citizen*, however,
   gave the prayer service full-page coverage, but on page 15, well after the
   front page coverage of the birthday cake and fireworks celebrations. See
   Connelley, "French, English Canadians Urged: Resolved Differences,"
   Ottawa Citizen 3 July 1967, 15, and Seale, "Queen Urges Understanding
   and Goodwill," *Globe and Mail* 3 July 1967, 8. Both the *Globe* and the *Citizen* highlighted the role and speech of the Queen.

6 Others have also chosen to use Expo 67 and the Centennial celebrations as
   windows through which to view Canadian culture in the 1960s. With particular relevance to this study, see Stackhouse, *Canadian Evangelicalism*,
   chap. 6; Kuffert, *A Great Duty*, chap. 6.

7 See, among others, Heaman, *The Inglorious Arts of Peace*; Walden, *Becoming
   Modern in Toronto*; Nelles, *The Art of Nation Building*; Davies, "The Politics
   of Participation"; Rydell and Gwinn, *Fair Representations*; Benedict,
   The Anthropology of World's Fairs.

8 For general reviews of the unrest of the 1960s, one can begin with Granatstein, *Canada, 1957–1967*, especially chaps. 3 and 8; Bothwell, Drummond,
   and English, *Canada since 1945*, part 5; Berton, *1967: The Last Good Year*,
   chap. 3. For a more detailed analysis of the changes to Canadian national
   symbols, see Breton, "Multiculturalism and Canadian Nation-Building,"
   27–67.

9 See Clarke, "English-Speaking Canada from 1854"; Grant, *The Church in
   the Canadian Era*, chaps. 9–10. See also Stackhouse, "The Protestant Experience in Canada since 1945," 206–12.

10 Grant, *The Church in the Canadian Era*, 213.

11 Philip Gleason has pointed this potential contradiction out in his recent
   study of the history of the term "pluralism." Gleason, *Speaking of Diversity*,
   especially chap. 3. Canadian scholars have long been making this point, as
   well. For recent examples, see Day, *Multiculturalism and the History of Canadian Diversity*, and Mackey, *The House of Difference*.

12 Granatstein, *Canada, 1957–1967*.

13 "Mainline" is a loose descriptor, but it remains a useful one. In this study,
   it will be used as a term inclusive of Canada's largest, oldest, and hence
   most publicly significant churches, the Roman Catholic Church, the
   United Church of Canada, the Anglican Church of Canada, and the Presbyterian Church of Canada. Convention Baptist Churches are often considered mainline, as well, but they are not a central focus of this study.

CHAPTER ONE

1 For one of the latest arguments from two key players in the debate, see Gauvreau and Christie, *A Full-Orbed Christianity.*

2 The two most popular examples of this kind of historical enquiry have been Cook, *The Regenerators,* and Marshall, *Secularizing the Faith.*

3 For others doing similar work on issues of religion, identity, and public religion, see Van Die, *Religion and Public Life in Canada;* Marks, *Revivals and Roller Rinks;* and Christie, *Households of Faith.*

4 Here I follow the work of sociologist José Casanova, who has argued that despite the worldwide process of modernization, religion has not disappeared today from public life but, rather, continues to resurface in ways ranging from fueling civil war to seeking to influence elections. Though differentiation – a process that leads to the gradual removal of religion from any direct involvement in such things as education, philanthropy, and the state – has indeed accompanied modernization, it has not always resulted in the privatization of belief. Casanova contends that scholars have often confused what could be considered possible with essential aspects of secularization. The privatization and loss of religious belief, while *possible* results of secularization, have not inevitably followed from it. In modernizing societies, many forms of religion have remained concerned about and involved in the shaping of public life. Thus, while the process of differentiation has removed religion to the voluntary sphere, it continues by its nature to speak out on public issues and to attempt to shape public life. See Casanova, *Public Religions in the Modern World,* part 1.

5 For the most thorough account of the Roman Catholic Church in Quebec, see Hamelin, *Histoire du catholicisme québécois,* 141–5. Two surveys of Roman Catholic and Protestant religion, in particular, have emphasized the 1960s as a crucial turning point. See Clarke, "English-Speaking Canada from 1854," and Grant, *Church in the Canadian Era.* On the separation of Roman Catholicism from French Canadian identities, see Mol, *Faith and Fragility,* 181–2.

6 Grant, *Church in the Canadian Era,* 204. See also Owram, *Born at the Right Time,* 109; Noll, *A History of Christianity in the United States and Canada,* 548.

7 Murphy and Perin, *A Concise History,* 369. On the American situation, see Hutchinson, *Between the Times;* Ellwood, *The Sixties Spiritual Awakening;* Wuthnow, *Restructuring of American Religion.* For comparisons of the Canadian and American situation, see Noll, *A History of Christianity in the United States and Canada,* especially part 5; Grant, "'At least you knew where you stood with them'"; Kim, "The Absence of Pan-Canadian Civil Religion." For a recent, though controversial, account of the British scene, see Brown, *The Death of Christian Britian.*

8 For an intriguing account of public religion in the Anglican tradition, see Westfall, "Constructing Public Religions at Private Sites," and Clarke, "Religion and Public Space in Protestant Toronto."

9 The civil religion debate in the United States began in earnest with Robert Bellah's "Civil Religion in America," published in 1967. Bellah has remained a key player in that debate since. See, for example, Bellah and Hammond, *Varieties of Civil Religion*. For a recent and very thorough review of the literature involved in the civil religion debate, see Cristi, *From Civil to Political Religion*.

10 Robert Wuthnow, for example, has recently defined public religion as involving "conceptions of the transcendent" that aim to shape a community's "destiny and sanction its highest values." See Wuthnow, *Producing the Sacred*, 3.

11 Ibid., 9.

12 Again in Wuthnow's words, public religion pertains "to the whole society or to some substantial segment of society," and it is "open and accessible" to all. Wuthnow, *Producing the Sacred*, 13.

13 For two insightful attempts to distinguish between various approaches to and forms of public religion, see Wilson, *Public Religion in American Culture*, chap. 7; Cristi, *From Civil to Political Religion*, 223–42.

14 Here I have followed Jonathan Wilson's four-part continuum of public religion. Wilson, *Public Religion in American Culture*, chap. 7.

15 Put in the language of sociological theories of religion, the prayer service was a blend of Durkheimian and Rousseauian forms of public religion that attempted to enunciate values and beliefs deemed to be at the heart of Canadian society and culture, all for the political purpose of strengthening and solidifying them. See Cristi, *From Civil to Political Religion*, for a clear description of the different views of civil religion held by Durkheim and Rousseau.

16 While they included a Durkheimian element of stating values and beliefs believed to be held by all fairgoers, they also represented the very different belief in transcendent principles and a transcendent being detached from the culture and society by which the culture and society can be judged. See Wilson, *Public Religion in American Culture*, chap. 7.

17 Anderson, *Imagined Communities*, 6.

18 Ibid.

19 See, for example, Hobsbawm, "Mass-Producing Traditions," and Gellner, *Nations and Nationalism*.

20 For a good summary of the literature on this point, see also McCrone, *The Sociology of Nationalism*, chap. 3. It should be noted that this is the viewpoint of a particular school of students of nationalism, often called modernists or constructionists. It is challenged by others who disagree with its dating of the birth of nationalism, as well as its reduction of nationalism

to only a tool of the modern state. I might also add the qualifying argument that nationalism has served equally well as a force for opposing political and economic elites. Here my point is simply to note the ways in which nationalisms and national identities are constructed entities serving the purpose of their creators.

21 Here I follow, among others, Eva Mackey's recent use and defense of the term "dominant culture." Mackey, *The House of Difference*.

22 Williams, *Problems in Materialism and Culture*, 38.

23 David Chennells has recently argued that the history of the politics of nationalism in Canada is one of political elites, particularly at the federal level, attempting to manage demands for exclusive forms of nationalism that most often came from more local, and sometimes provincial, populist sources. See Chennells, *The Politics of Nationalism in Canada*.

24 Colley, *Britons*.

25 Mol, *Faith and Fragility*, 2, 247.

26 Berger, *The Sacred Canopy*, 32–3. This understanding of the legitimating role of religion, offered earlier by Emile Durkheim, lies at the foundation of the concept of civil religion put forth by Robert Bellah in "Civil Religion in America."

27 For the role of public symbols and ritual in nation-building in the past, see also Hobsbawn, "Mass-Producing Traditions," 46, and Colley, *Britons*, chap. 5. On the importance of queen and Crown, the national anthem and the national flag to Canadian identity, see Mol, *Faith and Fragility*, 256–9.

28 Wuthnow, *Producing the Sacred*, 139.

29 Lukes, "Political Ritual and Social Integration," 301.

30 See Breton, "The Production and Allocation of Symbolic Resources"; "Multiculturalism and Canadian Nation-Building"; and "Intergroup Competition."

31 Breton, "The Production and Allocation of Symbolic Resources," 125.

32 Breton, "Intergroup Competition," 293.

33 Cohen, *The Symbolic Construction of Community*.

34 Alexander, "Citizen and Enemy as Symbolic Classification."

35 Spillman, *Nation and Commemoration*, 32. For an excellent cultural and political analysis of the 1937 Paris World's Fair, see Peer, *France on Display*.

36 See Heaman, *The Inglorious Arts of Peace;* Walden, *Becoming Modern in Toronto;* Nelles, *The Art of Nation Building;* and Rudin, *Founding Fathers*. For an excellent article-length study of the celebrations of Canada's Diamond Jubilee in 1927, see Cupido, "Appropriating the Past."

37 Heaman, *The Inglorious Arts of Peace*, 3.

38 For the specific use of the term "contested grounds," see Walden, *Becoming Modern in Toronto*, preface.

39 Cohen, *The Symbolic Construction of Community*, 37.

40 Hall, "Encoding, Decoding."

41 For a recent analysis of historical constructions of Canada, see Strong-Boag, et al., *Painting the Maple*.

CHAPTER TWO

1 Here I am drawing on the work of Charles Tilly, particularly his essay "Citizenship, Identity and Social History," 5–6. I was brought to Tilly's work by Gerald Friesen's *Citizens and Nation*, 225.
2 Québec, *Report of the Royal Commission of Inquiry on Constitutional Problems*.
3 Linteau, et al., *Quebec since 1930*, 282.
4 Trofimenkoff, *The Dream of Nation*, 274.
5 For this interpretation, see Franks, "Counting Canada," 5.
6 For a good collection of essays on English-speaking Catholics in Canada, for example, see Murphy and Stortz, *Creed & Culture*.
7 "Observations," *United Church Observer*, 1 February 1958, 5.
8 As the Canadian census of 1961 reported, 87 percent of Canadians had affiliated themselves with either the Roman Catholic, United, Anglican, Presbyterian, or Baptist Churches. When those affiliated with the Ukrainian Greek Roman Catholic, Pentecostal, Lutheran, Mennonite, and Greek Orthodox Churches were added to that number, the total ran up to 94 percent. See Legacy, *Historical Statistics of Canada*, series A164–184.
9 *United Church of Canada Yearbook, 1960*, 132.
10 For a detailed, yet brief, overview of religion in Canadian education, see Manzer, "Public Philosophy and Public Policy." See also Gidney and Millar, "The Christian Recessional in Ontario's Public Schools."
11 The story of Mrs Wilbert Dunn demonstrates the significance of such legislation. A Roman Catholic, Dunn had married a member of the United Church, and they had adopted a Roman Catholic child. In 1959, two years later, a Roman Catholic priest learned of the situation and contacted the Children's Aid Society to take the child away. When Dunn married a Protestant, the priest argued, she had left the Roman Catholic Church. The case went to court. See "Canadian Child Custody Case Stirs Controversy," *Pentecostal Testimony*, November 1959, 18.
12 Only after two appeals and a trip to the Ontario Court of Appeal in July of 1965 was the decision overturned. See *Regina v. Leach*, Ex parte Bergsma [1966] 1 O.R. 106.
13 As quoted in Kelley and Trebilcock, *The Making of the Mosaic*, 312.
14 Ibid., 328–9.
15 As quoted in Luciuk, *Searching for Place*, 209.
16 Moir, *Church and State in Canada*, xiii.
17 Norman, *Conscience of the State*, 184.
18 See Van Die, "The Marks of a Genuine Revival." See also Clarke, "English-Speaking Canada from 1854."

19 On the broader influence of the various churches in Canadian public life, start with Hamelin, *Histoire du catholicisme québécois*, vol. 2; Grant, "Religion and the Quest for a National Identity"; Gauvreau and Christie, *A Full-Orbed Christianity*; Hutchinson, "Religion, Morality and Law."

20 The close relationship between leaders of church and state institutions is argued in MacDowell, "United Church Support for Collective Bargaining in the 1940s," as well as in Campbell, "Presbyterians and the Canadian Church Union." See also the biographies of such leading churchmen as J.R. Mutchmor and A.B.B. Moore: Mutchmor, *Mutchmor*, and Moore, *Here Where We Live*. On university education in English Canada in the 1930s, see Axelrod, *Making a Middle Class*.

21 Porter, *The Vertical Mosaic*, 289–90, 389–90, 501.

22 Westfall, *Two Worlds*, 23.

23 On this point, see L.B. Kuffert's recent study of cultural critics in English-speaking Canada from 1939 to 1967. Kuffert, *A Great Duty*, chaps. 1 and 3. See also Paul Litt's study of the Royal Commission on National Development in the Arts, Letters, and Sciences (1949–51). Litt, *The Muses, the Masses and the Massey Commission*, 87–101. On the existence of a "moral imperative" in Canadian Protestant culture, see also McKillop, *A Disciplined Intelligence*, and Krygsman, "Freedom and Grace."

24 Katerberg, "Protecting Christian Liberty," 13.

25 See Balthazar, "The Faces of Quebec Nationalism"; Trofimenkoff, *The Dream of Nation*, chap. 14.

26 Perin, "French-Speaking Canada from 1840," 256. Perin adds that Léger's statement was characteristic of the Roman Catholic Church in Quebec of his day.

27 As quoted in Litt, *The Muses, the Masses and the Massey Commission*, 93.

28 From a scholarly perspective in 1950, Arthur Lower wrote that the "Protestant churches so far identify themselves with the state – it is *their* state – that divergence is hardly conceivable." Lower, "Religion and Religious Institutions," 93.

29 Mather, *Christianity and Politics*, 35.

30 The Roman Catholic Church, building on the papal encyclicals *Rerum Novarum* (1891) and *Quadragesimo Anno* (1931), was uncomfortable with political liberalism in a way in which the Protestant churches were not. Particularly in Quebec, it offered instead a corporatist view of society based on a "principle of subsidiarity" that was largely responsible for the church's continued dominance of healthcare, welfare, and education in Quebec into the 1960s. Baum, *Catholics and Canadian Socialism*, chap. 2, 78–9, 88–90, and Hamelin, *Histoire du catholicisme québécois*, 35–8, 251–6. Among the Protestant churches, differences were also apparent. Hubert Krygsman has argued convincingly that the Presbyterian Church of Canada took a more distanced position from the state after 1945 than did the United Church. See his "Freedom and Grace," especially part 3.

31 See Clifford, "His Dominion"; Kim, "The Absence of Pan-Canadian Civil Religion"; Perin, "Religion, Ethnicity and Identity."

32 For differences within the Protestant mainlines on the issue of the prohibition of alcohol, see Clarke, "English-Speaking Canada from 1854," 328.

33 See Quebec, *Report of the Royal Commission of Inquiry on Constitutional Problems*, vol. 2, 6–43; McRoberts, *Misconceiving Canada*, chap. 1.

34 See Barber, "Nationalism, Nativism, and the Social Gospel."

35 See Grant, "At least you knew where you stood with them"; Kim, "The Absence of Pan-Canadian Civil Religion."

36 In his recent analysis of the politics of Canadian nationalism, David Chennells makes the convincing point that in Canada, by necessity, the federal level of government had long attempted to dampen the influence of exclusive nationalisms, emanating from such places as Ontario and Quebec, on the nation as a whole. While local and even provincial politicians could be heavily influenced by exclusive nationalisms held by their more homogeneous electors, successful federal political parties worked hard to maintain a more inclusive nationalist perspective that could appeal to as many diverse local, provincial, and regional interests as possible. Chennells, *The Politics of Nationalism in Canada*.

37 Matheson, *Canada's Flag*, 180.

38 *Hansard*, 1 July 1942, 3836. Hanson was quoting Sir John A. Macdonald.

39 For this reference, see Faulkner, "For Christian Civilization," 3.

40 See Litt, *The Muses*, 212, 92–100.

41 For a contemporary argument for the importance of Christianity to the defense of Western civilization, see Mather, *Christianity and Politics*, chaps. 3–5.

42 Owram, *Born at the Right Time*, 162.

43 As quoted from Gidney and Millar, "The Christian Recessional in Ontario's Public Schools," 11.

44 Lower, "Religion and Religious Institutions," 19, 14.

45 Governor General Georges Vanier, a deeply devout Roman Catholic, in office from 1959 to 1967, spoke of "spiritual values" in his public addresses because "these could mean different things to different people and it was his business to speak, as far as possible, to all Canadians." Speaight, *Vanier*, 448.

46 Gordon Donaldson, "The 'Have-Nots' of Religion," *United Church Observer*, 15 June 1960, 9.

47 Bothwell, Drummond, and English, *Canada since 1945*, 247.

48 Clark, *Church and Sect in Canada*.

49 That analysis found its way into any number of other studies. See Wilson, *The Church Grows in Canada*; see also Moir, "The Sectarian Tradition in Canada."

50 For a good account of the issue of religious broadcasting in early radio from the regulator's perspective, see Johnston, "The Early Trials of Protestant Radio." See also Simpson, "Federal Regulation and Religious Broadcasting

in Canada and the United States," and Peers, *The Politics of Canadian Broadcasting, 1920–1951*, 257–61.

51 Miedema, "Preaching to the Nation." James Opp has argued that fundamentalist Christian groups were forced by government regulations to become less combative on commercial radio, as well as public radio, and that by 1938 much of the controversial and antagonistic tone of early broadcasts had been replaced by what Opp calls a "general evangelical message without … schismatic overtones." See Opp, "The New Age of Evangelism," 110–11.

52 Johnston, "The Early Trials of Protestant Radio," 401–2.

53 In a 1937 meeting with the heads of the largest Canadian churches, the chairman of the CBC, Leonard Brockington, noted that all "agreed that radio shall be used for reconciliation and healing and for the insistence on the eternal truths that unite us rather than on the transitory differences that divide us." For this story, see Peers, *The Politics of Canadian Broadcasting, 1920–1951*, 257–61.

54 Into the early 1960s in Quebec, a fear of causing religious offense to Roman Catholics kept the French-language CBC network from providing any airtime to French Protestants. By 1964 the United, Anglican, Baptist, Presbyterian, and Pentecostal Churches had formed a committee to work against this practice, and in that year the Pentecostal Assemblies of God passed a resolution condemning the religious discrimination. See the "Minutes of the 24th General Conference of the Pentecostal Assemblies of Canada," 17–22 September 1964, 5.

55 See, for example, John Stackhouse's account of the evangelicalism of the Prairie Bible Institute, a conservative Bible college in Three Hills, Alberta. Stackhouse, *Canadian Evangelicalism in the Twentieth Century*, 71–88.

56 Gauvreau and Christie, *A Full-Orbed Christianity*, 64.

57 For example, Russel Johnston argues that it was the anti-Catholic diatribes of Jehovah's Witnesses and of the notorious "Battling Baptist" T.T. Shields that led to the regulation of religious broadcasting on public radio. See Johnston, "The Early Trials of Protestant Radio."

58 As quoted in Plaxton, "The Whole Gospel for a Whole Nation," 215.

59 This is the perspective of a number of studies on the Canadian state. See Traves, *The State and Enterprise*; Moscovitch and Drover, "Social Expenditures and the Welfare State"; Struthers, *No Fault of Their Own*.

60 See Hodgetts, *From Arm's Length to Hands-On*. Hodgetts calls the state in this period an "enabler," not a doer.

61 See Campbell, *Canadian Political Facts, 1945–1976*, 52. This number includes employees of "departmental corporations and administrative, regulatory and special funds." The breakdown by five-year periods is as follows: 1945, 115,908; 1950, 127,196; 1955, 181,582; 1960, 182,305; 1965, 188,571; 1970, 244,197; 1975, 319,605.

62 Granatstein has argued that by the late 1950s, leading bureaucrats used to wielding significant power found their influence mitigated by a greater number of people involved in the federal state bureaucracy and by the weakening of personal relationships that had been so helpful in the past. Granatstein, *The Ottawa Men*, 253–4.

63 Zylberberg and Côté, "Les balises étatiques de la religion au Canada."

64 Restricted to those fields, the argument of Zylberberg and Côté seems to overstate the point for the Protestant churches. In the early twentieth century, in fact, the Protestant churches were some of the leading proponents of the expansion of the welfare state. See Gauvreau and Christie, *A Full-Orbed Christianity*, chap. 6.

65 This issue was the concern of cultural critics, as much as of the churches. See Kuffert, *A Great Duty*, chaps. 1–3. On the rising importance of social scientific experts in Canadian society, see Owram, *Born at the Right Time*, 21–2, chap. 2.

66 Plaxton, "The Whole Gospel for a Whole Nation," 239. Other historians have concurred. Grant, *The Church in the Canadian Era*, 165; Black, "Inwardly Renewed," 118.

67 Fairweather, "The Christian Message in Canada, 1967," 1–4.

68 For a particularly careful and brief sociological account of modernization and differentiation, see Casanova, *Public Religions in the Modern World*, 20–5. For studies of a differentiating Canadian society, see Gauvreau and Christie, *A Full-Orbed Christianity*, chap. 6; Owram, *The Government Generation*; Ferguson, *Remaking Liberalism*. On the shift within the churches to more "private," personal concerns, see Grant, *Church in the Canadian Era*, 173–4, 180; Clifford, "His Dominion," 35–43; and Gauvreau and Christie, *A Full-Orbed Christianity*, chap. 7.

69 Legacy, *Historical Statistics of Canada*, series A125-163.

70 See Francis, *National Dreams*, 80–3.

71 See, for example, Day, *Multiculturalism and the History of Canadian Diversity*; Iacovetta, "Making 'New Canadians'"; Badgley, "As long as he is an immigrant from the U.K."; and Cupido, "Appropriating the Past."

72 On the Hutterites and Doukhobors, see Jansen, *Limits on Liberty*. On Buddhists, note Canada's immigration laws, which heavily restricted entrance into the country of "Orientals," in Kelley and Trebilcock, *The Making of the Mosaic*, 321–8. On anti-Semitism in Canada, see Davies, *Anti-Semitism in Canada*; Abella and Troper, *None Is Too Many*.

73 Kelley and Trebilcock, *The Making of the Mosaic*, 319.

74 After 1955, the civil rights movement in the United States also helped to demonstrate the horrors of racial discrimination to Canadians and to provoke change.

75 Smith, "First Nations, Race and the Idea of a Plural Community," 234.

76 Kuffert, *A Great Duty*.

77 Owram, *Born at the Right Time*, chaps. 2, 5.

78 Kuffert, *A Great Duty*; Litt, *The Muses*, especially 94–101.

79 For this theme in the American context, see Brick, *Age of Contradiction*, 13–18. For an important Canadian critique of pragmatism and "technocracy" in the 1960s, see Grant, *Lament for a Nation*.

80 Grant, *The Church in the Canadian Era*, chap. 8; Owram, *Born at the Right Time*, 171–4; Brick, *Age of Contradiction*. Given the high degree of cultural overlap between Canada and the United States, I have drawn on Brick's work for insights into the Canadian scene, as well.

81 Owram, *Born at the Right Time*, 174; Brick, *Age of Contradiction*, xiv.

82 On the impact of these reformers and of the Quiet Revolution in Quebec, see Behiels, *Prelude to Quebec's Quiet Revolution*; McRoberts, *Quebec: Social Change and Political Crisis*. For an argument that reformers in Quebec were not driven by a secular agenda, see Gauvreau, "From Rechristianization to Contestation."

83 Vallières, *White Niggers of America*.

84 See Porter's, *The Measure of Canadian Society*, 159–60.

85 Luciuk, *Searching for Place*, especially chaps. 7–8, 10.

86 See Wangenheim, "The Ukrainians."

87 This quote was taken from an address of Yuzyk to the Canadian Association of Slavists in 1965. His paper was appropriately and prophetically called "Canada: A Multi-Cultural Nation." As quoted in Porter, *The Measure of Canadian Society*, 117.

88 Bialystok, *Delayed Impact*.

89 The *United Church Observer* made that association quite obvious. In November of 1957, it published the pictures of each minister in Prime Minister Diefenbaker's new cabinet and included each person's church affiliation. Under the name of Michael Starr, that famous Ukrainian, was the Ukrainian Orthodox Church. "The Queen's New Ministers," *United Church Observer*, 1 November 1957, 14–15.

90 Wangenheim, "The Ukrainians," 87.

91 Among Canadian Christian denominations, Pentecostals have been marked by their emphasis on "speaking in tongues," a phenomena of speech attributed to the power of the Holy Spirit. Though Pentecostals in Canada began organizing in 1909, the Pentecostal Assemblies of Canada, the largest Pentecostal denomination in Canada, was formed in 1919. In 1931, the PAOC had approximately 26,349 adherents. By 1951 it had grown to 95,131, and by 1961 it had reached 143,877. See the Census of Canada, 1931, 1951, 1961.

92 On the basis of the rapid growth of the Pentecostals, conservative scholar Henry P. Van Dusen placed them in the limelight by arguing in *Life* magazine in 1958 that they represented a "third force" in American religion, beside Protestants and Roman Catholics. Henry P. Van Dusen, "The Third Force," *Life*, 9 June 1958, 122–4. In response, Canadian Pentecostals actually argued that they were the *first* force. See Raymond L. Cox, "The Pentecostal Movement – Christendom's 'Third Force' or First Force?" *Pentecostal Testimony*, May 1959, 9, 28–9.

93 According to historian Robert Burkinshaw, Gagliardi's election, in particular, "seemed to signify a new position for Pentecostalism in BC." Burkinshaw, *Pilgrims in Lotus Land*, 169.

94 Miller, *Canadian Pentecostals*, 295.

95 See Kulbeck, "The Dangers of Social Climbing," *Pentecostal Testimony*, February 1958, 2.

96 After July 1959, the *Pentecostal Testimony* consistently included comment on Canada's birthday. See, for example, "Canada is Ninety-two Years Old," *Pentecostal Testimony*, July 1959, 2; "Implications of Dominion Day," *Pentecostal Testimony*, July 1961, 2.

97 See, for example, Frederick Leahy, "John Calvin's Social Consciousness," *Pentecostal Testimony*, October 1959, 4, 33; "Christian Social Conscience," *Pentecostal Testimony*, March 1961, 2; Earle E. Cairns, "The State, Church and Christian Citizen," and Walter Judd, "The Christian and Politics," *Pentecostal Testimony*, March 1962, 6–7.

98 The PAOC had been restricted to only one radio broadcast per year for the previous fourteen years and to very little presence at all on television. "Minutes of the 24th General Conference of the Pentecostal Assemblies of Canada," 17–22 September 1964, 12.

99 "French Protestant Broadcasts," *United Church Observer*, 1 January 1958, 6.

100 See Gidney and Millar, "The Christian Recessional in Ontario's Schools"; Grant, *The Church in the Canadian Era*, 179–80.

101 See Ontario, *Religious Information and Moral Development*.

102 Ibid., 14.

103 Ibid., 13–14. According to the report, some Christians in Ontario also "argued that religion belonged in the home and church and that … [religious instruction] might lead to religious dissension." *Religious Information and Moral Development*, 12.

104 Owram, *Born at the Right Time*, 105; Grant, *The Church in the Canadian Era*, 161–5; Stackhouse, "The Protestant Experience in Canada since 1945," 199–202.

105 Linteau, *Quebec since 1930*, chap. 24.

106 Owram, *Born at the Right Time*, 106–9; Grant, *The Church in the Canadian Era*, 161–5; Stackhouse, "The Protestant Experience in Canada since 1945," 205–8.

107 Polls showed Protestant weekly church attendance dropping from 60 percent in 1946 to 43 percent in 1956 and 32 percent in 1965. Bibby, *Fragmented God*, 17.

108 See the respective "Report of the Committee on Statistics and the State of the Church," General Synod of the Anglican Church of Canada, *Journal of Proceedings*, for 1965, 1967, and 1969.

109 McRoberts, *Quebec: Social Change and Political Crisis*, chaps. 3–4; Hamelin, *Histoire du catholicisme québécois*, chap. 3.

110 The following quotes are taken from the United States edition of the book. See Berton, *The Comfortable Pew*, 52.

Notes to pages 36-43

111 Ibid., 68.

112 Ibid., 108.

113 For such criticisms of the church in the nineteenth century, see Turner, *Without God, without Creed.*

114 Berton, *The Comfortable Pew*, viii.

115 United Church of Canada, *Why the Sea is Boiling Hot.*

116 Dion and O'Neill, *L'immoralité politique dans la province de Québec*, was originally supposed to be an in-house document of the Roman Catholic Church. It criticized the church's close ties to politics and suggested that they hampered its mission. When the press got hold of the document and published it, it caused quite a sensation as an open and powerful critique of the church by some of its own. The much more famous *Les Insolences de Frère Untel* (Montreal, 1960) was written by another priest, J.P. Desbiens, who was very unhappy with the state of education in Quebec. See also Harris, *Brief to the Bishops.*

117 Kilbourn, *The Restless Church.*

118 Young, "Theme and Variations," 288.

119 Jay, "Missiological Implications of Christianizing the Social Order," 278.

120 Young, "Theme and Variations," 288.

121 Kelley and Trebilcock, *The Making of the Mosaic*, 347.

122 Bumsted, *Peoples of Canada*, 369.

123 Owram, *Born at the Right Time*, 161.

124 Noll, *A History of Christianity*, 442.

125 Ibid., 548.

126 Berton, *1967*, 110, 161.

CHAPTER THREE

1 For the story of the development of Canada's flag, see Matheson, *Canada's Flag*; Granatstein, *Canada, 1957–1967*, 201–5.

2 Matheson, *Canada's Flag*, 24–38.

3 They also made sense in the realm of foreign affairs. Lester B. Pearson, prime minister from 1963 to 1967, was convinced that Canada needed its own national insignia, distinct from Britain's, when Egypt, during the Suez Crisis, "refused to accept Canadian troops for the United Nations Emergency Force because of their British insignia." It has also been suggested that the push for a new flag was at least partly intended to improve government morale and divert public attention from recent scandals that had badly hurt the Pearson Liberals. English, *The Worldly Years*, 289.

4 Ibid.

5 Matheson, *Canada's Flag*, xi.

6 For a sampling of those letters, see Matheson, *Canada's Flag*, 188–219.

7 Graratstein, *Canada, 1957–1967*, 202.

8 Ibid., 200.

9 Matheson, *Canada's Flag*, 3.
10 Ibid., 160.
11 Ibid., 165–6.
12 "The President's Address," The General Synod of the Anglican Church of Canada, *Journal of Proceedings* (1965), 8–13.
13 Matheson, *Canada's Flag*, 198.
14 Drawing on the work of others, Raymond Breton argues that the symbolic order of a nation includes its "collective identity ... represented in the multiplicity of symbols surrounding the rituals of public life, the functioning of institutions, and the public celebration of events, groups and individuals." It includes the "values and norms" and "customs and ways of doing things" of a nation that are most importantly "embedded in the forms and style of public institutions" such as government, school curricula, and the administration of justice. Breton, "The Production and Allocation of Symbolic Resources," 125.
15 Ninette Kelley and Michael Trebilcock have argued that those changes had as much to do with Canada's international reputation as they did with domestic affairs. See Kelley and Trebilcock, *The Making of the Mosaic*, 319.
16 Bothwell, Drummond, and English, *Canada since 1945*, 240, 256.
17 Behiels, "Lester B. Pearson and the Conundrum of National Unity, 1963–1968," 70.
18 English, *The Worldly Years*, 302.
19 Brodie and Jenson, *Crisis, Challenge and Change*, 247.
20 See Brick, *Age of Contradiction*, 1. Brick defines the "social sphere" as "extra-familial social institutions ... experiences enjoyed in public life, and ... demands for services and forms of human interaction that transcend the individualism of economic markets."
21 Hillmer, introduction, 16.
22 As quoted in Ayre, *Mr. Pearson and Canada's Revolution by Diplomacy*, 124.
23 Canada, Royal Commission on Bilingualism and Biculturalism, *A Preliminary Report*, 21–5, 151.
24 Horton, *André Laurendeau*, chap. 10; Pearson, *Mike*, vol. 3, 237.
25 Horton, *André Laurendeau*, 217.
26 House of Commons, *Debates*, 8 October 1971, 8546.
27 Ibid.
28 Pal, *Interests of State*, 251.
29 Goldstein, "Public Interest Groups and Public Policy," 142.
30 See Kelley and Trebilcock, *The Making of the Mosaic*, 349. See also Simeon and Robinson, *State, Society, and the Development of Canadian Federalism*, 155.
31 In 1950, for example, the government of Ontario passed a new Lord's Day Act that gave municipalities the right to decide on Sunday sports. Toronto immediately legalized them. Paul Laverdure, "Canada's Sunday."

32 See Appleby, *Responsible Parenthood*.

33 The statement was made in an interview in Ottawa on 12 December 1967.

34 Linteau, et. al., *Quebec since 1930*, 242. See also Hamelin, *Histoire du catholicisme québécois*, vol. 2, 134–6.

35 Black, *Duplessis*, 512.

36 Plaxton, "The Whole Gospel for a Whole Nation," 315, 328–9.

37 Laverdure, "Canada's Sunday."

38 See, in particular, David Plaxton's account of Gordon Sisco, general secretary of the United Church of Canada from 1936 to 1953. Plaxton, "The Whole Gospel for a Whole Nation," 322. For a good account of the rethinking of the relationship between Christianity and Canadian culture in the United and Presbyterian Churches in the postwar period, see Krygsman, "Freedom and Grace." On Catholic voices pushing for reform in Quebec, see Gauvreau, "From Rechristianization to Contestation."

39 Grant, *The Church in the Canadian Era*, 203.

40 Gauvreau and Christie, *A Full-Orbed Christianity*, chap. 6. See also Pulker, *We Stand on Their Shoulders*, 130.

41 Ibid., 172.

42 Plaxton, "The Whole Gospel for a Whole Nation," 287–336; Hamelin, *Histoire du catholicisme québécois*, 134.

43 The *United Church Observer* noted in 1957, for example, that "A-booming and a-building seems to describe the mood and the activity of Canadian churches as 1957 comes to a close ... We've scarcely seen a church which wasn't starting in on, in the midst of, or finishing up some ambitious project." "Observations," *United Church Observer*, 15 December 1957, 5. See also Grant, *The Church in the Canadian Era*, 160–3.

44 The publication of Reynolds, *Life and Death*, caused major waves in Canada's major daily newspapers because of some of its provocative and challenging statements on the topic. In the spring of 1958, the *Observer* also began publishing a series of provocative articles by A.J. Ebbutt with such titles as "Was Jesus Really Tempted?" and "Miracles: Fact or Fiction?" Those articles kicked off a passionate debate in the letters to the editor that was somewhat dampened when the editor himself chided those who were offended by arguing that Ebbut's ideas were nothing new and had been taught in theological colleges for years. He hoped the articles would "help bridge the gap between pulpit and pew." It was time, he clearly thought, to bring the masses up to date, whether they liked it or not. See the May through July 1958 issues of the *United Church Observer*. The editor's comments were made in "Observations," July 1958, 5.

45 "Report of the Board of Evangelism and Social Service," *The United Church of Canada Yearbook*, 1961, 139.

46 As quoted from Plaxton, "The Whole Gospel for a Whole Nation," 234.

47 General Synod of the Anglican Church of Canada, *Journal of Proceedings of the Twentieth Session* (1955), 181.

48 Or "The hour is not one of compromise" (my translation). Hamelin, *Histoire du catholicisme québécois*, 140.

49 Ibid., 152.

50 Grant, *The Church in the Canadian Era*, 170–1.

51 Hamelin, *Histoire du catholicisme québécois*, 176–8; Grant, *The Church in the Canadian Era*, 171.

52 Rouillard, "Major Changes in the Confederation des travailleurs catholiques du Canada."

53 Many noted the growing criticism of the church in this period. See, in particular, Behiels, "Quebec: Social Transformation and Ideological Renewal," and "Father Georges-Henri Lévesque and the Introduction of Social Sciences at Laval."

54 Hamelin, *Histoire du catholicisme québécois*, 226.

55 Moir, *Enduring Witness*, 257.

56 Seljak, "Why the Quiet Revolution was 'Quiet,'" 109–24; Baum, *The Church in Quebec*, chap. 1.

57 Grant, *The Church in the Canadian Era*, 185, 219.

58 According to historian Robert Merrill Black, "The sense of belonging to a worldwide church was formative for many of the present leaders of the Canadian church." Black, "Inwardly Renewed," 117. See also Grant, *The Church in the Canadian Era*, 185–219.

59 As one example, criticisms of the churchly status quo were rare in the *United Church Observer* in the late 1950s. Only one columnist, J.A. Davidson, seemed to consistently push his readers to recognize such things as the shallowness in some congregations and their elitist, "social club" character. See Davidson's column, "Ad Lib," *United Church Observer*, 1 January 1958 to 15 September 1960, 16.

60 For this take on *The Comfortable Pew* and for an argument that the churches started the reevaluation themselves, see Grant, *The Church in the Canadian Era*, 195.

61 "The President's Address," General Synod of the Anglican Church of Canada, *Journal of Proceedings* (1965), 7–8.

62 "Report of the Commission on the Ministry in the Twentieth Century to the Twenty-third General Council," 1.

63 Ibid., 2.

64 *The United Church of Canada Yearbook, 1968*, 10.

65 "Report of the Board of Evangelism and Social Service," *The United Church of Canada Yearbook, 1965*, 109.

66 Philip Jefferson, "What We Have Tried To Do," *Canadian Churchman* 92:4 (April 1965), 7.

67 Grant, *The Church in the Canadian Era*, 187.

68 Ibid., 189; Kilbourn, *Religion in Canada*, 68.

69 For a sustained argument concerning this change in the world-wide Roman Catholic Church, see Casanova, *Public Religions in the Modern World*. On the Canadian scene, see Hamelin, *Histoire du catholicisme québécois*, chap. 4; Baum, *The Church in Quebec*, chaps. 1–2; Seljak, "Why the Quiet Revolution Was 'Quiet'"; Appleby, *Responsible Parenthood*, 85.

70 On the approach of the Roman Catholic hierarchy in Quebec to the changes of both the 1950s and the 1960s and to Vatican II, see Hamelin, *Histoire du catholicisme québécois*, chaps. 3–4.

71 "Committee on Life and Mission," in "Guide to the Administrative History of the Presbyterian Church," Archives of the Presbyterian Church of Canada, 19.

72 William E. Hume, "The Care of Your Minister," *Presbyterian Record* 92:2 (April 1967): 10.

73 See Grant, *The Canadian Experience of Church Union*, 83.

74 Grant, *Church in the Canadian Era*, 192–3.

75 Hamelin, *Histoire du catholicisme québécois*, 227–9; Beaubien, *Towards Christian Unity in Canada*.

76 For a brief summary of the results of Vatican II, see Casanova, *Public Religions in the Modern World*, 71–4. For the documents prepared and released by the Council, see Abbott, *The Documents of Vatican II*. For a study of the Canadian Church and Vatican II, see Routhier, *L'Église canadienne et Vatican II*.

77 Grant, *Church in the Canadian Era*, 191.

78 Ibid., 190.

79 For a very brief summary of the theological trends of the 1960s, see Grant, *The Church in the Canadian Era*, 199. See also the *Canadian Journal of Theology* 13:1 (1967), which was dominated by existentialist themes.

80 Again, the *Canadian Journal of Theology* exhibited this line of thought. See Shaw, "The Basically Supernatural Character of the Christian Gospel," 259; see also Grant, *The Church in the Canadian Era*, 199.

81 Cox, *The Secular City*. Cox's term "secular city" became a theological catch phrase of the mid-1960s.

82 The leading academic voices of the Death of God theology were Thomas J.J. Altizer, William Hamilton, and Paul M. Van Buren. See, for example, Altizer and Hamilton, *Radical Theology and the Death of God*; Van Buren, *The Secular Meaning of the Gospel*.

83 See Harrison, *Let God Go Free*. The description is taken from "Toronto Priest's $ Bombshell," *Toronto Daily Star*, 24 April 1965, 23.

84 Editorial, "God: Dead or Alive?" *Canadian Churchman*, March 1966, 4.

85 For the controversy, see the March, April, and May 1966 issues of the *Canadian Churchman*. For Clark's response, see Howard. H. Clark, "A Pastoral Review of Theological Ferment," *Canadian Churchman*, May 1966, 9.

86 Grant, The *Church in the Canadian Era*, 198.

87 A survey of The *Canadian Churchman* in 1965 demonstrates this well.

88 Moir, *Enduring Witness*, 268.

89 The comment was widely reported by the press. See Warren Gerard, "Moderator Rejects Belief That Christ's Body Resurrected," *Globe and Mail*, 27 April 1965, 1; "Dr Howse Tells How He Views the Resurrection," *Toronto Daily Star*, 24 April 1965, 23; "Moderator Questions Physical Resurrection," St John's *Evening Telegram*, 23 April 1965, 20; "Moderator Raises Storm by Resurrection Statement," *Edmonton Journal* 24 April 1965, 31.

90 As quoted in Berton, *The Comfortable Pew*, xi.

91 For the Anglicans, see "Evangelicals Plan Fellowship Group," *Canadian Churchman*, May 1966, 6.

92 On this gap in the United Church, see Grant, "Roots and Wings."

93 The biographies of the moderators of the United Church from the late 1950s through to the 1970s reveal that the succession of men holding the top office of the church also held very different opinions on where the Church should go. See, respectively, MacQueen, *Memory Is My Diary*, vol. 2; Howse, *Roses in December*; Pope, *Clarence Mackinnon Nicholson*.

94 As quoted in Moir, *Enduring Witness*, 260–1.

95 "The President's Address," General Synod of the Anglican Church of Canada, *Journal of Proceedings of the Nineteenth Session* (1965), 13.

96 In 1960, for example, the United Church officially stated that in addition to total abstinence, drinking in moderation was an acceptable option. In 1965 it also gave its official approval to legal abortions in cases of rape or in cases where the mother's health was at risk. The 1967 Assembly of the Presbyterian Church supported therapeutic abortion. On the changing perspectives of the churches on contraception, see Appleby, *Responsible Parenthood*.

97 Reisner, *Strangers and Pilgrims*, 96.

98 Daly, *Remembering for Tommorrow*, 104. Under the old system, Daly remarks, a "scowl from a cardinal could kill a motion before it was even seconded." Under the new system, their power was significantly moderated.

99 Hamelin, *Histoire du catholicisme québécois*, 287.

100 Moir, *Enduring Witness*, 269–70.

101 United Church of Canada, *Report of the Commission on the Ministry in the Twentieth Century*, 6. The quote was taken from a radio program entitled "The Listener," which was heard on the BBC on 2nd March 1967.

102 Ibid.

103 Murphy and Perin, *A Concise History*, 366.

104 Appleby, *Responsible Parenthood*, 224.

105 Ibid., 85.

106 Murphy and Perin, *A Concise History*, 366.

107 That, according to José Casanova, was also precisely what happened in Roman Catholic churches around the world in the wake of Vatican II. See Casanova, *Public Religions in the Modern World*, chap. 5.

108 Black, "Inwardly Renewed," 129.

109 Murphy and Perin, *A Concise History*, 366. The significance of that transition from establishment church to defender of the weak was best demonstrated by the transformation in both style and subject matter of documents published by the Canadian Conference of Catholic Bishops in the 1950s and 1960s. See Sheridan, *Do Justice*, 41.

CHAPTER FOUR

1 The following account of the flame-lighting ceremony has been reconstructed from "PM Kindles Flame to Canada's Year," *Ottawa Citizen*, 3 January 1967, 3; Michael Gillan, "Cheers Ring Out as Prime Minister Puts Flame to Centennial Torch," *Globe and Mail*, 2 January 1967, 1, 2; Dennis Braithwaite, "Words Fail Us," *Globe and Mail*, 2 January 1967, 17.

2 "The Flame Lighting Ceremony, Parliament Hill, Eve of the Centennial, 31 December 1966," in Armitage, *Canadian Centennial Anthology of Prayer*, 10.

3 "Anthem for the Centennial of Canadian Confederation," in Armitage, *Canadian Centennial Anthology of Prayer*, viii.

4 Berton, *1967*, 13.

5 Pearson, *Words and Occasions*, 245.

6 See, for example, the *Ottawa Citizen*, 3 January 1967, 6.

7 Every province and territory was eligible for a maximum grant of 10.5 million dollars to construct a Confederation memorial building of some significant nature, and they all took advantage of the opportunity. See Aykroyd, *The Anniversary Compulsion*, appendix K, 200.

8 *Ottawa Citizen*, 3 January 1967, 6.

9 Peter Aykroyd lists the grand total of expenditures of the Centennial Commission as $359,456,592, in 1992 dollars. See Aykroyd, *The Anniversary Compulsion*, 197.

10 *Birthday of a Nation*, 1.

11 See Pearson, *Words and Occasions*, 234, as well as Bothwell, Drummond, and English, *Canada since 1945*, 271–3.

12 Pearson, *Words and Occasions*, 234.

13 Ibid., 234–6.

14 National Archives of Canada (NA), RG69, vol. 386, file 5, "Proceedings of the Fourth Meeting of the National Conference: Toronto, November 25–26, 1964."

15 Centennial Commission, *The Centennial Handbook*, 3.

16 Ibid., 27.

17 NA, RG69, vol. 386, file 5, "Proceedings of the Fifth Meeting of the National Conference: Regina, May, 11–12, 1965."
18 NA, RG69, vol. 389, "Minutes of the Meeting of the Board of Directors of the Centennial Commission, 25 November 1964."
19 Pal, *Interests of State*, 269. That thesis is also supported by Goldstein's, "Public Interest Groups and Public Policy," 142, but both authors ignore the role of citizen involvement and state intervention in the voluntary sector in the years leading up to and including the Centennial celebrations of 1967.
20 This is the central argument of Helen Davies in her doctoral thesis, "The Politics of Participation."
21 "Confederation Train on the Way West," *Globe and Mail*, Monday, 2 January 1967, 12.
22 NA, MG28 176, vol. 3, file, "Report – final – to BD of Dir. – 1967," 4.
23 One of the most innovative participating clergy, perhaps, was the Reverend Jim Liles of Browman, Manitoba. When his town held a privy-burning event to usher in the Centennial and a new age of central sewage treatment, Liles, the local United Church minister, delivered a tongue-in-cheek "funeral oration." See Berton, *1967*, 10–12.
24 See NA, MG28 176, vol. 3, file, "Report – final – to BD of Dir. – 1967," for an expansive list of religious activities aimed at celebrating the Centennial, as well as a record of numerous 1 July services.
25 See *Canadian Churchman*, December, 1966, 19; *Presbyterian Record*, January 1967, 7; *United Church Observer*, 15 December 1966, back page.
26 Having grown to twenty-eight members by the time of the April conference, the CIC reached a total of thirty-three member faiths by the middle of the Centennial year. Listed in alphabetical order, the member faiths were as follows: Anglican Church of Canada, Baptist Federation of Canada, Buddhist Churches of Canada, Byelorussian Authocephalic Orthodox Church, Canadian Jewish Congress, Canadian Unitarian Council, Canadian Yearly Meeting of the Religious Society of Friends, Christian and Missionary Alliance in Canada, Christian Science, Churches of Christ (Disciples), Church of Jesus Christ of Latter-Day Saints, Church of the Nazarene, Evangelical United Brethren, Fellowship of Evangelical Baptist Churches in Canada, Free Methodist Churches in Canada, Greek Orthodox Church, Islamic Community, Lutheran Council in Canada, Mennonite Central Committee of Canada, National Spiritual Assembly of the Baha'is of Canada, Pentecostal Assemblies of Canada, Presbyterian Church in Canada, Reformed Episcopal Church of Canada, Roman Catholic Church, Romanian Orthodox Episcopate of America, Salvation Army, Seventh-Day Adventist Church in Canada, Syrian Antiochian Orthodox Church, Ukrainian Catholic Church, Ukrainian Greek-Orthodox Church of Canada, Union of Spiritual Communities of Christ (Doukhobors), United Church of Canada, and Zoroastrians.

27 King, *From the Ghetto to the Main*, 242.

28 NA, MG28 I76, vol. 1, file 6–9, Minutes of Executive Meetings, 20 October 1965, 15 November 1965, 6 January 1966.

29 All the above information has been drawn from the papers of the Canadian Interfaith Conference, NA, MG28 I76.

30 NA, MG28 I76 vol. 11, file 2, "Memorandum to Management Committee on Church Centennial Participation in 1967," from Elliot, 14 October 1964.

31 NA, RG 69, vol. 386, file 5, "Minutes of the 3rd Meeting of the Standing Committee on Historical Activities of the National Conference on the Centennial of Confederation"; NA, MG28 I76, vol. 11, "Inter-Faith Steering Committee: Minutes of a Meeting on Tuesday, March 9, 1965 at the Chateau Laurier to Discuss Church Participation in the Centennial of Confederation," 6.

32 NA, MG28 I76, vol. 1, file 5, "Minutes of the Meeting of the Executive Committee, October 20, 1965."

33 NA, MG28 I76, vol. 1, file 1, "Memo to Father Mathieu [et al.] RE: July 22, 1965 Meeting of the Executive Committee of Inter-faith Conference," section 4.

34 NA, MG28 I76, vol. 11, file 2, "Memorandum to Management Committee on Church Centennial Participation in 1967," from Elliot, October 14, 1964.

35 NA, RG69, vol. 389, "Basic Objectives or Guidelines for the Centennial Commission," approved by the board of directors on 27 November 1964.

36 NA, MG28 I76, vol. 1, file 1, "Memorandum of Agreement," dated 14 December 1965.

37 NA, MG28 I76, vol. 3, file 2, "Report on the Inter-Faith Conference Activities Held in Ottawa on 5 July 1965."

38 NA, MG28 I76, vol. 4, file 6, Peter Aykroyd's address to the 26–27 April 1966 conference.

39 NA, MG28 I76, vol. 3, file 2, "Report on the Interfaith Conference Activities Held in Ottawa on July 5, 1965."

40 NA, MG28 I76, vol. 11, last file, "Church Can Help Bring Unity – Lamontagne," *Ottawa Citizen*, 6 July 1965, 5.

41 NA, MG28 I76, vol. 4, file 6, from the text of George Gauthier's speech to the 26–27 April 1966 Canadian Interfaith Conference.

42 NA, MG28 I76, vol. 11, "Inter-Faith Steering Committee: Minutes of a Meeting on Tuesday, March 9, 1965 at the Chateau Laurier to Discuss Church Participation in the Centennial of Confederation," 6.

43 Smith, "Celebrations and History on the Prairies," 56.

44 NA, RG69, vol. 386, file 5, "Minutes of the 3rd Meeting of the Standing Committee on Historical Activities of the National Conference on the Centennial of Confederation."

45 NA, MG28 176, vol. 1, file 1, "Memo to Father Mathieu [et al.] RE: July 22, 1965 meeting of Executive Committee of Inter-faith Conference," section 4.

46 Until the Trudeau era, Leslie Pal has recently argued, federal governments were willing to fund programs but not administrations in the voluntary sector, for fear that direct funding for organizations would entangle the government too closely in their affairs. See Pal, *Interests of State*, 104, 269.

47 Aykroyd, *The Anniversary Compulsion*, 144.

48 Expressed in 1967 dollars, the total expenditures of the Centennial Commission from 1963 to 1968 was close to an astounding $85 million. Within that sum, a total proposed grant to the CIC of $60,000 over three years was negligible. In 1992 dollars, the CIC received some $459,000. That grant compares with $604,202 spent on historical re-enactments, $489,632.00 on student involvement, and $835,724.00 on participation by Indians. See Aykroyd, *The Anniversary Compulsion*, appendices I to L.

49 NA, MG28 176, vol. 11, file 2, "Memorandum to the Board of Directors of the Centennial Commission on Interfaith Centennial Activities," from Elliot, 14 October 1964.

50 NA, MG28 176, vol. 1, file 1, "Memo to Father Mathieu [et al.] RE: July 22, 1965 meeting of Executive Committee of Inter-faith Conference," section 4.

51 NA, MG28 176, vol. 13, file "Centennial Commission, General Correspondence," letter from LeBlanc to Becker, 6 May 1966.

52 Johnston, "The Early Trials of Protestant Radio," 401–2.

53 NA, MG28 176, vol. 2, file 5, "Minutes of Meeting of Board of Directors of the Canadian Interfaith Conference, 19 September 1966."

54 NA, MG28 176, vol. 2, file 6, "Minutes of Meeting of Board of Directors of the Canadian Interfaith Conference, 23 November 1967." These comments are taken from a summary report by Gilstorf within the minutes.

55 NA, MG28 176, vol. 6, letter from Becker to Gauthier, October 26, 1966.

56 NA, MG28 176, vol. 2, file 6, "Minutes of Meeting of Board of Directors of the Canadian Interfaith Conference, November 23, 1967."

57 See Breton, "The Production and Allocation of Symbolic Resources," "Multiculturalism and Canadian Nation-Building," and "Intergroup Competition in the Symbolic Construction of Canadian Society."

58 Breton, "The Production and Allocation of Symbolic Resources," 127.

59 Any organized religion in Canada was welcome in the CIC.

60 Membership in the National Religious Advisory Council was originally restricted to the United, Anglican, Presbyterian, Baptist, and Roman Catholic Churches. The chair of the council (a member of one of those churches) was said to represent the other Canadian faith traditions not present. The CBC gave this organization the responsibility for dividing up free airtime for religious services on Sundays between Canada's religious groups. Miedema, "Preaching to the Nation."

61 An unnamed delegate to a CIC conference was reported as stating that "Ecumenical [*sic*] and Centennial comes at a providential time when the ecumenical spirit is beginning to be felt in the community, and we are blessed indeed when the Canadian Government is assisting our efforts." NA, MG28 176, vol. 11, last file, "Interim Report on Interfaith Seminar, July 5, 1965."

62. See Breton, "The Production and Allocation of Symbolic Resources," 136.

63 "Happy Centennial," *Ottawa Citizen*, 3 January 1967, 6.

64 Aykroyd, *The Anniversary Compulsion*, 134.

65 NA, MG28 176, vol. 1, file 1, "Memorandum of Agreement," dated 14 December 1965.

66 NA, MG28 176, vol. 1, file 10, "Canadian Interfaith Conference – Tentative Agenda – April 26–27, 1966."

67 NA, MG28 176, vol. 1, file 5, "Minutes of Executive Meeting, October 20, 1965."

68 The Pentecostal Assemblies of Canada, for example, was a member faith of the CIC, in spite of its denunciation of the ecumenical movement. See "Minutes of the 24th General Conference of the Pentecostal Assemblies of Canada," 17–22 September 1964, 8.

69 In the 1960s the "Islamic Community," listed as a member faith of the CIC, was small, had no central administration, and was made up mostly of an ethnically diverse group of recent postwar immigrants. See Abu-Lahan, "The Canadian Muslim Community."

70 Peter, "The Myth of Multiculturalism and Other Political Fables," 64.

71 Brotz, "Multiculturalism in Canada," 41–6; Kallen, "Multiculturalism," 60–8.

72 Bannerji, "On the Dark Side of the Nation."

73 Berry and Laponce, "Evaluating Research on Canada's Multiethnic and Multiculturalism Society," 9. See also Mackey, *The House of Difference*.

74 See Harney, "So Great a Heritage as Ours." As quoted from Paquet, "Political Philosophy of Multiculturalism," 67.

75 Day, *Multiculturalism and the History of Canadian Diversity*, and Mackey, *The House of Difference*.

76 NA, RG71, vol. 6, letter, Gilstorf to Becker, 20 February 1967.

77 Studies of the Roman Catholic Church, in particular, demonstrate how the changes it made in the 1960s were part of an attempt to retain their influence in Canadian public life. See Hamelin, *Histoire du catholicisme québécois*, 353–73; Baum, *The Church in Quebec*, 15–67.

78 See Legacy, *Historical Statistics of Canada*, series A164–184.

79 Grant, *The Church in the Canadian Era*, 204. For a more statistical discussion of the disintegration of influence of the large Christian Churches in Canadian society in the last two decades, see Bibby, *Fragmented Gods*, and *Unknown Gods*.

80 NA, MG28 176, vol. 2, file 6, "Minutes of 'After Conference Planning' Meeting of April 27, 1966." See the "Report of the Small Group Dialogue Committee," within the minutes.

81 As quoted in NA, MG28 176, vol. 2, file 5, "Minutes of the Board of Directors Meeting," September 19, 1966.

82 NA, MG28 176, vol. 8, speech to the Ottawa Diocesan Board of the Women's Auxiliary of the Anglican Church, 19 April 1967, entitled "Faith the Key to the Future."

83 NA, MG28 176, vol. 1, file 16, "Minutes of the Meeting of the Executive Board of the Canadian Interfaith Conference, February 15, 1967."

84 NA, RG69, vol. 392, executive committee document EC 67–52.

CHAPTER FIVE

1 NA, MG28 176, vol. 9, file "Baptists," letter from F. Bullen to Gilstorf, 26 October 1967.

2 NA, MG28 176, vol. 9, file "Evangelical Baptists," letter from C.A. Tipps to Gilstorf, 30 December 1966.

3 NA, MG28 176, vol. 27, file "Montreal Meeting, October 3, 1966," typewritten document describing 3 October meeting, no title, no date.

4 NA, MG28 176, vol. 27, file "Montreal Meeting, October 3, 1966," letter, Irénée Beaubien to Lavy M. Becker, 19 September 1966.

5 Ibid.

6 NA, MG28 176, vol. 27, file "Montreal Meeting, October 3, 1966," document, "Programme."

7 According to Louis Fosey-Foley, an article in *La Presse* claimed that distinction. See NA, MG28 176, vol. 27, file "Montreal Meeting, October 3, 1966," "Préparatifs en vue de la celebration interconfessionelle du centenaire," *La Presse*, 5 October 1966. The article dripped with sarcasm and poked fun at Lavy Becker for his inability to understand why Quebeckers did not share his own enthusiasm for the CIC and the Centennial. It also noted that when a Monsignor Leclerc of New Brunswick asked why Quebeckers were not more excited about the Centennial, journalists burst into laughter. It was clearly not a good day.

8 NA, MG28 176, vol. 6, letter from Gilstorf to A. Macdonald, 5 October 1966.

9 The following summary of the work of that committee is drawn from the "Report of the Primate's Proposals Committee on the Church's Observance of Canada's Centennial," *General Synod Journal, Twenty-first Session* (1962), 292–3.

10 Ibid., 293.

11 Ibid.

12 As noted in chapter 3, the Anglican World Congress was a very significant event in the life of the Anglican Church of Canada, absorbing a great deal

of its general office's energy in 1962 and 1963. A kind of Anglican version of Vatican II, it took place in Toronto in August of 1963 and involved 995 delegates and 393 official guests. See "Highlights of the Anglican Congress," *Canadian Churchman*, September 1963, 1.

13 "Report of the Primate's Proposals Committee," 293.

14 "Report of the Committee on the Observance of Canada's Centennial," *General Synod Journal, Twenty-second Session* (1965), 316–17.

15 "Report of the Budget Committee," *General Synod Journal, Twenty-second Session* (1965), 280–2.

16 "Report of the Committee on the Observance of Canada's Centennial," 317.

17 Ibid.

18 They accurately reflected the developments since 1961 of the decision of Canada to hold a world exposition in Montreal in 1967, as well as the rise into public life of a questioning and unsettled generation of youth.

19 "Report of the Committee on the Observance of Canada's Centennial," 317.

20 Formed in 1919, the Pentecostal Assemblies of Canada had 143,877 adherents in 1961, according to the national census in that year. By comparison, the Anglican Church of Canada was listed as having 2,409,068 adherents.

21 Pentecostal Assemblies of Canada (PAOC), Document Case 16, Series 2, Committees, file "Centennial Committee," document entitled "Minutes of the meeting of the Centennial Committee, June 8, 1966."

22 To pay for this, the committee urged Pentecostals to increase by 20 percent in 1967 their giving to world missions. PAOC, Document Case 16, Series 2, Committees, file "Centennial Committee," "Minutes – July 13, 1966."

23 PAOC, Document Case 16, Series 2, Committees, file "Centennial Committee," document entitled "Centennial Committee Report, 1966."

24 PAOC, Document Case 16, Series 2, Committees, file "Centennial Committee," "Minutes – August 12, 1966."

25 PAOC, Document Case 16, Series 2, Committees, file "Centennial Committee," "Minutes of the Meeting of the Centennial Committee of Nov. 3, 1966 at the National Office," 4.

26 PAOC, *Minutes of the 1966 General Conference of the Pentecostal Assemblies of Canada*, 15–16.

27 NA, MG28 I76, vol. 3, file 2, "Report on the Inter-Faith Conference Activities Held in Ottawa on July 5, 1965."

28 For a classic study of different nationalisms and nations in Canada, see Cook, *The Maple Leaf Forever*.

29 Documents Department, Stauffer Library, Queen's University, Centennial Commission Press Release, 25 April 1966.

30 NA, MG28 I76, vol. 3, file 2, "Report on the Inter-Faith Conference Activities Held in Ottawa on July 5, 1965."

31 Lavy Becker, "Chairman's Foreword," in Armitage, *Canadian Centennial Anthology of Prayer*, xiv–xv.

32 NA, MG28 176, vol. 3, file 2, "Report on the Inter-Faith Conference Activities Held in Ottawa on July 5, 1965."

33 Ibid.

34 NA, MG28 176, vol. 11, last file, "Interim Report on Interfaith Seminar, July 5, 1965."

35 NA, MG28 176, vol. 3, file 2, "Report on the Inter-Faith Conference Activities Held in Ottawa on July 5, 1965."

36 Grant, *The Church in the Canadian Era*, 194–5.

37 NA, MG28 176, vol. 10, file "Reformed Episcopal Church."

38 Ibid.

39 "31 Faiths Hold National Conference," *Canadian Baha'i News*, June 1966, 5.

40 NA, MG28 176, vol. 1, file 10, "Canadian Interfaith Conference – Tentative Agenda – April 26–27."

41 NA, MG28 176, vol. 9, letter from National Spiritual Assembly of the Baha'i faith to the CIC, 2 February 1967.

42 NA, MG28 176, vol. 9, letter from Local Spiritual Assembly of Saint John, NB, to National Spiritual Assembly, 9 March 1967.

43 "Interfaith – A Second Look," *Canadian Baha'i News*, July 1967, 6.

44 NA, MG28 176, vol. 11, "Inter-Faith Steering Committee: Minutes of a Meeting on Tuesday, March 9, 1965 at the Chateau Laurier to Discuss Church Participation in the Centennial of Confederation," 6.

45 The Lutheran Council joined the Anglicans in placing historical plaques on their churches, and for good reason. The year 1967 also marked the 450th anniversary of the Reformation and the beginning of the Lutheran Church. NA, MG28 176, vol. 3, file 2, in the appendices of the Minutes of the Meeting of the Board of Directors of the CIC, 23 November 1967.

46 Wilson, *The Church Grows in Canada*. In similar fashion, the Fellowship of Evangelical Baptist Churches had Leslie K. Tarr, the secretary of the denomination's Home Missions Board, write *This Dominion, His Dominion: The Story of Evangelical Baptist Endeavour in Canada*.

47 NA, MG28 176, vol. 10, file "Zoroastrians."

48 NA, MG28 176, vol. 4, file 6, summary of the 26–27 April 1966 conference by Lavy Becker.

49 NA, MG28 176, vol. 22, pamphlet "Community Demonstrations."

50 NA, MG28 176, vol. 21, pamphlet "Open House."

51 Documents Department, Stauffer Library, Queen's University, Centennial Commission press release, 679766/311e.

52 Ibid., 2.

53 Documents Department, Stauffer Library, Queen's University, Centennial Commission press release, 679666/312e.

54 Ibid.

55 Ibid., 2.
56 Armitage, *Canadian Centennial Anthology of Prayer*, xvii.
57 Ibid, xiv.
58 Ibid.
59 Ibid, 3.
60 Ibid, 9.
61 See Gilstorf's report on her Maritime trip in NA, MG28 176, vol. 26, "Nova Scotia Interfaith File," "Report to the Chairman and Board of Directors, the Canadian Interfaith Conference," 4 April 1966. For more detailed notes on her meetings in the various provinces, see the interfaith files of the various provinces in NA, MG28 176, vol. 26–30.
62 NA, MG28 176, vol. 3, file "Report – final – to Board of Directors – 1967," 5.
63 Ibid., appendix b, "Publication Distribution Table."
64 NA, MG28 176, vol. 26, file "Provincial Centennial Officials."
65 NA, MG28 176, vol. 3, file "Report – final – to Board of Directors – 1967," 25–30.
66 Ibid., 24.
67 Ibid., 25.
68 Ibid., 17–18.
69 Ibid., 20–1.
70 Ibid., 37–8.
71 Ibid., 41–2.
72 Ibid., 50.
73 Ibid., 36.
74 Ibid., 51.
75 This account of the Halifax-Dartmouth service can be found in NA, MG28 176, vol. 26, file "Nova Scotia Interfaith file," letter, Rev. Gordon W. Philpotts, Rector of St Paul's Anglican Church in Halifax, to Gilstorf, 27 October 1967.
76 The Canadian census of 1961 listed 78 percent of the population of the two towns with French as their "mother-tongue" and 13 percent with English.
77 The following account of events in Noranda and Rouyn has been constructed from a newspaper clipping in the CIC files. See NA, MG28 176, vol. 27, file "Quebec Centennial Release file," "Local Students Blamed for Filthy Letter to Clergymen," *Rouyn-Noranda Press*, 30 March 1967.
78 Ibid.
79 NA, MG28 176, vol. 27, file "Quebec Centennial Release file," C.R.L., "Did the Church Chicken Out?" *Rouyn-Noranda Press*, 30 March 1967.
80 Ibid, "Local Students Blamed for Filthy letter to Clergymen."
81 The following account of the events in Lethbridge draws on NA, MG28 176, vol. 29, "Alberta Interfaith File," article, "4,000 South Albertans Join in Common Prayer," *Lethbridge Herald*, 12 July 1967, and document, "Lethbridge Inter-faith Centennial Weekend, Sunday June 11, 1967, Massed Family Service of Thanksgiving and Re-dedication."

82 "4,000 South Albertans Join in Common Prayer," *Lethbridge Herald,* 12 July 1967.

83 The Canadian census of 1961 revealed that out of a total population of 35,454 Lethbridge residents, 78 percent belonged to the Anglican, Presbyterian, Baptist, Lutheran, Roman Catholic, or United Churches. The Mormon population, at 9 percent of the total, was the fourth largest single denomination, following the United Church (30 percent), the Roman Catholic Church (21 percent), and the Anglican Church (12 percent). Other Christian denominations together made up another 8 percent of the population (they were the Adventists, Christian Reformed, Church of Christ (Disciples), Brethren, Greek Orthodox, Jehovah's Witnesses, Mennonite, Pentecostal, Salvation Army, and Ukrainian (Greek) Catholics). *Census* (1961), table 45.

84 The 1961 Canadian census also listed Buddhists at 2 percent of the population, Jews at .5 percent, and "other" at just over 3 percent. Ibid.

85 NA, MG28 176, vol. 26, file "Nova Scotia Interfaith File," document, "Registrants, Nova Scotia Provincial Interfaith Meeting, March 18, 1966."

86 NA, MG28 176, vol. 26, file "Centennial News, Nova Scotia," letter, Becker to Rev. Gordon Philpott, 10 May 1967. Read in the light of Becker's letter, Philpott's summary of the event to the CIC at the end of the Centennial year seemed to try to present its own justification. The service was Christian, he said, but "an invitation to all denominations was extended."

87 Opposition to the concept of interfaith Centennial celebrations also seems apparent from the, albeit scarce, records of controversy at the provincial level in Nova Scotia. There, the provincial minister responsible for planning Centennial celebrations in the province refused to have anything to do with the CIC, but as one of his subordinates noted, "in this province every organized town, village and hamlet including our three cities are planning to have a non-denominational church service as part of their Celebration activities." See, respectively, NA, MG28 176, vol. 26, file "Nova Scotia Interfaith File," document, "Minutes of the Nova Scotia Provincial InterFaith Meeting, March 18, 1966"; ibid., letter, L.V. Hutt, the planning co-ordinator of the province's Confederation Centenary Celebration Committee, to Gilstorf, 20 April 1966.

88 Roblin's religious affiliation is unknown, but Kulbeck was a Pentecostal.

89 NA, MG28 176, vol. 28, file "Ottawa," document, "Interfaith Meeting," 27 April 1967.

90 From the article "Interfaith – A Second Look," *Canadian Baha'i News,* July 1967, 6.

91 NA, MG28 176, vol. 28, File "Ontario Interfaith File," letter, Daphne Clayton, North Bay, to Gilstorf, 10 January 1967.

92 NA, MG28 176, vol. 3, file "Report – Final – to Board of Directors – 1967," appendix, "National Spiritual Assembly of the Baha'is of Canada."

93 NA, MG28 I76, vol. 1, file 18, letter from Becker to the Ministerial Association of Yellowknife, NWT, 22 February 1967.

94 As quoted in NA, MG28 I76, vol. 27, file "Quebec Centennial Release File," "Local Students Blamed for Filthy letter to Clergymen."

95 LeBlanc and Edinborough, *One Church, Two Nations?* 176.

96 NA, MG28 I76, vol. 6, memorandum from Gilstorf to Becker, 11 October 1966.

97 Ibid.

98 See Hamelin, *Histoire du catholicisme québécois*, chaps. 3–4; Grant, *The Church in the Canadian Era*, 227–8.

99 NA, MG28 I76, vol. 2, file 11, "Final Board Meeting, Canadian Interfaith Conference – November 23, 1967," 4.

CHAPTER SIX

1 From the Expo theme song, see *Expo 67, Montréal, Canada: The Memorial Album*, 38.

2 This metaphor was common in the Centennial year.

3 That transformation required twenty-five million truckloads of landfill, much of which came from the excavation of Montreal's new subway system which would, in turn, help bring 52 million people through Expo's gates. To pay for all of this, a funding formula was worked out between the three levels of government that left the federal government paying 50 percent of the bills, the province of Quebec 37.5 percent, and the city of Montreal 12.5 percent. See NA, RG71 vol. 10, file 6, document "General Report 1: First Meeting of Private Exhibitors, June 21 to 23, 1965," opening address by R.F. Shaw, deputy commissioner general.

4 Fulford, *This Was Expo*, 27.

5 Such was the description of Donald F. Theall, head of the English department at McGill University. Fulford, *This Was Expo*, 70.

6 These were the words of Robert Fulford, a correspondent at Expo 67 for four months for the *Toronto Star*. Fulford, *This Was Expo*, 79, 201.

7 Ibid., 78.

8 Berton, *1967*, 256. Confirming Berton's sentiments, the 1 July 1999 issue of *Maclean's* named Expo 67 and the Centennial celebrations one of the twenty-five most significant Canadian events of the twentieth century.

9 For a study of the prehistory of the CNE, see Walden, *Becoming Modern in Toronto*.

10 Philippe de Gaspé Beaubien, the man who ran Expo 67 once it was open, pushed for La Ronde against opposition in the CCWE. An amusement park was thought to be too commercial and cheap for the exposition. To convince one naysayer, Beaubien took him to Tivoli Gardens in Copenhagen for the weekend. He got his amusement park. See Berton, *1967*, 271.

11 For a brief summary and photographs of each national pavilion, see
    Expo 67, Montréal, Canada: The Memorial Album.

12 See *Expo 67, Montréal, Canada: The Memorial Album*, 265–8. There, the So-
    viet Pavilion is referred to as one of the most comprehensive at the fair,
    but it was not the most exciting or engaging. A theatre at the centre of the
    pavilion, for example, held lectures on such things as "the economics of
    the USSR today" (268). The majority of the displays were overwhelmingly
    industrial; they used complex instruments and had a serious scientific
    tone.

13 Berton, *1967*, 273. According to Berton, the New York World's Fair of
    1964–65 drew in 446,953 visitors on its best day.

14 According to Findling's *Historical Dictionary of World's Fairs and Exposi-
    tions, 1851–1988*, Expo 67 had the largest attendance of world's fairs up to
    that point, approximately 55 million visitors. The next world exposition in
    Osaka, Japan, in 1970 surpassed Expo 67 with over 64 million in atten-
    dance. See Findling, *Historical Dictionary*, appendix B, 380.

15 As quoted in Berton, *1967*, 274.

16 Ibid.

17 Rydell and Gwinn, *Fair Representations*, 4.

18 Benedict, *The Anthropology of World's Fairs*, 6–7.

19 Heaman has also argued that indoctrination was challenged by the reluc-
    tance of many fairgoers to simply listen and learn. They brought their
    own ideas to the fair. Heaman, *The Inglorious Arts of Peace*, 78.

20 Nelles, *The Art of Nation-Building*, 168.

21 *Expo 67, Montréal, Canada: The Memorial Album*, 38.

22 Canadian World Exhibition Corporation Act, 11 Elizabeth II, 1962, c.12,
    sec. 3 (1).

23 Newman, *The Distemper of Our Times*, 424.

24 Fulford, *This Was Expo*, 201.

25 Judy LaMarsh, "A Message from the Secretary of State," *Expo 67: Official
    Guide*, 290.

26 When the Canadian Corporation for the 1967 world exposition was origi-
    nally formed by the government to plan the fair in 1962, Prime Minister
    Diefenbaker appointed two party stalwarts and successful businessmen to
    its top posts. Paul Bienvenue, the commissioner general, was a spaghetti
    manufacturer, while his deputy, C.F. Carsley, was in the vinegar business.
    Both men were loyal conservatives from Montreal, but according to Pierre
    Berton, neither was able to weather the infighting and indecision that sur-
    rounded the early days of their corporation. In August of 1963, with rela-
    tively little accomplished, both men resigned. See Berton, *1967*, 257–9.

27 Even Expo director George Hees later noted that it "was my opinion that
    there was not the slightest chance for Expo. Our chances were zero, nil."

The *Toronto Star*, for its part, argued that the "simplest thing is to call the whole thing off." Both are quoted in Pevere and Dymond, "When We Were Fab: Expo 67," 52.

28 Dupuy was chargé d'affaires to numerous besieged governments in London during the Second World War and the Canadian ambassador to the Netherlands in 1947 and to Italy in 1952. See *Who's Who in Canada* (1966–68), 1028.

29 Directly under Dupuy was Robert Shaw, the deputy commissioner general and vice-president of the corporation. A professional engineer and builder who had risen from the ranks of day labourer to company president in the course of his brilliant career, Shaw was an extremely capable administrator and a man well chosen for the gargantuan task of building Expo 67 in the middle of the St Lawrence (*Canadian Who's Who*, vol. 10 (1964–66), 996. Andrew Kniewasser, a former commercial counsellor and close associate of Dupuy's in Paris, was named general manager of the fair. Pierre de Bellefeuille, a former editor of the French version of *Maclean's*, was put in charge of the theme pavilions. Phillipe de Gaspé Beaubien, a young, independently wealthy, charismatic man and a dynamic speaker, became the director of operations and the person most responsible for selling the fair to visitors. Colonel Edward Churchill, a retired permanent army officer who had helped build airfields during the war, was recruited to engineer the actual construction of the site. The management team of Expo 67 was close-knit, capable, and determined. They called themselves *les Durs*, or the tough guys. See Dupuy, *Expo 67, ou la découverte de la fierté*, 27–8; Berton, *1967*, 264–6.

30 Or, a crisis of development that crosses my country (my translation). Dupuy, *Expo 67*, 18.

31 [Expo 67] could be a unifying factor among all Canadians. While working together on a large project of national and international significance, Canadians would prove that collaboration, comprehension, and understanding were possible between them and that that could be the true way of celebrating the Centenary of Canadian Confederation. (my translation). Dupuy, *Expo 67*, 18.

32 Your country needs you. (my translation). Ibid., 31.

33 Ibid., 32–3.

34 NA, RG71, vol. 73, file 1200-P-0061, pt. 3, "Pavillon Chrétien," letter, Andrew Kniewasser to Robert F. Kramer, S.J., of Loyola College, 13 July 1965.

35 The following is drawn from the in-depth description (including photographs) of the Canada Pavilion in *Expo 67, Montréal, Canada: The Memorial Album*, 109–17, and from Expo's "Information Manual." See NA, RG71, vol. 9, file 1, document, "Information Manual," section 26, "Pavilion of Canada."

36 Expo 67 and the Canada Pavilion, it needs to be noted, were planned by two different groups of people. Dupuy and his team of *les Durs* were responsible for the construction and management of the entire Expo site and specifically for the theme pavilions, but not for the Canada Pavilion.
37 Brown and Lucien Parizeau, associate commissioner general, wrote a three-paragraph introduction to a series of souvenir booklets that described the Canada Pavilion. Two of those booklets were Bush and Lacoste, *My Home, My Native Land,* and Sinclair, *Change Comes to Canada*.
38 Anything less, of course, would have been inappropriate for the host country. The Canada Pavilion covered forty-five thousand square metres of ground on the western tip of Île Notre Dame.
39 NA, RG71, vol. 9, file 1, document, "Information Manual," s26, 5.
40 Richler, "Expo 67," 116.
41 NA, RG71, vol. 9, file 1, document, "Information Manual," s26, 4.
42 Photographs of these "roots" can be found in the middle pages of *My Home, My Native Land*.
43 NA, RG71, vol. 9, file 1, document, "Information Manual," s26, 6.
44 Ibid.
45 *Expo 67, Montréal, Canada: The Memorial Album,* 114.
46 Ibid., 112.
47 Ibid., 114.
48 See Bush, "The Land and the Growth."
49 That was how Robin Bush summarized the Canadian history portion of the pavilion, quoting, in part, from Donald Crowlis. See Bush, "The Land and the Growth," 5.
50 Sinclair, *Change Comes to Canada,* 31.
51 This was also a message portrayed in the official Canada Day celebrations at Expo. The afternoon's entertainment began with a show entitled "Canadians of Tomorrow," which emphasized Canadian youth. Significantly, the Ontario Pavilion also portrayed a very youthful, energetic, and creative image.
52 For photographs and a description of the American pavilion, see Fulford, *This Was Expo*.
53 NA, RG71, vol. 9, file 1, document, "Information Manual," s26, 6.
54 Lacoste, "The People Tree," 19.
55 Ibid., 21.
56 Ibid., 23.
57 Not only British or French (my translation). Other "roots" were translated more directly. For example, "Our Work Pattern" was followed by "Nos occupations sont diverses" (Our occupations are diverse; my translation). Again, see the photographs in the middle section of *My Home, My Native Land*.
58 *Expo 67, Montreal, Canada: The Memorial Album,* 114.
59 NA, RG71, vol. 9, file 1, document, "Information Manual," s26, 6.

60 Ibid.

61 See *Expo 67, Montreal, Canada: The Memorial Album*, 265–8.

62 One could also argue, of course, that in placing religion in a chapel, pavilion planners subtly declared that it had little to do with the other economic, political, or social concerns of the pavilion. The more important point, I would argue, is that they included religion at all.

63 For this account of the meeting, see Jean Drapeau's introduction to *Terre des Hommes/Man and His World: Official Guide*, 35.

64 See Berton, *1967*, 257.

65 See Roy, "The Theme Unfolded by Gabrielle Roy," 30.

66 Ibid., 28.

67 Ibid., 30.

68 Ibid., 26.

69 Before 1946, Canada could not be crossed by car, and the Trans-Canada Highway was not completely paved until 1967. For car registrations and road building in post-1945 Canada, see Bloomfield, MacPherson, and Neufeld, "The Growth of Road and Air Transport." On the building of new schools, see ibid., *Born at the Right Time*, 115–24.

70 On the impact of technological change on the Canadian home, see ibid., 73–4.

71 Galbraith, *The Affluent Society*.

72 Brick, *Age of Contradiction*, xiv.

73 Ibid., 98.

74 Large scale "slum clearance" and urban redevelopment was widespread in the 1960s. Toronto levelled the old homes of Regent Park South and replaced them with clusters of two-storey apartment structures and playgrounds. Windsor created a low-cost rental housing area called Glengarry Court. In Halifax, a ten-block "slum area" was levelled and replaced with low-cost housing and industry and renamed Mulgrave Park. Montreal called its project Les Habitations Jeanne-Mance. From 1961 to 1968, in fact, the National Film Board produced a number of short films on each of these projects and others across the country in a series called *A Report on Development*. See the National Film Board website, http://www.nfb.ca/FMT/E/seri/R/A_Report_on_Redevelopment.html.

75 Berman, *All That Is Solid Melts into Air*, 68.

76 See Kuffert, *A Great Duty*; Brick, *Age of Contradiction*, 13–17.

77 Kuffert, *A Great Duty*; Brick, *Age of Contradiction*, 13–17; Owram, 203–7, chap. 9.

78 See, especially, the book after which Expo was named, Saint Exupéry, *Terre des hommes*. Saint Exupéry was a pilot himself and wrote from his own experience.

79 *Expo 67, Montréal, Canada: The Memorial Album*, 54.

80 *General Rules and Regulations* (Canadian Corporation for the 1967 World Exposition), 1.

81 *Expo 67, Montréal, Canada: The Memorial Album,* 54.

82 Pierre Dupuy, "Message from Commissioner General," in *Expo 67: Official Guide,* 2.

83 See Roy, "The Theme Unfolded"; *Expo 67, Montréal, Canada: The Memorial Album,* 38; Berton, *1967,* 258. On the themes of previous world fairs, see Benedict, *The Anthropology of World's Fairs,* 35–6; Findling, *Historical Dictionary of World's Fairs and Expositions.*

84 Schroeder-Gudehus and Cloutier, "Popularizing Science and Technology during the Cold War."

85 That was how it was described by Mr Deschatelets in what became a prolonged debate about the symbol in the House of Commons. The symbol was attacked for, among other things, being unintelligible, "un-Canadian," and "beatnik" in style. See House of Commons, *Debates,* 20 December 1964, 6225–32.

86 *General Rules and Regulations,* 1.

87 *Expo 67, Montréal, Canada: The Memorial Album,* 38.

88 L.B. Kuffert also argues that Expo 67's approach to scientific and technological progress was ambivalent and focused not on science itself, but on how human beings might control it. Kuffert, *A Great Duty,* 229–32.

89 Benedict, *The Anthropology of World's Fairs,* 36.

90 House of Commons, *Debates,* 20 December 1963, 6226.

91 *General Rules and Regulations,* 1.

92 NA, RG71, vol. 73, file 1200-p-0061 pt 1, "Pavillon Chrétien," document "Projet d'une lettre de S.E. M. Pierre Dupuy, commissaire de l'expo 1967, à S.E. le Cardinal Paul-Émile Léger, Archeveque de Montreal."

93 Unifying forces of the future (my translation). CCE, file 31.30, "Entrevue avec S.E. M. Pierre Dupuy," 23 March 1964.

94 Findling, *Historical Dictionary of World's Fairs and Expositions,* 325.

95 Burton Benedict makes this point and notes the uniqueness of Expo 67 in this context. Benedict, *Anthropology of World's Fairs,* 14.

96 Schroeder-Gudehus and Cloutier, "Popularizing Science and Technology during the Cold War."

97 Roy, "The Theme Unfolded," 32.

98 The following description is drawn from NA, RG71, vol. 12, file 5, document "Theme Exhibit Text."

99 Ibid., 17b.

100 Benedict, *The Anthropology of World's Fairs,* 36.

101 NA, RG71, vol. 12, file 5, document "Theme Exhibit Text," 23.

102 Ibid., 27.

103 Ibid., 35.

104 *Expo 67: Official Guide,* 58.

105 NA, RG71, vol. 12, file 5, document "Theme Exhibit Text," 48–9.

106 Dupuy wanted to discuss his "desire to see at Expo the construction of an immense altar ... where at certain times the Catholics could have a mass one evening at midnight, at other times the Protestants would have their worship, at other moments the Jews, etc."CCE, File 31.30, "Entrevue avec S.E. M. Pierre Dupuy," 23 March 1964.

107 NA, RG71, vol. 73, file 1200-p-0061 pt 1, "Memoire sur un projet de Pavillon Oecumenique a L'Exposition Universelle – Montreal, 1967," 25 September 1964.

108 "My recent rounds in various countries made me feel that the current time waits much on the Christian West," Dupuy wrote in a draft letter to Cardinal Léger in 1964. "I feel that Expo can pose gestures of great consequence for the future. As the Commissioner General, I consider the Pavilion of Unity as the one that responds best to the general theme of Expo" (my translation). NA, RG71, vol. 73, file 1200-p-0061, pt 1, draft letter, "Projet d'une lettre de S.E. M. Pierre Dupuy, commissaire de l'expo 1967, à S.E. le Cardinal Paul-Émile Léger, Archeveque de Montréal."

109 Pierre Dupuy, "Preface," in Expo 67, Montréal, Canada: The Memorial Album.

110 As quoted in Berton, 1967, 274.

111 As quoted in Fulford, This Was Expo, 29.

112 As quoted in Berton, 1967, 275.

113 Fulford, Remember Expo, 8–9.

114 Ibid., 31.

115 Expo 67, Montréal, Canada: The Memorial Album, 5.

CHAPTER SEVEN

1 Buddhism and Islam were present at the fair, but as aspects of national pavilions, not as world religions in pavilions of their own.

2 See, for example, Heaman, The Inglorious Arts of Peace, 78.

3 Expo 67, Montréal, Canada: The Memorial Album, 54. See also Roy, "The Theme Unfolded by Gabrielle Roy," 30. L.B. Kuffert has recently argued that the willingness of Expo organizers to entertain, as well as instruct, typified a change of tactics among cultural critics in the 1960s. Instead of simply calling on Canadians from on high to recognize the value of what might be termed high culture (as they had done in previous decades), critics began to attempt to elevate mass culture by drawing on its appeal – by making elements of high culture more popular in form and content. Kuffert, A Great Duty, chap. 6.

4 NA, RG71, vol. 81, file 1200-S-0090, "Sermons from Science pt 1," letter, G.V. Gordon to W.N.A. Chipman, 6 November 1963. In this letter, Gordon and Chipman discussed "an exchange of correspondence between Mr. Stanley and Mr. Paul Bienvenue dated April 4th, 1963 and Mr. C.F. Carsley's reply of April 9th, 1963."

5 NA, RG71, vol. 73, file 1200-p-0061, pt 1, "Pavillon Chrétien," letter, H.V. Gilbert to M. Paul Bienvenu, Commissioner General, 9 May 1963.

6 NA, RG71, vol. 73, file 1200-p-0061, pt 1, "Pavillon Chrétien," letter, J.H. Berger, President of the Synagogue Council of Greater Montreal, to Bienvenu, 15 May 963.

7 NA, RG71, vol. 73, file 1200-p-0061, pt 1, "Pavillon Chrétien," letter, Letendre to Gilbert on behalf of Shaw, 2 December 1963.

8 When the Roman Catholic Church offered official greetings to the General Assembly of the Presbyterian Church in 1967 with the approval of the Presbyterian church's executive but not the Assembly itself, 45 out of the 170 in attendance were upset. See "General Assembly," *Presbyterian Record* (July-August, 1967), 8–13. According to an article in the *Pentecostal Testimony*, Quebec was a nation in "spiritual darkness" that needed "to be won for Christ." Evangelist G.W. Brooks, "Quebec – Land of Opportunity," *Pentecostal Testimony* (NA, 1962), 10.

9 Grant, *The Church in the Canadian Era*, 188–92.

10 NA, RG71, vol. 73, file 1200-p-0061, pt 1, "Pavillon Chrétien," letter, Irénée Beaubien, Diocesan Ecumenical Commission, to M. Philippe Beaubien, 19 November 1963.

11 For the early story of Beaubien's ecumenical group, see Beaubien, "Le pavillon chrétien de l'Expo '67: 30e anniversaire."

12 NA, RG71, vol. 73, file 1200-p-0061, pt 1, "Pavillon Chrétien," memo, Letendre to Shaw, 5 December 1963.

13 NA, RG71, vol. 73, file 1200-p-0061, pt 1, "Pavillon Chrétien," memo, Dupuy to Letendre, 6 December 1963.

14 NA, RG71, vol. 73, file 1200-p-0061, pt 1, "Pavillon Chrétien," memo, Letendre to Kniewasser, 18 February 1964.

15 In the end, the pavilion was cooperatively built by eight Christian churches: the Roman Catholic Church, the United Church, the Anglican Church, the Presbyterian Church, the Canadian Lutheran Council, the Eastern Association of Churches of the Baptist Convention of Ontario and Quebec, the Greek-Orthodox Church, and the Ukrainian Greek-Orthodox Church.

16 CCE, file 31.30, "Entrevue avec S.E. M. Pierre Dupuy," 23 March 1964.

17 A pavilion reuniting all the confessions (my translation). NA, RG71, vol. 73, file 1200-p-0061, pt 1, "Pavillon Chrétien," memo, de Bellefeuille to Kniewasser, 2 April 1964.

18 NA, RG71, vol. 73, file 1200-p-0061, pt 1, "Pavillon Chrétien," memo, G. Bertrand to M.M. Boudriau, "Centre oecuménique de Montréal," 5 May 1964.

19 NA, RG71, vol. 73, file 1200-p-0061, pt 1, "Pavillon Chrétien," letter, Rev. Paul Gibson to de Bellefeuille, 30 June 1964.

20 NA, RG71, vol. 73, file 1200-p-0061, pt 1, "Pavillon Chrétien," letter, Rev. Paul Gibson to de Bellefeuille, 30 June 1964, 1.

21 Ibid.

22 NA, RG71, vol. 73, file 1200-p-0061, pt 1, "Pavillon Chrétien," de Belle-feuille to Rev. Paul Gibson, 3 August 1964.

23 There isn't room to precede the work of the centuries. We will therefore hold ourselves to ecumenism between Christians (my translation). NA, RG71, vol. 73, file 1200-p-0061, pt 1, "Pavillon Chrétien," letter, Dupuy to Pére Beaubien, 4 July 1964.

24 See NA, RG71, vol. 14, file 6, document "Expo Digest, vol. 2, no. 1, Jan. 6, 1965."

25 See Order-in-Council PC 1966–2453. The Christian Pavilion was the only nonnational pavilion to receive a "national day." Given the pavilion's pre-carious financial situation, the gift of tax exemption was particularly im-portant. "I am convinced that it was due to your efforts that the Christian Pavilion was able to obtain this very great privilege," the Christian Pavil-ion's new commissioner general wrote to Dupuy upon hearing the good news. NA, RG71, vol. 73, file 1200-p-0061, pt 4, "Pavillon Chrétien," letter, Horace Boivin to Pierre Dupuy, Jan. 9, 1967.

26 The inclusion of the Christian Pavilion among national and theme pavil-ions was commonplace, even in publications outside the CCWE. See *Mon-tréal, Expo 67, Man and His World*, 35.

27 NA, RG71 vol. 73, file 1200-p-0061, pt 1, "Pavillon Chrétien," letter, Robert Letendre to Pitcher, 16 October 1964.

28 NA, RG71, vol. 11, file 7, document "Private Pavilions." See the unnum-bered page titled "Christian Pavilion." Thanks to the personal endorse-ment of Dupuy, the Christian Pavilion was also quietly permitted to build on over 60 percent of its lot, a very clear infraction of the rules governing all other pavilions. See NA, RG71, vol. 73, file 1200-p-0061, pt 2, letter, Roger M. Desy to M. Paul Buisson, 5 April 1965. Indicating the potential conflict this permission could cause, the letter was marked "EXPO CONFI-DENTIEL – A NE PAS PUBLIER," and stamped in large letters, "RE-STRICTED."

29 The minutes of the decision listed three factors: "le champs d'action de ce Comité, l'absence de representants des religions non-Chrétien-nes au Comité, ainsi que du voisinage du pavillon des Nations-Unies près du pavillon de l'Unité Chrétienne" the sphere of action of the Committee, the absence of representatives of other non-Christian reli-gions on the Committee, as well as the vicinity of the United Nations Pavilion close to the Pavilion of Christian Unity; my translation. See NA, RG71, vol. 73, file 1200-p-0061, pt 1, "Pavillon Chrétien," docu-ment, "Pavillon de l'Unité Chrétienne," from the Comité de Direction, 27 October 1964.

30 NA, RG71, vol. 81, file 1200-s-0017, "Salvation Army," Contact Report of Vallée and Salvation Army, 17 December 1963.

31 NA, RG71, vol. 73, file 1200-p-0061, pt 1, "Pavillon Chrétien," letter, Leten-dre to Walter A. Schultz, executive secretary of the Division of Public

Relations for the Canadian Lutheran Council, 8 January 1964. Letendre referred to the committee as if it was an official arm of the CCWE.

32 NA, RG71, vol. 81, file 1200-s-0017, "Salvation Army," Contact Report of Vallée and Salvation Army, 17 December 1963; NA, RG71, vol. 73, file 1200-p-0061, pt 1, "Pavillon Chrétien," letter, Letendre to Walter A. Schultz, executive secretary of the division of public relations for the canadian Lutheran Council, 8 January 1964.

33 NA, RG71, vol. 73, file 1200-p-0061, pt 1, "Pavillon Chrétien," memo, Letendre to Shaw, 5 December 1963.

34 See NA, RG71, vol. 73, file 1200-p-0061, pt 1, "Pavillon Chrétien," "Christian Pavilion Project at Expo 67 – Fifth Meeting of the Board of Directors of the Pavilion," 1 October 1964.

35 Channelling Christian groups through the Christian Pavilion actually resulted, in the Canadian Lutheran Council's case, in an addition to the Christian Pavilion's membership roster.

36 The complete correspondence between the Salvation Army and the CCWE is contained in NA, RG71, vol. 81, file 1200-s-0017, "Salvation Army."

37 NA, RG71 vol. 78, file 1200-p-0201, "Prairie Bible Institute." When Abbé Martucci of the Christian Pavilion wrote to the institute to say there would be no room for individual booths in the pavilion, the institute was not heard from again. NA, RG71, vol. 78, file 1200-p-0201, "Prairie Bible Institute," Martucci to Callaway, 22 February 1966.

38 See, in particular, NA, RG71, vol. 73, file 1200-P-0061, pt 2, "Pavillon Chrétien," Desjardins on Letendre's behalf, to Toronto, 17 February 1965; "Contact Report," 19 February 1965, on a meeting between Roger Desy and M. Roland Corriveau of the Mormons, 18 February 1965.

39 NA, RG71, vol. 81, file 1200-s-0102, "Seventh Day Adventist Church Inc., Canada."

40 NA, RG71, vol. 62, file 1200-c-0089, "Graham, Billy," document, "Contact Report," for appointment with Captain Jack Barr, 25 August 1964 with Claude Lacombe and Robert Letendre.

41 NA, RG71, vol. 62, file 1200-c-0089, "Graham, Billy," memo, de Bellefeuille to Letendre, 26 August 1964.

42 NA, RG71, vol. 62, file 1200-c-0089, "Graham, Billy," memo, Bertrand to de Bellefeuille, 8 September 1964.

43 The project of a Pavilion of Christian Unity which will be prepared by serious representatives of serious religion (my translation). NA, RG71, vol. 81, file 1200-s-0090, "Sermons from Science pt 1," memo, de Bellefeuille to Letendre, 26 August 1964.

44 "A delaying tactic" (my translation). Ibid.

45 We do not have anything to lose even if Graham wants to make a fuss. We will be able to answer him that thanks to our Ecumenical Committee we have already chosen Christ (my translation). Ibid.

46 NA, RG71, vol. 81, file 1200-c-0089, "Graham, Billy," "Contact Report," Robert Letendre with George Wilson and Leighton Ford, 30 November 1964. The fact that Letendre himself had actually assigned a lot to another religious group, the Sermons from Science organization, nearly six months before did not seem to strike him as a contradiction.

47 NA, RG71, vol. 62, file 1200-c-0089, "Graham, Billy," letter, Leighton Ford to Lantier, 8 January 1965.

48 Shaw wrote a draft of a letter that may have been edited and corrected by de Bellefeuille. It was never sent. NA, RG71, vol. 62, file 1200-c-0089, "Graham, Billy," letter, Shaw to Wilson, stamped 15 March 1965.

49 NA, RG71, vol. 62, file 1200-c-0089, "Graham, Billy," memo, Kniewasser to Shaw, 8 March 1965.

50 Ibid.

51 NA, RG71, vol. 62, file 1200-c-0089, "Graham, Billy," Shaw to George Wilson, 11 May 1965.

52 On Mennonite relations with the state, see Jansen, *Limits on Liberty.*

53 NA, RG71, vol. 73, file 1200-P-0061, pt 3, "Pavillon Chrétien," letter, J.M. Klassen to Mitchell Sharp, minister of trade and commerce, 13 August 1965.

54 NA, RG71, vol. 62, file 1200-c-0089, "Graham, Billy," article, "A Boon for Religion," *Toronto Star*, 27 November 1965.

55 NA, RG71, vol. 62, file 1200-c-0089, "Graham, Billy," letter, Earl Hawkey of Bancroft, ON, to Prime Minister Pearson, 22 January 1966.

56 NA, RG71, vol. 73, file 1200-P-0061, pt 3, "Pavillon Chrétien," Sharp to Klassen, 24 August 1965.

57 NA, RG71, vol. 62, file 1200-c-0089, "Graham, Billy," letter, Robert H. Winters to Hawkey, 23 February 1966.

58 A list of the board of directors of the pavilion and their occupations reveals that thirteen of the fourteen men were in business. Among them were Stan Mackey, the chairperson and an executive officer of Iberville Williams Textiles; Malcolm Spankie, a staff engineer with Sun Life Assurance; Dr William Weaver, director of research for Canada Cement; and A.A. Kimber, purchasing agent for A.R. Lite Manufacturing.

59 This account of the early beginnings of the Sermons from Science Pavilion draws on interviews between the author and some of its key leaders, Stan Mackey (Toronto 1996), Malcolm Spankie (Toronto 1996), and William Weaver (Montreal 1996). It is also supported by John Stackhouse's brief look at the Sermons from Science Pavilion in *Canadian Evangelicalism in the Twentieth Century*, 114–20.

60 That reservation was reported at a board meeting. See CD, in box entitled "Board Minutes," document, Meeting of Board of Directors, 10 June 1964.

61 NA, RG71, vol. 81, file 1200-s-0090, "Sermons from Science pt 1," memo, Kneiwasser to de Bellefeuille, 28 August 1964.

62 NA, RG71, vol. 81, file 1200-s-0090, "Sermons from Science pt 1," memo, Bertrand for Dupuy to de Bellefeuille, 8 September 1964.

63 We have all agreed not to accept as exhibitors Billy Graham and the other evangelistic, eccentric groups, he wrote. The question, then, was whether or not Sermons from Science belonged to the same category. In de Belle-feuille's eyes, the answer to that question was yes and no. Although he recognized that the Sermons from Science group was attached to the Moody Bible Institute, an institute that was patronized by a certain number of religious groups, including evangelistic and eccentric organizations, de Belle-feuille argued that the principal work of Sermons from Science consists of showing films and other presentations popularizing science. He continued, It is therefore the quality of the films and other popular science presentations that in my opinion is the factor that makes the group an acceptable exhibitor. There is no question, in the Sermons from Science Pavilion, of diffusing evangelistic sermons in the style of Billy Graham. (my translations). NA, RG71, vol. 81, file 1200-s-0090 "Sermons from Science pt 1," memo, de Bellefeuille to Kniewasser, 16 September 1964.

64 Keith Price, the general manager of the pavilion, said as much when he wrote to Stan Turner of the CCWE to explain the lack of advertising about the second portion of the pavilion, the evangelistic film. "We feel that the interest in the second auditorium will be created whilst the primary audience sits fascinated by the main presentation," he explained. There was no advertisement of the second aspect of the pavilion because "to publicize the nature of this beforehand may well defeat our object by causing people to 'miss out' [on] a 'religious' pavilion." NA, RG71, vol. 81, file 1200-s-0090, letter, Keith A. Price to P.S. Turner, 22 February 1967.

65 CD, in box marked "Board Minutes," minutes of board of directors meeting, 15 December 1964.

66 Kee, "Revivalism." For a similar argument in the American context, see Moore, *Selling God*.

67 For the harsh treatment of Protestant evangelicals in Quebec, see Renfree, *Heritage and Horizon*, 273–4, 300. Ray Blakke also briefly mentions the fact that some Fellowship Baptist ministers were imprisoned in the 1950s for door-to-door evangelism. See Blaake, *Espoir pour la ville*, 222.

68 See the "Minutes of the 24th General Conference of the Pentecostal Assemblies of Canada," 17–22 September 1964, 5.

69 A constant peril (my translation). Hamelin, *Histoire du catholicisme québé-cois*, 207.

70 Apparently concerned only about the scientific films, the Expo corporation had gone so far as to gather a number of scientists to review them in early 1964. Their report had been positive. The scientific assessment is referred to in NA, RG71, vol. 81, file 1200-s-0090, "Sermons from Science pt 1," memo, de Bellefeuille to Bertrand, 20 October 1964.

71 CCWE officials wanted the two to merge, but they also wished to have "le bénéfice de vos commentaires avant de faire une recommandation au Commissaire général de l'exposition" (the benefit of your comments before making recommendation to the commissioner general of the exposition; my translation) who would make the final call on the participation of the Sermons from Science group. See, respectively, NA, RG71, vol. 81, file 1200-s-0090 "Sermons from Science pt 1," memo, de Bellefeuille to Kneiwasser, 16 September 1964; memo, Bertrand to de Bellefeuille, 22 September 1964; memo, de Bellefeuille to Bertrand, 20 October 1964; NA, RG71, vol. 81, file 1200-s-0090, "Sermons from Science pt 1," letter marked "Expo-Confidentiel," Bertrand to Martucci, 23 October 1964.

72 See, respectively, CD, in box marked "Board Minutes," minutes of meeting of 19 March 1964; "Report of the Jointly-Sponsored Meeting of the Pavilion of Unity and the Sermons of Science Committee, April 6, 1964." See also, in the library of the Canadian Centre for Ecumenism in Montreal (CCE), file 31.31, "Pavillon Chrétien – Expo 67, Comités," minutes of "Joint Meeting of the Research Committee (nineteenth meeting), Expo 67 Pavilion of Unity and the Board of Directors, 'Sermons from Science' 1967," 9 June 1964.

73 Bound by their Christian consciences, which told them (in spite of the policy of the CCWE) that the Christian Pavilion had no particular monopoly on the expression of the Christian faith, several persons on the board argued that if the Christian Pavilion said no to Sermons from Science, it could be saying no to an avenue through which God himself might have been able to work. See NA, RG71, vol. 73, file 1200-p-0061 pt 1, "Pavillon Chrétien," document, "Pavillon Chrétien, Expo' 67: lére Réunion du Comité de Gestion," 4 November 1964.

74 Gerard Bertrand read a newspaper article in late October that explicitly said that the group already had a pavilion. NA, RG71, vol. 81, file 1200-s-0090, "Sermons from Science pt 1," memo, Bertrand to de Bellefeuille, 29 October 1964.

75 NA, RG71, vol. 81, file 1200-s-0090, Sermons from Science pt 1," Stan Mackey to Letendre, 3 December 1964.

76 The Commissioner General is not at all convinced that it would be desirable to give a pavilion to this organization (my translation). NA, RG71, vol. 81, file 1200-s-0090, "Sermons from Science pt 1," memo, Bertrand to de Bellefeuille, 29 October 1964.

77 NA, RG71, vol. 81, file 1200-s-0090, "Sermons from Science pt 1," memo, Bertrand to Letendre, 16 December 1964.

78 NA, RG71, vol. 73, file 1200-p-0061, pt 2, document, "Details of Request to the Board of Governors Policy concerning Christian Churches Participation," 25 March 1965, 2.

79 NA, RG71, vol. 81, file 1200-S-0090, "Sermons from Science pt 1," memo, Bertrand to Letendre, 16 December 1964.

80 NA, RG71, vol. 81, file 1200-S-0090, "Sermons from Science pt 1," letter, de Bellefeuille to Mackey, 8 March 1965. De Bellefeuille had earlier inquired of a colleague if "nous avons informé les Sermons de la Science qu'ils devraient se contenter de vulgarisation scientifique et s'abstenir de proselytisme ('counselling')?" (we have informed Sermons from Science that they must content themselves with scientific popularization and abstain from proselytizing; my translation). NA, RG71, vol. 81, file 1200-S-0090, "Sermons from Science pt 1," handwritten note, de Bellefeuille to Letendre, 28 December 1964.

81 A copy of McCabe's original letter was not found in the Expo files, but Kniewasser's response to that letter made its concerns very clear. NA, RG71, vol. 73, file 1200-p-0061, pt 1, "Pavillon Chrétien," Kniewasser to Mr Michael McCabe, exec. assistant to the minister of trade and commerce, 20 July 1964.

82 Sharp was the MP for the predominantly Jewish riding of Eglinton in Toronto. See Tulchinsky, *Branching Out*, 293.

83 NA, RG71, 84-85/031, vol. 73, file 1200-p-0061, pt 1, "Pavillon Chrétien," letter, Kniewasser to Michael McCabe, 20 July 1964.

84 NA, RG71, 84-85/031, vol. 73, file 1200-p-0061, pt 1, "Pavillon Chrétien," letter, Michael McCabe to Kniewasser, 4 August 1964.

85 Dupuy described his efforts himself. See Dupuy, *Expo 67*, 60.

86 Ibid., 23.

87 For a description of the two pavilions, see *Expo 67, Montréal, Canada: The Memorial Album*, 203–4, 259–60.

88 Because it would not be enough for me to have obtained the Christian Pavilion ... it was necessary that the other religions, too, would be able to make known the role they have played in the spiritual solidarity between men (my translation). Dupuy, *Expo 67*, 60.

89 Another religion to the common denominator of spiritual forces (my translation). Ibid., 23.

90 The 1961 Canadian census found only 11,611 Buddhists (.06 percent of the population) in the country and not enough Muslims to list them separately. Since Confucians, listed at 5,089, were the smallest individual group on the list, Muslims were below that number. In 1971, 16,175 Buddhists were found, and Muslims remained unnumbered. 1971 Census of Canada, table 9.

91 In 1964, Saul Hayes, of the Canadian Jewish Congress, wrote about the "anxiety of the Religious Welfare Committee of the Canadian Jewish Congress as regards plans of the Israel Government" at Expo. They were evidently concerned about having a place for worship, as well as a place offering kosher food. By June 1965, Israel had agreed to add a kosher res-

taurant, but the chapel was rejected. See in the archives of the Canadian Jewish Congress in Montreal (CJC), CA, vol. 92, file 1079 "Pavilion of Judaism, Expo 67, 1964–1966," letter, Canada-Israel Development Ltd to Saul Hayes, 3 January 1964; CJC, CA, vol. 92, file 1079 "Pavilion of Judaism, Meetings, 1965–1967," "Minutes of Meeting of Special Committee on World's Fair ... June 29, 1965."

92 NA, RG71, vol. 74, file 1200-P-0067, "Pavilion of Judaism," letter, Shaw to Mr Micheal Garber, president of the Canadian Jewish Congress, 15 July 1965; CJC, CA, vol. 92, file 1079 "Programme, Jewish Pavilion Expo 67," "Minutes of Meeting of the Officers of the Canadian Jewish Congress," 15 July 1966.

93 Sam Steinberg, owner of a grocery store chain, Rabbi Shuchat of Congregation Shaar Hashomayim, and Saul Hayes of the Canadian Jewish Congress all played prominent roles in pushing the pavilion to completion. In October 1965 a committee was talking seriously about building a separate pavilion, and Shuchat was insisting that it include a chapel. According to the minutes of a later meeting of the Canadian Jewish Congress, that body agreed to support a pavilion of Judaism at Expo 67, though not financially, at a meeting on 15 November 1965. See, respectively, CJC, CA, vol. 92, file 1079, "Pavilion of Judaism, Meetings, 1965–1967," "Minutes of Meeting of Ad Hoc Committee on Expo Held Oct. 25, 1965; CJC, CA, vol. 92, file 1079, "Programme, Jewish Pavilion Expo 67," "Minutes of Meeting of the Officers of the Canadian Jewish Congress," 15 July 1966.

94 See Tulchinsky, *Branching Out*, chaps. 10–11, for a thorough account of the changes in the postwar Canadian Jewish Community.

95 See Legacy, *Historical Statistics of Canada*, series A164-184.

96 NA, RG71, vol. 11, file 1, document, "Expo 67 Information Manual," s81a.

97 CJC, CA, 1967, vol. 2, file 20, "House of Judaism Newsclippings, 1967," document, "Shaar Hashomayim Bulletin, Pavilion of Judaism."

98 Steinberg was the owner and president of Steinberg's Limited, a Canadian chain store enterprise encompassing 170 supermarkets and 15 department stores in Quebec, New Brunswick, and Ontario. Appointed a member of the Canada Council in 1962, Steinberg had the wealth and prestige needed to push the project through to completion. He became the president of the Foundation of Judaism and gave a substantial sum of money to pay down the deficit of the pavilion when Expo closed (interview between author and Rabbi Shuchat, Montreal, 1996). Charles Lazarus, a member of the editorial department of the *Montreal Star* and a Jew himself, criticized the pavilion organizers for not working harder to involve the whole Canadian community in the Expo project. Instead, he noted, they sought most of their funds in Montreal. See CJC, CA, 1967, vol. 2, file 20D, Charles Lazarus, "The Jewish Presence at Expo 67"; CJC, CA, vol. 92, file 1079, "Expo 67 clippings," Charles Lazarus, "In My View," *Canadian Jewish Chronicle*, 21 October 1966.

CHAPTER EIGHT

1 When a model of the building was revealed in mid-February, 1966, it received a picture and article in everything from the *B.C. Catholic* to the *Globe and Mail* and *Le Devoir*. See, respectively, NA, RG71, vol. 405, file "Christian Pavilion Newspaper Clips, 1966–1967": article "No Religion "Sold" at Expo '67," *B.C. Catholic*, 3 March 1966; "Plan Silence Room in Expo 'Church,' *Globe and Mail*, 15 February 1966; "Le Pavillon Chrétien à l'Expo 67," *Le Devoir*, 15 February 1966.

2 The latter was chosen as the pavilion's symbol because no denomination could claim it as its own. In the shape of a capital T, the tau cross was considered a universal ecumenical symbol of the Christian faith.

3 This description has largely drawn on photographs of the interior of the pavilion in the collection of the Canadian Centre for Ecumenism in Montreal.

4 Those churches were, again, the Roman Catholic Church, the United Church, the Anglican Church, the Presbyterian Church, the Canadian Lutheran Council, the Eastern Association of Churches of the Baptist Convention of Ontario and Quebec, the Greek-Orthodox Church, and the Ukrainian Greek-Orthodox Church.

5 Called *The Eighth Day* and produced by Charles Gagnon, copies of the film are still available for viewing through the Canadian Film Gallery in Toronto.

6 NA, RG71, vol. 405, file "Christian Pavilion, Newspaper Clips, 1966–67," article, Un Chrétien, "Pavillon Chrétien," *L'Action*, 31 May 1967.

7 See, respectively, NA, RG71, vol. 405, file "Christian Pavilion, Newspaper Clips, 1966–67," article, Woulter de Wet, "Christian Pavilion Surprises," *Montreal Star*, 17 April 1967; "Shocking: Frankness of Christian Pavilion Astounds Newsmen," *Ottawa Journal*, 15 April 1967; "Expo's 'Shock' Pavilion," *Toronto Telegram* 15 April 1967.

8 NA, RG71, vol. 405, file, "Christian Pavilion, Newspaper Clips, 1966–67," letter to the editor, Mr and Mrs Gordan Chase, "Blasphemy," *Toronto Telegram*, Friday, 2 June 1967; article, Don Gain, "Christian Pavilion at Expo Shows All Life As It Is," *Victoria Colonist*, 26 August 1967.

9 CCE, document 505, article, Hugh McCullum, "Christian Pavilion a Shocker," *Montreal Churchman* 94:6 (June 1967).

10 NA, RG71, vol. 405, file "Christian Pavilion, Newspaper Clips, 1966–67," article, Rev. Lindsay Howan, "Shock Pagoda," under "The Letterbox," *Windsor Star*, 17 May 1967.

11 NA, RG71, vol. 405, file "Christian Pavilion, Newspaper Clips, 1966–67," article, Dorothy Chrisholm, "Christian Pavilion Enigma: No Place to Rest," *Canadian Register* (Kingston), (1 July 1967).

12 NA, RG71, vol. 405, file "Christian Pavilion, Newspaper Clips, 1966–67," article, Martin O' Malley, "A Christian Trip to Hell and Back," *Globe and Mail*, 24 March 1967.

13 As quoted in Chrisholm, "Christian Pavilion Enigma."

14 NA, RG71, vol. 405, file "Christian Pavilion, Newspaper Clips, 1966–67," article, Claude Gendron,"Au pavillon chrétien: une experience réaliste; mais le visiteur verra-t-il le message qu'on veut transmettre?" *La Presse*, 6 May 1967.

15 Talk of financial crisis first became widespread in national church offices in 1964 and 1965. Yearly increases in giving were no longer keeping up with the rate of inflation in some institutions, and shortfalls required cutbacks in programs. See "Report of the Budget Committee," General Synod of the Anglican Church of Canada, *Journal of Proceedings of the Twenty-first Session* (1959), 251–6; "Report of the Budget Committee," *Journal of Proceedings* (1962), 230–4; "Report of the Budget Committee," *Journal of Proceedings* (1965), 280–2. See also the "Information and Stewardship Report," in *The United Church of Canada Yearbook* (1961–65).

16 "Report of Committee on Statistics and State of the Church," *Journal of Proceedings* (1967), 214–60.

17 See Stackhouse, "The Protestant Experience in Canada since 1945," 205–9; Hamelin, *Histoire du catholicisme québécois*, 312–13.

18 Berton, *The Comfortable Pew*; Berton et al., *Why the Sea is Boiling Hot*.

19 The religious tumult of the period even made it to television. In the fall of 1965, the CBC launched a four-part television series that interviewed leading theologians of the day, such as Paul Tillich and John Robinson. Hosted by Kenneth Bagnell, the assistant to the editor of the United Church *Observer*, the series was appropriately called *Ferment*. For two reviews of the series, see Patricia Clark's regular column in the *United Church Observer*, August 1965, 6, and "The Editor's Observations," *United Church Observer*, August 1965, 7.

20 CCE, file 31.35, "Pavillon Chrétien – Expo 67 – Projet – Historique – Evolution," document entitled "The Holy Spirit's Gamble," by Jean Martucci, n.d., 4.

21 As quoted in O' Malley, "A Christian Trip to Hell and Back."

22 Cox, *The Secular City*.

23 Ibid., 2.

24 As quoted ibid., 2.

25 Ibid., 4.

26 As quoted in NA, RG71, vol. 405, file "Christian Pavilion, Newspaper Clips, 1966–67," article, "Christian Pavilion: A Challenge," *Muenster Prairie Messenger* (Saskatchewan), 2 March 1966.

27 NA, RG71, vol. 73, file 1200-P-0061, pt 1, document, "Report of the Rev. Jean Martucci to the Meeting of the Board of Directors on June 26, 1964," marked "CONFIDENTIAL" and "Translation," 1.

28 CCE, file 31.35, "Pavillon Chrétien – Expo 67 – Projet – Historique – Evolution," document, Jean Martucci, "The Holy Spirit's Gamble," n.d., 4.

29 As quoted in "Christian Pavilion, Expo 67," Canadian Catholic Institutions (March-April 1967), n.p.
30 See CCE, file 31.31, minutes of a meeting of the board of directors, 20 May 1964. See attached, "Communiqué de M. l'abbé Jean Martucci au nom de S.E. le cardinal Paul-Émile Léger, le 20 mai 1964."
31 See NA, RG71, vol. 73, file 1200-P-0061, pt 1, document, "Un Pavillon de l'Unité: Second Meeting of the Board of Directors of the Pavilion with the Research Committee, May 20, 1964"; document, "Pavillon Oecuménique: Fourth Meeting of the Board of Directors of the Pavilion, July 21, 1964."
32 NA, RG71, vol. 73, file 1200-P-0061, "Pavillon Chrétien, pt 1," document, "Project of the Christian Pavilion." This document was written by the representatives of the pavilion's research committee on 22 July 1964.
33 For an example of the ongoing debate on this issue, see NA, RG71, vol. 73, file 1200-P-0061, pt 1, document, "Un Pavillon de l'Unité: Second Meeting of the Board of Directors of the Pavilion with the Research Committee, May 20, 1964."
34 NA, RG71, vol. 73, file 1200-P-0061, pt 3, document, "Meeting of the Programme-Construction Committee, Sept. 15, 1965."
35 In an interview with the author, Rev. Ralph Watson, former chair of the program Committee for the pavilion, explained that some members of the committee were never very excited about Gagnon's plans but simply accepted them as the only compromise that would make an ecumenical pavilion possible.
36 NA, RG71, vol. 405, file "Christian Pavilion, Newspaper Clips, 1966–67," article, "God Focuses Right and Wrong," En Ville, 11 June 1966.
37 See NA, RG71, vol. 73, file 1200-P-0061, pt 3, document, "Meeting of the Programme-Construction Committee, Sept. 15, 1965."
38 "A member of the committee developing the pavilion [stated] that they were concerned that it would not merely be 'a humanist' pavilion," the article read, "and were developing strong Christian statements involving such basic concepts as original sin." NA, RG71, vol. 405, file "Christian Pavilion, Newspaper Clips, 1966–67," article, "Hell and Back Expo Church Theme," Toronto Telegram, 15 February 1966.
39 According to the Reverend Ralph Watson, the Reverend Douglas Smith, a United Church minister and chair of the management committee, was most opposed to where the pavilion had gone, but all were uneasy to varying degrees. To keep things together, Watson sent a letter of assurance to the heads of the various churches. Interview with Rev. Ralph Watson, Montreal, February 1996.
40 CCE, file 31.30, "Pavillon Chrétien – Expo 67 – Correspondence," document, A.C. Roberts, "Questions That Are Currently Being Asked with Some Frequency," n.d. The document was prepared for speakers promoting the pavilion.

41 This interpretation of Gagnon is grounded in several recorded exchanges between him and the pavilion's board of directors. It has also been supported by the recollections of Irénée Beaubien, gathered in an interview with him in Montreal in February 1996 and in an interview with Rev. Ralph Watson, a United Church clergyman and chairperson of the programming committee in its early days, in Montreal in February 1996.

42 NA, RG71, vol. 405, file "Christian Pavilion, Newspaper Clips, 1966–67," article, "God focuses Right and Wrong," *En Ville*, 11 June 1966.

43 NA, RG71, vol. 405, file "Christian Pavilion, Newspaper Clips, 1966–67," article, Dave MacDonald, "Expo's Shock Pavilion," *Ottawa Citizen* (22 April 1967).

44 CCE, file 31.30, "Pavillon Chrétien – Expo 67 – Correspondence," document, "Questions That Are Currently Being Asked with Some Frequency."

45 *Canadian Churchman*, May 1967, 23.

46 As quoted in NA, RG71, vol. 405, file "Christian Pavilion, Newspaper Clips, 1966–67," article, "Christian Pavilion Provides Contrast at Expo," *Echoes* (Toronto), spring 1967.

47 L.B. Kuffert has recently argued that the Christian Pavilion typified a common critical response to the relationship between science and religion in the 1950s and 1960s: that science was limited in its ability to satisfy the emotional and spiritual needs of humanity – a task that only religion could accomplish. Kuffert, *A Great Duty*, chap. 3, 133.

48 NA, RG71, vol. 405, file "Christian Pavilion, Newspaper Clips, 1966–67," article, Aubrey Wice, "Clerics Rap Expo Pavilion," *Ottawa Journal*, 20 May 1967, 51. The reaction of Timotheos indicates that communication between the church representatives planning the pavilion and their respective churches was not always clear.

49 Wice, "Clerics Rap Expo Pavilion."

50 NA, RG71, vol. 405, file "Christian Pavilion, Newspaper Clips, 1966–67," article, Ted Greenslade, "Expo Christian Pavilion Hits Hard at Viewers," *Cornwall Standard-Freeholder*, 26 May 1967.

51 CCE file 31.35, untitled compilation, 2.

52 NA, RG71, vol. 405, file "Christian Pavilion, Newspaper Clips, 1966–67," article, Rev. A.C. Forrest, "Is Expo's Salute to Christianity Tasteless, Obscene?" from the series "A Minister Answers Back," *Toronto Daily Star*, 21 June 1967. A CCWE publication, "Expo after 100 days," also noted a breakdown by generation in reactions to the pavilion. While visitors between eighteen and thirty-five were overwhelmingly positive about their experience, those between thirty-five and fifty were critical but continued to "support the innovations applied to spreading the Gospels in an electronic age." Visitors fifty and over were clearly "split over the radical departure from the more conventional ways of getting the Christian message across." NA, RG71, vol. 40, file 4, "Expo after 100 days," 27.

53 NA, RG71, vol. 405, file "Christian Pavilion, Newspaper Clips, 1966–67," article, "Christian Pavilion Blasted by Canon," *Sudbury Star*, 22 July 1967.

54 NA, RG71, vol. 405, file "Christian Pavilion, Newspaper Clips, 1966–67," article, Jane Scott, "...and It's Vulgar," *Toronto Telegram*, 27 May 1967.

55 NA, RG71, vol. 405, file "Christian Pavilion, Newspaper Clips, 1966–67," letter to the editor, Leonard Wheeler, *Canadian Churchman*, September 1967.

56 NA, RG71, vol. 405, file "Christian Pavilion, Newspaper Clips, 1966–67," letter to the editor, Rev. W.O. Weathers, "Sharp Criticism," *Montreal Star*, 21 August 1967.

57 See also NA, RG71, vol. 405, file "Christian Pavilion, Newspaper Clips, 1966–67," article, Carol Dicks, "Pavilion's Message Deep, but Elusive to Many," *Canadian Register* (Kingston), 7 October 1967.

58 Forrest, "Is Expo's Salute to Christianity Tasteless, Obscene?" *Toronto Daily Star*, 21 June 1967.

59 As quoted in NA, RG71, vol. 405, file "Christian Pavilion, Newspaper Clips, 1966–67," article, "Lessons Must Not Be Ignored," *Kelowna Courier* (Kelowna, BC), 2 September 1967.

60 NA, RG71, vol. 405, file "Christian Pavilion, Newspaper Clips, 1966–67," article, "Christian Pavilion Takes Shape As United Witness at Expo 67," *Canadian Mennonite*, 1 March 1966.

61 Howan, "Shock Pagoda," n.p. Contrary to Howan's insinuation, the Christian Pavilion did not promote any particular church either.

62 This description of Speake's live performances is drawn from a combination of first-hand reports and interviews and the Moody Bible Institute film *Facts of Faith*. Made in 1956, the film featured Dr Irwin Moody himself, but it followed the same story line, used the same experiments, and made the same points as Dr Speake's show.

63 The Moody Bible Institute still sells these films, now transferred to video and called "classics." The descriptions have been drawn from a Moody Institute promotional booklet, "Moody Video: Learn Something Good Today," n.d., sent to the author.

64 This description of Ford's nine-minute address is taken from a viewing of the film itself, now held in the archives of Christian Direction, Montreal.

65 NA, RG71, vol. 503, file "Sermons from Science, "Newspaper Clips," article, "This Pavilion Could Be a Sleeper but ... NO ONE SLEEPS HERE!" *En Ville*, 24 June 1967.

66 NA, RG71, vol. 503, file "Sermons from Science, Newspaper Clips," article, Aubrey Wice, "Where Evangelistic Pitch Doesn't Ditch Tourists," *Toronto Telegram*, 3 June 1967, D16.

67 NA, RG71, vol. 81, file 1200-s-0090, document, promotional booklet, "Sermons from Science."

68 NA, RG71, vol. 81, file 1200-s-0090, document, address of Robert Shaw to the Sermons from Science Press Conference, untitled, 12 May 1965.

69 NA, RG71, vol. 81, file 1200-s-0090, letter, Keith A. Price to P.S. Turner, 22 February 1967.

70 The *Evangelical Christian*, for example, quite typically noted that "In distinction from the so-called Christian Pavilion, which only portrays man in his world of emptiness, frustration and fear, Sermons from Science provide the answer to man and his need: Jesus Christ." NA, RG71, vol. 503, file "Sermons from Science, Newspaper Clips," article, "Sermons from Science," *Evangelical Christian*, September 1967.

71 NA, RG71, vol. 405, file "Christian Pavilion Newspaper Clips, 1966–67," article, Jacques Quay, "Sermons de la Science versus Pavillon Chrétien," *Le Magazine Maclean*, August 1967.

72 NA, RG71, vol. 73, file 1200-p-0061, pt 1, "Pavillon Chrétien," "Minutes of the 1ère Réunion du Comité de Gestion pour la Pavillon Chrétienne, Nov. 4, 1964."

73 NA, RG71, vol. 73, file 1200-p-0061, pt 1, "Pavillon Chrétien," document, "Minutes of the First Meeting of the Board of Directors, Nov. 4, 1964." See NA, RG71, vol. 73, file 1200-p-0061, pt 1, "Pavillon Chrétien," document, "Christian Pavilion Project at Expo 67," "Fifth Meeting of the Board of Directors of the Pavilion," 1 October 1964.

74 CD, in box titled "Board Minutes," document, minutes of the board of directors meeting, 3 August 1964.

75 In November 1964, in Montreal's Anglican House, Bothwell also hosted the meeting of 125 clergy and 50 laymen that was planned to raise support for the Sermons from Science pavilion. NA, RG71, vol. 81, file 1200-s-0090, "Sermons from Science pt 1," document, "Report of Clergy Meeting" by Malcolm Spankie, attached to letter, Malcolm Spankie to Robert Letendre, 3 December 1964.

76 CD, in box titled "Board Minutes," document, minutes of the board of directors meeting, 5 October 1964.

77 CD, in box titled "Board Minutes," document, minutes of the board of directors meeting, 20 June 1964. While official support of the Presbyterian Church as a whole would go only to the Christian Pavilion, the Montreal Presbytery of the Presbyterian Church chose to support both the Christian Pavilion and Sermons from Science. CD, in box titled "Board Minutes," document, minutes of the executive committee meeting, 28 September 1964.

78 CD, in box titled "Board Minutes," document, minutes of the board of directors meeting, 5 October 1964.

79 Carpenter, *Revive Us Again*, 125.

80 NA, RG71, vol. 503, file "Sermons from Science, Newspaper Clips," article, Aubrey Wice, "A Slice of Expo," *Toronto Telegram*, 28 January 1967.

81 For a similar take on differences between mainline and conservative evangelical approaches to culture in the 1945–60 period, see Block, "Boy Meets Girl."

82 For a very thorough account of the relationship between evangelicalism and science, see Gauvreau, *The Evangelical Century.*

83 Stackhouse, *Canadian Evangelicalism in the Twentieth Century,* 115.

84 John Stackhouse makes this argument, and a review of the newspaper clippings held in the Expo Corporation files confirms it. See Stackhouse, *Canadian Evangelism in the Twentieth Century,* 15.

85 Howan, "Shock Pagoda."

86 The original projections were listed at a board of directors meeting in January of 1967. See CD, in box entitled "Board Minutes," document, minutes of the board of directors meeting, 16 January 1967. For the final numbers, see "Sixty-Seven Miracles at Expo 67," a souvenir booklet published by the pavilion and given to all of its supporters in December of 1967. The copy I viewed is in the personal possession of Stan Mackey.

87 NA, RG71, vol. 40, file 4, document, "Expo after 100 days," 28.

88 NA, RG71, vol. 503, file "Sermons from Science, Newspaper Clips," article, Charles Lazarus, "$500,000 Pavilion for Expo Planned by Christian Laymen," *Montreal Star,* 13 May 1965.

89 NA, RG71, vol. 503, file "Sermons from Science, Newspaper Clips," article, Charles Lazarus, "Expo 67 Countdown: 158 days to Go," *Montreal Star,* 21 November 1966.

90 CD, in box entitled, "Board Minutes," attachment to the minutes of the board of directors meeting, 3 August 1964, entitled, "Dr R. Gordon Jones." See also the minutes of the 31 August 1964 and 5 October 1964 board meetings.

91 "The [fundraising] method which generally works was to stress the opportunity which Sermons from Science provides to reach French Roman Catholics on a larger scale than has been possible in the past," the minutes recalled. CD, box titled "Board Minutes," document, minutes of board of directors meeting, 13 December 1965. See also CD, box titled "Board Minutes," document, minutes of meeting with IVCF counseling committee, 6 October 1965.

92 See the chapter devoted to French Canada in Tarr, *This Dominion, His Dominion,* 160. According to an article in the *Pentecostal Testimony,* Quebec was a nation in "spiritual darkness" that needed "to be won for Christ." Evangelist G.W. Brooks, "Quebec – Land of Opportunity," *Pentecostal Testimony,* January 1962, 10.

93 "The pavilion seems to be making its biggest impact on the French Canadians in Quebec," The *Canadian Mennonite* of Manitoba quoted a counsellor at the pavilion. "We have also recorded the decision of a priest." NA, RG71, vol. 503, file "Sermons from Science, Newspaper Clips," article, Leroy Unrau, "Response to Sermons from Science was beyond the Fondest Hopes," *Canadian Mennonite,* 31 October 1967.

94 CD, box titled "Board Minutes," document, "Follow-up." See also CD, box titled "Board Minutes," document, minutes of board of directors meeting, 16 November 1965.

95 NA, RG71, vol. 503, file "Sermons from Science, Newspaper Clips," letter to the editor, J. George Teplick, MD, "Finds Sermons in Science One Discordant Note," *Montreal Gazette*, 9 May 1967.

96 See also the negative review of the pavilion in NA, RG71, vol. 503, file "Sermons from Science, Newspaper Clips," letter to the editor, B. Gardner, "More Views on 'Sermons from Science'," *Montreal Gazette*, Monday, 22 May 1967.

97 CD, in box marked, "Board Minutes," document, Minutes of Board of Directors Meeting," 6 February 1967. Notably, the pavilion did get slapped on the wrist for this literature but claimed ignorance. NA, RG71, vol. 81, file 1200-s-0090, "Sermons from Science pt 2," document, internal memo, P.S. Turner to P. de G. Beaubien, 8 May 1967.

98 Just gathering the number of people required to staff the pavilion required major cross-country support. Since the program of the pavilion required three five-hour shifts of twenty counsellors and ten hosts and hostesses every day, it had to have ninety volunteers a day to function well. In the months leading up to Expo, in fact, Sermons from Science people across the country trained around five thousand people to work as counsellors in the pavilion. NA, RG71, Acc. no. 84-85\031, file 1200-s-0090, "Sermons from Science pt 1," letter, Keith Price to P.S. Turner, 30 March 1967.

99 See the "Minutes of the 24th General Conference of the Pentecostal Assemblies of Canada," 17–22 September 1964, 8.

100 Stackhouse, *Canadian Evangelicalism in the Twentieth Century*, 116. According to Stackhouse, the Brethren were able to contribute such a large percentage of the pavilion's finances because many of their congregations had volunteer ministers who were not paid a salary.

101 NA, RG71, vol. 81, file 1200-s-0090, document, promotional booklet, "Sermons from Science."

102 NA, RG71, vol. 503, file "Sermons from Science, Newspaper Clips," article, Rev. D.L. Patterson, Lambeth Bible Church, "The Way of Life," *Lambeth News*, 31 Mar 1966.

103 NA, RG71, vol. 503, file "Sermons from Science, Newspaper Clips," article, "Thanks to Sacrifice of Montreal Businessmen, There'll Be an Expo Pavilion on *Canada's Ideology*," *En Ville*, 11 June 1966, 11.

104 Tarr, *This Dominion, His Dominion*, 172.

105 Editorial, "Implications of Dominion Day," *Pentecostal Testimony*, July 1961, 2.

106 See, for example, Frederick Leahy, "John Calvin's Social Consciousness," *Pentecostal Testimony*, October, 1959, 4, 33 (written as a comment on Reformation Day, 31 October); "Christian Social Conscience," *Pentecostal Testimony*, March 1961, 2; Earle E. Cairns, "The State, Church and Christian Citizen," and Congressman Walter Judd, MD, "The Christian and Politics," *Pentecostal Testimony*, March 1962, 6–7.

107 "Implications of Dominion Day."

108 Grant, *Church in the Canadian Era*, 221.

109 See Stackhouse, *Canadian Evangelicalism in the Twentieth Century*, 114–20.

110 Carpenter, *Revive Us Again*, 140.

111 See the "Minutes of the 24th General Conference of the Pentecostal Assemblies of Canada," 17–22 September 1964, 8.

112 CD, in box entitled "Board Minutes," document, minutes of the board of directors meeting, 5 July 1965.

113 CD, in box entitled "Board Minutes," document, minutes of the board of directors meeting, 13 December 1965.

114 CD, in box entitled "Board Minutes," document, minutes of meeting with IVCF counselling committee, 6 Octobre 1965.

115 CD, in box entitled "Board Minutes," document, minutes of the board of directors meeting, 29 January 1966.

116 CD, in box entitled "Board Minutes," document, minutes of the board of directors meeting, 22 August 1966.

117 NA, RG71, vol. 503, file "Sermons from Science, Newspaper Clips," article, "400 training as Expo Counselors," *Kitchener-Waterloo Record*, 18 March 1967.

118 NA, RG71, vol. 503, file "Sermons from Science, Newspaper Clips," article, "Seek Counselors, Ushers for Expo Science Sermons," *Standard-Freeholder*, 15 October 1966.

119 CD, in box entitled, "Board Minutes," document, minutes of the board of directors meeting, 13 December 1965.

120 NA, RG71, vol. 503, file "Sermons from Science, Newspaper Clips," article, "Worthy Contribution," *The War Cry*, 28 October 1967.

121 CD, promotional document, "10,000% is possible: St Luke 8:8."

122 The description of the Pavilion of Judaism has been drawn from the following documents: Canadian Jewish Congress archives (CJC) collection, CA, vol. 92, file 1079, "Pavilion of Judaism, Expo 67, 1965–1967," document "Story Line Theme, Pavilion of Judaism, Visual Exhibit," 23 February 1966; NA, RG71, vol. 455, file "Judaism Pavilion," press release, Kenneth Johnstone, INFORMEDIA, "The Pavilion of Judaism"; NA, RG71, vol. 455, file "Judaism Pavilion," press release, Kenneth Johnstone, INFORMEDIA, "Exhibits in the Pavilion of Judaism – Expo 67"; NA, RG71, vol. 74, file 1200-P-0067, "Pavilion of Judaism," document "Pavilion of Judaism"; CJC, CA, vol. 92, file 1079, "Pavilion of Judaism, Expo 67, 1965–1967," document "Pavilion of Judaism at Expo 67 – Program Schedule: May-June;" CJC, 1967, vol. 2 file 20d, document, Moses Rowell, "The Eternal Light: Expo 67 Pavilion of Judaism, a View of the Ages"; CJC, 1967, vol. 2, file 20d, document "Canadian Jewish Congress Presents the Message of Judaism to Man and His World: Highlights of the Pavilion of Judaism at Expo 67."

123 NA, RG71, vol. 455, file "Judaism Pavilion," press release, Kenneth Johnstone, INFORMEDIA, "The Pavilion of Judaism," 2.

124 Ibid.

125 CJC, CA, vol. 92, file 1079, "Pavilion of Judaism, Expo 67, 1965–1967," document "Storyline Theme, Pavilion of Judaism, Visual Exhibit," 23 February 1966.

126 Ibid.

127 Ibid., 5.

128 An article in *Montreal-Matin*, for example, compared the Christian Pavilion and the Sermons from Science Pavilion and found both wanting. The Pavilion of Judaism, it argued, harboured the only truly sacred space on the whole Expo site. NA, RG71, vol. 455, file "Judaism, Pavilion of: Newspaper Clips," article, "À l'Expo, Rencontre avec le sacré," *Montreal-Matin*, 14 November 1967; see also Jane Scott, "God's Plan in Focus at Expo," *Toronto Telegram*, 20 May 1967; Charles Wilkinson, "The Jews: Expo Pavilion Tells of Faith, Courage and Grief," *Hamilton Spectator* 24 June 1967.

129 The Pavilion of Judaism was not without some controversy, however. Charles Lazarus, editor of the *Montreal Star* quoted above, proved to be a significant critic of the pavilion planners, but only in the Jewish press and not in his regular column in the *Star*. He disliked the solely religious focus of the pavilion, demanding more cultural displays to fill out the image of the Jew. He also criticized what he considered to be the dominance of wealthy Jewish entrepreneurs in Montreal in the organization of the pavilion and lamented that most of its support was based among them. See CJC, CA, 1967, vol. 2, file 20D, Charles Lazarus, "The Jewish Presence at Expo 67"; CJC, CA, vol. 92, file 1079 "Expo 67 Clippings," Charles Lazarus, "In My View," *Canadian Jewish Chronicle*, 21 October 1966.

130 The temple, in fact, got its own exclusive press release. See NA, RG71, vol. 455, file, "Judaism Pavilion," press release, Kenneth Johnstone, INFORMEDIA, "Temple of Jerusalem in Pavilion of Judaism."

131 When the Pavilion of Judaism was previewed for the press about a week before opening day, reporters invariably picked up on the model of the temple or on some of the pavilion's historical treasures. See, NA, RG71, vol. 455, file, "Judaism Pavilion," photographs, *St Catherines Standard*, 21 April 1967, and the *Sherbrooke Record*, 21 April 1967; article, Charles Lazarus, "Countdown, 7 Days to Go," *Montreal Star*, 21 April 1967; "Pavilion of Judaism, Expo 67," in Spotlight, *Congress Bulletin*, March 1967.

132 NA, RG71, vol. 455, file, "Judaism Pavilion," press release, Kenneth Johnstone, INFORMEDIA, "The Pavilion of Judaism," 2.

133 NA, RG71, vol. 74, file 1200-P-0067," Pavilion of Judaism," document, "Pavilion of Judaism," 2.

134 "Story Line Theme, Pavilion of Judaism, Visual Exhibit," 5.

135 Ibid.

136 Again, the Jewish contribution to the debate on the place of religion in public education in Ontario stands as a prominent example.

137 See Tulchinsky, *Branching Out*, 276.

138 Ibid., xvii.

139 Ibid., 275.

140 "Legislation on Hate Propaganda Promised," *Congress Bulletin* 22:7 September-October 1966, 1.

141 On the impact of anti-Semitism on the Canadian Jewish community in the early 1960s, see Bialystok, *Delayed Impact*, chap. 4.

142 Tulchinsky, *Branching Out*, 276–80.

143 Ibid., 289. Alongside the Bronfman family came Sam Steinberg and the Reichmann family, for example.

144 NA, RG71, vol. 74, file 1200-P-0067, "Pavilion of Judaism," document entitled "A Proclamation of Faith and Thanksgiving on the Occasion of the National Bi-centenary of Canadian Jewry," in folder entitled "Excerpts from the Beginning of Canadian Jewry: Canadian Centennial Year, Pavilion of Judaism at Expo 67, Montreal, April 28 to Oct. 27, 1967," 9.

145 As noted in the last chapter, while the Pavilion of Judaism originated with the Canadian Jewish Congress, the major national institution of Canadian Jews, the bulk of its financial support came from Montreal and, more specifically, from a few very wealthy men. Steinberg was first among them.

146 NA, RG71, vol. 74, file 1200-P-0067, "Pavilion of Judaism," biography of Sam Steinberg.

147 Bialystok, *Delayed Impact*, chaps. 3–5.

148 NA, RG71, vol. 455, file "Judaism Pavilion," article, "Sam Steinberg and Expo," *Canadian Jewish News*, 14 April 1967.

149 CJC, CA, vol. 92, file 1079 "Pavilion of Judaism, Expo 67, correspondence," letter, Sam Steinberg to Mr Ray Wolfe, Oshawa Wholesale Limited, 8 August 1966.

CONCLUSION

1 Fulford, *Remember Expo*, 8.

2 Pearson, *Words and Occasions*, 275.

3 Owram, *Born at the Right Time*, chap. 11.

4 Berton, *1967*.

5 Granatstein, *Canada, 1957–1967*, chap. 11; Banting, "Images of the Modern State," 9.

Bibliography

ARCHIVAL COLLECTIONS

ANGLICAN CHURCH OF CANADA ARCHIVES, TORONTO
Church's Observance of Canadian Centenary Papers
General Synod Papers

BAPTIST FEDERATION OF CANADA ARCHIVES, HAMILTON
Exhibits (Expo '67) Papers

CANADIAN CENTRE FOR ECUMENISM, MONTREAL (CCE)
Christian Pavilion Papers

CANADIAN CONFERENCE OF CATHOLIC BISHOPS, OTTAWA
Centennial of Canada Papers
Expo 67 Papers

CANADIAN COUNCIL OF CHURCHES, OTTAWA
Canadian Centenary Committee Papers

CANADIAN JEWISH CONGRESS, MONTREAL (CJC)
Centennial Project Papers
Pavilion of Judaism, Expo 67 Papers

CHRISTIAN DIRECTION, MONTREAL (CD)
Sermons from Science Papers

NATIONAL ARCHIVES OF CANADA (NA)
Centennial Commission Papers
Canadian Corporation for the 1967 World Exposition Papers
Canadian Interfaith Conference Papers

PENTECOSTAL ASSEMBLIES OF CANADA, TORONTO
Records of the Canadian Centennial Council
Records of the Centennial Committee

PRESBYTERIAN CHURCH OF CANADA ARCHIVES, TORONTO
Correspondence, Christian Pavilion
Committee on History Minutes

UNITED CHURCH ARCHIVES OF THE MONTREAL/OTTAWA CONFERENCE
Records of Proceedings, Montreal Presbytery, 1965–67

UNITED CHURCH OF CANADA ARCHIVES, TORONTO
Centennial Committee Papers

OFFICIAL SOURCES

Acts and Proceedings of the General Assembly of the Presbyterian Church of Canada
Baptist Convention of Ontario and Quebec Yearbook
General Synod of the Anglican Church of Canada, Journal of Proceedings
Minutes of the General Conference of the Pentecostal Assemblies of Canada
United Church of Canada Yearbook

PRIMARY AND SECONDARY SOURCES

Abbott, Walter M., ed. *The Documents of Vatican II.* New York: Guild 1966.
Abella, Irving, and Harold Troper. *None Is Too Many: Canada and the Jews of Europe, 1933–1948.* Toronto: Lester & Orphen Dennys 1982.
Abu-Laban, Yasmeen. "Keeping 'em Out: Gender, Race, and Class Biases in Canadian Immigration Policy." In Veronica Stron-Boag, et al., eds., *Painting the Maple: Essays on Race, Gender and the Construction of Canada*. Vancouver: University of British Columbia Press 1998, 69–84.
Abu-Lahan, Baha. "The Canadian Muslim Community: The Need for a Survival Strategy." In E. Waugh, et al., eds., *The Muslim Community in North America*. Edmonton: University of Alberta Press 1983, 75–92.
Airhart, Phyllis. "'As Canadian as Possible under the Circumstances': Reflections on the Study of Protestantism in North America." In Harry Stout and D.G. Hart, eds., *New Directions in American Religious History*. Oxford: Oxford University Press 1997: 116–37.
Airhart, Phyllis, and Roger Hutchinson. "Introduction." *Toronto Journal of Theology* 12, no. 2 (1996): 155–7.
Aldwinckle, R.F. "Did Jesus Believe in God? Some Reflections on Christian Atheism." *Canadian Journal of Theology* 13, no. 1 (1967): 19–30.

Alexander, Jeffrey. "Citizen and Enemy as Symbolic Classification: On the Polarizing Discourse of Civil Society." In Michèle Lamont and Pierre Fournier, eds., *Cultivating Differences: Symbolic Boundaries and the Making of Inequality*. Chicago: University of Chicago Press 1992, 289–308.

Alford, Robert R. "The Social Bases of Political Cleavage in 1962." In John Meisel, ed., *Papers on the 1962 Election*. Toronto: University of Toronto Press 1964, 203–34.

Allen, Richard. "Providence to Progress: The Migration of an Idea in English Canadian Thought." In William Westfall, et al., eds., *Religion/Culture: Comparative Canadian Studies*. Ottawa: Association of Canadian Studies 1985, 33–46.

– *The Social Passion: Religion and Reform in Canada, 1914–1928*. Toronto: University of Toronto Press 1971.

Altizer, Thomas J., and William Hamilton. *Radical Theology and the Death of God*. Indianapolis, IN: Bobbs-Merrill 1966.

Anderson, Benedict. *Imagined Communities: Reflections on the Origin and Spread of Nationalism*. Revised ed. New York: Verso 1991.

Anderson, Grace M. "Voting Behaviour and the Ethnic Religious Variable: A Study of a Federal Election in Hamilton, Ontario." *Canadian Journal of Economics and Political Science* 32, no. 1 (February 1966): 27–37.

Anderson, Robert, and Eleanor Wachtel, eds. *The Expo Story*. Madeira Park, BC: Harbour Publishing 1986.

Anglican Church of Canada. The Council for Social Service. "'Canada: Unity in Diversity': Report of Submission to the Royal Commission on Biculturalism and Bilingualism, 1965." *Bulletin* 91 (June 1965).

– "The Church in the World: A Symposium on the Role of the Institutional Church in Our Society." *Bulletin* 189 (November 1964).

– "The Church's Mission in Urban Industrial Society." *Bulletin* 176 (January 1960).

Appel, Fredrick. "Instrumentalist and Interpretive Approaches to Quebec Political Culture: A Critical Analysis." In Alain-G. Gagnon, ed., *Quebec: State and Society*. 2d ed. Scarborough, ON Nelson Canada 1993, 130–45.

Appleby, Brenda. *Responsible Parenthood: Decriminalizing Contraception in Canada*. Toronto: University of Toronto Press 1999.

Armitage, Ramsay, ed. *Canadian Centennial Anthology of Prayer*. Ottawa: Mutual Press 1967.

Armstrong, Joe C.W. *Farewell the Peaceful Kingdom: The Seduction and Rape of Canada, 1963–1994*. Toronto: Stoddart Publishing 1995.

Aster, Howard. "Nationalism and Communitarianism." In Wallace Gagne, ed., *Nationalism, Technology and the Future of Canada*. Toronto: Macmillan, 1976, 52–74.

Audi, Robert, and Nicholas Wolterstorff. *Religion in the Public Square: The Place of Religious Convictions in Political Debate*. New York: Rowman and Littlefield 1997.

Axelrod, Paul. "Higher Education, Utilitarianism, and the Acquisitive Society: Canada, 1930–1980." In Michael S. Cross and Gregory S. Kealey, eds., *Modern Canada, 1930–1980*. Toronto: McClelland and Stewart 1984, 179–205.

– *Making a Middle Class: Student Life in English Canada during the Thirties*. Montreal and Kingston: McGill-Queen's University Press 1990.

Axelrod, Paul, and John G. Reid. "Introduction." In Paul Axelrod and John G. Reid, eds., *Youth, University and Canadian Society: Essays in the Social History of Higher Education*. Montreal and Kingston: McGill-Queen's University Press 1989, xi–xxx.

Aykroyd, Peter. *The Anniversary Compulsion: Canada's Centennial Celebration, a Model Mega-Anniversary*. Toronto: Dundurn Press 1992.

Ayre, W. Burton. *Mr Pearson and Canada's Revolution by Diplomacy*. Montreal: Wallace Press 1966.

Azzi, Stephen. "'It Was Walter's View': Lester Pearson, the Liberal Party and Economic Nationalism." In Norman Hillmer, ed., *Pearson: The Unlikely Gladiator*. Montreal and Kingston: McGill-Queen's University Press 1999, 104–116.

– *Walter Gordon and the Rise of Canadian Nationalism*. Montreal and Kingston: McGill-Queen's University Press 1999.

Badgley, Kerry. "'As Long As He Is an Immigrant from the U.K.': Deception, Ethnic Bias, and Milestone Commemoration in the Department of Citizenship and Immigration, 1953–1965." *Journal of Canadian Studies* 33, no. 3 (fall 1998), 130–49.

Balthazar, Louis. "The Faces of Quebec Nationalism." In Alain-G. Gagnon, ed., *Quebec: State and Society*. 2d ed. Scarborough, ON: Nelson Canada 1993, 2–17.

Bannerji, Himani. "On the Dark Side of the Nation: Politics of Multiculturalism and the State of 'Canada.'" *Journal of Canadian Studies* 31, no. 3 (fall 1996), 103–28.

Banting, Keith. "Images of the Modern State: An Introduction." In Keith Banting, ed., *State and Society in Comparative Perspective*. Toronto: University of Toronto Press 1986, 1–20.

Barber, Marilyn. "Nationalism, Nativism, and the Social Gospel." In Richard Allen, ed., *The Social Gospel in Canada*. Ottawa: National Museums of Canada 1975, 186–226.

Baum, Gregory. "Catholicism and Secularization in Quebec." In David Lyon and Marguerite Van Die, eds., *Rethinking Church, State, and Modernity: Canada between Europe and America*. Toronto and Buffalo: University of Toronto Press 2000, 149–65.

– *Catholics and Canadian Socialism: Political Thought in the Thirties and Forties*. Toronto: James Lorimer 1980.

– *The Church in Quebec*. Ottawa: Novalis 1991.

- "Social Catholicism in Nova Scotia." In Peter Slater, ed., *Religion and Culture in Canada*. Canadian Corporation for Studies in Religion 1977, 117–48.
- "The Survival of Canada and the Christian Church." In Gregory Baum, Ronald Sutherland, and Louis LeBlanc, *The Survival of Canada and the Christian Church: Conference*. Toronto: St Michael's College 1973.

Beaubien, Irénée. "Le pavillon chrétien de l'Expo '67: 30e anniversaire." *Aujourd'hui Credo* (Publication of the United Church of Canada, Consistoire Laurentienne) (July-August 1997): 7–8.
- *Towards Christian Unity in Canada: A Catholic Approach*. Montreal: Palm Publisher 1956.

Behiels, Michael. "Father Georges-Henri Lévesque and the Introduction of Social Sciences at Laval, 1938–55." In Paul Axelrod and John G. Reid, eds., *Youth, University and Canadian Society: Essays in the Social History of Higher Education*. Montreal and Kingston: McGill-Queen's University Press 1989, 320–41.
- "Lester B. Pearson and the Conundrum of National Unity, 1963–1968." In Norman Hillmer, ed., *Pearson: The Unlikely Gladiator*. Montreal and Kingston: McGill-Queen's University Press 1999, 68–82.
- "Quebec: Social Transformation and Ideological Renewal, 1940–1976." In Michael D. Behiels, ed., *Quebec since 1945: Selected Readings*. Toronto: Copp Clark Pitman 1987, 21–45.

Belanger, Andre-J. "Quebec: Not that Unique, nor that Alone." In Alain-G. Gagnon, ed., *Quebec: State and Society*. 2d ed. Scarborough, ON: Nelson Canada 1993, 146–57.

Bell, David V.J. *The Roots of Disunity: A Study of Canadian Political Culture*. 2d ed. Toronto: Oxford University Press 1992.

Bellah, Robert. "Civil Religion in America." *Daedalus* 96: 1–21.
- "New Religious Consciousness and the Crisis in Modernity." In Robert N. Bellah and Phillip E. Hammond, eds., *Varieties of Civil Religion*. San Francisco: Harper and Row 1980, 167–87.

Bellah, Robert, and Phillip E. Hammond, eds. *Varieties of Civil Religion*. San Francisco: Harper and Row 1980.

Benedict, Burton. *The Anthropology of World's Fairs: San Francisco's Panama Pacific International Exposition of 1915*. Berkeley: Scolar Press 1983.

Berger, Carl. "The True North Strong and Free." In Peter Russell, ed., *Nationalism in Canada*. Toronto: McGraw-Hill 1966, 3–26.

Berger, Peter. "The Relevance Bit Comes to Canada." In William Kilbourn, ed., *The Restless Church: A Response to the Comfortable Pew*. Toronto: McClelland and Stewart, 1966, 75–9.
- *The Sacred Canopy: Elements of a Sociological Theory of Religion*. Toronto: Doubleday 1967.

Berman, Marshall. *All That Is Solid Melts into Air: The Experience of Modernity*. New York: Penguin Books 1988.

Berry, J.W., and J.A. Laponce. "Evaluating Research on Canada's Multiethnic and Multicultural Society: An Introduction." In J.W. Berry and J.A. Laponce, eds., *Ethnicity and Culture in Canada: The Research Landscape.* Toronto: University of Toronto Press 1994, 3–16.

Berton, Pierre. *1967: The Last Good Year.* Toronto: Doubleday Canada 1997.

– *The Comfortable Pew: A Critical Look at Christianity and the Religious Establishment in the New Age.* New York: J.B. Lippincott Company 1965.

– *Voices from the Sixties: Twenty-Two Views of a Revolutionary Decade.* New York: Doubleday 1967.

Berton, Pierre, et. al. *Why the Sea is Boiling Hot: A Symposium on the Church and the World.* The Board of Evangelism and Social Service, The United Church of Canada 1965.

Bialystok, Franklin. *Delayed Impact: The Holocaust and the Canadian Jewish Community.* Montreal and Kingston: McGill-Queen's University Press 2000.

Bibby, Reginald. *Fragmented Gods: The Poverty and Potential of Religion in Canada.* Toronto: Irwin Publishing 1987.

– "Religion and Modernity: The Canadian Case." *Journal for the Scientific Study of Religion* 18, no. 1 (March 1979): 1–17.

– *Unknown Gods: The Ongoing Story of Religion in Canada.* Toronto: Stoddart 1993.

Bibby, Reginald W., and Merlin B. Brinkerhoff. "The Circulation of the Saints." *Journal for the Scientific Study of Religion* 12 (1973): 273–83.

– "Circulation of the Saints, 1966–1990: New Data, New Reflection." *Journal for the Scientific Study of Religion* 33 (September 1994): 273–80.

Bird, Frederick, and William Reimer. "New Religious and Para-Religious Movements in Montreal." In Stewart Crysdale and Les Wheatcroft, eds., *Religion and Canadian Society.* Toronto: Macmillan of Canada 1976, 307–20.

Birthday of a Nation: The Story of Canada's Centennial. Time International of Canada 1968.

Blaake, Ray. *Espoir pour la ville: Dieu dans la cité.* Quebec City: La Clairière 1994.

Black, Conrad. *Duplessis.* Toronto: McClelland and Stewart 1977.

Black, Robert Merrill. "Inwardly Renewed: The Emergence of Modernity in the Diocese of Toronto, 1939–1989." In Alan L. Hayes, ed., *By Grace Coworkers: Building the Anglican Diocese of Toronto 1780–1989.* Toronto: Anglican Book Centre, 1989, 97–140.

Block, Tina. "'Boy Meets Girl': Constructing Heterosexuality in Two Victoria Churches, 1945–1960." *Journal of the Canadian Historical Association* 10 (1999): 279–96.

Bloomfield, Gerald, Murdo Macpherson, and David Neufeld, "The Growth of Road and Air Transport, Plate 53." In Donald Kerr and Derych W. Holdsworth, eds., *Historical Atlas of Canada, III: Addressing the Twentieth Century, 1891–1961.* Toronto: University of Toronto Press 1990.

Blumstock, Robert. "Canadian Civil Religion." In W.E. Hewitt, ed., *The Sociology of Religion: A Canadian Focus.* Toronto: Butterworths 1993, 173–94.

Bothwell, Robert, Ian Drummond, and John English. *Canada since 1945: Power, Politics and Provincialism.* Revised ed. Toronto: University of Toronto Press 1989.

Boulding, Kenneth E. *The Meaning of the Twentieth Century: The Great Transition.* New York: Harper and Row 1964.

Breton, Raymond. "From Ethnic to Civic Nationalism: English Canada and Quebec." *Ethnic and Racial Studies* 11 no. 1 (January 1988): 85–102.

– "Intergroup Competition in the Symbolic Construction of Canadian Society." In Peter S. Li, ed., *Race and Relations in Canada.* 2n ed. Oxford: Oxford University Press 1999, 291–315.

– "Multiculturalism and Canadian Nation-Building." In Alan Cairns and Cynthia Williams, eds., *The Politics of Gender, Ethnicity, and Language in Canada.* Toronto: University of Toronto Press 1986, 27–67.

– "The Production and Allocation of Symbolic Resources: An Analysis of the Linguistic and Ethnocultural Fields in Canada." *Canadian Review of Sociology and Anthropology* 21, no. 2 (1984): 123–44.

Breuilly, John. "Nationalism and the State." In Roger Michener, ed., *Nationality, Patriotism and Nationalism.* St Paul, Mn: Paragon House 1993, 19–48.

Brick, Howard. *Age of Contradiction: American Thought and Culture in the 1960s.* New York: Twayne Publishers 1998.

Brodie, Janine, and Jane Jenson. *Crisis, Challenge and Change: Party and Class in Canada Revisited.* Ottawa: Carleton University Press 1988.

Brotz, Howard. "Multiculturalism in Canada: A Muddle." *Canadian Public Policy* 6, no. 1 (winter 1980), 41–6.

Brown, Callum. *The Death of Christian Britain: Understanding Secularization, 1800–2000.* New York: Routledge 2001.

Bryden, P.E. *Planners and Politicians: Liberal Politics and Social Policy, 1957–68.* Montreal and Kingston: McGill-Queen's University Press 1997.

Brym, Robert J., William Shaffir, and Morton Weinfeld. *The Jews in Canada.* Toronto: Oxford University Press 1993.

Bumsted, J.M. *The Peoples of Canada: A Post-Confederation History.* Toronto: Oxford University Press 1992.

Burkinshaw, Robert K. *Pilgrims in Lotus Land: Conservative Protestantism in British Columbia, 1917–1981.* Montreal and Kingston: McGill-Queen's University Press 1995.

Burnet, Jean. "Taking into Account the Other Ethnic Groups and the Royal Commission on Bilingualism and Biculturalism." In James S. Frideres, ed., *Multiculturalism and Intergroup Relations.* New York: Greenwood Press 1989, 9–18.

Bush, Robin. "The Land and the Growth," In *My Home, My Native Land: A People, Their Land, Their Growth.* Montreal: Canadian Government Pavilion, Expo 67, n.d., 3–17.

Cairns, Alan. "The Embedded State: State-Society Relations in Canada." In Keith Banting, ed., *State and Society: Canada in Comparative Perspective.* Toronto: University of Toronto Press 1986, 53–86.

Cairns, Alan, and Cynthia Williams. "Constitutionalism, Citizenship and Society in Canada: An Overview." In Alan Cairns and Cynthia Williams, eds., *Constitutionalism, Citizenship, and Society in Canada.* Toronto: University of Toronto Press 1985, 1–50.

Caldwell, M. Alice. *The Nine Mile River Church: Now and Then.* N.p. 1969.

Caloren, Fred. "Nationalism in Quebec, 1967." In W.E. Mann, ed., *Canada: A Sociological Perspective.* Toronto: Copp Clark 1968, 498–506.

Campbell, Colin. *Canadian Political Facts, 1945–1976.* Toronto: Methuen Publications 1977.

Campbell, Douglas F. "Presbyterians and the Canadian Church Union: A Study in Social Stratification." *Canadian Society of Presbyterian History Papers* (1991): 1–32.

Careless, J.M.S. "'Limited Identities' in Canada." *Canadian Historical Review* 50, no. 1 (March 1969): 1–10.

Canada. Royal Commission on Bilingualism and Biculturalism. *A Preliminary Report of the Royal Commission on Bilingualism and Biculturalism.* Ottawa: Queen's Printer 1965.

– *Report of the Royal Commission on Bilingualism and Biculturalism.* Book 4, *The Contribution of the Other Ethnic Groups.* Ottawa: Queen's Printer 1969.

Canadian Catholic Conference. *Contraception, Divorce, Abortion: Three Statements.* Ottawa: Canadian Catholic Conference 1968.

– "Labour Day Message, 1962: Socialization." In E.F. Sheridan, ed., *Do Justice! The Social Teaching of the Canadian Catholic Bishops (1945–1986).* Sherbrooke, Qc, and Toronto: Éditions Paulines and the Jesuit Centre for Social Faith and Justice 1987, 91–4.

– "Labour Day Message, 1963: Indispensable Collaboration between Public Authorities and Intermediate Organizations." In E.F. Sheridan, ed., *Do Justice! The Social Teaching of the Canadian Catholic Bishops (1945–1986).* Sherbrooke, Qc, and Toronto: Éditions Paulines and the Jesuit Centre for Social Faith and Justice 1987, 95–103.

– "Labour Day Message, 1967: The Economic Condition of the Canadian Family." In E.F. Sheridan, ed., *Do Justice! The Social Teaching of the Canadian Catholic Bishops (1945–1986).* Sherbrooke, QC, and Toronto: Éditions Paulines and the Jesuit Centre for Social Faith and Justice 1987, 135–41.

– "On Development and Peace." In E.F. Sheridan, ed., *Do Justice! The Social Teaching of the Canadian Catholic Bishops (1945–1986).* Sherbrooke, QC, and Toronto: Éditions Paulines and the Jesuit Centre for Social Faith and Justice 1987.

– "On the Occasion of the Hundredth Year of Confederation." In E.F. Sheridan, ed., *Do Justice! The Social Teaching of the Canadian Catholic Bishops*

(1945–1986). Sherbrooke, QC, and Toronto: Éditions Paulines and the Jesuit Centre for Social Faith and Justice 1987, 122–34.

Canadian Corporation for the 1967 World Exposition. *General Rules and Regulations*. N.p., n.d.

– *Information Manual, Universal and International Exhibition of 1967, Montreal, April 28–October 27*. N.p., n.d.

Canadian Government Pavilion. *My Home, My Native Land: A People, Their Land, Their Growth*. Montreal: Canadian Government Pavilion, Expo 67. N.d.

Carpenter, Joel A. *Revive Us Again: The Reawakening of American Fundamentalism*. Oxford: Oxford University Press 1997.

Carrington, Philip. *The Anglican Church in Canada*. Toronto: Collins 1963.

Carter, Stephen. *The Culture of Disbelief: How American Law and Politics Trivialize Religious Devotion*. New York: Basic Books 1993.

Casanova, José. *Public Religions in the Modern World*. Chicago: University of Chicago Press 1994.

Centennial Commission. *The Centennial Handbook*. Ottawa: The Centennial Commission 1964.

Chagnon, Roland. "Les nouvelles religions dans la dynamique socio-culturelle récente au Québec." In W. Westfall et al., eds., *Religion/Culture: Comparative Canadian Studies*. Ottawa: Association of Canadian Studies 1985, 118–51.

Chennells, David. *The Politics of Nationalism in Canada: Cultural Conflict since 1760*. Toronto: University of Toronto Press 2001.

Choquette, Robert. "The Canadian Churches, Bilingualism and Multiculturalism." In Keith A. McLeod, ed., *Multiculturalism, Bilingualism and Canadian Institutions*. Toronto: Governing Council of the University of Toronto 1979, 61–8.

– "Christ and Culture during 'Canada's Century.'" In Jay P. Dolan and James P. Wind, eds., *New Dimensions in American Religious History: Essays in Honor of Martin E. Marty*. Grand Rapids, MI: William B. Eerdmans Publishing 1993, 83–102.

Chorney, Harold, and Andrew Molloy. "Boss Politics in Montreal and Quebec Nationalism, Jean Drapeau to Jean Dore: From the Pre-Modern to the Post-Modern." In Alain-G. Gagnon, ed., *Quebec: State and Society*. 2d edition. Scarborough, ON: Nelson Canada 1993, 64–80.

Christian, William. *George Grant: A Biography*. University of Toronto Press 1993.

Christie, Nancy, ed. *Households of Faith: Family, Gender and Community in Canada, 1760–1969*. Montreal and Kingston: McGill-Queen's University Press 2002.

Clark, S.D. *Church and Sect in Canada*. Toronto: University of Toronto Press 1948.

- *The Developing Canadian Community.* 2d ed. Toronto: University of Toronto Press 1968.
- "Movements of Protest in Postwar Canadian Society." In R. Douglas Francis and Donald B. Smith, eds., *Readings in Canadian History: Post-Confederation.* 2d ed. Toronto: Holt, Rinehart and Winston of Canada 1986, 578–92.

Clarke, Brian. "English-Speaking Canada from 1854." In Terrence Murphy and Roberto Perin, eds. *A Concise History of Christianity in Canada.* Toronto: Oxford University Press 1996, 261–360.

- "Religion and Public Space in Protestant Toronto, 1880–1900." In M. Van Die, ed., *Religion and Public Life in Canada: Historical and Comparative Perspectives.* Toronto: University of Toronto Press 2001, 69–86.

Clifford, N.K. "His Dominion: A Vision in Crisis." In Peter Slater, ed., *Religion and Culture in Canada.* Canadian Corporation for Studies in Religion 1977, 24–43.

- "The Interpreters of the United Church of Canada." *Church History* 46, no. 2 (June 1977): 203–14.

Cohen, A.P. *The Symbolic Construction of Community.* New York: Tavistock Publications 1985.

Cohen, Naomi W. *Jews in Christian America: The Pursuit of Religious Equality.* Oxford: Oxford University Press 1992.

Colley, Linda. *Britons: Forging the Nation, 1707–1837.* London: Yale University Press 1992.

Collins, Robert. *The Holy War of Sally Ann: The Salvation Army in Canada.* Saskatoon, SK: Western Producer Prairie Books 1984.

Comeau, Paul. "Multiculturalism and Bilingualism at the Community Level." In Keith A. McLeod, ed., *Multiculturalism, Bilingualism and Canadian Institutions.* Toronto: Governing Council of the University of Toronto 1979, 37–41.

Cook, Ramsay. *The Maple Leaf Forever: Essays on Nationalism and Politics in Canada.* Toronto: Macmillan of Canada 1971.

- *The Regenerators: Social Criticism in Late Victorian English Canada.* Toronto: University of Toronto Press 1985.

Courcy, Raymond. "L'Église Catholique au Québec: De la fin d'un monopole au redéploiement dans une société plurielle." In W. Westfall, et al., eds., *Religion/Culture: Comparative Canadian Studies* Ottawa: Association of Canadian Studies, 1985, 86–98.

Cox, Harvey. *The Secular City: Secularization and Urbanization in Theological Perspective.* New York: Macmillan 1965.

Creighton, Donald. *Canada's First Century: 1867–1967.* Toronto: Macmillan of Canada 1970.

Crerar, Duff. "The Church in the Furnace: Canadian Anglican Chaplains Respond to the Great War." *Journal of the Canadian Church Historical Society* 35, no. 2 (October 1993): 75–104.

Cristi, Marcela. *From Civil to Political Religion: The Intersection of Culture, Religion and Politics.* Waterloo, ON: Wilfrid Laurier University Press 2001.

Crunican, Paul. *Priests and Politicians: Manitoba Schools and the Election of 1896.* Toronto: University of Toronto Press 1974.

Crysdale, Stewart. *The Changing Church in Canada.* Toronto: United Church Publishing House 1965.

Cupido, Robert. "Appropriating the Past: Pageants, Politics, and the Diamond Jubilee of Confederation." *Journal of the Canadian Historical Association* 9 (1998): 155–86.

– "'Sixty Years of Canadian Progress': The Diamond Jubilee and the Politics of Commemoration." *Canadian Issues/Thèmes Canadiens* 20 (1998): 19–33.

Currie, Raymond F. "Belonging, Commitment, and Early Socialization in a Western City." In Stewart Crysdale and Les Wheatcroft, eds. *Religion and Canadian Society.* Toronto: Macmillan of Canada 1976, 462–78.

Dahlie, Jorgen, and Tissa Fernando. "Reflections on Ethnicity and the Exercise of Power: An Introductory Note." In Jorgen Dahlie and Tissa Fernando, eds., *Ethnicity, Power and Politics in Canada.* Vol. 8. Toronto: Methuen Publications 1981, 1–5.

Daly, Bernard. "Immigration Policy: Its Impact on Canadian Society." In Keith A. McLeod, ed., *Multiculturalism, Bilingualism and Canadian Institutions.* Toronto: Governing Council of the University of Toronto 1979, 27–31.

– *Remembering for Tomorrow: A History of the Canadian Conference of Catholic Bishops, 1943–1993.* Ottawa: Canadian Conference of Catholic Bishops 1995.

Davies, Alan, ed. *Anti-Semitism in Canada: History and Interpretation.* Waterloo, ON: Wilfrid Laurier University Press 1992.

Davies, Helen. "The Politics of Participation: A Study of Canada's Centennial Celebration." PhD diss., University of Manitoba, 1999.

Davis, Kenneth R. "The Struggle for a United Evangelical Baptist Fellowship, 1953–1965." In Jarold K. Zeman, ed. *Baptists in Canada: Search for Identity amidst Diversity.* Burlington, ON: Welch Publishing 1980, 237–66.

Dawson, Michael. *The Mountie: From Dime Novel to Disney.* Toronto: Between the Lines 1998.

Day, Richard J.F. *Multiculturalism and the History of Canadian Diversity.* Toronto: University of Toronto Press 2001.

Debicki, Marek. "The Double Mythology of Multiculturalism in Canada." In Stella Hryniuk, ed., *Twenty Years of Multiculturalism: Successes and Failures.* Winnipeg: St John's College Press, 1992, 29–35.

Demerath, N.J., and Rhys H. Williams. "Religion and Power in the American Experience" In Thomas Robbins and Dick Anthony, eds., *In God We Trust: New Patterns of Religious Pluralism in America.* New Brunswick, NJ: Transaction Publishers 1990, 427–48.

Desbiens, J.P. *Les Insolences de Frère Untel.* Montreal: Les Éditions de l'Homme 1960.

Dickstein, Morriss. "From the Thirties to the Sixties: The New York World's Fair in its Own Time." In Robert Rosenblum, ed., *Remembering the Future: The New York World's Fair from 1939 to 1964.* New York: Rizzoli International Publications 1989, 21–45.

Diefenbaker, John G. *One Canada: Memoirs of the Right Honourable John G. Diefenbaker.* Vol. 3. Scarborough, ON: Macmillan-NAL Publishing 1977.

Dion, Gérald. "The Church and the Conflict in the Asbestos Industry." In Pierre Elliot Trudeau, ed., *The Asbestos Strike.* Toronto: James Lewis and Samuel 1974, 205–25.

Dion, Gérard, and Louis O'Neill. *L'immoralité politique dans la province de Québec.* Montreal: Comité de moralité publique 1956.

Dogan, Mattei. "Introduction: Strains on Legitimacy." In Mattei Dogan, ed., *Comparing Pluralist Democracies: Strains on Legitimacy.* London: Westview Press 1988, 1–18.

Douglas, Pauline, and Vera Manuel. "The Show but Not the Substance: The Question of Native Participation." In Robert Anderson and Eleanor Wachtel, eds., *The Expo Story.* Madeira Park, BC: Harbour Publishing 1986, 189–214.

Doull, James. "The Theology of the Great Society." *Canadian Journal of Theology* 13, no. 1 (1967): 5–18.

Drainville, Dennis. *Poverty in Canada: A Discussion Paper Prepared for the Primate of the Anglican Church of Canada and the Board of Directors of Stop 103.* Toronto: Anglican Book Centre 1985.

Druick, Zoë. "'Ambiguous Identities' and the Representation of Everyday Life: Notes toward a New History of Production Policies at the National Film Board of Canada." *Canadian Issues/Thèmes Canadiens* 20 (1998): 125–37.

Dumont, Fernand. "Transformation within the Relegous Culture of Francophone Quebec." In W. Westfall, et al., eds., *Religion/Culture: Comparative Canadian Studies.* Ottawa: Association of Canadian Studies 1985, 22–32.

– "Une Révolution Culturelle?" In Fernand Dumont et al., eds., *Idéologies au Canada Francais, 1940–1976.* Vol. 1, *la Presse – la Littérature.* Québec: Les Presses de l'Université Laval 1981, 5–32.

Dumont, Fernand, and Guy Rocher. "An Introduction to a Sociology of French Canada." (Originally published 1961). In Marcel Rioux and Yves Martin, eds., *French Canadian Society.* Vol. 1. Toronto: McClelland and Stewart, 1964, 178–200.

Dupuy, Pierre. *Expo 67, ou la découverte de la fierté.* Montreal: Les Éditions la Presse 1972.

Ellis, Walter E. "Fragmented Baptists: The Poverty and Potential of Baptist Life in Western Canada." In David T. Priestley ed., *Memory and Hope:*

Strands of Canadian Baptist History. Waterloo, ON: Wilfrid Laurier University Press 1996, 111–22.

Ellwood, Robert S. *The Fifties Spiritual Marketplace: American Religion in a Decade of Conflict.* New Brunswick, NJ: Rutgers University Press 1997.

– *The Sixties Spiritual Awakening: American Religion Moving from Modern to Postmodern.* New Brunswick, NJ: Rutgers University Press 1994.

English, John. *Shadow of Heaven: The Life of Lester B. Pearson.* Vol. 1. London: Vintage UK 1990.

– *The Worldly Years: The Life of Lester B. Pearson.* Vol. 2. Toronto: Alfred A. Knopf Canada 1992.

Evenson, G.O. *Adventuring for Christ: The Story of the Evangelical Lutheran Church of Canada.* Calgary: Foothills Lutheran Press 1974.

Expo 67, Montréal, Canada: The Memorial Album of the First Category Universal and International Exhibition Held in Montréal from the Twenty-Seventh of April to the Twenty-Ninth of October, 1967. Canada: Thomas Nelson and Sons 1968.

Expo 67: Official Guide. Montreal: Maclean-Hunter 1967.

Exposition Universelle et Internationale de Bruxelles, 1958. Vol. 3, *Les Participations Étrangères et Belges.* Etablissements Généraux d'Imprimerie à Bruxelles 1958.

Fachenhiem, Emil L. "A Jew Looks at Christianity and Secular Liberalism." In William Kilbourn, ed., *The Restless Church: A Response to the Comfortable Pew.* Toronto: McClelland and Stewart 1966, 86–99.

Fairweather, Eugene. "The Catholic Tradition." In William Kilbourn, ed., *The Restless Church: A Response to the Comfortable Pew.* Toronto: McClelland and Stewart 1966, 65–71.

– "The Christian Message in Canada, 1967: A Critical Glance at the Canadian Scene." *Canadian Journal of Theology* 13, no. 1 (1967): 1–4.

– "The Christian Moralist in 1966: Some Random Reflections and Queries." *Canadian Journal of Theology* 12, no. 4 (1996): 227–8.

Falardeau, Jean-Charles. "The Changing Social Structures of Contemporary French-Canadian Society." (Originally published 1953). In Marcel Rioux and Yves Martin, eds. *French Canadian Society.* Vol. 1. Toronto: McClelland and Stewart 1964, 106–122.

– "The Role and Importance of the Church in French Canada." (Originally published 1952). In Marcel Rioux and Yves Martin, eds. *French Canadian Society.* Vol. 1. Toronto: McClelland and Stewart 1964, 342–57.

Faulkner, C.T. "For Christian Civilization: Churches and Canada's War Effort, 1939–1942." PhD diss. University of Chicago 1975.

Ferguson, Barry. *Remaking Liberalism: The Intellectual Legacy of Adam Shortt, O.D. Skelton, W.C. Clark, and W.A. Mackintosh.* Montreal and Kingston: McGill-Queen's University Press 1993.

Findling, John E., ed. *Historical Dictionary of World's Fairs and Expositions, 1851–1988.* New York: Greenwood Press 1990.

Fornäs, Johan. *Cultural Theory and Late Modernity.* London: Sage Publications 1995.

Foster, Kate. *Our Canadian Mosaic.* Toronto: Dominion Council, YWCA, 1926.

Fowler, Albert G. "Following in the Footsteps of our Lord: Canadian Army Chaplains in Korea, 1950–53." *Journal of the Canadian Church Historical Society* 35, no. 2 (October 1993), 122–31.

Francis, Daniel. *National Dreams: Myth, Memory and Canadian History.* Vancouver: Arsenal Pulp Press 1997.

Francis, R. Douglas et al., eds. *Destinies: Canadian History since Confederation.* Toronto: Harcourt Canada 2000.

Franks, C.E.S. "Counting Canada: One, Two, Four, Ten and More." In M.P. Singh and Chandra Mohan, eds., *Regionalism and National Identity: Canada-India.* Delhi: Pragati Publications 1994, 1–20.

Fraser, Brian J. "Christianizing the Social Order: T.B. Kilpatrick's Theological Vision of the United Church of Canada." *Toronto Journal of Theology* 12, no. 2 (1996): 189–200.

Fraser, Nancy. "Rethinking the Public Sphere: A Contribution to the Critique of Actually Existing Democracy." In Simon During, ed., *The Cultural Studies Reader.* 2d ed., London and New York: Routledge 1999, 518–36.

Friesen, Gerald. *Citizens and Nation: An Essay on History, Communication, and Canada.* Toronto: University of Toronto Press 2001.

Frye, Northrop. *The Modern Century: The Whidden Lectures, 1967.* Oxford: Oxford University Press 1967.

Fulford, Robert. *Remember Expo: A Pictorial Record.* Toronto: McClelland and Stewart 1968.

– *This Was Expo.* Toronto: McClelland and Stewart 1968.

Gagne, Wallace, ed. *Nationalism, Technology and the Future of Canada.* Toronto: The Macmillan Company of Canada 1976.

Galbraith, John Kenneth. *The Affluent Society.* Boston: Houghton Mifflin, 1958.

Gans, Herbert J. *Popular Culture and High Culture: An Analysis and Evaluation of Taste.* New York: Basic Books 1975.

Gauvreau, Michael. "Beyond the Half-Way House: Evangelicalism and the Shaping of *English Canadian Culture.*" Acadiensis 20, no. 2 (1991): 158–76.

– *The Evangelical Century: College and Creed in English Canada from the Great Revival to the Great Depression.* Montreal and Kingston: McGill-Queen's University Press 1991.

– "From Rechristianization to Contestation: Catholic Values and Quebec Society, 1931–1970." *Church History* 69, no. 4 (December 2000): 803–33.

Gauvreau, Michael, and Nancy Christie. *A Full-Orbed Christianity: The Protestant Churches and Social Welfare in Canada, 1900–1940.* Montreal and Kingston: McGill-Queen's University Press 1996.

Gehrig, Gail. *American Civil Religion: An Assessment.* Society for the Scientific Study of Religion 1979.

Gellner, Ernest. *Nations and Nationalism.* Ithaca, NY: Cornell University Press 1983.

Gibbon, J.M. *Canadian Mosaic: The Making of a Northern Nation*. Toronto: McClelland and Stewart 1938.

Gidney, Catharine. *The Long Eclipse: The Liberal Protestant Establishment and the Canadian University, 1920–1970*. Montreal and Kingston: McGill-Queen's University Press 2005.

– "Poisoning the Student Mind? The Student Christian Movement at the University of Toronto, 1920–1965." *Journal of the Canadian Historical Association* 8 (1997): 147–63.

Gidney, R.D., and W.P.J. Millar. "The Christian Recessional in Ontario's Public Schools." In M. Van Die, ed., *Religion and Public Life in Canada: Historical and Comparative Perspectives*. Toronto: University of Toronto Press 2001, 275–93.

Gillespie, William. "The Recovery of Ontario's Baptist Tradition." In David T. Priestley, ed., *Memory and Hope: Strands of Canadian Baptist History*. Waterloo, ON: Wilfrid Laurier University Press 1996, 25–38.

Gleason, Philip. *Speaking of Diversity: Language and Ethnicity in Twentieth Century America*. Baltimore, MD: Johns Hopkins University Press 1992.

Goldstein, Jonah. "Public Interest Groups and Public Policy: The Case of the Consumers' Association of Canada." *Canadian Journal of Political Science* 12 (March 1979): 137–55.

Gougeon, Gilles. *A History of Quebec Nationalism*. Trans. Louisa Blair, Robert Chodos, and Jane Ubertino. Toronto: James Lorimer 1994.

Grace, Sherrill, and Gabriele Helms. "Documenting Racism: Sharon Pollock's *The Komagata Maru Incident*." In Veronica Strong-Boag, et al., eds., *Painting the Maple: Essays on Race, Gender and the Construction of Canada*. Vancouver: University of British Columbia Press 1998, 85–99.

Graham, Ron. *God's Dominion: A Skeptic's Quest*. Toronto: McClelland and Stewart 1990.

Granatstein, J.L. *Canada 1957–1967: The Years of Uncertainty and Innovation*. Toronto: McClelland and Stewart 1986.

– *The Ottawa Men: The Civil Service Mandarins, 1935–57*. Toronto: Oxford University Press 1982.

Granatstien, J.L., et al. *Twentieth Century Canada*. 2d ed. Toronto: McGraw-Hill Ryerson 1986.

Grant, George. *Lament for a Nation: The Defeat of Canadian Nationalism*. Toronto: McClelland and Stewart 1965.

– *Technology and Empire*. Concord, ON: House of Anansi Press 1969.

Grant, John Webster. "'At least you knew where you stood with them': Reflections on Religious Pluralism in Canada and the United States." *Studies in Religion* 2, no. 4 (1973): 340–51.

– *The Canadian Experience of Church Union*. London: Lutterworth Press 1967.

– *Church in the Canadian Era*. Burlington, ON: Welch Publishing 1988.

– "From Revelation to Revolution: Some Thoughts on the Background of the Social Gospel." *Toronto Journal of Theology* 12:2 (1996): 159–68.

– "Religion and the Quest for a National Identity: The Background in Canadian History." In Peter Slater, ed., *Religion and Culture in Canada*. Canadian Corporation for Studies in Religion 1977, 7–23.

– "Roots and Wings." Theme address delivered to the Annual General Meeting – Division of Ministry Personnel and Education, 18–19 February 1989.

Guindon, Hubert. "The Social Evolution of Quebec Reconsidered." *Canadian Journal of Economics and Political Science* 26 (November 1960): 533–51.

Habermas, Jürgen. "Modernity: An Unfinished Project." In Charles Jencks, ed., *The Post-Modern Reader*. New York: St Martin's Press 1992, 158–69.

Hale, Katherine. *Canada's Peace Tower and Memorial Chamber*. Toronto: Mundy-Goodfellow 1935.

Hall, Douglas John. *The End of Christendom and the Future of Christianity*. Valleyforge, PA: Trinity Press International 1997.

Hall, Stuart. "Encoding, Decoding." In Simon During, ed., *The Cultural Studies Reader*. 2d ed. London and New York: Routledge 1999, 507–17.

Hamelin, Jean. *Histoire du catholicisme québécois, le XXe siècle*. Vol. 2, *De 1940 à nos jours*. Montreal: Les Éditions du Boréal Express 1984.

Hamilton, T.J. "The Delicate Equilibrium: Canada's Protestant Chaplains during the Second World War." *Journal of the Canadian Church Historical Society* 35: 2 (October 1993): 105–21.

Hammond, Phillip E., Amanda Porterfield, James G. Moseley, Jonathan D. Sarna. "Forum: American Civil Religion Revisited." *Religion and American Culture* 4 (1994): 1–23.

Handy, Robert T. *A Christian America: Protestant Hopes and Historical Realities*. Oxford: Oxford University Press 1984.

– "Dominant Patterns of Christian Life in Canada and the United States: Similarities and Differences." In William Westfall, et al., eds., *Religion/Culture: Comparative Canadian Studies*. Ottawa: Association for Canadian Studies 1985, 344–55.

– *Undermined Establishment: Church-State Relations in America, 1880–1920*. Princeton, NJ: Princeton University Press 1991.

Harney, R.F. "'So Great a Heritage as Ours': Immigration and the Survival of the Canadian Polity." *Daedalus* 117, no. 4 (fall 1988): 51–97.

Harris, Paul T., ed. *Brief to the Bishops: Canadian Catholic Laymen Speak Their Minds*. Toronto: Catholic Information Centre 1965.

Harrison, Ernest. *Let God Go Free*. Anglican Church of Canada 1965.

Harshaw, William E. *A Transforming Influence: A Biographical Memoir of Archbishop Howard C. Clark*. Toronto: The Harfolk Press 1993.

Hastings, Adrian. *The Construction of Nationhood: Ethnicity, Religion and Nationalism*. Cambridge: Cambridge University Press 1997.

Hayes, Alan L. "Repairing the Walls: Church Reform and Social Reform, 1867–1939." In Alan L. Hayes, ed., *By Grace Coworkers: Building the Anglican Diocese of Toronto, 1780–1989*. Toronto: Anglican Book Centre 1989, 43–96.

Heaman, E.A. *The Inglorious Arts of Peace: Exhibitions in Canadian Society during the Nineteenth Century.* Toronto: University of Toronto Press 1999.

Hebert, Raymond. "Francophone Perspectives on Multiculturalism." In Stella Hryniuk, ed., *Twenty Years of Multiculturalism: Successes and Failures.* Winnipeg: St John's College Press 1992, 59–72.

Henry, Frances, and Carol Tator. "State Policy and Practices as Racialized Discourse: Multiculturalism, the Charter and Employment Equity." In Peter S. Li, ed., *Race and Relations in Canada.* 2d ed. Oxford: Oxford University Press 1999, 88–115.

Hewitt, W.E., ed. *The Sociology of Religion: A Canadian Focus.* Toronto: Butterworths Canada 1993.

Hillier, Harry. "Civil Religion and the Problem of National Unity: The 1995 Quebec Referendum Crisis." In David Lyon and Marguerite Van Die, eds., *Rethinking Church, State, and Modernity: Canada between Europe and America.* Toronto and Buffalo: University of Toronto Press 2000, 166–187.

Hillmer, Norman. "Introduction: Pearson and the Sense of Paradox." In Norman Hillmer, ed., *Pearson: The Unlikely Gladiator.* Montreal and Kingston: McGill-Queen's University Press 1999, 3–18.

Hobsbawm, Eric. "Mass-Producing Traditions: Europe, 1870–1914." In Eric Hobsbawm and Terrence Ranger, eds., *The Invention of Tradition.* Cambridge: Cambridge University Press 1983, 263–307.

Hodgetts, J.E. *The Canadian Public Service: A Physiology of Government, 1867–1970.* Toronto: University of Toronto Press 1973.

– *From Arm's Length to Hands-On: The Formative Years of Ontario's Public Service, 1867–1940.* Toronto: University of Toronto Press 1995.

Hollinger, David. "Jewish Intellectuals and the de-Christianization of American Public Life in the Twentieth Century." In Harry Stout and D.G. Hart, eds., *New Directions in American Religious History.* Oxford: Oxford University Press 1997, 462–84.

Horne, Donald. *Public Culture: An Argument with the Future.* 2d ed. London: Pluto Press 1995.

Horton, Donald J. *André Laurendeau: French Canadian Nationalist, 1912–1968.* Toronto: Oxford University Press 1992.

Howard, Keith. "100 Huntley Street and the Interfaith Pavilion Controversy." In Robert Anderson and Eleanor Wachtel, eds., *The Expo Story.* Madeira Park, BC: Harbour Publishing 1986, 173–88.

Howse, E.M. *Roses in December: The Autobiography of Ernest Marshall Howse.* Winfield, BC: Wood Lake Books 1982.

Hutchinson, Roger. "Christianizing the Social Order: A Three-Dimensional Task." *Toronto Journal of Theology* 12, no. 2 (1996): 227–36.

– *Prophets, Pastors and Public Choices: Canadian Churches and the Mackenzie Valley Pipeline Debate.* Waterloo, ON: Wilfrid Laurier University Press 1992.

- "Religion, Morality and Law." In Peter Slater, ed., *Religion and Culture in Canada*. Canadian Corporation for Studies in Religion 1977: 187–224.

Hutchinson, William R., ed. *Between the Times: The Travail of the Protestant Establishment in America, 1900–1960*. Cambridge: Cambridge University Press 1989.

Iacovetta, Franca. "Making 'New Canadians': Social Workers, Women, and the Reshaping of Immigrant Families." In Franca Iacovetta, Paula Draper, and Robert Ventresco, eds., *A Nation of Immigrants: Women, Workers and Communities in Canadian History, 1840s-1960s*. Toronto: University of Toronto Press 1998, 482–513.

James, William C. *Locations of the Sacred: Essays on Religion, Literature, and Canadian Culture*. Waterloo, ON: Wilfrid Laurier University Press 1998.

Jamison, Andrew, and Ron Eyerman. *Seeds of the Sixties*. Berkeley: University of California Press 1994.

Jansen, William. *Limits on Liberty: The Experience of Mennonite, Hutterite and Doukhobor Communities in Canada*. Toronto: University of Toronto Press 1990.

Jasen, Patricia. "'In Pursuit of Human Values (or Laugh When You Say That)': The Student Critique of the Arts Curriculum in the 1960s." In Paul Axelrod and John G. Reid, eds., *Youth, University and Canadian Society: Essays in the Social History of Higher Education*. Montreal and Kingston: McGill-Queen's University Press 1989, 247–74.

Jay, C. Douglas. "Missiological Implications of Christianizing the Social Order with Special Reference to the United Church of Canada." *Toronto Journal of Theology* 12:2 (1996): 275–84.

Jencks, Charles. "The Post-Modern Agenda." In Charles Jencks, ed. *The Post-Modern Reader*. New York: St Martin's Press 1992, 10–39.

Jenson, Jane. "Naming Nations: Making Nationalist Claims in Canadian Public Discourse." *Canadian Review of Sociology and Anthropology* 30, no. 3 (1993): 337–58.

Jiwani, Yasmin. "On the Outskirts of Empire: Race and Gender in Canadian T.V. News." In Veronica Strong-Boag, et al., eds., *Painting the Maple: Essays on Race, Gender and the Construction of Canada*. Vancouver: University of British Columbia Press 1998, 53–68.

Johnson, Douglas W., and George W. Cornell. *Punctured Preconceptions: What North American Christians Think about the Church*. New York: Friendship Press 1972.

Johnston, Richard. "The Reproduction of Religious Cleavage in Canadian Elections." *Canadian Journal of Political Science* 18 (March 1985): 99–113.

Johnston, Russell. "The Early Trials of Protestant Radio, 1922–1938." *Canadian Historical Review* 75, no. 3 (1994): 376–402.

Joint Strategy Committee of the Canadian Council of Churches and of the Canadian Catholic Conference. "'Poverty and Conscience: Towards a Coalition for Development': Report of a Joint Strategy Committee of the Canadian Council of Churches and of the Canadian Catholic Conference: To All Concerned Canadians, May 30, 1969." In E.F. Sheridan, ed., *Do Justice! The Social Teaching of the Canadian Catholic Bishops (1945–1986)*. Sherbrooke, QC, and Toronto: Éditions Paulines and the Jesuit Centre for Social Faith and Justice 1987, 155–74.

Jones, Peter. "Theology and Ethnicity." In Keith A. McLeod, ed., *Multiculturalism, Bilingualism and Canadian Institutions*. Toronto: Governing Council of the University of Toronto 1979, 53–60.

Kaill, Robert C. "The Impact of Clerical Attitudes and Liberalism on Ecumenism." In Stewart Crysdale and Les Wheatcroft, eds., *Religion and Canadian Society*. Toronto: Macmillan of Canada 1976, 398–410.

Kallen, Evelyn. "Multiculturalism: Canada's Response to Racial and Ethnic Diversity." In M.P. Singh and Chandra Mohan, eds., *Regionalism and National Identity: Canada-India*. Delhi: Pragati Publications 1994, 60–8.

– "Synagogues in Transition: Religious Revival or Ethnic Survival." In Stewart Crysdale and Les Wheatcroft, eds., *Religion and Canadian Society*. Toronto: Macmillan of Canada 1976, 278–88.

Kaplan, William. *State and Salvation: The Jehovah's Witnesses and Their Fight for Civil Rights*. Toronto: University of Toronto Press 1989.

Katerberg, William H. "Protecting Christian Liberty: Mainline Protestantism, Racial Thought and Political Culture in Canada, 1918–1939." *Historical Papers 1995: Canadian Society for Church History*, 5–34.

Kawamura, Leslie J. "Buddhism in Southern Alberta." In Peter Slater, ed., *Religion and Culture in Canada*. Canadian Corporation for Studies in Religion 1977, 492–506.

Kee, Kevin. "Revivalism: The Marketing of Protestant Religion in English-Speaking Canada, 1884–1957." PhD diss., Queen's University, Kingston, ON, 1999.

Kelley, Ninette, and Michael Trebilcock. *The Making of the Mosaic: A History of Canadian Immigration Policy*. Toronto: University of Toronto Press 1998.

Kelly, Séan, and Ron Wareham. *Man and His World Inside Out: A Review of Montreal's Man and His World*. Montreal: Atlantis Enterprises 1968.

Keohane, Kieran. *Symptoms of Canada: An Essay on the Canadian Identity*. Toronto: University of Toronto Press 1997.

Kernaghan, William David Kenneth. "Freedom of Religion in the Province of Quebec with Particular Reference to the Jews, Jehovah's Witnesses and Church-State Relations, 1930–1960." PhD diss., Duke University, 1966. Reproduced by University Microfilms, Ann Arbor, MI.

Kicksee, Richard. "'Scaled Down to Size': Contested Liberal Common Sense and the Negotiation of 'Indian Participation' in the Canadian Centennial Celebrations and Expo '67, 1963–1967," MA thesis, Queen's University, Kingston, ON, 1995.

Kilbourn, William. "An Interview with Harvey Cox." In William Kilbourn, ed., *The Restless Church: A Response to the Comfortable Pew.* Toronto: McClelland and Stewart 1966, 169–72.

– "Introduction." In William Kilbourn, ed., *Canada: A Guide to the Peaceable Kingdom.* Toronto: Macmillan 1970, xi–xviii.

– ed. *Religion in Canada: The Spiritual Development of a Nation.* Toronto: McClelland and Stewart 1968.

– *The Restless Church: A Response to the Comfortable Pew.* Toronto: McClelland and Stewart 1966.

Kilgour, David. *Inside Outer Canada.* Edmonton: Lone Line Publishing 1990.

Kim, Andrew. "The Absence of Pan-Canadian Civil Religion: Plurality, Duality and Conflict in Symbols of Canadian Culture." *Sociology of Religion* 54 (1993): 257–75.

King, Joe. *From the Ghetto to the Main: The Story of the Jews of Montreal.* Montreal: Montreal Jewish Publication Society 2001.

Klein, Milton M. "Mythologizing the U.S. Constitution." *Soundings* 78 (spring 1995): 169–88.

Kollar, Nathan R. "The Death of National Symbols: Roman Catholicism in Quebec." In P.D. Phan, ed., *Ethnicity, Nationality and Religious Experience.* New York: University Press of America 1991, 289–311.

Kostash, Myrna. *Long Way from Home: The Story of the Sixties Generation in Canada.* Toronto: J. Lorimer 1980.

Kröller, Eva-Marie. "Expo '67: Canada's Camelot?" *Canadian Literature/ Littérature canadienne* 152/153 (spring/summer 1997): 36–51.

Krygsman, Hubert. "Freedom and Grace: Mainline Protestant Thought in Canada, 1900-1960." PhD diss., Carleton University, 1997.

Kuffert, L.B. *A Great Duty: Canadian Responses to Modern Life and Mass Culture, 1939–1967.* Montreal and Kingston: McGill-Queen's University Press 2003.

Kulbeck, Gloria G. *What God Hath Wrought: A History of the Pentecostal Assemblies of Canada.* Toronto: The Pentecostal Assemblies of Canada 1958.

Lacoste, Norbert. "The People Tree." In *My Home, My Native Land: A People, Their Land, Their Growth.* Montreal: Canadian Government Pavilion, Expo 67, n.d., 19–26.

LaMarsh, Judy. *Memoirs of a Bird in a Gilded Cage.* Toronto: McClelland and Stewart 1968.

Lane, Grace. *Brief Halt at Mile 50.* Toronto: The United Church Publishing House 1974.

Lanken, Dane. "Remembering the Magic of Expo 67." *Canadian Geographic* 112, no. 4 (July/August 1992): 76–82.

Larsen, V.W. *The Minister and the Church: An Exploratory Study of Some Characteristics and Attitudes of United Church of Canada Clergymen in Manitoba and Saskatchewan.* Saskatoon: Centre for Community Studies 1964.

Lautard, Jugh, and Neil Guppy. "Revisiting the Vertical Mosaic: Occupational Stratification among Ethnic Groups." In Peter S. Li, ed., *Race and Relations in Canada*. 2d ed. Oxford: Oxford University Press 1999, 219–52.

Laverdure, Paul. "Canada on Sunday: The Decline of the Sabbath, 1900–50." PhD diss., University of Toronto 1990.

– "Canada's Sunday: The Presbyterian Contribution, 1875–1950." In William Klempa, ed., *The Burning Bush and a Few Acres of Snow: The Presbyterian Contribution to Canadian Life and Culture*. Ottawa: Carleton University Press 1994, 83–100.

LeBlanc, Louise. "The Church and Reconciliation." In Gregory Baum, Ronald Sutherland, and Louis LeBlanc, *The Survival of Canada and the Christian Church: Conference*. Toronto: St Michael's College 1973.

LeBlanc, Philip, and Arnold Edinborough, eds. *One Church, Two Nations?* Don Mills, ON: Longmans Canada 1968.

Lee, Anne, and Linda Cardinal. "Hegemonic Nationalism and the Politics of Feminism and Multiculturalism in Canada." In Veronica Strong-Boag et al., eds., *Painting the Maple: Essays on Race, Gender and the Construction of Canada*. Vancouver: University of British Columbia Press 1998, 215–37.

Legacy, F.H., ed. *Historical Statistics of Canada*. 2d ed. Statistics Canada 1983.

Li, Peter S. *The Making of Post-War Canada*. Toronto: Oxford University Press 1996.

– "The Multiculturalism Debate" In Peter S. Li, *Race and Relations in Canada*. 2d ed. Oxford: Oxford University Press 1999, 148–77.

Linteau, Paul-Andre, et al. *Quebec since 1930*. Trans. by Robert Chodos and Ellen Garmaise. Toronto: James Lorimer 1991.

Litt, Paul. *The Muses, the Masses, and the Massey Commission*. Toronto: University of Toronto Press 1992.

Loney, Martin. "A Political Economy of Citizen Participation." In Leo Panitch, ed., *The Canadian State: Political Economy and Political Power*. Toronto: University of Toronto Press 1977, 446–66.

Lougheed, Richard. "Anti-Catholicism among French-Canadian Protestants." *Historical Papers 1995: Canadian Society of Church History*, 161–80.

Lower, Arthur R.M. "Church and State in Canada." Ottawa: Dominion-Chalmers United Church 1965.

– "Religion and Religious Institutions." In Welf H. Heick, ed., *History and Myth: Arthur Lower and the Making of Canadian Nationalism*. Vancouver: University of British Columbia Press 1975, 75–96.

Lucas, Rex A. "Religious Differentiation and Conflict in Single-Industry Communities." In Stewart Crysdale and Les Wheatcroft, eds., *Religion and Canadian Society*. Toronto: Macmillan 1976, 268–77.

Luciuk, Lubomyr Y. *Searching for Place: Ukrainian Displaced Persons, Canada, and the Migration of Memory*. Toronto: University of Toronto Press 2000.

Lukes, S. "Political Ritual and Social Integration." *Sociology* 9 (1975): 289–308.

Lupul, Manoly. "Political Implementation of Multiculturalism." *Journal of Canadian Studies* 17, no. 1 (spring 1982): 93–102.

Lyotard, Jean-Francois. "Answering the Question: What is Postmodernism?" In Charles Jencks, ed., *The Post-Modern Reader*. New York: St Martin's Press 1992, 138–50.

MacAdam, Murray. "The Canadian Churches' Ecumenical Coalitions for Social Justice." *Scarboro Missions* (February 1995): 15–7.

MacDowell, Laurel Sefton. "United Church Support for Collective Bargaining in the 1940s." *Toronto Journal of Theology* 12, no. 2 (1996): 251–63.

Mackey, Eva. *The House of Difference: Cultural Politics and National Identity in Canada*. University of Toronto Press 2002.

MacLean, Allan. *The First Hundred Years, 1877–1977: Tabernacle United Church of Canada, Belleville, Ontario*. Kingston: Hanson and Edgar 1977.

MacQueen, Angus James. *Memory Is My Diary*. Vol. 2. Hantsport, NS: Lancelot Press 1991.

Mahon, Rianne. "Canadian Public Policy: The Unequal Structure of Representation." In Leo Panitch, ed., *The Canadian State: Political Economy and Political Power*. Toronto: University of Toronto Press 1977, 166–98.

"Man and His World": A Series of Prayer Gatherings for the Success of the Christian Pavilion at Expo 67. Booklet prepared jointly by Montreal Ecumenical Centre, Greater Montreal Council of Churches, and Christian Pavilion. N.p., n.d.

Manent, Pierre. *An Intellectual History of Liberalism*. Trans. by Rebecca Balinski. Princeton: Princeton University Press 1994.

Mann, Donald R. Whyte. "Religion and the Rural Church." In W.E. Mann, ed., *Social and Cultural Change in Canada*. Vol. 1. Toronto: Copp Clark 1970, 156–69.

Mann, W.E., ed. *Social and Cultural Change in Canada*. Vol. 1. Toronto: Copp Clark 1970.

Manzer, Ronald. "Public Philosophy and Public Policy: The Case of Religion in Canadian State Education." *British Journal of Canadian Studies* 7, no. 2 (1992): 248–76.

Marks, Lynne. *Revivals and Roller Rinks: Religion, Leisure and Identity in Late-Nineteenth-Century Small-Town Ontario*. Toronto: University of Toronto Press 1996.

Marsden, George. *The Soul of the American University: From Protestant Establishment to Established Unbelief*. Oxford: Oxford University Press 1994.

Marshall, David. *Secularizing the Faith: Canadian Protestant Clergy and the Crisis of Belief, 1850–1940*. Toronto: University of Toronto Press 1992.

Marshall, Joan. *A Solitary Pillar: Montreal's Anglican Church and the Quiet Revolution*. Montreal and Kingston: McGill-Queen's University Press 1995.

Marty, Martin. *The One and the Many: America's Struggle for the Common Good*. Cambridge, MA: Harvard University Press 1997.

− "Religion in America since Mid-Century." *Daedalus* 111 (winter 1982): 149–63.

Mason, Ian M. "Religious Revival and Social Transformation: George Pidgeon and the United Church of Canada in the 1930s." *Toronto Journal of Theology* 12, no. 2 (1996): 213–21.

Masurek, Kas. "Defusing a Radical Social Policy: The Undermining of Multiculturalism." In Stella Hryniuk, ed., *Twenty Years of Multiculturalism: Successes and Failures*. Winnipeg: St John's College Press 1992, 17–29.

Mather, G.B., ed. *Christianity and Politics*. National Evangelistic Mission Committee, United Church of Canada, 1960.

Mathers, Donald. "... Not by Sight: Some Sermons and Occasional Talks of Donald Mathers." Published by his Friends, 1974.

Matheson, John. *Canada's Flag: A Search for a Country*. Belleville, ON: Mika Publishing 1986.

Mathews, Robert, and Cranford Pratt, eds., *Church and State: The Christian Churches and Canadian Foreign Policy*. Proceedings of a Consultation, Toronto, Canada, 28 September 1982. Canadian Institute of International Affairs 1982.

McCall, Christina. "The Unlikely Gladiators: Pearson and Diefenbaker Remembered." In Norman Hillmer, ed. *Pearson: The Unlikely Gladiator*. Montreal and Kingston: McGill-Queen's University Press 1999, 58–67.

McCrone, David. *The Sociology of Nationalism: Tommorrow's Ancestors*. London: Routledge 1998.

McDermott, Mark C., James A. Patrick, and Barrie A. Wilson. "A Bibliography of the 'New Theology': Introduction and Part One: Some Historical Antecedents." *Canadian Journal of Theology* 13, no. 1 (1967): 57–63.

McDonald, Lynn. "Religion and Voting: A Study of the 1968 Canadian Federal Election in Ontario." *Canadian Review of Sociology and Anthropology* 8, no. 3 (August 1971): 164–84.

McKay, Ian. *The Challenge of Modernity: A Reader on post-Confederation Canada*. Toronto: McGraw-Hill Ryerson 1992.

− *The Quest of the Folk: Anti-modernism and Cultural Selection in Twentieth Century Nova Scotia*. Montreal and Kingston: McGill-Queen's University Press 1994.

McKenna, Robert, and Susan Purcell. *Drapeau*. Toronto: Clarke, Irwin 1980.

McKillop, A.B. *A Disciplined Intelligence: Critical Inquiry and Canadian Thought in the Victorian Era*. Montreal and Kingston: McGill-Queen's University Press 1979.

McKinnon, Alastair. "Barth's Relation to Kierkegaard: Some Further Light." *Canadian Journal of Theology* 13, no. 1 (1967): 31–42.

McNaught, Kenneth. "The National Outlook of English-Speaking Canadians." In Peter Russell, ed., *Nationalism in Canada*. Toronto: McGraw-Hill 1966, 61–71.

McRoberts, Kenneth. *Misconceiving Canada: The Struggle for National Unity.* Toronto: Oxford University Press 1997.

Meisel, John. *The Canadian General Election of 1957.* Toronto: University of Toronto Press 1962.

– ed. *Papers on the 1962 Election.* Toronto: University of Toronto Press 1964.

Menendez, Albert J. *Church and State in Canada.* New York: Prometheus Books 1996.

Merkl, Peter H. "Comparing Legitimacy and Values among Advanced Democratic Countries." In Mattei Dogan, ed., *Comparing Pluralist Democracies: Strains on Legitimacy.* London: Westview Press 1988, 19–64.

Miedema, Gary. "For Canada's Sake: The Centennial Celebrations of 1967, State Legitimation, and the Restructuring of Canadian Public Life," *Journal of Canadian Studies* 34, no. 1 (spring 1999): 139–60.

– "God in the Centennial: Religion and the State in the Canadian Interfaith Conference, 1965–1967." *Historical Papers 1996: Canadian Society of Church History,* 38–56.

– "Preaching to the Nation: The National Religious Advisory Council of the CBC, 1938–1970." Unpublished paper delivered to the Canadian Society of Church History, Halifax, May 2003.

Miller, J.P. "Anti-Catholicism in Canada from the British Conquest to the Great War." In Terrence Murphy and Gerald Stortz, eds., *Creed and Culture: The Place of English-Speaking Catholics in Canadian Society 1750–1930.* Montreal and Kingston: McGill-Queen's University Press 1993, 25–49.

Miller, J.R. *Shingwauk's Vision: A History of Native Residential Schools.* Toronto: University of Toronto Press 1996.

Miller, Thomas William. *Canadian Pentecostals: A History of the Pentecostal Assemblies of Canada.* Mississauga, ON: Full Gospel Publishing House 1994.

Mitchell, Tom. "'The Manufacture of Souls of Good Quality': Winnipeg's 1919 National Conference on Canadian Citizenship, English-Canadian Nationalism, and the New Order after the Great War." *Journal of Canadian Studies* 31, no. 4 (winter 1996–97): 5–28.

Moir, J.S. "*The Canadian Baptist* and the Social Gospel Movement, 1879–1914." In Jarold K. Zeman, ed., *Baptists in Canada: Search for Identity amidst Diversity.* Burlington, ON: Welch Publishing 1980, 147–60.

– *Enduring Witness: A History of the Presbyterian Church in Canada.* Bryant Press 1975.

– "The Sectarian Tradition in Canada." In J.W. Grant, ed., *The Churches and the Canadian Experience: A Faith and Order Study of the Christian Tradition.* Toronto: The Ryerson Press 1963, 119–32.

– ed. *Church and State in Canada: 1627–1867.* Toronto: McClelland and Stewart 1967.

Mol, Hans. *Faith and Fragility: Religion and Identity in Canada.* Burlington, ON: Trinity Press 1985.

Mol, Hans. "Major Correlates of Churchgoing in Canada." In Stewart Crysdale and Les Wheatcroft, eds., *Religion and Canadian Society*. Toronto: Macmillan of Canada 1976, 241–54.

Montréal, Expo 67, Man and His World. France: Banque Nationale de Paris 1967.

Monsma, Stephen V., and J. Christopher Soper. *The Challenge of Pluralism: Church and State in Five Democracies*. New York: Rowman and Littlefield 1997.

Moore, A.B.B. *Here Where We Live: An Autobiography*. Toronto: The United Church Publishing House 1988.

Moore, R. Laurence. *Selling God: American Religion in the Marketplace of Culture*. New York: Oxford University Press 1994.

Morgan, Cecelia. *Public Men and Virtuous Women: The Gendered Language of Religion and Politics in Upper Canada, 1791–1850*. Toronto: University of Toronto Press 1996.

Morgan, Nicole. *Implosion: An Analysis of the Growth of the Federal Public Service in Canada (1945–1985)*. Montreal: Institute for Research on Public Policy 1986.

Moscovitch, Allan, and Glenn Drover. "Social Expenditures and the Welfare State: The Canadian Experience in Historical Perspective." In A. Moscovitch, ed., *The Benevolent State: The Growth of Welfare in Canada*. Toronto: Garamond Press 1987.

Mosse, George. *Confronting the Nation: Jewish and Western Nationalism*. Hanover, NH: Brandeis University Press 1993.

Motz, Arnell, ed. *Reclaiming a Nation: The Challenge of Re-Evangelizing Canada by the Year 2000*. Richmond, BC: Church Leadership Library 1990.

Moyles, R.G. *The Blood and Fire in Canada: A History of the Salvation Army in the Dominion, 1882–1976*. Toronto: Peter Martin Associates 1977.

Mulgrew, Ian. "And Now for a Paid Political Announcement." In Robert Anderson and Eleanor Wachtel, eds. *The Expo Story*. Madeira Park, BC: Harbour Publishing 1986, 45–64.

Munro, Fraser. *These Forty Years*, and Grace Lane, *A Dream Walks*. Toronto: United Church Publication House 1965.

Munro, John. "Multiculturalism: The Policy." In Keith A. McLeod, ed., *Multiculturalism, Bilingualism and Canadian Institutions*. Toronto: Governing Council of the University of Toronto 1979, 12–15.

Murphy, Terrence, and Roberto Perin, eds. *A Concise History of Christianity in Canada*. Toronto: Oxford University Press 1996.

Murphy, Terrence, and Gerald Stortz, eds. *Creed & Culture: The Place of English-Speaking Catholics in Canadian Society, 1750–1930*. Montreal and Kingston: McGill-Queen's University Press 1993.

Mutchmor, J.R. *Mutchmor: The Memoirs of James Ralph Mutchmor*. Toronto: The Ryerson Press 1965.

Nelles, H.V. *The Art of Nation Building: Pageantry and Spectacle at Quebec's Tercentenary.* Toronto: University of Toronto Press 1999.

Nett, Emily M. *Canadian Families: Past and Present.* 2d ed. Toronto: Harcourt, Brace 1993.

Neumann, Peter D. "The Scope and Application of Salvation in the Pentecostal Assemblies of Canada – Doubts and Hopes: An Analysis of Articles Appearing in the *Pentecostal Testimony.*" MTS thesis, Toronto School of Theology, 1998.

Newman, Peter C. *The Distemper of Our Times: Canadian Politics in Transition, 1963–68.* Toronto: McClelland and Stewart 1968.

– *Renegade in Power: The Diefenbaker Years.* Toronto: McClelland and Stewart 1963.

Ng, Roxana. *The Politics of Community Services: Immigrant Women, Class and State.* Toronto: Garamond Press 1988.

Nock, David. "Cult, Sect and Church in Canada: A Re-Examination of Stark and Bainbridge." *Canadian Review of Sociology and Anthropology* 24 (November 1987): 514–25.

Noll, Mark. *A History of Christianity in the United States and Canada.* Grand Rapids, MI: William B. Eerdmans 1992.

Norman, E.R. *The Conscience of the State in North America.* Cambridge: Cambridge University Press 1968.

Official Souvenir Book: New York World's Fair. New York: Exposition Publications 1939.

Olsen, Dennis. "The State Elites." In Leo Panitch, ed., *The Canadian State: Political Economy and Political Power.* Toronto: University of Toronto Press 1977, 199–224.

Ontario. Committee on Religious Education in the Public Schools of the Province of Ontario. *Religious Information and Moral Development: The Report of the Committee on Religious Education in the Public Schools of the Province of Ontario, 1969.* Ontario Department of Education 1969.

Opp, James W. "The New Age of Evangelism: Fundamentalism and Radio on the Canadian Prairies, 1925–1945." *Historical Papers 1994: Canadian Society of Church History,* 99–119.

Orsi, Robert A., ed. *Gods of the City: Religion and the American Urban Landscape.* Bloomington, IN: Indiana University Press 1999.

Ostry, Bernard. *The Cultural Connection: An Essay on Culture and Government Policy in Canada.* Toronto: McClelland and Stewart 1978.

O'Toole, Roger. "Religion in Canada: Its Development and Contemporary Situation." *Social Compass* 43, no. 1 (1996): 119–34.

Outhwaite, William. *The Habermas Reader.* Cambridge: Polity Press 1996.

Owen, Michael. "'Keeping Canada God's Country': Presbyterian School-Homes for Ruthenian Children." In Dennis L. Butcher et al., eds., *Prairie Spirit: Perspectives on the Heritage of the United Church in the West.* Winnipeg: University of Manitoba Press 1985, 184–201.

Owram, Doug. *Born at The Right Time: A History of the Baby-Boom Generation*. Toronto: University of Toronto Press 1996.

- *The Government Generation: Canadian Intellectuals and the State, 1900–1945*. Toronto: University of Toronto Press 1986.

Pal, Leslie A. *Interests of State: The Politics of Language, Multiculturalism, and Feminism in Canada*. Montreal and Kingston: McGill-Queen's University Press 1993.

Palmer, Howard. *Immigration and the Rise of Multiculturalism*. Toronto: Copp Clark 1975.

- "Mosaic Versus Melting Pot? Immigration and Ethnicity in Canada and the United States." In Eli Mandel and David Taras, eds., *A Passion for Identity: Introduction to Canadian Studies*. Toronto: Methuen Publications 1987, 82–96.

Paquet, Gilles. "Political Philosophy of Multiculturalism." In J.W. Berry and J.A. Laponce, eds., *Ethnicity and Culture in Canada: The Research Landscape*. Toronto: University of Toronto Press 1994, 60–80.

Peake, Frank A. "Taught in Christ: Christian Education in the Diocese of Toronto." In Alan L. Hayes, ed., *By Grace Coworkers: Building the Anglican Diocese of Toronto, 1780–1989*. Toronto: Anglican Book Centre 1989, 261–86.

Pearson, Lester B. *Mike: The Memoirs of the Right Honourable Lester B. Pearson*. Vol. 3. Toronto: University of Toronto Press 1975.

- *Words and Occasions: An Anthology of Speeches and Articles Selected from His Papers by the Right Honourable L.B. Pearson*. Toronto: University of Toronto Press 1970.

Peer, Shanny. *France on Display: Peasants, Provincials, and Folklore in the 1937 Paris World's Fair*. New York: State University of New York Press 1988.

Peers, Frank W. *The Politics of Canadian Broadcasting, 1920–1951*. Toronto: University of Toronto Press 1969.

Perin, Roberto. "Religion, Ethnicity and Identity: Placing the Immigrants within the Church." In W. Westfall et al., eds., *Religion/Culture: Comparative Canadian Studies*. Ottawa: Association of Canadian Studies 1985, 212–32.

- *Rome in Canada: The Vatican and Canadian Affairs in the Late Victorian Age*. Toronto: University of Toronto Press 1990.

Peter, Karl. "The Myth of Multiculturalism and Other Political Fables." In Jorgen Dahlie and Tissa Fernando, eds., *Ethnicity, Power and Politics in Canada*. Vol. 8. Toronto: Methuen Publications 1981, 56–74.

Pevere, Geoff, and Greig Dymond. "When We Were Fab: Expo 67." In *Mondo Canuck: A Canadian Pop Culture Odyssey*. Scarborough, ON: Prentice Hall Canada 1996, 50–5.

Plaxton, David. "The Whole Gospel for a Whole Nation: The Cultures of Tradition and Change in the United Church of Canada and its Antecedents, 1900–1950." PhD diss., Queen's University, Kingston, ON, 1997.

Pope, William, ed. *Clarence Mackinnon Nicholson*. Hantsport, NS: Lancelot Press 1981.

Porter, John. *The Measure of Canadian Society: Education, Equality, Opportunity.* Ottawa: Carleton University Press 1987.

– *The Vertical Mosaic: An Analysis of Social Class and Power in Canada.* Toronto: University of Toronto Press 1965.

– Board of Evangelism and Social Action. *A Declaration of Faith Concerning Church and Nation.* Toronto: The Board of Evangelism and Social Action of the Presbyterian Church in Canada 1955.

– "Manual on Christian Social Action, January 1970: Statements on Social Questions by the Board of Evangelism and Social Action and Recommendations Adopted by General Assemblies of The Presbyterian Church in Canada." Toronto: The Board of Evangelism and Social Action of the Presbyterian Church of Canada, n.d.

Presthus, Robert Vance. *Elite Accommodation in Canadian Politics.* Toronto: Macmillan 1973.

Priestley, David T., ed. *Memory and Hope: Strands of Canadian Baptist History.* Waterloo, ON: Wilfrid Laurier University Press 1996.

Promey, Sally M. "'Triumphant Religion' in Public Places: John Singer Sargent and the Boston Public Library Murals." In Jay P. Dolan and James P. Wind, eds., *New Dimensions in American Religious History: Essays in Honor of Martin E. Marty.* Grand Rapids, MI: William B. Eerdmans 1993, 3–27.

Pulker, Edward. *We Stand on Their Shoulders: The Growth of Social Concern in Canadian Anglicanism.* Toronto: Anglican Book Centre 1986.

Purdy, J.D. *Townsend of Huron.* London, ON: The Althouse Press 1992.

Québec. *Report of the Royal Commission of Inquiry on Constitutional Problems.* Québec 1956.

Raboy, Marc. "The Media in Quebec." In Alain-G. Gagnon, ed., *Quebec: State and Society.* 2d ed. Scarborough, ON: Nelson Canada 1993, 158–72.

Radcliffe, Sarah, and Sallie Westwood. *Remaking the Nation: Place, Identity and Politics in Latin America.* New York: Routledge 1996.

Rawls, John. *Political Liberalism.* New York: Columbia University Press 1993.

Rawlyk, George, ed. *The Canadian Protestant Experience, 1760–1990.* Burlington, ON: Welch Publishing 1990.

Reaven, Sheldon J. "New Frontiers: Science and Technology at the Fair." In Robert Rosenblum, ed., *Remembering the Future: The New York World's Fair from 1939 to 1964.* New York: Rizzoli International Publications 1989, 75–105.

Redekop, John H. "The Involvement of Canadian Mennonites with Non-Mennonite National Religious Bodies." In Abe Dueck ed., *Canadian Mennonites and the Challenge of Nationalism.* Winnipeg: Manitoba Mennonite Historical Society 1994, 111–27.

Reeve, Ted. "Advocating for the Welfare State in Canada: Institutional Responses of the United Church of Canada in the Late 1930s." *Toronto Journal of Theology* 12, no. 2 (1996): 237–49.

Regehr, T.D. *Mennonites in Canada, 1939–1970: A People Tranformed*. Toronto: University of Toronto Press 1996.

Regenstreif, Peter. *The Diefenbaker Interlude: Parties and Voting in Canada*. Toronto: Longmans 1965.

Reilly, Brent. "Baptists and Organized Opposition to Roman Catholicism, 1941–1962." In Jarold K. Zeman, ed., *Costly Vision: The Baptist Pilgrimage in Canada*. Burlington, ON: Welch Publishing 1988, 181–98.

Reimers, Al. *God's Country: Charismatic Renewal*. Burlington, ON: G.R. Welch 1979.

Reisner, M.E. *Strangers and Pilgrims: A History of the Anglican Diocese of Quebec, 1793–1993*. Toronto: Anglican Book Centre 1995.

Renfree, Harry A. *Heritage and Horizon: The Baptist Story in Canada*. Mississauga, ON: Canadian Baptist Federation 1988.

Resnick, Philip. *The Land of Cain: Class and Nationalism in English Canada, 1945–1975*. Vancouver: New Star Books 1977.

– *The Masks of Proteus: Canadian Reflections on the State*. Montreal and Kingston: McGill-Queen's University Press 1990.

– *Thinking English Canada*. Toronto: Stoddart Publishing 1994.

Reynolds, A.G., ed. *Life and Death: A Study of the Christian Hope*. The Committee on Christian Faith of the United Church of Canada 1959.

Richler, Mordecai. "Expo '67." In Robert Fulford, ed., *The Great Comic Book Heroes and Other Essays*. Toronto: McClelland and Stewart 1978, 104–18.

Richmond, Anthony H. "Immigration and Pluralism in Canada." In W.E. Mann, ed., *Social and Cultural Change in Canada*. Vol. 1. Toronto: The Copp Clark Publishing Company 1970, 81–95.

Rioux, Marcel. "Youth in the Contemporary World and in Quebec." In W.E. Mann, ed. *Social and Cultural Change in Canada*. Vol. 1. Toronto: The Copp Clark Publishing Company 1970, 302–15.

Robertson, Roland. "Church-State Relations and the World System." In Thomas Robbins and Roland Robertson, eds., *Church-State Relations: Tensions and Transitions*. Oxford: Transaction Books 1987, 39–51.

– "General Considerations in the Study of Contemporary Church-State Relationships." In Thomas Robbins and Roland Robertson, eds., *Church-State Relations: Tensions and Transitions*. Oxford: Transaction Books 1987, 5–11.

Robinson, John A.T. "Religion without Dogma." In William Kilbourn, ed., *The Restless Church: A Response to the Comfortable Pew*. Toronto: McClelland and Stewart 1966, 55–61.

Rocher, Guy. "A Half-Century of Cultural Evolution in Quebec." In Michael D. Behiels, ed., *Quebec since 1945: Selected Readings*. Toronto: Copp Clark Pitman 1987, 289–99.

Rogers, Randal Arthur. "Man and His World: An Indian, A Secretary and a Queer Child: Expo 67 and the Nation in Canada." MA thesis, Concordia University 1999.

Rosenblum, Robert, ed. *Remembering the Future: The New York World's Fair from 1939 to 1964*. New York: Rizzoli International Publications 1989.

Rossiter, Sean. "The Shape of Things to Come – Architecture." In Robert Anderson and Eleanor Wachtel, eds., *The Expo Story*. Madeira Park, BC: Harbour Publishing 1986, 101–24.

Rotstein, Abraham. "The 20th Century Prospect: Nationalism in a Technological Society." In Peter Russell, ed., *Nationalism in Canada*. Toronto: McGraw-Hill 1966, 341–63.

Rouillard, Jacques. "Major Changes in the Confederation des Travailleurs Catholiques du Canada, 1940–1960." In Michael D. Behiels, ed., *Quebec since 1945: Selected Readings*. Toronto: Copp Clark Pitman 1987, 111–32.

Roy, Gabrielle. "The Theme Unfolded by Gabrielle Roy." In *Terre des Hommes/Man and His World*. Canadian Corporation for the 1967 World Exhibition, 1967, 21–60.

Roy, Maurice, Archbishop of Quebec. *The Parish and Democracy in French Canada*. Toronto: University of Toronto Press 1950.

Rubens, Lisa. "Re-Presenting the Nation: The Golden Gate International Exhibition." In Robert W. Rydell and Nancy Gwinn, eds., *Fair Representations: World's Fairs and the Modern World*. Amsterdam: VU University Press 1994, 121–39.

Rudin, Ronald. *Founding Fathers : The Celebration of Champlain and Laval in the Streets of Quebec, 1878–1908*. Toronto: University of Toronto Press 2003.

– *Making History in Twentieth Century Quebec*. Toronto: University of Toronto Press 1997.

– "Marching and Memory in Early Twentieth-Century Quebec: La Fete-Dieu, La Saint-Jean-Baptiste, and Le Monument Laval." *Journal of the Canadian Historical Association* 10 (1991): 209–35.

Ruggle, Richard I. "Canadian Chaplains: A Special Issue." *Journal of the Canadian Church Historical Society* 35, no. 2 (October 1993): 65–74.

Russell, Peter. "Conclusion." In Peter Russell, ed., *Nationalism in Canada*. Toronto: McGraw Hill 1966, 364–76.

– ed. *Nationalism in Canada*. Toronto: McGraw-Hill 1966.

Rutherdale, Robert. "Canada's August Festival: Communitas, Liminality, and Social Memory." *Canadian Historical Review* 77, no. 2 (June 1996): 221–49.

Rutherford, Paul. *When Television Was Young: Primetime Canada, 1952–1967*. Toronto: University of Toronto Press 1990.

Ryan, Claude. "Lester B. Pearson and Canadian Unity." In Norman Hillmer, ed., *Pearson: The Unlikely Gladiator*. Montreal and Kingston: McGill-Queen's University Press 1999: 83–103.

Rydell, Robert W. *All the World's a Fair: Visions of Empire at American International Expositions, 1876–1916*. Chicago: University of Chicago Press 1984.

Rydell, Robert W., and Nancy Gwinn, eds. *Fair Representations: World's Fairs and the Modern World*. Amsterdam: VU University Press 1994.

Saint Exupéry, Antoine de. *Terre des homes*. Paris: Gallimard 1939.

Sawatsky, Rodney J. "Canadian Mennonite Nationalism? The 49th Parallel in the Structuring of Mennonite Life." In Abe Dueck, ed., *Canadian Mennonites and the Challenge of Nationalism*. Winnipeg: Manitoba Mennonite Historical Society 1994, 89–110.

Sayre, Patricia A. "Personalism." In Philip L. Quinn and Charles Taliaferro, eds., *A Companion to Philosophy of Religion*. Cambridge, MA: Blackwell Publishers 1997, 129–35.

Schecter, Stephen. "Capitalism, Class, and Educational Reform in Canada." In Leo Panitch, ed., *The Canadian State: Political Economy and Political Power*. Toronto: University of Toronto Press 1977, 446–72.

Schmidt, Leigh Eric. *Consumer Rites: The Buying and Selling of American Holidays*. Princeton: Princeton University Press 1995.

Schroeder-Gudehus, Brigitte, and David Cloutier. "Popularizing Science and Technology during the Cold War: Brussels 1958." In Robert W. Rydell and Nancy Gwinn, eds., *fair Representations: World's Fairs and the Modern World*. Amsterdam: VU University Press 1994, 157–80.

Schwartz, Mildred A. *Public Opinion and Canadian Identity*. Berkeley: University of California Press 1967.

Seiler, Robert M., and Tamara P. Seiler. "The Social Construction of the Canadian Cowboy: Calgary Exhibition and Stampede Posters, 1952–1972." *Journal of Canadian Studies* 33, no. 3 (fall 1998): 51–82.

Seljak, David. "The Jesuit Journal *Relations*, 1959–1969: Modernity, Religion and Nationalism in Quebec." *Historical Papers 1993: Canadian Society of Church History*, 187–203.

– "Religion, Nationalism and the Break-up of Canada." In John Coleman and Miklos Tomka, eds., *Religion and Nationalism*. London: SCM Press 1995, 68–76.

– "Why the Quiet Revolution Was 'Quiet': The Catholic Church's Reaction to the Secularization of Quebec after 1960." *Études d'Histoire Religieuse* 62 (1996): 109–24.

Sharp, Mitchell. *Which Reminds Me: A Memoir*. Toronto: University of Toronto Press 1994.

Shaw, J.M. "The Basically Supernatural Character of the Christian Gospel." *Canadian Journal of Theology* 12, no. 4 (1996): 259–66.

Sheridan, E.F., ed. *Do Justice! The Social Teaching of the Canadian Catholic Bishops (1945–1986)*. Sherbrooke, QC, and Toronto: Éditions Paulines and the Jesuit Centre for Social Faith and Justice 1987.

Sider, E. Morris. *The Brethren in Christ in Canada: Two Hundred Years of Traditions and Change*. Nappanee, IN: Evangel Press 1988.

Simeon, Richard, and Ian Robinson. *State, Society, and the Development of Canadian Federalism*. Toronto: University of Toronto Press 1990.

Simpson, John. "Federal Regulation and Religious Broadcasting in Canada and the United States." In W. Westfall et al., eds., *Religion/Culture: Comparative Canadian Studies* Ottawa: Association of Canadian Studies 1985, 152–63.

Sinclair, Lister. *Change Comes to Canada, Challenge of Changing Times: A Personal Glance.* Montreal: Canadian Government Pavilion, Expo 67. N.d.

Sissons, C.B. *Church and State in Canadian Education.* Toronto: The Ryerson Press 1959.

Smith, Allan. "First Nations, Race and the Idea of a Plural Community: Defining Canada in the Postmodern Age." In Stella Hryniuk, ed., *Twenty Years of Multiculturalism: Successes and Failures.* Winnipeg: St John's College Press 1992, 233–54.

– "National Images and National Maintenance: The Ascendancy of the Ethnic Idea in North America." *Canadian Journal of Political Science* 14, no. 2 (June 1981): 227–58.

Smith, Anthony D. *Nations and Nationalism in a Global Era.* Cambridge: Polity Press 1995.

Smith, David E. "Celebrations and History on the Prairies." *Journal of Canadian Studies* 7, no. 3 (fall 1982): 45–57.

Smith, Edward. "Planning for People: The Gaspé Project." In W.E. Mann, ed., *Social and Cultural Change in Canada.* Vol. 1. Toronto: Copp Clark 1970, 170–7.

Smith, Glenn. "Towards a Contextual Praxis for the Urban French World: A Case Study to Engage Christian Direction, Inc., with Montreal, Quebec." Doctor of Ministry thesis, Northern Baptist Theological Seminary, 1991.

Smith, Raymond R. "A Heritage of Healing: Church Hospital and Medical Work in Manitoba, 1900–1977." In Dennis Butcher et al., eds., *Prairie Spirit.* Winnipeg: University of Manitoba Press 1985, 265–83.

Speaight, Robert. *Vanier: Soldier, Diplomat and Governor General: A Biography.* Great Britain: Collins and Harvill Press 1970.

Spillman, Lyn. *Nation and Commemoration: Creating National Identities in the United States and Australia.* Cambridge: Cambridge University Press 1997.

Stackhouse, John Jr. *Canadian Evangelicalism in the Twentieth Century: An Introduction to Its Character.* Toronto: University of Toronto Press 1993.

– "The Protestant Experience in Canada since 1945." In G.A. Rawlyk, ed., *The Canadian Protestant Experience, 1760–1990.* Burlington, ON: Welch Publishing 1990, 198–252.

Stairs, Denis. "Lester B. Pearson and the Meaning of Politics." In Norman Hillmer, ed., *Pearson: The Unlikely Gladiator.* Montreal and Kingston: McGill-Queen's University Press 1999, 30–50.

Stiller, Brian Carl. "The Evolution of Pentecostalism: From Sectarianism to Denominationalism, with Special Reference to the Danforth Gospel Temple, 1922–1968." Master of Religion thesis, Wycliffe College, 1975.

– *From the Tower of Babel to Parliament Hill: How to Be a Christian in Canada Today.* Toronto: Harper Collins 1997.

Stonecipher, Branwen, and Kate Slater. "If You're White You Can't Be Pagan." In Caterina Pizanias and James S. Frideres, eds., *Freedom within the Margins: The Politics of Exclusion.* Calgary: Detselig Enterprises 1995, 15–30.

"The Story of the United Church at Morven, 1856–1966: Prepared at the Request of the United Church Women of Canada." N.p. 1967.

Strange, Carolyn, and Tina Loo. *Making Good: Law and Moral Regulation in Canada, 1867–1939.* Toronto: University of Toronto Press 1997.

Strong-Boag, Veronica, et al., eds. *Painting the Maple: Essays on Race, Gender and the Construction of Canada.* Vancouver: University of British Columbia Press 1998.

Struthers, James. *No Fault of Their Own: Unemployment and the Canadian Welfare State, 1914–1941.* Toronto: University of Toronto Press 1983.

Stryckman, Paul, and Robert Gaudet. "Priests under Stress." In Stewart Crysdale and Les Wheatcroft, eds., *Religion and Canadian Society.* Toronto: Macmillan of Canada 1976, 336–45.

Stursberg, Peter. *Roland Michener: The Last Viceroy.* Toronto: McGraw-Hill Ryerson 1989.

Suter, Bruno, and Peter Knapp. *Osaka: 500 Pictures of the Osaka Expo 70.* Paris: Hermann Éditeurs des Sciences et des Arts 1970.

Sutherland, Ronald. "Christianity in Canada and the Canadian Mystique." In Gregory Baum, Ronald Sutherland, and Louis LeBlanc, *The Survival of Canada and the Christian Church: Conference.* Toronto: St Michael's College, 23–25 February 1973.

Sweet, Leonard. "The 1960s: The Crisis of Liberal Christianity and the Public Emergence of Evangelicalism." In George Marsden, ed., *Evangelicalism and Modern America.* Grand Rapids, MI: Eerdmans 1984.

Swidler, Ann. "Culture in Action: Symbols and Strategies." *American Sociological Review* 51 (1986): 273–86.

Tarr, Leslie K. *This Dominion, His Dominion: The Story of Evangelical Baptist Endeavour in Canada.* Fellowship of Evangelical Churches in Canada 1968.

Taylor, Charles. "Alternative Futures: Legitimacy, Identity and Alienation in Late Twentieth Century Canada." In Alan Cairns and Cynthia Williams, eds., *Constitutionalism, Citizenship and Society in Canada.* Toronto: University of Toronto Press 1985, 183–225.

– "A Canadian Future?" In *Reconciling the Solitudes: Essays on Canadian Federalism and Nationalism.* Montreal and Kingston: McGill-Queen's University Press 1993, 23–39.

– "Nationalism and the Political Intelligentsia: A Case Study." In W.E. Mann, ed., *Social and Cultural Change in Canada.* Vol. 1. Toronto: Copp Clark 1970, 274–87.

Tepper, Elliot L. "Immigration Policy and Multiculturalism." In J.W. Berry and J.A. Laponce, eds., *Ethnicity and Culture in Canada: The Research Landscape.* Toronto: University of Toronto Press 1994, 95–123.

Terre des Hommes/Man and His World: Official Guide. City of Montreal 1968.

Thomas, M.M. "Changes in Function and Understanding of the State in the Modern World." In *Church and State: Opening a New Ecumenical Discussion.* Faith and Order Paper, no. 85, World Council of Churches 1978, 19–28.

Thompson, K.A. "Religious Organizations: The Cultural Perspective." In G. Salaman and K. Thompson, eds., *People and Organizations*. Essex: Longman 1973, 273–86.

Thomson, Dale C. *Louis St Laurent: Canadian*. Toronto: Macmillan of Canada 1967.

Threinen, Norman J., ed. *In Search of Identity: A Look at Lutheran Identity in Canada*. Winnipeg: Lutheran Council in Canada 1977.

Tillotson, Shirley. "Citizen Participation in the Welfare State: An Experiment, 1945–57." *Canadian Historical Review* 75, no. 4 (1994): 511–42.

Tilly, Charles. "Citizenship, Identity and Social History." In Charles Tilly, ed., *Citizenship, Identity and Social History*. Cambridge: Press Syndicate of the University of Cambridge 1996, 1–18.

Traves, Tom. *The State and Enterprise: Canadian Manufacturers and the Federal Government, 1917–1931*. Toronto: University of Toronto Press 1979.

Trofimenkoff, Susan Mann. *The Dream of Nation: A Social and Intellectual History of Quebec*. Toronto: Macmillan of Canada 1982.

– *Stanley Knowles: The Man from Winnipeg North Centre*. Saskatoon: Western Producer Prairie Books 1982.

Trudeau, Pierre Elliot. "Canada and French-Canadian Nationalism." In William Kilbourn, ed., *Canada: A Guide to the Peaceable Kingdom*. Toronto: Macmillan of Canada 1970, 14–17.

– "The Province of Quebec at the Time of the Strike." In Pierre Elliot Trudeau et al., *The Asbestos Strike*. Toronto: James Lewis and Samuel 1974, 1–82.

Tulchinsky, Gerald. *Branching Out: The Transformation of the Canadian Jewish Community*. Toronto: Stoddart Publishing 1998.

– *Taking Root: The Origins of the Canadian Jewish Community*. Toronto: Lester 1992.

Turner, Bryan S. "Religion, State and Civil Society: Nation-Building in Australia" In Thomas Robbins and Roland Robertson, eds, *Church-State Relations: Tensions and Transitions*. Oxford: Transaction Books 1987, 233–51.

– "Religion, State Formation, and White-Settler Societies: With Special Reference to Australia." In Mark Bax, Peter Kloos, and Adrianus Koster, eds., *Faith and Polity*. Amsterdam: VU University Press 1992, 27–51.

Turner, Frederick C. "Basic Values: Religion, Patriotism, and Equality." In Mattei Dogan, ed., *Comparing Pluralist Democracies: Strains on Legitimacy*. London: Westview Press 1988, 181–201.

Turner, James. *Without God, Without Creed: The Origins of Unbelief in America*. Baltimore, MD: The Johns Hopkins University Press 1985.

Underhill, Frank. "Foreword." In Peter Russell, ed., *Nationalism in Canada*. Toronto: McGraw-Hill 1966, xvi–xx.

United Church of Canada. *Creeds: A Report of the Committee on Christian Faith*. United Church of Canada 1969.

- Board of Evangelism and Social Service. "Bilingualism and Biculturalism: Recent Statements of the United Church of Canada." N.p., n.d.
- Commission on the Ministry in the Twentieth Century. *Report of the Commission on the Ministry in the Twentieth Century to the Twenty-third General Council.* United Church of Canada 1968.
- Commission on World Mission. *World Mission: Report of the Commission on World Mission.* Toronto: United Church of Canada 1966.

United Church of Canada, City of Kingston, Ontario, Survey of the Churches. Report of the Director to the Survey Committee, November 1964.

Vallières, Pierre. *White Niggers of America.* Trans. by Joan Pinkam. Toronto: McClelland and Stewart 1971.

Valverde, Mariana. *The Age of Light, Soap and Water: Moral Reform in English Canada, 1885–1925.* Toronto: McClelland and Stewart 1991.

Van Buren, Paul M. *The Secular Meaning of the Gospel.* New York: Macmillan 1963.

VanderVennen, Robert E., ed. *Church and Canadian Culture.* New York: University Press of America 1991.

Van Die, Marguerite. *An Evangelical Mind: Nathanael Burwash and the Methodist Tradition in Canada, 1839–1918.* Montreal and Kingston: McGill-Queen's University Press 1989.
- "'The Mark of a Genuine Revival': Religion, Social Change, Gender and Community in Mid-Victorian Brantford, Ontario." *Canadian Historical Review* 79, no. 3 (September 1998): 524–63.
- "'A Woman's Awakening': Evangelical Belief and Female Spirituality in Mid-Nineteenth-Century Canada." In Wendy Mitchison et al., eds., *Canadian Women: A Reader.* Toronto: Harcourt Brace 1996, 49–67.
- ed. *Religion and Public Life in Canada: Historical and Comparative Perspectives.* Toronto: University of Toronto Press 2001.

Van Dusen, Henry P. "The Third Force." *Life,* 9 June 1958, 122–4.

Vipond, Mary. "Canadian National Consciousness and the Formation of the United Church of Canada." In Mark McGowan and David Marshall, eds., *Prophets, Priests and Prodigals: Readings in Canadian Religious History, 1608 to Present.* Toronto: McGraw-Hill Ryerson 1992, 167–83.

Vischer, Lucas. "Introduction." In *Church and State: Opening a New Ecumenical Discussion.* Faith and Order Paper, no. 85, World Council of Churches 1978, 7–18.

Voisine, Nive. *Histoire de L'Église catholique au Québec (1608–1970).* Montreal: Éditions Fides 1971.

Wachtel, Eleanor. "Expo 86 and World's Fairs." In Robert Anderson and Eleanor Wachtel, eds., *The Expo Story.* Madeira Park, BC: Harbour Publishing 1986, 19–44.

Walden, Keith. *Becoming Modern in Toronto: The Industrial Exhibition and the Shaping of a Late Victorian Culture.* Toronto: University of Toronto Press 1997.

Waldo, Myra. *Japan Expo '70 Guide*. London: Collier-Macmillan 1970.

Wangenheim, Elizabeth. "The Ukrainians: A Case Study of the 'Third Force.'" In Peter Russell, ed., *Nationalism in Canada*. Toronto: McGraw-Hill 1966, 72–90.

Ward, Barbara. "The First International Nation." In William Kilbourn, ed., *Canada: A Guide to the Peaceable Kingdom*. Toronto: Macmillan 1970, 45–8.

Watkins, Melville. "Technology and Nationalism." In Peter Russell, ed., *Nationalism in Canada*. Toronto: McGraw-Hill 1966, 284–301.

Weithman, Paul J. "Introduction: Religion and the Liberalism of Reasoned Respect." In Paul J. Weithman, ed., *Religion and Contemporary Liberalism*. Notre Dame, IN: University of Notre Dame Press 1997.

Westfall, William. "Constructing Public Religions at Private Sites: The Anglican Church in the Shadow of Disestablishment." In M. Van Die, ed., *Religion and Public Life in Canada: Historical and Comparative Perspectives*. Toronto: University of Toronto Press 2001, 23–49.

– *Two Worlds: The Protestant Culture of Nineteenth Century Ontario*. Montreal and Kingston: McGill-Queen's University Press 1989.

Westhues, Kenneth. "The Adaptation of the Roman Catholic Church in Canadian Society." In Stewart Crysdale and Les Wheatcroft, eds, *Religion and Canadian Society*. Toronto: Macmillan 1976, 290–306.

Westphal, Merold. "Phenomenology and Existentialism." In Philip L. Quinn and Charles Taliaferro, eds., *A Companion to Philosophy of Religion*. Cambridge, MA: Blackwell 1997, 143–9.

Whitaker, Reginald. *The Government Party: Organizing and Financing the Liberal Party of Canada, 1930–1958*. Toronto: University of Toronto Press 1977.

Whitaker, Reginald, and Gary Marcuse. *Cold War Canada: The Making of a National Insecurity State, 1945–1957*. Toronto: University of Toronto Press 1994.

Whitney, Allison. "Labyrinth: Cinema, Myth and Nation at Expo 67." PhD Diss., McGill University 1999.

Whyte, Donald R. "Religion and the Rural Church." In W.E. Mann, ed., *Social and Cultural Change in Canada*. Vol. 1. Toronto: Copp Clark 1970, 156–69.

Wicker, Hans-Rudulf. "Introdution: Theorizing Ethnicity and Nationalism." In Hans-Rudolf Wicker, ed., *Rethinking Nationalism and Ethnicity: The Struggle for Meaning and Order in Europe*. New York: Berg 1997, 1–42.

Williams, John R. "Religion in Newfoundland." In Peter Slater, ed., *Religion and Culture in Canada*. Canadian Corporation for Studies in Religion 1977, 95–116.

– ed. *Canadian Churches and Social Justice*. Toronto: Anglican Book Centre and James Lorimer 1984.

Williams, Raymond. *Problems in Materialism and Culture: Selected Essays*. London: Verso 1980.

Wilson, Douglas J. *The Church Grows in Canada*. Toronto: Ryerson Press 1966.

Wilson, John F. *Public Religion in American Culture*. Philadelphia: Temple University Press 1979.

Woolf, Stuart, ed. *Nationalism in Europe, 1815 to the Present*. New York: Routledge 1996.

Wright, Robert. *A World Mission: Canadian Protestantism and the Quest for a New International Order, 1918–1939*. Montreal and Kingston: McGill-Queen's University Press 1991.

Wuthnow, Robert. *Producing the Sacred: An Essay on Public Religion*. Chicago: University of Illinois Press 1994.

– *Restructuring of American Religion: Society and Faith since World War II*. Princeton: Princeton University Press 1988.

Yengoyan, Aram A. "Culture, Ideology and World's Fairs: Colonizer and Colonized in Comparative Perspectives." In Robert W. Rydell and Nancy Gwinn, eds., *Fair Representations: World's Fairs and the Modern World*. Amsterdam: VU University Press 1994, 62–83.

Young, Pamela Dickey. "Theme and Variations: The Social Gospel in a New Key." *Toronto Journal of Theology* 12, no. 2 (1996): 285–90.

Zeman, Jarold K. "Building a Future on the Past." In David T. Priestley, ed., *Memory and Hope: Strands of Canadian Baptist History*. Waterloo, ON: Wilfrid Laurier University Press 1996 11–24.

– ed. *Baptists in Canada: Search for Identity amidst Diversity*. Burlington, ON: Welch 1980.

Zolf, Dorothy, and Paul W. Taylor. "Redressing the Balance in Canadian Broadcasting: A History of Religious Broadcasting Policy in Canada." *Studies in Religon* 182 (spring 1989): 153–70.

Zylberberg, Jacques, and Pauline Côté, "Les balises étatiques de la religion au Canada." *Social Compass* 40, no. 4 (1993): 529–53.

Index

abortion: changing positions of mainline churches on, 60, 226n96
adoption: and influence of religion on policy, 16
affluence: in 1950s and 1960s, 31, 42, 46, 127–8; at end of 1960s, 205
Aitken, Jonathan, 115
Anderson, Benedict, 8
Anglican Church of Canada: and the Canadian Interfaith Conference, 83, 99; and the Christian Pavilion, 141–2; and decline in the 1960s, 35, 167; and moral legislation, 62; and planning for the Centennial year, 92–3; and postwar revival, 34; privileged position in dominant culture, 18, 27; and racial and religious discrimination in postwar period, 51; and religious broadcasting on the CBC, 217n54, 230n60; response of leadership to changes of 1950s and 1960s, 53–7, 58–9, 61, 63; and the Sermons from Science Pavilion, 182; tension within over response to changes of 1950s and 1960s, 59–60.

See also Anglican World Congress, The Comfortable Pew, ecumenism, mainline churches
Anglican World Congress, 53, 54, 92, 232n12
Aykroyd, Peter, xxi, 76, 227n9, 230n48

Baha'i faith, National Spiritual Assembly of the: facing resistance to interfaith cooperation, 99, 109–11, and participation in the Canadian Interfaith Conference, 98
Baptist Convention of Ontario and Quebec: and Christian Pavilion, 244n15; as mainline church, 210n13; and the New Curriculum, 59
Baptist Federation of Canada: as member of Canadian Interfaith Conference, 89–90; and the Sermons from Science Pavilion, 182
Beaubien, Irénée, xxiv; and early ecumenism in Montreal, 57; and message of Christian Pavilion, 167; and origins of Christian Pavilion, 140–3
Beaubien, Philippe de Gaspé, 237n10, 239n29

Becker, Lavy N., xii–xv, 72–3, 83; on CIC programs, 97, 101–2; on Christian exclusivity in the Centennial, 110–11, 232n7; on the existence of the CIC beyond the Centennial year, 87
Behiels, Michael, 45
Bellah, Robert, 212n9, 213n26
Benedict, Burton, 117, 129, 242n95
Berger, Peter: and public religion, 9; and the response to The Comfortable Pew, 37–8
Berton, Pierre: and the end of the 1960s, 205; response to Expo 67, 115; and unrest of the 1960s, 40. See also The Comfortable Pew
Bienvenue, Paul, 118, 238n26
Bilingualism and Biculturalism Commission. See Royal Commission on Bilingualism and Biculturalism
Boivin, Horace, xxiv, 173
Bonhoeffer, Dietrich, 58, 167–8
Bothwell, William, xxiv, 155, 182, 257n75
Breton, Raymond: and the definition of "symbolic